OVERVIEW OF COMPETITION LAW IN BRAZIL

IBRAC

Desde 1992

Instituto Brasileiro de Estudos de Concorrência,
Consumo e Comércio Internacional

Edited by
Cristianne Zarzur, Krisztian Katona and Mariana Villela

OVERVIEW OF COMPETITION LAW IN BRAZIL

Contributors

Ana Paula Martinez
Aurélio Santos
Barbara Rosenberg
Bruno de Luca Drago
Caio Mario da Silva Pereira Neto
Carlos Francisco de Magalhães
Cristiano Rodrigo Del Debbio
Daniel Andreoli
Eduardo Caminati Anders
Eduardo Frade Rodrigues
Erika Vieira Sang
Fabíola Cammarota de Abreu
Fabricio Antonio Cardim de Almeida
Filippo Maria Lancieri
Francisco Niclós Negrão
Gabriel Nogueira Dias
Guilherme Morgulis
João Marcelo Lima
Joyce Midori Honda
Leonardo Maniglia Duarte
Luís Henrique Perroni Fernandes
Marcela Abras Lorenzetti
Marcelo Calliari
Marcio Bueno
Marcio Dias Soares
Marcos Exposto
Marcos Paulo Verissimo
Maria Eugênia Novis
Mariana Tavares de Araujo
Mauro Grinberg
Paulo Eduardo Lilla
Paulo Leonardo Casagrande
Pedro Paulo Salles Cristofaro
Priscila Brolio Gonçalves
Renata Fonseca Zuccolo
Renê Guilherme S. Medrado
Ricardo Botelho
Rodrigo Alves dos Santos
Sandra Terepins
Vinicius Marques de Carvalho

IBRAC
Desde 1992
Instituto Brasileiro de Estudos de Concorrência, Consumo e Comércio Internacional

EDITORA SINGULAR

2015

Dados Internacionais de Catalogação na Publicação (CIP)

O967 Overview of competition law in Brazil. / São Paulo : IBRAC/Editora Singular, 2015.

448 p.

ISBN: 978-85-86626-74-6

Edited by: Cristianne Zarzur, Krisztian Katona and Mariana Villela.

Contributors: Ana Paula Martinez, Aurélio Santos, Barbara Rosenberg, Bruno de Luca Drago, Caio Mario da Silva Pereira Neto, Carlos Francisco de Magalhães, Cristiano Rodrigo Del Debbio, Daniel Andreoli, Eduardo Caminati Anders, Eduardo Frade Rodrigues, Erika Vieira Sang, Fabíola Cammarota de Abreu, Fabricio Antonio Cardim de Almeida, Filippo Maria Lancieri, Francisco Niclós Negrão, Gabriel Nogueira Dias, Guilherme Morgulis, João Marcelo Lima, Joyce Midori Honda, Leonardo Maniglia Duarte, Luís Henrique Perroni Fernandes, Marcela Abras Lorenzetti, Marcelo Calliari, Marcio Bueno, Marcio Dias Soares, Marcos Exposto, Marcos Paulo Verissimo, Maria Eugênia Novis, Mariana Tavares de Araujo, Mauro Grinberg, Paulo Eduardo Lilla, Paulo Leonardo Casagrande, Pedro Paulo Salles Cristofaro, Priscila Brolio Gonçalves, Renata Fonseca Zuccolo, Renê Guilherme S. Medrado, Ricardo Botelho, Rodrigo Alves dos Santos, Sandra Terepins, Vinicius Marques de Carvalho.

1. Direito da concorrência, Brasil. 2. Concorrência, Brasil. 3. Direito econômico. 4. Direito econômico internacional. I. Instituto Brasileiro de Estudos de Concorrência, Consumo e Comércio Internacional – IBRAC (Ed.). II. Editora Singular (Ed.).

CDD: 341.3787

CDU: 339.137:34(81)

CDU: 929

Revisora: Christina Rostworowski da Costa
Diagramação: Microart Design Editorial
Capa: Aeroestudio

IBRAC
Rua Cardoso de Almeida, 788, cj 121
05013-001 – São Paulo-SP
Tel. (11) 3872-2609
www.ibrac.org.br
ibrac@ibrac.org.br

Editora Singular
www.editorasingular.com.br
singular@editorasingular.com.br

TABLE OF CONTENTS

ABOUT IBRAC

The Brazilian Institute of Studies on Competition, Consumer Affairs and International Trade – **IBRAC** is a nonprofit private entity established in 1992 to foster the development of research, studies and debates involving competition, consumer law issues and international trade.

In order to achieve that end, IBRAC has played an active role in the interaction with the Brazilian antitrust authorities (Conselho Administrativo de Defesa Econômica – CADE) and a number of other governmental and non-governmental institutions, all of which have translated into constant meetings and workshops to discuss specific topics of relevant subjects.

In addition, IBRAC also promotes events, notably the International Seminar on Competition Defense, which is held every year with the attendance of illustrious panelists from Brazil, and from many other jurisdictions that interact with the Brazilian antitrust system, notably the United States of America, the European Community, countries in Latin America and Asia.

IBRAC is basically a forum for discussion. Within this context it also maintains a permanent university extension course on antitrust law in São Paulo, whose classes are given by leading professionals and authorities in the Brazilian competition segment, and we promote our own publication, *Revista do IBRAC*, which is one of the leading publications in the area in Brazil.

This year, we have decided to innovate, putting together a book containing articles on topics on antitrust law that affect both Brazilian and foreign companies doing business in Brazil, written by associates of IBRAC, all of which have been working with antitrust law in Brazil for many years. The idea was to organize a publication in English which would be accessible to the international antitrust community and foster knowledge and discussion on the development of antitrust in Brazil.

For this project, we have been honored to work together with Krisztian Katona, Counsel for International Antitrust in the Federal Trade Commission's Office of International Affairs, who co-edits the publication and who has helped conceive, coordinate and execute the project. We have also been honored to receive contributions from Mr. Vinicius Marques de Carvalho, President of CADE's Tribunal, and to Mr. Eduardo Frade Rodrigues, General Superintendent of CADE, who have agreed to participate in a specific Q&A section. We are grateful for the time and energy they have dedicated to this publication.

We are extremely proud of this high-quality work, prepared with enthusiasm, which we feel and expect will be helpful to bring more light to the discussions being held in the competition field in Brazil.

We hope that you enjoy this journey. For further information on IBRAC, please visit our website at ***www.ibrac.org.br***, or write to ***ibrac@ibrac.org.br***.

April 2015

Cristianne Zarzur – *President*

Mariana Villela – *Director of Publications*

FOREWORD

Brazil's rapid development in the global competition arena in recent years has impressed all observers. In a remarkably short period of time, the Brazilian competition regime has expanded in both breadth and depth, while also witnessing reforms that changed the nature and functioning of the entire system. The result is a considerably more mature legal and regulatory structure, one that now rivals the most advanced antitrust and competition regimes in the world.

Working with a number of emerging competition regimes, I have watched with respect Brazil's progress accelerate. As part of its transition to a market-based economy in the 1990s, Brazil was one of the first Latin American countries to create an active competition enforcement system. However, since 1994, Brazil's antitrust regime consisted of three agencies with overlapping enforcement responsibilities, resulting in lengthy reviews and significant backlogs in merger and conduct investigations. These and other important areas were promptly recognized as needing improvement by practitioners, scholars, and international organizations, even as the system made steady and remarkable progress over the years.

The structure changed dramatically with the adoption of the 2011 competition law. Following an institutional reform that unified all antitrust enforcement functions in a single agency, today's Brazilian regime boasts a modern competition authority (Conselho Administrativo de Defesa Econômica - CADE) with streamlined decision-making processes, a significantly reduced backlog in investigations, and a number of notable organizational improvements. The new law also addressed another bottleneck of the previous regime by creating a pre-merger notification system with fixed deadlines in place of post-merger notification. Having removed the largest problems of the old regime, the 2011 reform set the legal and institutional foundation for further progress. Indeed, CADE recently released a number of regulations addressing substantive and procedural issues, developments keenly watched by practitioners, businesses, and scholars.

However, challenges remain. For example, a number of important issues in merger (*e.g.*, gun-jumping, remedies) and cartel (*e.g.*, leniency) enforcement require additional guidance and further clarification of the rules. Increasing awareness of the benefits of competition in the business community and promoting competition compliance will be an ongoing challenge, also to be coordinated with compliance with anti-corruption rules. Additionally, CADE faces significant resource challenges in view of its increased prominence and responsibilities.

In light of this progress, the *Overview of Competition Law in Brazil* provides a much-needed and timely roadmap to a rapidly changing landscape in Brazilian merger, unilateral conduct, and cartel enforcement. It also addresses important enforcement and policy developments in the areas of private damages, vertical price restraints, and standard essential patents and FRAND commitments. Companies doing business in Brazil and their counsel should carefully consider the impact of these developments in light of the country's increasing importance on the global stage of antitrust enforcement, as also evidenced by CADE imposing the highest cartel penalties worldwide in 2014.

This compendium, prepared by Brazil's leading competition experts, will provide invaluable guidance for international practitioners about how best to identify and minimize antitrust risks when dealing with this key jurisdiction. The publication also features detailed interviews with CADE's President and Superintendent, in which they share their views of the recent antitrust reforms and challenges CADE and the Brazilian competition policy system are facing.

The *Overview of Competition Law in Brazil* will undoubtedly be a keystone work and resource in the field, and one on which international antitrust and competition practitioners of all varieties can rely.

April 2015

KRISZTIAN KATONA, U.S. Federal Trade Commission*

Washington, DC

* The views are of the author's alone and do not necessarily represent those of the U.S. Federal Trade Commission or any of its individual Commissioners.

ABOUT THE EDITORS

CRISTIANNE ZARZUR is a partner at Pinheiro Neto Advogados where she focus on competition matters, acting on the following areas: merger clearance; non-merger counseling/investigations (cartel investigations, leniency applications, settlement agreements, abuse of dominant position, exclusionary practices, etc.); and compliance programs. Ms. Zarzur has a LL.B. degree from the Mackenzie University, São Paulo (1995) and a specialization degree in economics from the Getulio Vargas Foundation (1996). Her international experience includes participation in several seminars (ABA, IBA, ICN). In addition, Ms. Zarzur joined the competition and intellectual property law firm Howrey Simon Arnold & White, LLP as a foreign associate at 2000/2001. Ms. Zarzur is currently the president of the Brazilian Institute of Competition and Consumer Relations – IBRAC. She is listed in several publications such as Chambers Global (Tier 1 in Competition in Brazil), Who's Who Legal, PLC Which Lawyer, Expert Guides – Women in Business Law, among other publications.

KRISZTIAN KATONA is Counsel for International Antitrust at the U.S. Federal Trade Commission, where he is responsible for multilateral antitrust affairs and bilateral cooperation with European competition authorities. Prior to joining the FTC in 2006, he worked in the Washington, DC office of Weil, Gotshal & Manges LLP. Mr. Katona holds law degrees from the University of Virginia School of Law, the University of Konstanz, Paris II Panthéon-Assas University, and ELTE University. He is admitted to the bars of the State of New York, the U.S. Supreme Court, and England and Wales. He serves as a Vice-Chair of the ABA Antitrust Section's International Committee.

MARIANA VILLELA is a partner in the antitrust/competition law, litigation and corporate integrity groups of Veirano Advogados. She holds Masters and Doctor (Ph.D) degrees in Commercial Law from the Law School of the University of São Paulo (USP), with emphasis in Competition Law, and an LL.M. degree (Masters of Law, with merits) from the London School of Economics and Political Sciences (LSE), University of London. She is currently Director of Publications of the Brazilian Institute of Competition and Consumer Relations – IBRAC.

ABOUT THE AUTHORS

ANA PAULA MARTINEZ is a partner with Levy & Salomão Antitrust and Compliance practice groups. She worked with the Brazilian federal administration from 2007 to 2010 in competition, regulation, anti-corruption and money laundering matters. She co-headed the cartel sub-group of the ICN with the US DoJ. She is a member of the IBA and of the ABA Sections of Antitrust Law, and of the Advisory Board of IBRAC. Named "Lawyer of the Year 40 and under" at 2014 GCR Awards, she has been included by GCR on its lists "Top Women in Antitrust" and "40 under 40". She is licensed to practice in Brazil and NY and was an associate with Cleary Gottlieb Steen and Hamilton in Brussels. Ms. Martinez served as an advisor to Unctad, to the World Bank and to the Government of Colombia. Currently she is a non-governmental advisor to the ICN. She holds a LL.M. from USP and from Harvard and a Ph.D. from USP (http://www.levysalomao.com.br/professionals/name/ana-paula-martinez).

AURÉLIO SANTOS is the leading partner of Cascione, Pulino, Boulos & Santos Advogados antitrust practice area. He has extensive experience in representing clients in complex antitrust matters and has been recognized among the best Competition and Antitrust lawyers in Brazil by Chambers and Partners, Latin Lawyer, Global Competition Review among others. LL.B., Law School of the University of São Paulo. Master of Laws (LL.M.), Law School of the University of São Paulo. Non-governmental advisor, 2010 Annual Conference of the International Competition Network (ICN) and Member of the Brazilian Institute for the Study of Competition, Consumer Affairs, and International Trade (IBRAC) (www.cpbs.com.br).

BARBARA ROSENBERG is a partner at Barbosa, Müssnich & Aragão Advogados, where she heads the Competition Law practice. Previously, during three years (2003-2005), Barbara was the head of the Antitrust Division within the Secretariat of Economic Law of the Ministry of Justice (SDE/MJ). She has a bachelor degree and a Ph.D. from the University of São Paulo (USP) and an LL.M. from the University of California at

Berkeley. Barbara is the Vice-President of IBRAC; a "Non-Governmental Advisor" of the International Competition Network and a Member to the Internacional Task Force of the Antitrust Section. Barbara has been recognized by a number of publications, such as Chambers Latin America and Global Competition Review, as a prominent lawyer in her field and she was awarded the "Best Lawyer of the Year – Under 40" granted by GCR Award in 2011.

Bruno de Luca Drago has been practicing in the area of Competition Law for more than 13 years, including activities related to notifications of mergers and acquisitions to CADE, international and local cartels, and abuse of dominant position. Bruno's experience involves several economy sectors, such as pharmaceutical, chemical, automotive, civil construction, health, agribusiness, and transportation, among others. Bruno was an associate attorney at Howrey LLP, in Brussels (2005/2006) and in Washington, D.C. (2007). Member of IBRAC and the Competition Bar Commission. Bruno graduated from PUC-SP Law School; holds a post-graduation in Finance Administration at FIA/FEA, a LL.M. in Competition Law from the King's College of London, and a Ph.D. in Commercial Law with major in Competition Law at University of São Paulo (http://www.demarest.com.br).

Caio Mario da Silva Pereira Neto is an expert on competition law and regulation, with extensive experience in both the private and public sectors. Before founding Pereira Neto | Macedo he held office as Director for Competition at the Secretariat of Economic Law of the Brazilian Ministry of Justice (SDE). Caio holds a J.D. from the University of São Paulo, and LL.M. and J.S.D. degrees from Yale Law School, where he was a Fulbright Scholar. He was also a fellow at the Information Society Project of Yale Law School. He is a professor at FGV Direito SP, where he teaches Antitrust, Regulation and Administrative Law, in both graduate and undergraduate courses. Caio is the author of a book, as well as several articles and book chapters published in Brazil and abroad.

Carlos Francisco de Magalhães is considered a pioneer in Competition Law in Brazil, being the creator and founder of IBRAC (Brazilian Institute of Competition, Consumption and International Trade Studies), author of dozens of articles, studies and opinions about Competition Law, all published in specialized magazines and journals since 1970. Member of several governmental committees that amended the Competition Defense

Federal Law, specially the Bill that originated most of the current statutory provisions, he drafted the part that sets forth the definitions of offenses and the submission of concentration acts to the analysis of the Brazilian System of Competition Defense.

Cristiano Rodrigo Del Debbio graduated from Pontifical Catholic University of São Paulo (PUC). Master's Degree in Civil Procedure from University of São Paulo (USP) and LL.M. by the University of Chicago (UC). Has extensive experience in complex commercial, antitrust and consumer litigation, including class-action suits and collective claims, before judicial and administrative authorities, involving banking and credit cards, telecommunications, automotive, food industry and health insurance. Collaborated in the updating of Vol. XV of the *Treatise of Private Law* by Pontes de Miranda, released by Revista dos Tribunais (2013).

Daniel Andreoli. Partner at the Antitrust Law Practice at Tozzini Freire Advogados. LL.M. in Corporate and Commercial Law from King's College London of the University of London. Graduate of the Law School of Pontifícia Universidade Católica de São Paulo (PUC-SP). Vice-president of the Antitrust Group of the São Paulo Section of the Brazilian Bar Association (CECORE/OAB-SP). Member of the Board of IBRAC.

Eduardo Caminati Anders. Lawyer. Antitrust Director of the IBRAC (Instituto Brasileiro de Estudos de Concorrência, Consumo e Comércio Internacional); Vice-President of the Council of IBRAC, 2010/2011. Member of the Applied Corporate Law Institute – IDSA (Instituto de Direito Societário Aplicado). He is also member of the Antitrust Committee of the São Paulo Bar Association (CECORE); President of CECORE, 2010/2012. Author of books and legal papers. Partner at Lino, Beraldi, Belluzzo e Caminati Advogados (http://lbba.com.br/english/eduardo-caminati).

Eduardo Frade Rodrigues is the Acting General Superintendent of the Brazilian Administrative Council for Economic Defense - CADE (since June 2014). He has previously worked as Deputy Superintendent (2012-2014), as an advisor for CADE's Commissioners (2007-2011) and participated in a secondment at the Canadian Competition Bureau (2008). He also headed a unit of the Civil Aviation Regulatory Policy Secretariat (2011-2012). He holds bachelor degrees in Law by the University CEUB in Brasilia and in International Relations by the University of Brasilia, is graduated in Competition Policy by the Getulio Vargas Foundation and is currently a LL.M. candidate at the University of Brasilia. He also attended an Advanced Regulatory Policy course at the George Washington University and a Public Administration course at the Brazilian National School of Public Administration, among others.

Erika Vieira Sang is member of the Antitrust Law Practice at Lefosse Advogados. Erika specializes in competition law, particularly focused on the notification of national and foreign transactions to the Brazilian Competition Defense System and client defense in anticompetitive practices investigations, as well as compliance programs and consultations regarding competition matters. She holds a LL.B from the Universidade Presbiteriana Mackenzie and has a diploma in Competition Law at the São Paulo Law School of the Fundação Getulio Vargas – *GVlaw* Graduate Program.

Fabíola Cammarota de Abreu is a partner of Souza, Cescon, Barrieu & Flesch Advogados (Souza Cescon) since 2005. She holds a law degree from the Catholic University of São Paulo (PUC/SP), 1996. She is Postgraduate in Comparative Law by Anglia Polytechnic University, Cambridge, UK, 1998. She is an M.B.A. candidate reading at The University of Manchester (England), UK, since 2013 and certified by the Compliance Certification Board of the Society of Corporate Compliance and Ethics (SCCE) as a Certified Compliance & Ethics Professional. She is member of the Brazilian Bar Association, the Brazilian Institute of Competition, Consumer and International Trade – IBRAC, the American Bar Association (ABA) and the International Bar Association (IBA). She joins the Task Force on Antitrust Compliance and Advocacy of the International Chamber of Commerce (ICC). She is the head of the Competition Department of Souza Cescon. For more information please *see* www.souzacescon.com.br.

Fabricio Antonio Cardim de Almeida is the head of the antitrust practice at Stocche Forbes Advogados in São Paulo, Brazil. He holds a J.D. and a LL.M. from University of São Paulo's Law School and a LL.M. from Columbia Law School. Fabricio has previously worked as an International Antitrust Consultant in the U.S. Federal Trade Commission's Office of International Affairs. He is a member of IBRAC and of the ABA Section of Antitrust Law and serves as a NGA to the International Competition Network. Fabricio is admitted to the bar of the State of São Paulo, Brazil (http://www.stoccheforbes.com.br/en/teams/fabricio-a-cardim-de-almeida.html).

FILIPPO MARIA LANCIERI specializes in competition law and regulation. Before becoming an associate at Pereira Neto | Macedo he worked at the legal department of a renowned international investment bank. Filippo holds a J.D. from FGV Direito SP (during which he spent a semester at New York University School of Law) and Masters in Economics from INSPER – Instituto de Ensino e Pesquisa (also in São Paulo). Filippo is the winner of the BM&F Bovespa-FGV-2010 paper competition prize, and has published articles in competition and regulation in Brazil and abroad.

FRANCISCO NICLÓS NEGRÃO is magna cum laude highest honors Economics B.A. from Brandeis University (BU), with Justice Brandeis Scholarship. Master's degree in International Economics and Finance from Brandeis University GSIEF, with a semester at Università Commerciale Luigi Bocconi. Bachelor of Laws from Centro Universitário de Brasília (CEUB). Certified Compliance and Ethics Professional (CCEP) from the Society for Commercial Compliance and Ethics (SCCE). Finance and Control Analyst of the Brazilian Treasury Secretariat at the Ministry of Finance (2003-2004), acting in the negotiation of foreign funding operations with international organizations. Phi Beta Kappa. Morris and Anna Feldberg Award for excellence in Economy.

GABRIEL NOGUEIRA DIAS is distinguished for his academic expertise and intense professional engagement in highly complex cases of our important clients. Graduate by the University of São Paulo (USP), he was granted a LL.M. and a LL.D. by the Law School of Bonn – Germany. He acted as adviser to the President of the Administrative Counsel of Economic Defense (CADE) and, while occupying such position, was directly responsible for the development of new Resolutions and Opinions. Currently, Gabriel Nogueira Dias is also a director of IBRAC. Visiting Professor in several Schools, he is the author of several articles as well as an awarded book published by the distinguished German Publisher Mohr Siebeck.

GUILHERME MORGULIS is an Associate lawyer at Barbosa, Müssnich & Aragão Advogados in the Competition Law practice area. He has worked in law firms in corporate law, civil litigation, international trade and antitrust and is a member of the Brazilian Bar Association (OAB). Guilherme has a Law Degree from the University of São Paulo Law School (USP) and was a visiting student at the Georgetown Center for Transnational Legal Studies in London.

João Marcelo Lima is an associate at Mattos Filho's Antitrust practice group. He holds an LL.B. from Fundação Getulio Vargas and is an M.A. candidate at the same institution. Additional information is available at: http://www.mattosfilho.com.br/pages/Profile.aspx?Profile=401&Nome=Jo%C3%A3o%20Marcelo%20da%20Costa%20e%20Silva%20Lima.

Joyce Midori Honda is a partner of the competition law practice group of Souza, Cescon, Barrieu & Flesch Advogados (Souza Cescon), based in São Paulo. Joyce received a law degree from the Catholic University of São Paulo (PUC/SP) in 2001 and holds an LL.M. degree from the London School of Economics and Political Science (LSE) and a postgraduate degree in Economic Law from Fundação Getulio Vargas (FGV). In 2007, she was at the Brazilian Permanent Mission to the World Trade Organization (WTO) in Geneva acting in cases involving international trade law. She is a member of the board of IBRAC, a member of the Competition and Regulatory Committee of the Brazilian Bar Association (OAB) and joins the Task Force on Antitrust Compliance and Advocacy of the International Chamber of Commerce (ICC). For more information please *see* www.souzacescon.com.br.

Leonardo Maniglia Duarte is a lawyer at Veirano Advogados and focuses his practice on the areas of competition law and regulatory law in Brazil. Leonardo holds an LL.M. degree in comparative law, concentrating on antitrust law and mergers and acquisitions, from the University of Miami – School of Law (Coral Gables-FL, United States), and a specialization degree in competition law and regulatory law from the University of Lisbon (Lisbon, Portugal). Leonardo is the author of several articles on competition law published in Brazil and abroad. For additional information, please *see* http://www.veirano.com.br/eng/professionals/view/leonardo_duarte.

Luís Henrique Perroni Fernandes is an associate at Pinheiro Neto Advogados. Mr. Fernandes focuses his practice on competition and international trade matters. Mr. Fernandes received an LL.B. degree from the Catholic Law School in São Paulo (2014). He Medrado is admitted to practice law in Brazil. He can be reached at lfernandes@pn.com.br.

Marcela Abras Lorenzetti is an intern at Grinberg e Cordovil, a competition and trade law boutique in São Paulo, Brazil since 2012. She is a last-year law student at Pontifícia Universidade Católica de São Paulo.

Marcelo Calliari: Partner and Head of the Antitrust Law Practice at TozziniFreire Advogados. Doctor of Laws degree in International Law from University of São Paulo (USP). LL.M. degree from Harvard University. Graduate of the Law School of University of São Paulo (USP). Vice-chair of the Trade and Customs Law Committee of the International Bar Association (IBA). Former President of IBRAC.

Marcio Bueno: Partner at the Antitrust Law Practice at TozziniFreire Advogados. Graduate of the Law School of Pontifícia Universidade Católica de São Paulo (PUC-SP). Former Vice-president of the Antitrust Group of the São Paulo Section of the Brazilian Bar Association (CECORE/OAB-SP). Director of IBRAC.

Marcio Dias Soares is a partner at Mattos Filho's Antitrust practice group. He holds an LL.B. and a Post-Graduate degree from Universidade do Estado do Rio de Janeiro, as well as an LL.M. from Columbia Law School. Additional information is available at: http://www.mattosfilho.com.br/Documents/Socios-en-us/MARCIO%20DIAS.pdf.

Marcos Exposto is an Associate lawyer at Barbosa, Müssnich & Aragão Advogados in the Competition Law practice area. He is a member of the Brazilian Bar Association (OAB), as well as of OAB's Competition and Regulation Committee. Marcos has a Law Degree from the University of São Paulo Law School (USP) (2006) and an LL.M. in Competition, Innovation and Information Law from New York University (2012).

Marcos Paulo Verissimo is a partner at Machado Meyer. He specializes in constitutional law and economic law, including both competition and regulation matters. Marcos was active in the Brazilian Public Administration as a commissioner at the Brazilian Administrative Council for Economic Defense (CADE) and played a pivotal role in CADE's restructuring process following the new Brazilian Antitrust Law in 2011. Marcos was also Head of Office at the Brazilian Development Bank (BNDES), acting in the forefront of major infrastructure projects. Marcos received his LL.B., LL.M. and Ph.D. degrees from University of São Paulo, were he is a tenured professor. He was a visiting Scholar at Yale University Law School in 2005. http://www.machadomeyer.com/lawyers/marcos-paulo-verissimo.

Maria Eugênia Novis is a partner at Machado Meyer Advogados. She possesses vast experience in merger cases, antitrust investigations and antitrust risk assessment, as well as in trade defense matters. Maria Eugênia is ranked by Chambers Latin America as a leading lawyer in the antitrust field in Brazil. She received her Bachelor of Laws degree from Universidade Federal da Bahia and her LL.M. degree in International Business Law from the University of Leiden, in the Netherlands. Maria Eugênia did an internship at the Brazilian Mission to the World Trade Organization in Geneva in 2004. She has been a member of the Deliberative Committee of Brazilian Institute for Competition, Consumer Relations and International Trade Studies (IBRAC) since 2012 (http://www.machadomeyer.com/lawyers/maria-eugenia-novis).

Mariana Tavares de Araujo is a partner with the Antitrust, Product Liability and Compliance practice groups of Levy & Salomão Advogados. Ms. Araujo worked with the Brazilian federal administration for nine years with special focus on competition, product liability and regulation. She attended meetings of the OECD's Committee on Competition and co-headed with the US DoJ the cartels sub-group of the ICN. Ms. Araujo provides counseling to the World Bank, co-chairs the IBA Working Group on International Cartels and is a member of the ABA International Cartel Task Force. GCR named her on its list of the "Top 100 Women in Antitrust" and she has been nominated by the members of the Latin American Corporate Counsel Association for inclusion in its list "LACCA Approved". Ms. Araujo holds a LL.M. from the Georgetown University (http://www.levysalomao.com.br/professionals/name/mariana-tavares-de-araujo).

Mauro Grinberg is the senior partner at Grinberg e Cordovil, a competition and trade law boutique in São Paulo, Brazil. He is a former Commissioner of the Brazilian Antitrust Agency, and a former Attorney of the Treasury. He has been a frequent contributor to specialized publications, including Cartel Regulation of Global Competition Review. He has been mentioned by most publications, including Global Competition Review, Legal 500 and Chambers and Partners, as one of the leading antitrust lawyers in Brazil. Among others, he has extensive works on cartels. Besides being a member both of International Bar Association (Antitrust Committee) and American Bar Association (Antitrust Section), he is a founder, a former President and a Board Member of IBRAC, the main Brazilian antitrust think tank (http://gcalaw.com.br/equipe/diretoria/mauro-grinberg).

Paulo Eduardo Lilla is head of the Antitrust Law Practice at Lefosse Advogados in São Paulo. Paulo holds a Ph.D. and a Master Degree in International Law at University of São Paulo – USP and is also a Professor of Law at Fundação Getulio Vargas Business School – FGV/EAESP. He was a Visiting Scholar at Stanford Law School (Winter-Spring 2012). Paulo is an expert in Competition Law, particularly focused on national and cross-border transactions' notifications to the Brazilian Competition Defense System and client defense in anticompetitive practices investigations. He is particularly knowledgeable about matters involving the interface between Antitrust Law and Intellectual Property and he has published several academic works. Paulo is also experienced in Regulatory Law, Intellectual Property, Anti-Bribery & Compliance and International Business Law. He is a member of the São Paulo Attorneys Institute (IASP) and the Brazilian Institute of Studies of Competition Law, Consumer Relation and International Trade Law (IBRAC).

Paulo Leonardo Casagrande is a specialist in Competition and Regulation, with an extensive expertise in both the private and public sectors. Before becoming a partner at Pereira Neto | Macedo he worked both at the Secretariat of Economic Law of the Brazilian Ministry of Justice (SDE), where he was in charge of implementing the new unit responsible for investigating bid rigging, and at an important international law firm in Brussels, Belgium. Paulo holds a J.D. and a J.S.D. in Economic Law from University of São Paulo, and a LL.M. in Law and Economics from the Universities of Hamburg and Manchester. He is an lecturer of Brazilian Society of Public Law (SBDP) and has written several articles on competition law and regulation, published in Brazil and abroad.

Pedro Paulo Salles Cristofaro is a Brazilian lawyer admitted in Rio de Janeiro and São Paulo, partner at Lobo e Ibeas Advogados (www.loboeibeas.com.br), professor of regulatory and antitrust Law at the Catholic University of Rio de Janeiro (PUC-Rio) and invited lecturer at the Master II Droit du Commerce International at the University Paris Ouest Nanterre La Défense, France (Dec. 2014). He is a member of the Board of the "Instituto Brasileiro de Estudos das Relações de Concorrência e de Consumo – IBRAC", vice-chairman of the Legal Committee of the American Chamber of Commerce in Rio de Janeiro (AMCHAM), member of the American Bar Association and former member of the Legal Education Committee of the Brazilian Bar Association (Rio de Janeiro Section).

Priscila Brolio Gonçalves (br.linkedin.com/pub/priscila-gonçalves/7/9a7/1b4/em) practices economic law, with focus on competition and regulation, distribution agreements, consumer relations and public biddings. Besides providing consultancy to Brazilian and foreign companies, Ms. Gonçalves acts before the antitrust authorities, representing corporate clients in merger notifications and behavior cases. Ms. Gonçalves has been in practice since 1998. She holds a LL.M. (2002) and a Ph.D. (2008) in Commercial Law, and was a Visiting Researcher at London School of Economics and Political Science (2007). Ms. Gonçalves has published two books (*Fixação e Sugestão de Preços de Revenda em Contratos de Distribuição*, 2002, and *A Obrigatoriedade de Contratar no Direito Antitruste*, 2008) and several articles on competition and antitrust issues. She is a Member of IBRAC, of the Antitrust Economic Regulation Studies Committee of the Brazilian Bar Association, São Paulo section (CECORE/OAB/SP), and a Member of the American Bar Association (Antitrust and International Sections). She has been a partner at law firm Vella Pugliese Buosi e Guidoni (http://www.vpbg.com.br/our-team.php) in São Paulo and Brasília since 2008.

Renata Fonseca Zuccolo is a senior associate at Mattos Filho's Antitrust practice group. She holds an LL.B. from Pontifícia Universidade Católica de São Paulo, a specialist Degree in Economic Law and Regulation from GVLAW and an LL.M. from King's College London. Additional information is available at: http://www.mattosfilho.com.br/pages/Profile.aspx?Profile=343&Nome=Renata%20Fonseca%20Zuccolo%20Giannella.

Renê Guilherme S. Medrado is a partner of Pinheiro Neto Advogados. Mr. Medrado has been with the firm since 1995, where he is a partner since 2009. He counsels multinational corporations, companies, trade associations, on international trade and competition matters, and litigates disputes over such matters. Mr. Medrado has years of experience in competition law matters, having counseled and represented companies in important merger cases, as well as in several cartel investigations. Mr. Medrado received an LL.B. degree from the Catholic University in São Paulo (1997), and an Executive MBA from Insper (2002). He received an LL.M. from Columbia University School of Law (2003), where he graduated with honors (Harlan Fiske Stone scholar). Mr. Medrado also received his Ph.D. from the University of São Paulo (USP) Law School in 2011. Mr. Medrado is admitted to practice law in Brazil and in the State of New York (USA), and is recognized by many publications as a leading lawyer in Brazil in his areas of practice. He can be reached at rmedrado@pn.com.br (http://www.pinheironeto.com.br/advogado/rene-g-s-medrado).

Ricardo Botelho is partner of Cascione, Pulino, Boulos & Santos Advogados. He represents clients in antitrust investigations and merger review processes and advises in preventive counseling on practices and compliance programs. He also assists clients in international trade and commercial defense matters and market regulation issues, including insurance law matters. Recognized among the best Competition and Antitrust lawyers by The Legal 500 and by Latin Lawyer 250. LL.B., Law School of the University of São Paulo. Master in Business Economics, Fundação Getúlio Vargas (FGV-SP). Post-graduate in EU Competition Law, King's College London, UK. Member of the Council of IBRAC (www.cpbs.com.br).

Rodrigo Alves dos Santos is a lawyer at Veirano Advogados and focuses his practice on the areas of competition and anticorruption law. Rodrigo holds an LL.B. degree from the Law School of Centro Universitário de Brasília. Rodrigo is the author of articles on competition law in Brazil. For additional information, please *see* http://www.veirano.com.br/eng/professionals/view/rodrigo_santos.

Sandra Terepins is an Associate lawyer at Barbosa, Müssnich & Aragão Advogados in the Competition Law practice area. She is a member of the Brazilian Bar Association (OAB). Sandra has a Law Degree from the Pontifícia Universidade Católica de São Paulo (PUC-SP) (2006), a Master in Business Economics Degree from the Fundação Getulio Vargas de São Paulo (FGV/SP) (2010), and an LL.M. focused in Antitrust Law from Georgetown University (2011).

Vinicius Marques de Carvalho. First and current President of CADE under the new competition law (Law 12,529/11). Former Secretary of Economic Law of the Ministry of Justice (2011-2012). Former Commissioner of CADE (2008-2011). Chief of Staff of the Special Secretariat for Human Rights of the Presidency of the Republic (2007-2008). Public Policies and Government Management Specialist (EPPGG) since 2006. Ph.D. in Commercial Law, University of São Paulo Law School. Ph.D. in Economic Compared Law, Paris I University (Panthéon-Sorbonne).

QUESTIONS & ANSWERS

Vinicius Marques de Carvalho

I. In your view, since the entering into effect of Law 12,529/11, in May, 2012, what have been the most relevant developments and achievements in competition policy in Brazil?

First and foremost, the most relevant development, and achievement, in competition policy in Brazil, with the entry into effect of Law 12,529/11, the Brazilian Competition Law, was the institutional reorganization of the Brazilian System for the Defense of Competition, which created the new CADE. The new CADE, with the structure and organization we know today, brought together the investigatory and decision-making powers of competition enforcement, leading to increased efficiency, coherence and effectiveness to competition policy and enforcement in Brazil.

Under the new law, a two-tiered agency was created, with the investigatory aspect of proceedings mostly concentrated in the General Superintendence, and the complex analysis, decision-making and normative competences mostly focused in the Tribunal. Such institutional reorganization set the stage for an important reallocation of resources and an increased robustness of CADE's competition enforcement activity. This was rooted not only in the increased specialization of the General Superintendence in matters of investigative practice, and greater resources for the Tribunal to focus on more impactful issues for the Brazilian competition authority, it was also rooted in the creation of an independent Economic Studies Department, which contributes increasingly with sophisticated economic analysis to CADE decisions. CADE decisions have become stronger, more robust and quicker.

Among the substantive changes that accompanied that law, perhaps the most significant is that the new Competition Law established the pre-merger notification regime, setting new thresholds for compulsory notification, and implementing a non-stop deadline of 330 days for a final decision to be issued by CADE.

The impact of this change in the competition community, and indeed in the economy, was very significant, considering that the previous system was a stop-the-clock post-merger review system, in which a given merger could be handled by up to three different institutions and took, on average, 155 days. Complex mergers could take up two years to be decided.

Before the entry into force of the law, there was a great deal of concern regarding whether CADE would be able to deal with the influx of mergers to review, analyzing and deciding on them within a reasonable time frame. In response to that, CADE sought to reassure the competition community and pledged to approve fast-track mergers in less than 30 days.

Not only did we achieve this immediately following the entry into effect of the new system, we have been able to maintain this maximum to this day. This statistic relates to cases which currently represent almost 90% of mergers reviewed by CADE. Ordinary cases are currently reviewed in 65 days, on average. Challenged or complex mergers, which may require further analysis, negotiation of remedies and are decided upon by the Tribunal, are reviewed in just over 200 days, on average.

CADE managed to achieve and maintain this efficiency with normative guidance and predictability of the system, by way of resolutions, as well as with an organizational design that privileged the screening and triage of fast-track cases and the handling of the remaining cases by four units specialized in particular economic sectors. This institutional design allowed for CADE to increase the speed in the analysis of merger review without compromising the quality of its work. This organizational structure also allowed CADE to eliminate its significant merger backlog.

The amount of information parties were required to provide CADE in their pre-merger notification was also essential to ensuring the efficiency of the system once the merger was notified. CADE provided a self-assessment opportunity to merging parties, as to whether they would provide a fast-track or an ordinary notification form, which had varying degrees of compulsory information. As a merger notification is only complete once

CADE considers the notification form is duly completed with room for pre-notification interaction between the merging parties and the authority, CADE ensured that it would have necessary information to adequately deal with the merger review. In complex cases, of course, further requests for information would still be inevitable.

In the legal framework of Law 12,529/11, legislators also opted for changing the notification criteria of mergers by eliminating the market share criteria and applying a turnover threshold to more than one party of the operation. This legal change was responsible for a substantial decline of the number of cases submitted to CADE and reflects the option, even on the legislative level, for identifying and prioritizing the most relevant competition cases for the economy and consumers.

In addition to this, the decision-making process regarding mergers created important institutional efficiencies. As the large majority of merger cases may now be decided by the General Superintendence, under the supervision of the Tribunal, the Tribunal focuses on only the challenged and complex cases. This allows for the Tribunal to focus its resources on those cases that will have the greatest impact on the market and to Brazilian consumers.

In fact, among all mergers challenged since 2012, all but one of them resulted in a settlement with remedies, rather than imposed restrictions or a merger block – a reflection of the maturity of the system and the openness to negotiating innovative solutions.

These developments also allowed CADE to become a more active player in terms of cooperating with its international counterparts. With a post-merger review system, it was more difficult for CADE to cooperate with other agencies that carried out pre-merger reviews and were tackling the same merger, since coordinating the timetable of the analyses was a challenge. On implementing a pre-merger review, with consolidated practice and world-class review times, CADE was able to engage in international cooperation in the past three years with agencies from all over the world in merger review, among which are the European Commission's DG Competition, the United States agencies FTC and DOJ and other Latin American agencies. In 2014, CADE cooperated in 13 merger cases. In 2015, so far 7 merger cases have required international cooperation.

As regards anti-competitive conducts, the developments and achievements have also been substantial, benefited in large part by the gain in efficiency from the elimination of the merger backlog and the filtering of cases that reach the Tribunal. Whereas in 2011, only 16 anticompetitive practice cases were tried by the Tribunal, 38 administrative proceedings in antitrust were tried in 2014, and 57 cases in 2015.

The organizational set up in the new CADE strongly contributed to these results. The creation of the General Superintendence as the investigatory body as regards antitrust investigations, with a significant degree of independence from the Tribunal regarding the opening of proceedings, how they are conducted thereafter and the recommendation to the Tribunal to file or to sanction a particular investigated conduct. The Tribunal, which was previously overloaded with older long-running investigations, was able, in the past years, to move beyond this and focus on cases that bring more impact to the institution and to the economy and create relevant precedent. In the past, for instance, a large majority of proceedings tried in the Tribunal were filed (up to 85%), whereas in 2013 and 2014, 64% of the administrative proceedings decided by the Tribunal led to convictions. This does not indicate a more aggressive competition enforcement trend, but rather that the Tribunal's efforts are being focused on cases that are more likely to be harmful to the Brazilian economy and to Brazilian consumers.

The internal organization of the General Superintendence, and in particular the implementation of a triage unit for receiving and screening complaints and leniency applications, as well as identifying and prioritizing harmful, stronger cases contributed to this. The prioritization and screening policies seeks to avoid cases with little change of success, that is, which have apparently little evidence, and the subsequent squander of scarce resources.

In 2014, for instance, CADE applied, for the first time ever, structural remedies in a cartel case, along with historic fines, in the cement cartel case. The final decision of this case is still pending following a motion for clarification to CADE. CADE also decided various high-profile, complex cartel cases in bid-rigging, opening administrative proceedings against several multinational companies in alleged cartel behavior in train and subway procurements.

CADE also contributed significantly to providing legal certainty for companies when assessing their liability in competition law infringements with resolutions. For example, in 2012, the resolution which set out branches of economic activity, cited in the Brazilian competition law as the basis for setting fines, ensured a much higher level of predictability and certainty in considering eventual fines for competition enforcement.

In parallel to the previously mentioned developments and achievements, CADE also increased its international cooperation in antitrust proceedings, benefiting from its clearer, more structured and organized proceedings which followed from the new Brazilian competition law and the institutional reorganization. In 2014, CADE cooperated in 3 conduct cases with authorities from other countries, whereas until March of 2015, CADE has cooperated internationally in 5 conduct cases.

In addition to competition enforcement, the developments and achievements of the past three years have not only brought added efficiency, and effectiveness to CADE's competition enforcement, but have allowed both CADE's Superintendence and Tribunal to explore other areas of competition policy and enforcement.

In terms of cartel detection, the General Superintendence created, in 2013, an Intelligence Unit, which is charged with *ex officio* cartel detection, particularly in public procurement. This is based on a dual track approach of, on the one hand, creating partnerships with public institutions that can provide the data on public procurements in Brazil and, on the other hand, developing the procedures, based on international best practice, and the technological means, to apply screens to the data and identify potential misconduct.

Despite important advances in that area, CADE's Leniency Program continues to be a fundamental part of cartel detection in Brazil. It has evolved throughout these years, and is today a more mature instrument, in which CADE has become increasingly aware of the importance of effectively evaluating which leniency applications to accept, and which are simply insufficient. In 2014, the number of leniency applications continues on an increasing trend, and reflects CADE's sound resolve in maintaining the integrity of the program.

The freeing up of resources also allowed CADE to develop its alternative case resolution mechanisms, namely its new Settlements Program. In the resolution passed in 2013, CADE changed the rules for settlements in investigations of anticompetitive conducts by way of Cease and Desist Agreements (TCC, in its acronym in Portuguese).

The new provisions rule that, in order to settle in antitrust proceedings involving cartels, the parties must confess their participation in the practice and cooperate with the investigation if the proceeding is still in its investigatory stage. It also requires the immediate suspension of the conduct.

Although there was a concern among that the confession requirement could dissuade parties from seeking settlements with CADE, the results of the settlements program so far have been very positive. For CADE, settlements reduce prosecution costs and avoid lengthy battles in court, and also contribute to more robust decisions, all the while desincentivizing anticompetitive behavior with the payment of a pecuniary contribution to the Brazilian Diffused Rights Fund. For the parties, the new settlements policy brought legal certainty to the instrument and gave a structured, transparent avenue to quick case resolution, through a negotiation process with CADE. The settlements program was particularly important in providing a lifeline to parties as a complement to CADE's Leniency Program, which grants immunity only for first-in applicants.

The number of settlements signed, and its increase, is a reflection of its success. In 2014, CADE signed 38 TCCs, 22 of which were in cartel investigations.

With experience in applying the new Brazilian Competition Law, CADE also took the opportunity to provide clarification and further legal certainty and guidance on issues of competition policy and enforcement. These have included various clarifications to both the Brazilian Competition Law, as well as to CADE's Internal Regulation (*Regimento Interno do CADE – RICADE*).

I would highlight, among others I have already mentioned, that in terms of clarifications of the law, CADE published Resolution No. 10 in 2014, which clarified the issue of notification of associative contracts, foreseen in the competition law but without a clear definition of the concept of associative contracts. Resolution No. 10 defined the circumstances in which these contracts should be notified to the authority to be analyzed.

In addition to these developments in competition policy and enforcement, CADE continues to work to improve the efficiency of its management and procedures. In January 2015, Resolution No. 11 implemented the Electronic Information System, SEI in its acronym in Portuguese, as the official system of the agency for document management. This widespread organizational shift to paperless internal procedures aims to significantly reduce the duration of competition cases, as well as allowing for management information on CADE's performance and competition enforcement activity. SEI also allows for companies involved in CADE investigations online access to file.

In conclusion, since the entry into effect of the new law, the new CADE has matured into an institution and to enable the consolidation of a more efficient competition defense policy, which can be proved by CADE's latest numbers and by its priorities in the recent years.

II. How do you view the role of CADE's Tribunal in the context of the current organizational structure of the Brazilian Competition Defense System?

The role of the Tribunal in the context of the current organizational structure of the Brazilian Competition Defense System is to steer and guide competition policy and enforcement. The Tribunal is the highest decision-making body in CADE and the body which is responsible for providing normative provisions for competition enforcement in Brazil. Its main responsibility is to supervise competition enforcement within CADE, and to be more effective and efficient in trying the cases brought to it, which are effectively the most relevant cases at CADE, with the greatest impact on the economy and consumers.

In fact, the importance of the Tribunal stems not only from its position with CADE's organizational structure, but also due to its very nature. The Tribunal is a collegial body composed, in full quorum, by 6 Commissioners and a President, who usually come from legal and economic academic backgrounds, and with diverse professional experience. This difference of opinions, of points of view and of expertise, contribute to profound discussions on competition cases, and lead to better, stronger decisions in every case CADE tries.

In terms of competition enforcement, then, CADE's Tribunal has two important functions, that of supervision of decisions taken within the General Superintendence, and the trial of challenged merger proceedings and antitrust proceedings.

While under the repealed law (Law 8,884/94) the Secretariat for Economic Law (*Secretaria de Direito Econômico* – SDE) and the Secretariat for Economic Monitoring *(Secretaria de Acompanhamento Econômico* – SEAE) had no power of decision and only issued opinions on the cases they handled, under the new Law, the General Superintendence may approve mergers and decide to file an administrative investigation or its preparatory procedures when it considers that there is a lack of grounds to proceed. This option reduces the number of cases submitted to the Tribunal, which now has more room to focus on select cases, those most relevant cases which have survived the triage process.

However, the system implemented has various checks and balances built in. In order to ensure that certain decisions (mergers approved or investigative proceedings filed by the General Superintendence) are not limited solely to the General Superintendence, the new legal framework established an arrogation (*avocação*) mechanism. Through it the Tribunal may, upon request and reasoned decision of one of its Commissioners, submit a merger approved by the General Superintendence to trial, as well as request the analysis of an administrative investigation or of an administrative investigation preparatory procedure filed by the General Superintendence.[1] Such a mechanism enables the Tribunal to supervise decision-making in CADE on the whole, while focusing on the most relevant competition cases.

As for the caseload of the Tribunal itself, the new institutional framework has allowed only the most relevant cases to reach the highest level in CADE. This has various implications for the Tribunal's role in the current organizational structure.

Firstly, the reallocation of resources has allowed the Tribunal to have a greater role in actively approaching those complex competition cases which are judged by it with robust, sound legal and economic reasoning.

---

1 According the Brazilian Competition Law, once the administrative investigation is requested, the Reporting Commissioner shall have thirty (30) business days to either i) confirm the dismissal decision of the General Superintendence, as well as, if deemed necessary, provide grounds for its decision; or ii) transform the administrative investigation into administrative proceedings, determining that a complementary fact-finding be performed, being also possible, at its criteria, to require that the General Superintendence performs it, stating the points in controversy and specifying the measures to be taken.

The reallocation of resources has also allowed the Tribunal to ensure relevant precedent, predictability and legal certainty and to provide and promote innovative solutions which have a real impact on the Brazilian economy, with benefits to the Brazilian consumer.

This is an important development, particularly in comparison with the past, in which three different organizational bodies carried out competition policy and enforcement, sometimes leaving room for grey areas and contradicting interpretations. CADE now has the tools and framework to reflect carefully on competition cases to provide coherent, consistent and robust legal precedent in Brazil – a unified competition policy.

This is an essential part of what I would consider the Tribunal's second role in the current organizational system, which is that of promoting compliance and enriching the normative framework of competition policy in Brazil.

When firms are more aware of the benefits of competition, the rules of competition, as well as have legal certainty on the interpretation of the law, and how CADE will go about investigating and sanctioning particular conducts, it makes it easier for them to comply with competition law. It is essential that companies feel confident enough to do this, and to self-evaluate their own risk of infringing competition rules, so that they may effectively implement internal compliance programs.

For instance, a recently enacted CADE resolution sets out the rules on the consultation procedure, provided by Law 12,529/11, whereby parties can consult CADE's Tribunal on the interpretation of the competition law. It is an extremely useful tool to encourage companies to engage with CADE to clarify issues related to the scope of the provisions of Brazilian competition legislation.

Within CADE, the development of this guidance is a multi-actor process, which includes the involvement of the technical bodies of CADE in international benchmarking and incorporating CADE's experience and common practice. All of the guidelines and resolutions are also subject to public consultation and reviewed in order to engage in a fruitful dialogue with the competition community in seeking to promote a solid, robust normative framework for competition enforcement. This guidance are then discussed and approved within the Tribunal, which is ultimately responsible for ensuring the consistency and cohesion of the normative framework provided by CADE, and which will then take those same guidelines and resolutions into account upon deciding competition cases.

These efforts have been reflected in a number of normative guidelines and resolutions CADE has published in the past years, and will continue to be an important part of the Tribunal's work in the coming years.

III. Since the coming into effect of Law 12,529/11, the number of cases submitted to CADE's Administrative Tribunal has decreased substantially. How has this been affecting the analysis of the cases by the Tribunal?

The reduced number of cases submitted to the Tribunal has not meant a declining workload for CADE's Tribunal Commissioners. In fact, it has freed up resources for the Tribunal to take on its role at the helm of competition policy and enforcement.

This has been carried out on two main dimensions, that of concentrating on the cases with most impact with CADE, both in merger review and antitrust, and that of creating a robust normative framework, guiding and promoting a more mature competition policy and competition culture in Brazil.

Firstly, then, as previously mentioned, the Tribunal can focus on developing robust decisions, with dedicated resources on profoundly analyzing issues of economic analysis and legal precedent.

Upon receiving a case from the General Superintendence, whether it is a challenged merger or an antitrust administrative proceeding, the Tribunal then takes the opportunity to provide for ample analysis of the case, taking into consideration the parties' defense. The means available to carry out this more profound analysis are greatly increased, particularly in terms of antitrust proceedings, allowing the Tribunal to go deeper in its analysis.

Before the case reaches the Tribunal floor, there are various discussions among Tribunal members to discuss the merit of the case, and the potential solutions on the table so as to provide full information and disclosure to the Tribunal members, allowing for quicker, more efficient handling of the case within the Tribunal, and a more profound collegial discussion and decision on it. This has also allowed for the Tribunal to more effectively deal with alternative case resolution mechanisms, such as the new settlements program, which has seen very positive developments since its implementation in 2013.

Also, besides allowing the allocation of resources in the most relevant competition cases and assuring greater equilibrium between the analysis of mergers and conducts, the reduction of cases submitted to CADE's Tribunal also enabled it to proactively regulate the new Law.

As mentioned above, since Law 12,529/11 came into force, CADE enacted a series of resolutions targeted at clarifying the provisions set out in it. The agency's commitment to mitigate legal uncertainty is, in fact, strictly connected with the lower number of cases currently judged by CADE: clearer criteria on what should and should not be notified to the authority increases predictability and leads to more objectivity on the side of companies, thereby reducing notifications by default.

IV. CADE has issued several regulations in the last years to try to provide more guidance and predictability regarding certain provisions of Law 12,529/11. Do you plan or expect new regulations to be enacted in the near future?

Since the enactment of the new competition law, CADE has worked to hold a constant and open dialogue with the economic and legal community that work with CADE in order to perfect the agency's rules and provide guidance on the application of competition law. Various resolutions were enacted by CADE's Tribunal setting out rules of legal clarification on specific subjects, such as the need for notification of associative contracts and on consultations to CADE's Administrative Tribunal on the application of the competition legislation.

CADE is currently undertaking significant efforts in a new phase of developing guidance for companies, and the legal community, as a means of providing a roadmap for companies of CADE's understanding on particular issues of the application of competition law, allowing stakeholders to better assess the risk inherent to their actions. This reinforces legal certainty and promotes more effective compliance with competition rules, with increased and improved awareness of the rules of competition. There are three guides currently being developed.

The first guide on gun jumping, already near conclusion, seeks to guide private agents, to promote legal certainty, to reduce merger transaction costs, and to facilitate the legal integration of activities of economic agents. The guide aims to establish parameters in which merging parties can base themselves when designing a merger transaction. The guide is being developed based on CADE's experience since the enactment of Law 12,529/11 and on international benchmarking. The guide should be concluded in the first semester of 2015.

The second guide being developed gives guidance to companies on complying with competition law. It aims to provide a framework whereby companies can regulate themselves, internally implementing competition compliance programs and incorporating compliance with competition law into the corporate identity of the company. Thus, companies would be able to assess their own actions and monitor their behavior to prevent potentially infringing competition rules and being investigated for an anticompetitive conduct. The guide also seeks to promote the importance of compliance with competition law as a key factor to the maintenance of a competitive environment in Brazil. CADE aims to have a first draft of the compliance guide in the first semester of 2015 in order to invite comments from stakeholders in the second semester and complete the guide until the end of the year.

The third guide, which is due to be published in 2016, is on the implementation of antitrust remedies. The project to develop the guide is being carried out with the support of the United Nations Development Program – UNDP, which finances specialized consulting. There is currently an open selection process to hire a specialist consultant to develop the guide within CADE.

V. What do you think are the main challenges that the Brazilian Competition Defense System faces today and how do you think they can be overcome?

The challenges that CADE faces today are to maintain what has grown into a mature, consolidated institutional practice of competition enforcement and to enhance our capacity, both in our current areas of work, as well as exploring new areas for CADE activity.

In terms of investigative capacity, CADE must maintain its current very successful merger review regime, with short average durations and robust decisions, with successful negotiation of remedies packages. CADE should always strive to make the system more efficient for its stakeholders, and for its institutional performance, but it should also expand its activity to the detection of non-notifiable mergers that may still have harmful impact on competition, and identifying gun jumping.

Regarding antitrust, very significant developments have been made in the past years, but there is still work to be done. CADE is working, and must continue its efforts, to reduce the backlog of cases, some of which are indeed very long-running, and to reduce the time it takes to investigate and decide upon antitrust cases, particularly cartels.

It must also enhance its cartel detection initiatives, with a renewed commitment to its Leniency Program, but also with the development of technological and human resources to expand its activity in the *ex officio* detection of cartels, which it has begun to do in the Intelligence Unit of the General Superintendence. This point is especially important with the current anti-corruption agenda in Brazil, and the reinforced cooperation and dialogue between agencies that deal with areas of law enforcement that are related to corruption and competition, as well as with procurement agencies.

CADE must also increase its capacity to deal with a greater influx of leniency applications as Brazilian companies internalize competition compliance programs, open and investigate more cases while maintaining or even reducing the duration of cases, as well as engage in more settlement negotiations. This is particularly important when considering the significant backlog of conduct cases CADE still has.

Also, at the beginning of this year, CADE successfully carried out a very important IT organizational reform with the implementation of SEI, the Electronic Information System, making all of CADE's administrative and case proceedings paperless. This important step brings increased efficiency and productivity internally and online access to file and to CADE decisions to anyone who consults it. The next challenge in this field is to expand this system to allow for online notification of mergers and the electronic submission of documents to CADE.

To overcome these myriad challenges, CADE needs to be able to expand its human resource base. For instance, in comparison to other competition agencies, among the best in the world, CADE has an extremely low case handler to case ratio, at 0.8 case handlers to an abuse of dominance case, compared to DG COMP's 5.3 case handlers per abuse of dominance case, and 0.4 case handlers to a merger review, in comparison to 2.7 case handlers per merger case in the EU.

With reinforced human resources, CADE could also invest in enhancing its internal knowledge and expertise of particular markets and relevant areas for CADE's activity. This would be very useful, for instance, in public procurement, as CADE is combating bid-rigging both in its enforcement agenda, and as part of its cartel detection.

Finally, there is the challenge of raising awareness of the benefits of competition to the business community and promoting competition compliance, as a means to consolidating the competition culture in Brazil. We have registered that there has been an increasing concern from the competition community regarding compliance with competition rules, a trend influenced by CADE's enforcement activity but also with the current widespread trend regarding compliance with anti-corruption legislation, as well.

The seminar on *Competition and Compliance*, held in August in São Paulo, was an important launch to the dialogue between CADE and the business community regarding what should constitute a competition compliance program and how CADE should participate in promoting competition compliance. Following from that, CADE is now developing a guide for competition compliance, which is due to be published at the end of the year, following public consultations. This is particularly important in approaching competition culture in Brazil as a whole, looking beyond competition enforcement, and advocating for the importance of internalizing the benefits of competition in the values of companies in Brazil – the beginning of a stronger competition culture in Brazil.

VI. How do you see the developments of competition policy for the next few years?

On a global level, one of the main developments of the next few years will be reinforced international cooperation and procedural convergence, particularly in conduct cases. In the past, we have seen international cooperation in mergers become a successful case study, with cross-border mergers being increasingly effectively tackled by competition authorities across the globe. International cartels have also had their moment in stimulating international convergence and coordination among agencies. However, as we see an increasing trend in the investigation of national cartels, rather than international, as a likely consequence of the renewed efforts in combating bid-rigging in public procurement, the attention of international cooperation will likely shift towards unilateral conduct. This is particularly true when we look at global markets which are emerging in the competition policy discussions on a global level, such as the digital economy.

In Brazil, competition policy in the next few years will evolve on various fronts, as a consequence of political and institutional context, as Brazil takes a step beyond effective public enforcement and as companies begin to internalize the importance of complying with competition law.

Firstly, the interaction of competition law with other areas of law is gaining increasing relevance, and will continue to do so in the coming years. This is particularly relevant given the context of the strong public agenda in the fight against corruption. The subway car cartel case and the "Operation Car Wash" case show the growing importance of this interaction. This will mean that CADE will need reinforced dialogue with other institutions such as the Federal Comptroller-General's Office (*Controladoria Geral da União – CGU*), the Federal Public Prosecutor's Office (*Ministério Público*) and the judiciary. It will be essential to work to raise awareness among these institutions of the importance of instruments such as leniency, and maintaining the integrity of the program. This has already begun in Brazil with the newly adopted anti-corruption legislation establishing a leniency program within CGU.

On a similar note, private enforcement will also gain importance in Brazil. The claim for damages by private parties following competition infringements is rare in Brazil. However, these types of claims will become more common, particularly as regards claims for damages in bid-rigging cases where the appellant is the State. This will likely lead to an in-depth discussion of the legislative framework for private enforcement regarding infringement of competition rules, including the calculation of damages.

Looking at the business side of things, and as previously mentioned, companies in Brazil are increasingly showing concern with regards to competition compliance, clearly in a wider context of concern with compliance of other types of legislation. CADE is already participating in this discussion, and is taking an active role in providing guidance on competition compliance, and may work with other institutions, as well as the private bar, to give guidance to companies on how best to promote internal compliance.

In fact, CADE has made an important effort in the consolidation of competition policy in Brazil through its consistent, coherent and robust competition enforcement and also through its normative agenda of developing guidance and bringing legal clarity to the business community. In the next few years, we will see the effects of this agenda, and the consolidation of this competition policy, with CADE leading the way to faster, more efficient and more effective enforcement and the consolidation of a competition culture in Brazil.

* * *

QUESTIONS & ANSWERS

Eduardo Frade Rodrigues

I. In your view, since the entering into effect of Law 12,529/11, in May, 2012, which have been the most relevant developments and achievements in competition policy in Brazil?

The first and most obvious development relates to the rationalization of the structure of the Brazilian system, switching from a system in which mergers and conducts were handled by three different bodies, to one in which this analysis is conducted within a single body: CADE. Although CADE is divided in two levels (Tribunal and General Superintendence), the legislator required that only the most complex cases reach the Tribunal, meaning that in practice the majority of cases are dealt with solely by the General Superintendence. Besides the obvious gains in simplicity and speed, such structure also permitted greater and easier interaction between the bodies' staff, leading to a smother decision process, easier and faster solution of administrative and case matters, and generating a more consensual and consistent competition policy.

MERGERS

The first most significant developments and achievements were clearly derived from the new merger review process. The transformation by the Law of a post-merger review system into a pre-merger review framework, with pre-established and non-suspensory review deadlines, was in itself a development, but also a challenge. The challenge was greater yet when CADE understood the need to go beyond what was required by Law (which stipulates mergers must be reviewed within 330 days), and committed itself to review simple mergers in less than 30 days (and ordinary mergers in significantly less than 330 days, in most cases).

The achievements in this field are perhaps the most evident in light of Brazil's new competition policy. In 2011, before the new Law came into effect, merger review periods averaged 155 days (complex mergers could take over two years to be decided on). From the beginning of the new system to this day, all fast-track cases – which account for 80% to 90% of total mergers reviewed by CADE – are decided in a maximum of 30 days. Ordinary cases are reviewed in an average of 65 days, whereas challenged and complex mergers are analyzed in a little over 200 days on average.[1]

Such results were achieved through a mix of regulation changes and new management frameworks which are now institutionalized within CADE: the already mentioned rationalization of the Competition System's structure; the update of minimum turnovers parties must achieve in order for a merger to be deemed notifiable; clear and objective categorization of ordinary and fast-track cases; enforcement of rules that require parties to provide minimum information when notifying a transaction; creation of a unit responsible for screening notified transactions and quickly reviewing fast-track cases; and the division of units responsible for analyzing ordinary cases observing economic sectors' criterion. During these past three years, other new regulations and regulation revisions were carried out in order to provide clearer rules regarding merger notification and analysis.

Within relatively little time, competition policy related to mergers also achieved new, interesting and positive developments regarding challenged mergers: it is a notable feature that, with a single exception, all mergers challenged by CADE in the new system (approximately 16 from 2012 to 2014) resulted in settlements, as opposed to imposed restrictions or blockages. The new framework also incentivized greater interaction and coordination between CADE and international antitrust authorities during common merger reviews, including the coordination of remedies. At the same time, such interaction and experience has immensely improved the design and implementation of remedies by CADE in comparison to past precedents.

Still in the merger arena, more recent developments are related to the quality of the merger review, which has been benefitting from a consistently

1 Numbers referring to 2014.

more frequent and profound use of CADE's Economics Department during the analysis.

CONDUCTS

Legislative changes in the structure of Brazil's competition policy system also favored the rationalization of anticompetitive conducts' assessments, for similar reasons. In particular, the fact that the Tribunal now concentrates especially in advanced stages of administrative proceedings, and at the same time spends less of its resources analyzing simple mergers, allowed a significant boost in the trial of conduct cases. Between 2013 and 2014, CADE's Tribunal tried an average of 47 administrative proceedings per year. The annual average of the previous three years was around 16. Also, in the previous years, the vast majority of tried proceedings ended up filed (approximately 85%), which meant CADE was concentrating most of its resources on cases that posed no harm to competition. During 2013 and 2014, however, this tendency was reversed: over 64% of tried administrative proceedings generated convictions.

This should not be read as an aggravation of competition policy resulting from a more rigorous approach towards the merits of conduct cases. Rather, such a switch resulted mainly from the new policy adopted by the General Superintendence, of case screening and prioritization. The idea behind it was the recognition that CADE's investigative units had too big of a backlog of conduct cases, opened and carried out too many investigations in weak cases (with poor evidence) and thus failed to concentrate its resources (and the Tribunal's resources) on strong, impactful cases.

Especially during the first year following the implementation of the new regime, there was a considerable effort within the General Superintendence to eliminate a portion of its backlog (whether by filing weak cases or by finishing assessments in order to send cases to the Tribunal). Between 2012 and 2013, the backlog was reduced by nearly a third, and has not increased significantly since, meaning the case stock is balanced.

At the same time, a triage unit, responsible for receiving and screening complaints of conduct cases, was created. The philosophy passed along to this unit, as well as to the other investigators within the General Superintendence, is to avoid carrying out investigations that do not present real chances of success, meaning, for instance, cases that pose doubtful competition harms and cases accompanied by weak evidence or with little chances of obtaining reasonable evidence. As a result of such policy, although the General Superintendence receives the same amount of complaints as in the past (or even more), the number of investigations that are actually turned into administrative proceedings, the procedure when the authority understands there is enough evidence to pose charges against parties, and which starts a formal process of defense, final opinion and mandatory trial by the Tribunal, was cut by over a third.

At the same time, however, the number of administrative proceedings assessed by the General Superintendence and sent to the Tribunal for trial is approximately double. In nearly 75% of such cases, the General Superintendence's opinion converges towards convictions. In sum, within the new system the competition policy towards conducts developed to one in which, although the number of initial complaints has only slightly increased, resources are mainly focused on stronger, potentially harmful cases, that tend to be delivered faster.

Regarding the duration of investigations, by the end of 2014, approximately 50% of the General Superintendence's backlog was composed of investigations dated one year old, whereas in 2013 one-year old investigations accounted for only 28% of the total stock. Nearly 70% of the investigations by the end of 2014 were less than 3 years old. By the end of the 2013, these accounted for 54%.

Speaking of investigations, the Superintendence has started efforts to develop and improve its investigative tools and capacity, directing personnel specifically to this task. In this arena, internal procedures regarding dawn raids have significantly improved the efficiency and efficacy of the operations, as well as lessened negative outcomes derived from judicial questioning of the search measures. The intelligence analysis of apprehended evidence and others has also become more efficient.

Although discovery of cases *ex officio* has been a continuous goal, with concrete outcomes, the leniency program remains a central and vital tool in cartel detection, with increasing resources being devoted to it. In continuation of the efforts and results constructed over the past decade, as of the new system's implementation, the leniency program has shown signs of maturity and development. There is today a continuous inflow of leniency applications, approximately 25% bigger than a couple of years ago and perhaps around 50% greater than in the past. These include international cartels, showing Brazil's growing importance in the international antitrust scenario, and an increasingly reasonable number of domestic cartels, which means leniency is becoming more common within national boundaries. It is also important to notice that the General Superintendence, since the new regime, has adopted a more rigorous approach towards leniency applications, meaning that the bar has been set higher when deciding whether or not to accept a proposal, based both on the demonstration of potential damages within Brazil and on the quality and robustness of the history of conduct and evidence presented.

Finally, one of the main developments in competition policy towards anticompetitive conducts relates to CADE's settlement policy, which has gone through important changes, especially in relation to cartels, and generated visible outcomes. In sum, clearer and more objective and predictable rules that pre-defined settlements procedures, discount rates on the applicable fine (considering if the applicant was the first, second, third-in, etc.) and requirements (confession and collaboration) have considerably boosted the number of settlements, which in 2014 (approximately 40 settlements) was more than six times larger than the average of previous years. The feared unattractiveness of the new policy regulation, because of the confession requirement in cartel cases, did not occur, and parties and authority found a common ground that allows companies and individuals to terminate prosecution against them, at the same time that CADE reduces prosecution costs, avoids long judicial battles, significantly improves cases (because of collaboration and confession requirements) and punishes cartel behavior through the collection of substantial pecuniary contributions.

As a result of the increase of both settlements and tried cases, fines and contributions collected by CADE have been significantly boosted, demonstrating important developments in terms of effectiveness in the investigation and sanctioning of anticompetitive conducts, especially cartels.

II. How do you view the role of the Office of the Superintendence General (Superintendência Geral do CADE – "SG") in enforcing and framing competition policy within the current structure of the Brazilian Competition Defense System? How does the SG interact with the other entities of the Brazilian Competition Defense System?

The General Superintendence is CADE's heart. Every single merger and conduct case starts there and is treated there. Equally importantly, most mergers and conducts are also terminated within the Superintendence. The most important conduct cases are deferred to the Tribunal, which has the ultimate say when a fine must be applied, as are challenged mergers, which can only be subject to remedies by way of a Tribunal decision. Commissioners can also arrogate any of the General Superintendence's cases that would not necessarily have to be decided upon by the Tribunal. Therefore, besides being the invested body of applying remedies and fines, the Tribunal plays a significant role of surveillance, of creating jurisprudence and of guiding CADE's competition policy as a whole (another important tool was recently given to the Tribunal, with the regulation of consultation proceedings, through which parties can directly request the Tribunal's view regarding a specific competition matter).

Nonetheless, the fact is that in practice only a small minority of cases is deferred to the Tribunal in the form of administrative proceedings of conducts and challenged mergers. The arrogation of cases by the Tribunal is also rare. This is indeed how the system is intended to work, bringing more speed to decisions and filtering the Tribunal's analysis. It leaves, however, a great deal of responsibility to the Superintendence's work.

In practice, it is the General Superintendence who assesses the necessity of conducting a deeper analysis of a merger or to dismiss it as a simple case. The opinion of the General Superintendence on whether or not to challenge a merger, or to agree to a settlement, has significant weight in the eyes of the Tribunal, who has the task of hearing all parties involved and deciding on the case. Similarly, it is the Superintendence who decides whether or not to pursue and deepen a conduct investigation, to publicize or not to publicize investigations, to conduct a dawn raid, to sign or not to sign a leniency agreement and so on. Once more, the Superintendence's final opinion for filing, conviction or settling is also very relevant.

As mentioned before, the General Superintendence plays a crucial part on setting the pace and the tone of CADE's work load. A change of policy in which the General Superintendence decides to pursue more investigations and to open more administrative proceedings that are later deferred to the Tribunal can overload the entire system, as well as pose unduly burdens to private parties. A change of policy in the opposite direction can empty CADE and its competition policy, undermining enforcement. A healthy middle ground can make the system work properly.

By focusing investigation efforts in a certain economic sector, or gathering similar investigations (as opposed to randomly setting opinions over spaced periods of time), the General Superintendence also has a great deal of say in the competition policy to be enforced.

In order for the system to work adequately, all these powers must be accompanied by careful institutional arrangements. A set of policies that allow institutional strength, proper and transparent assessment of cases, due process and concrete supervision by the Tribunal and private parties is necessary.

It is important to have in mind that unlike the Tribunal, which is composed by a group of Commissioners that make joint decisions, the General Superintendence's decisions are formally taken by a single person: the General Superintendent, which in theory could compromise self-surveillance. In practice, however, all cases are conducted by career staff and are accompanied by substantial technical opinions of CADE's employees, which significantly mitigates the risk of the Superintendent misconducting cases. This is how it should be. It is crucial, therefore, that continuous investments are made in CADE's staff and its institutional body.

The quality of the General Superintendence's technical staff and proper participation of CADE's other technical bodies, such as the Economics Department and the Attorney-General's Office in the assessment of cases is crucial in order to guarantee that enough analysis (and qualified analysis) will be made, as to allow the Superintendent, Commissioners and third parties to have the necessary information in order to be able to assess whether or not a certain case requires closer attention. Weak analyses diminish transparency, surveillance and speed.

The Law provides the Tribunal, involved agents and third parties important supervision mechanisms, in the form of arrogations, appeals and others. In order for these to work, due process and transparency are crucial. It is important to say that, besides having almost all of its decisions published in the Official Journal, the General Superintendence formally informs the Tribunal of all mergers approved and all conduct cases filed (including simple proceedings and confidential ones), in order to allow Commissioners to question and eventually arrogate cases. Also, a direct and frequent contact between Tribunal members and the Superintendent with purposes of transparency and accountability is crucial. In cases where settlements are proposed within the General Superintendence, for instance, this interface tends to be particularly important.

Lastly, as in other jurisdictions, in its daily work the General Superintendence is constantly faced with anticompetitive behaviors and frameworks derived not from private conducts, but from public legislations, regulations and actions, which call for advocacy measures. Within the Brazilian competition policy system, advocacy work is conducted by the Ministry of Finance, which demands an interaction between CADE and the Ministry's staff.

III. What are the main policy goals for the SG for the next few years? What do you think are the main challenges that the SG faces today and how does it plan to overcome them?

In the past three years CADE has effected most of its necessary regulations and institutional reforms. The transition challenge has been overcome and the new system is implemented. The agenda tends to then switch more heavily from discussions of institutional reforms to CADE's finalistic purpose: detecting, assessing and delivering cases that properly inhibit anticompetitive structures and behaviors.

This does not mean that regulation revisions or new regulations should stop. On the contrary, CADE has already pronounced intentions of eventually setting clearer rules or guidelines regarding topics such as new horizontal merger analysis, gun jumping, remedies, definitions of control, compliance, leniency, the solidification of the 30 day review period for fast-track mergers and others, all of which interest and directly impact the General Superintendence's work. It does not mean either that important institutional frameworks and policies adopted in the transition can be neglected. On the contrary, management mechanisms such as merger and conducts screening units, backlog balance and prioritization policies must be constantly and permanently applied and cared for.

Also, a great deal of work is required in order to maintain the benefits achieved during the first few years. The maintenance of the average merger review periods achieved is a must, as well as great challenge. From 2013 to 2014, the percentage of ordinary cases in comparison to fast-track cases literally doubled,[2] meaning the General Superintendence's merger units

2 The maintenance of the percentage of amendments requested by the General

had double the work. The average review period only slightly increased, showing an adequate response of the competition authority to the challenge posed. Nonetheless, especially considering probable increases in the number of notified mergers in the future, the maintenance of the favorable merger statistics will depend on adequate case management, investments in staff's technical capacity, appropriate use of precedents and information, efficient interaction with the Economics Department, merging parties and third parties, and especially on the maintenance of the screening and prioritization of conduct cases, so as to take advantage of scarce resources to merger analysis. Evidently, relevant human resources increases will at some point be a necessity.

Still in the mergers field, in its current position in the national and international spheres, the Brazilian competition authority cannot afford to stay behind the main antitrust agencies in the world when it comes to delivering proper quality analysis of mergers and applying adequate remedies. A policy of constant and increasing training, updating and interaction with international counterparts is necessary, and there is a concrete will to further improve the quality of merger assessments.

Converging with an eventual regulation of merger remedies, there is no doubt that although the content and procedure regarding remedies (especially through settlement) has greatly improved in the past years, there is considerable room for greater standardization, transparency, predictability and speediness of remedies procedures, negotiation and construction.

A successful competition policy towards anticompetitive conducts within the General Superintendence depends on the adequate maintenance of the screening and prioritization process, avoiding the pursuit of weaker cases and maintaining the balance between cases entering and exiting the General Superintendence.

As mentioned before, following the major institutional reforms, attention is now drawn to other aspects, particularly related to CADE's main purpose. Regarding conducts, this means being able to open

Superintendence in the notification phase, and the very small number of decisions transforming fast-track cases into ordinary cases indicate that such switch is not related to more rigorous rules or enforcement by the SG, but rather, to a natural complexity of merger cases notified during the past year.

relevant investigations and deliver effective actions against anticompetitive behaviors. The main policy goal, therefore, must be related to the purpose of generating more cases, in a greater variety of markets, including other geographical areas in the country and with large impacts over consumers. There is no doubt that in the past years CADE has significantly improved its insertion in such scenarios, taking part in some of the most impactful cases in Brazil, related to extremely important markets. Such exposure brings challenges, but also an opportunity of attracting new significant cases.

Regarding abuse of dominance cases, the General Superintendence's policy, that combines resource prioritization and the search for strong, impactful investigations means, most likely, a more careful choice of cases, but with real, relevant potential.

In terms of cartels, without putting aside efforts to continuously strengthen its leniency program, there has been a deliberate decision within CADE's General Superintendence to pursue other forms of cartel detection, relying on its own tools. This has always been an important aspect of Brazil's antitrust practice, which has generated and continues to generate strong investigations without the use of leniency. Nonetheless, an effort to develop the General Superintendence's investigative capacity has already started and must be further developed. This includes improving intelligence tools, staff training and economic techniques of cartel detection, including the screening of public databases.

The General Superintendence's recent and most impactful cases, and such investigation efforts, are closely drawn to tackling bid-rigging in public procurements, a field with great antitrust potential and significant relevance, which should continue to merit CADE's close attention.

When it comes to effectiveness, an obvious issue, until recently neglected due to other urgent necessities, has to do with the speediness of investigations. It is no surprise that, not unlike other administrative and judicial forums in Brazil, administrative proceedings within CADE historically take too long, significantly undermining decisions' effectiveness. At least two outcomes of CADE's recent reorganization have bore positive fruits in this arena: a relevant portion of the backlog of old cases has been terminated (as demonstrated earlier) and new cases tend to move faster within the new structure and framework. Nonetheless, the challenge remains: there still is a relevant backlog of cases and proceedings which still need to move faster. Part of the challenge is being overcome through unfinished backlog reduction efforts, prioritization of resources and focused case management. At some point, however, further improvements will obviously have to rely on increases of human resources.

Antitrust in Brazil has immense potential. Brazil is a large country, with a gigantic consumer market and an equally important economy. Concentrated markets are common, competition culture, even amongst large firms, is poorly developed, and competition law is still vaguely understood in many portions of the country. All of these features create conditions for significant anticompetitive behaviors. Especially when looking from inside, CADE's potential is even greater. CADE's recognition has grown, the number of complaints and leads with good potential is constant, the leniency program has matured and investigative capacity is continuously improving. There is still room to profit from such potential within CADE's current structure. Once again, however, a more significant step, that allows for a larger number of investigations, processing of further impactful cases, self-detection of cartels, more frequent dawn raids and more effective treatment of evidence will depend on a larger staff of qualified case handlers. It is only natural that a stronger human resources policy, accompanied by budgetary capacity, is one of the main challenges to be overcome.

Two other central policy issues relate, of course, to CADE's leniency program and settlement procedures, which will be discussed in the next question.

IV. How do you evaluate the effectiveness of the current legal framework and policy for the execution of leniency agreements and settlements? Do you believe that there is room for improvement in terms of creating the right incentives to increase leniency applications and negotiable resolutions in the investigations?

As previously mentioned, the recent changes in CADE's settlements policy have significantly increased the use of this tool, both in the benefit of parties and the investigations. Most recently, efforts to improve settlements have switched to thinking of new ways of facilitating, speeding up and posing less burden to the negotiation process. This calls, in particular, for the construction of standards and possibly clearer guidelines regarding the calculation of pecuniary contributions. The cost-benefit of entering or pursuing a settlement negotiation in certain cases is also an important variable.

CADE's leniency program, as demonstrated earlier, has significantly developed and seems to have achieved a mature stage. Applications are constant and generate high quality investigations. There is no doubt, however, that there is significant room for the program to increase and develop further cases.

On the one hand, such a process is directly linked with CADE's capability to deliver impactful cases, thus advertising and encouraging leniencies. At the same time, the General Superintendence has already announced its intentions to provide guidelines that allow for greater transparency, predictability and safety regarding leniency proceedings, which in its view might encourage and strengthen the program. Most of these guidelines do no tend to bring new features to the program, but rather, to provide a clearer and safer understanding of the process and of the rules involved. Some of these aspects, however, do present clarification of topics that perhaps are not yet entirely solidified, due to the lack of clear precedents, as is the case of the "leniency plus" instrument.

Another topic that has received a great deal of attention within the General Superintendence relates to safety aspects of leniency, especially regarding confidentiality rights. New proceedings that include clearer custody chains, treatment of documents and information, and closer follow up and awareness when dealing with other public agents involved, such as public prosecutors and judges, have already been adopted. Projects involving the mapping of eventual safety weaknesses within CADE (including information security) have already begun, as well as projects for the training of CADE's personnel in such fields. Advocacy aspects related to educating prosecutors, police agents and judicial authorities on the importance of confidentiality issues must be a constant feature as well.

* * *

INTRODUCTION

Fabricio Antonio Cardim de Almeida

In its 2010 Peer Review Report on competition law and policy in Brazil, the Organization for Economic Cooperation and Development ("OECD") affirmed that "the competition policy system [in Brazil] [had] made steady, even remarkable, progress."[1] In February 2011, Global Competition Review ("GCR") awarded for the first time the Brazilian Administrative Council for Economic Defense (*Conselho Administrativo de Defesa Econômica* – "CADE") with the prize of the "Agency of the Year, Americas".[2] In June 2013, GCR also rated for the first time CADE with 4 stars out 5 possible, ranking the agency among the top twelve enforcers of antitrust laws around the globe.[3]

Although Brazilian antitrust laws enforcement and policy have been increasingly recognized as effective, it has not been always like this. The first Antitrust Act was introduced in Brazil in 1962.[4] However, it was only in the 90s – with the opening of Brazilian economy – that the antitrust laws started to be relatively enforced by the authorities.

---

1 Org. for Econ. Cooperation and Dev., Competition Law and Policy in Brazil - A Peer Review 9 (2010) [hereinafter OECD 2010 Peer Review Report], *available at* http://www.oecd.org/daf/competition/45154362.pdf.

2 *GCR 2011 Award Winners Announced*, Global Competition Rev. (Feb. 7, 2011), http://globalcompetitionreview.com/news/article/29705/gcr-2011-award-winners-announced/.

3 *Brazil's Administrative Council for Economic Defence, Rating Enforcement*, Global Competition Rev. (2013), *available at* http://globalcompetitionreview.com/surveys/article/33566/brazils-administrative-council-economic-defence/.

4 Lei No. 4.137, de 10.09.1962, Diário Oficial da União [D.O.U.] de 12.09.1962 (Braz.).

For 17 years, since it was approved in 1994, Law No. 8,884[5] provided for the legal framework under which enforcement developed. However, this legal framework showed limitations and inefficiencies throughout the years due to two main reasons: (i) the lack of a pre-merger control regime; and (ii) the overlapping roles played by different authorities.

Under the regime of Law No. 8,884/94, the antitrust laws in Brazil were enforced by three different agencies: (i) the Economic Monitoring Office under the Ministry of Finance ("SEAE"); (ii) the Economic Law Office under the Ministry of Justice ("SDE"); and (iii) CADE, a federal independent agency under the supervision of the Ministry of Justice. This institutional design created inefficiencies to the system, as the agencies played overlapping roles throughout the process of review of antitrust cases, and that negatively affected the timing of review of the cases. For instance, in 2011 (the last full year in which Law No. 8,884/94 was effective), the antitrust agencies in Brazil used to take, in average, 154 days to approve a transaction under its post-merger control regime.[6]

Aiming to exclude the abovementioned two main "bottlenecks" out of the system, Congress approved in 2011 the "new Antitrust Act" ("Law No. 12,529/11").[7] The "new CADE" under Law No. 12,529/11 incorporated the antitrust division of SDE and is now formed by two main bodies: (i) the General Superintendence ("SG") and (ii) the Administrative Tribunal. CADE also has (i) a Chief Economist's Office; (ii) a General Attorney's Office ("ProCADE"); and (iii) a Public Prosecutor Office ("MPF"). SEAE is still accountable for "competition advocacy" activities under the new regime.

After the third anniversary of Law No. 12,529/11, this publication puts Brazilian Antitrust Law into perspective. It is clear that Brazilian Antitrust Law has been developing quite impressively in the past 20 years.

---

5 Lei No. 8.884, de 11 de Junho de 1994, Diário Oficial da União [D.O.U.] de 13.6.1994 (Braz.).

6 Vinicius Marques de Carvalho, Chairman, Conselho Administrativo de Defesa Econômica, Address at the IBRAC's 20th International Seminar on Competition Policy: Balanço do CADE (Oct. 31, 2014), at 20, *available at* http://www.ibrac.org.br/Uploads/Eventos/20SeminarioConcorrencia/PALESTRAS/%C3%9Altimo%20Painel.

7 Lei No. 12.529, de 30 de Novembro de 2011, Diário Oficial da União [D.O.U.] de 2.12.2011 (Braz.).

The last three years of the new law have kept the pace of development and have also brought some very positive changes, such as a more rational and efficient institutional design as well as a quick review of simple cases under the pre-merger control regime. In 2012, the same year Law No. 12,529 became effective, the amount of time in average that CADE took to clear a transaction under its new pre-merger control regime significantly dropped to 21 days.[8]

The new institutional design of CADE has already proved to be better than the previous one as it eliminated the overlapping activities played by the different agencies. However, there are also challenges ahead for CADE to preserve the outcomes of the new system.

In 2014, CADE put together a number of regulations addressing important issues in the merger control area, such as (i) acquisitions of minority interests,[9] (ii) transactions involving investment funds,[10] (iii) transactions involving capital markets,[11] and (iv) associative agreements.[12] It is important that CADE follows up closely the implementation of these new rules and constantly evaluate whether they are achieving the expected results.

Cartel behavior is another area where CADE has been very active in the past decades, since the implementation of the leniency and settlement policies in 2000.[13] Law No. 12,529/11 has put a framework in place that allows CADE to continue anti-cartel enforcement efforts. Since Law No.

---

8 Vinicius Marques de Carvalho, Chairman, Conselho Administrativo de Defesa Econômica, Address at the IBRAC's 20th International Seminar on Competition Policy: Balanço do CADE (Oct. 31, 2014), at 20, *available at* http://www.ibrac.org.br/Uploads/Eventos/20SeminarioConcorrencia/PALESTRAS/%C3%9Altimo%20Painel. In 2014 (until Oct. 29, 2014), the simple transactions (reviewed under CADE's fast track procedures) took 20.7 days in average to be cleared and those more complex (reviewed under CADE's ordinary procedures) took 77.4 days in average. *Id.*, at 19.

9 Resolução CADE No. 09, de 1º de outubro de 2014, Diário Oficial da União [D.O.U.] de 7.10.2014 (Braz.).

10 *Id.*

11 *Id.*

12 Resolução CADE No. 10, de 29 de outubro de 2014, Diário Oficial da União [D.O.U.] de 4.11.2014 (Braz.).

13 Lei No. 10.149, de 21 de dezembro de 2000, Diário Oficial da União [D.O.U.] de 22.12.2000 (Braz.).

12,529/11 became effective, and until May 16, 2014, CADE had imposed a total amount of BRL 593,578,973.21[14] as fines in conduct cases.[15] According to a study conducted by the Global Competition Review, in 2014, CADE and Korea Fair Trade Commission ("KFTC") imposed US$2.6 billion in penalties, breaking previous records and accounting for just under half the worldwide amount.[16]

Nonetheless, there are also challenges ahead for CADE in the area of anti-cartel enforcement. The amount of time spent by CADE to conclude an investigation on cartel behavior is still very high,[17] and CADE has just started its investigations in two high profile cartel cases in Brazil which tend to be among the most important cases in CADE's history.[18]

In addition to the traditional areas where CADE has been enforcing antitrust laws, there are other topics which may increasingly attract the attention of the antitrust community, such as the interaction between competition law and anticorruption law, unilateral behavior/vertical (price) restraints, judicial review of CADE's decisions, private antitrust enforcement/damages claims, among others. Some of these topics are treated in this book.

---

14 USD 268,466,292.72 (USD 1.00 = BRL 2.2110, Central Bank of Brazil, May 16, 2014).

15 Vinicius Marques de Carvalho, Chairman, Conselho Administrativo de Defesa Econômica, Address: Balanço do biênio da Lei 12,529/11 e perspectivas da defesa da concorrência no Brasil (May, 2014), at 13, *available at* http://www.cade.gov.br/upload/Balanço%202%20anos%20nova%20lei.pdf.

16 *Brazil, Korea impose half of world's $5.3 billion cartel fines*, Global Competition Rev. (Jan. 7, 2015), http://globalcompetitionreview.com/news/article/37717/brazil-korea-impose-half-worlds-53-billion-cartel-fines/.

17 In 2013, for instance, 39% of the conduct cases ruled by CADE had more than 5 years of investigations and 13% more than 10 years. In 2014, the percentages were 22% (more than 5 years) and 4% (more than 10 years). *See* Vinicius Marques de Carvalho, Chairman, Conselho Administrativo de Defesa Econômica, Address at the IBRAC's 20th International Seminar on Competition Policy: Balanço do CADE (Oct. 31, 2014), at 8-10, *available at* http://www.ibrac.org.br/Uploads/Eventos/20SeminarioConcorrencia/PALESTRAS/%C3%9Altimo%20Painel. Despite the efforts of CADE to try to reduce the timing of investigations in conduct cases, that was still a relevant number of cases which took more than 5 and 10 years to be concluded.

18 The subway cartel case (CADE, ex officio, Administrative Proceeding No. 08700.004617/2013-41) (March 19, 2014) and the Petrobras cartel case.

The development of antitrust laws in Brazil in the past 20 years has not been immune from criticism, as some of the articles in this publication will address. Although the balance in CADE's account is very positive, there are still lessons that can be learned from the past. The greater relevance CADE has in the international scenario, higher are the challenges.

In one of the few articles which address the issue of rating competition agencies, William E. Kovacic explains the difficulty of measuring the work of these agencies:

> *"The field of competition policy lacks such standards, yet the absence of well-defined, generally accepted scoring rules does not inhibit commentators from providing confident assessments of how well specific competition agencies are doing their jobs."*[19]

In a recent speech to commemorate U.S. Federal Trade Commission's ("FTC") one hundred anniversary, Commissioner Maureen K. Ohlhausen analyzed several aspects of the agency which led to its current success. One of the ideas she emphasized is that "a leading competition agency like the FTC must have the courage to fail from time to time."[20]

It is certainly not the intent of this introduction to rate CADE's work neither to rank it in comparison to other agencies around the globe. However, given the use of these measures by some institutions[21] – and sometimes even by the agencies[22] –, it is important to further discuss the achievements and challenges of one agency throughout a more substantial analysis that may go beyond the numbers and general impressions collected by those sources. Hopefully, this may be one of the benefits of this publication: to put CADE's recognizable work into perspective and analyze the significant developments in the past as well as identify the challenges ahead.

---

19 William E. Kovacic, *Rating The Competition Agencies: What Constitutes Good Performance?*, 16 Geo. Mason L. Rev. 903, 903 (2009).

20 Maureen K. Ohlhausen, Comm'r, U.S. Fed. Trade Comm'n, Speech at the ABA Section of Antitrust Law Fall Forum 2014: How to Measure Success: Agency Design and the FTC at 100, (Nov. 6, 2014), at 11, *available at* http://www.ftc.gov/system/files/documents/public_statements/597191/141106ftcat100fallforum.pdf.

21 *E.g.*, *supra* note 3.

22 *See, e.g.*, CADE, Press Release, CADE é Avaliado Com Quatro Estrelas Em Ranking Internacional de órgãos antitruste (Jun. 6, 2013), *available at* http://www.cade.gov.br/Default.aspx?7fb243d62ee338fb0e3b0d253c03.

The development of antitrust laws in Brazil during the past 20 years is a result of the engagement and the hard work of both officials at the agencies and lawyers and economists from the private bar. This publication combines the views of both enforcers and practitioners towards past achievements and challenges ahead of antitrust laws in Brazil. In the Q&A section, CADE's top enforcers provide their views on the most relevant developments and achievements under the new law and address the main issues and challenges they envisage for CADE in the next years. Next, members from the private bar in Brazil discuss in a number of articles several issues related to merger control, cartel behavior and other areas which may increasingly attract the attention of the antitrust community in Brazil.

It is a promising publication which allows the international antitrust community to be in touch with the main aspects of the Brazilian antitrust laws that are currently being discussed in the country at the same time it gives an opportunity for the authors (both officials at the antitrust agencies and members from the private bar in Brazil) to discuss their experience and challenges ahead.

* * *

Chapter I

CONTROVERSIAL ISSUES IN MERGER REVIEW: PRACTICAL ASPECTS

MARIA EUGÊNIA NOVIS
MARCOS PAULO VERISSIMO

I. Introduction

CADE the Brazilian Antitrust Agency,[1] was organized over fifty years ago with a very broad statutory mandate, which included some sort of merger control authority since the beginning of the 1960s. In fact, Law 4,137 (1962) provided CADE with wide-ranging authority to fight the abuse of monopoly power, which pursuant to Article 2 could consist in the dominance of national markets by means of acquisitions of assets, shares or rights over already established businesses, or transactions such as mergers, incorporations, or any other form of business concentration. In practice, however, CADE's powers to review mergers remained dormant for almost 30 years, and only came into life in the beginning of the 1990s in the context of the larger process of liberalization of the Brazilian economy.

The efforts to establish a free market economy in Brazil included the reduction of important barriers to foreign trade, the elimination of price control in major sectors of the economy, privatizations, and the promotion of free competition. Accordingly, the first major reform in Brazilian antitrust law came early in the 1990s by means of Law 8,158 (1991). Three

1 CADE is the Portuguese acronym for "Administrative Council for Economic Defense", which is the official designation of the Brazilian agency.

years later, Brazil successfully established a fully functional merger control system under Law 8,884 (1994) (the "Former Antitrust Law"), which consolidated the protection of free competition as one of the pillars of the country's economy.

The Former Antitrust Law attracted the attention of the business and antitrust communities to its provisions both in Brazil and abroad. In the course of almost 18 years, more than 7,000 domestic and foreign transactions were filed with the Brazilian antitrust authorities, and CADE was often praised by international publications for its achievements, becoming gradually deemed as one of the most active and prominent antitrust agencies in developing countries, and more recently in the world.[2]

Notwithstanding the overall positive experience of the first years of merger control in Brazil, the Former Antitrust Law had a number of flaws deriving mainly from the inefficiencies associated to the existence of multiple and overlapping agencies, the adoption of inadequate filing thresholds, and the limitations faced by CADE to prevent structural distortions to competition under a post-merger review regime.

In fact, law reform started to be discussed only a few years after the entry into force of the Former Antitrust Law,[3] and finally materialized in May 2012 when a long awaited new statute – Law 12,529/11 (hereinafter, the "Antitrust Law") – entered into force.

The Antitrust Law brought noticeable developments in the field of merger control, including the incorporation of the two other agencies previously in charge of antitrust investigations (the Secretariat of Economic Law – SDE and the Secretariat for Economic Monitoring – SEAE) into

---

2 In 2011, the Global Competition Review (GCR), one of the most influential publications in the antitrust field, granted the award of Agency of the Year in the Americas to CADE, and its 2014 survey placed CADE among the ten best antitrust agencies in the world. In addition, CADE is today vice-chairing the Steering Group of the International Competition Network.

3 The institutional change and the adoption of a pre-merger regime had been discussed since 2000, when a Ministerial Work Group was established to discuss the creation of the then-called National Agency for Consumer and Competition Defense. For details on this effort, *see* for instance the article Ana Paula Martinez, *Merger Control in Brazil: Past, Present and Future in* IBRAC Review n. 18, July-December 2010.

CADE, thus creating a larger and unified antitrust agency, and adopting new merger filing thresholds, and above all, adopting a suspensory regime.

Shortly after the entry into force of the Antitrust Law, CADE issued Resolution 2 (2012) to clarify material and procedural aspects of merger filings. Almost two and half years later, this regulation was amended by Resolution 9 (2014).

After a short period of time, the major positive effects of the Antitrust Law are already noticeable. The new filing thresholds enabled CADE to focus its efforts on more important cases, avoiding the review of transactions with little chances of impacting competition in domestic markets. Following the entry into force of the Antitrust Law, the overall number of merger filings dropped by almost half, decreasing from 626 in 2012 to 377 in 2013. Moreover, the number of merger cases reviewed each year by CADE's Administrative Court dropped from 731 to only 31 from 2012 to 2014, according to the agency's official figures, which resulted in a clearly better use of its scarce resources.[4]

CADE has also proved in the past few years that it can clear simple, fast-track cases under the new regime in a reasonable timeframe of about 30 days, eliminating a previously wide-spread concern that the suspensory regime in Brazil could entail a material delay in the closing of relevant transactions falling under CADE's jurisdiction.

Unfortunately, new statutes sometimes contain grey zones that require interpretation, clarification, and occasionally regulation. As mentioned above, CADE has made a preliminary effort to provide some of the required clarifications by means of Resolution 2 (2012) and Resolution 9 (2014). As one may easily imagine, however, these efforts have not completely eliminated all the uncertainties found in the Antitrust Law. Similarly to other administrative regulations, CADE's regulations also have their own zones of vagueness and ambiguity. Therefore, sometimes the assessment on whether a given transaction is subject to mandatory filing with CADE, which should be a simple and straightforward task for antitrust experts, still poses challenges to local practitioners, who often have different interpretations on the legal and regulatory criteria.

4 Under the new regime, most of the merger review cases are decided by CADE's General Superintendent, and are no longer referred for a decision at the Administrative Court level.

Although this is not a special feature of the Brazilian laws, insofar as potentially disputing interpretations on the meaning of legal provisions are almost inherent to the application of the law in general, uncertainties of this nature may have a negative impact on businesses, reason for which regulators should do their best to keep them to a minimum acceptable level.

Under a scenario of successful implementation of merger control in Brazil, coupled with the significant developments achieved in the past few years, solving and clarifying some of the major issues that still lead to controversies in daily practice seems to be a desirable and feasible task, especially considering that no legislative process would be required.

In view of this background, and aiming to contribute to the process of further clarifying the new merger review regulations in Brazil, this paper will address three major practical controversies associated to the current mandatory filing requirements. Following this introduction, Section II discusses the so-called effects test, whose broad scope persists under the Antitrust Law. Section III approaches the notion of economic concentration, as defined in the statutory law and CADE's regulation, which still poses some important interpretative doubts. Section IV addresses certain practical issues associated to the calculation of turnover thresholds. Finally, Section V summarizes the conclusions drawn.

II. The Effect Requirement

Apart from the changes in turnover thresholds, the basic jurisdictional framework set forth by the Former Antitrust Law remained unchanged under the Antitrust Law, which provides that (i) the law applies to practices performed fully or partially in Brazil or that produce or may produce effects in the national territory, and (ii) a foreign company that conducts transactions or has branches, agencies, subsidiaries, offices, establishments, agents or representatives in Brazil shall be deemed domiciled in national territory.

By adopting the effects doctrine of jurisdiction, Brazilian lawmakers have disregarded where the merger is taking place and the nationality of the merging parties focusing only on the merger's ability to produce effects in Brazil.

Under this legal framework, it is widely accepted that the so-called "effects test" may be met in two circumstances. The first is when the merger produces direct effects in Brazil, i.e., when the merging parties are either organized in Brazil or have a branch, agency, subsidiary, office, establishment, agent or representative in the country. The second is when the merger produces indirect effects in the country. This situation is usually associated to foreign transactions in which the target has export sales to Brazil.

However, jurisdiction based on local activities or exports without any clear local nexus rule or *de mininis* threshold has proved to be inadequate. Since 1994, the broad and vague language of the antitrust law has been imposing unnecessary burdens on some merging parties and requiring the use of CADE's resources without any corresponding enforcement benefit. This conclusion is supported by a number of filings for the purchase of companies with extremely low sales to Brazil and relative to the organization of joint ventures among companies that simply met the general turnover threshold requirements, regardless of whether Brazilian assets were being contributed to the joint venture, or whether it would compete in the Brazilian market or serve local customers.[5]

In this sense, the Brazilian jurisdictional standards are still inconsistent with the best practices for merger filings recommended by international discussion forums. For instance, according to the International Competition Network ("ICN"), when countries are exercising their sovereignty with respect to the application of their own laws to mergers, jurisdiction should only be asserted with respect to the transactions that have an appropriate nexus with the reviewing jurisdiction.[6] In other words, no merger filing should be required where the transaction is unlikely to have a significant, direct and immediate economic effect within the Brazilian territory.

The US antitrust laws expressly exempt transactions involving foreign firms with trivial sales or assets in the United States. Likewise, the European Union's notification thresholds require a significant amount of sales within the European Union. However, CADE has not specified the

---

5 CADE, *Reuters Limited and Equant Finance B.V.* Reporting Commissioner Celso Fernandes Campilongo (Merger No. 08012.001783/00-68) (Jan. 10, 2001); CADE, *CCR España and Camargo Correa S.A.* Reporting Commissioner Alessandro Octaviani Luis (Merger No. 087006929/2012-17) (Sept. 12, 2012).

6 *Available at* http://www.internationalcompetitionnetwork.org/uploads/library/doc588.pdf.

amount of exports or sales in Brazil that constitute cognizable effects for purposes of jurisdiction yet.[7]

This situation persists under the Antitrust Law, despite the adoption of a twofold turnover threshold under which a filing with CADE is required when at least one of the groups involved in the merger has registered gross turnover or volume of sales in the country, in the year preceding the transaction, of at least BRL 750 million and at least another group involved in the merger has registered gross turnover or volume of sales in the country, in the year preceding the transaction, of at least BRL 75 million. Such turnover thresholds take into consideration the Brazilian activities of the buyer group and the seller group as a whole, instead of looking specifically at the target's activities. As such, so far, the new turnover thresholds have not been able to screen out transactions that are unlikely to result in appreciable competitive effects within Brazil.

As far as this point is concerned, the major criticism should certainly be directed towards the wording of the Antitrust Law itself, which determined that the lower threshold requirement applies to any of the groups involved in the merger, when in fact it would have been much better to apply it to the target entity. This would also be in line with the ICN recommendations, which state that a merger filing should not be required solely on the basis of the acquiring firm's local activities, but also on the relevant local activities of the acquired party, calculated on the basis of the local sales or assets of the business being acquired.

The good news is that CADE has recently devoted some attention to the local nexus issue and has dismissed some joint venture filings. One of them involved the organization of a greenfield joint venture for the provision of automotive services in Europe.[8] The second one involved the consolidation of control over a 50%-50% joint venture that has no local activities in Brazil or sales to Brazil.[9] In both precedents, even though the

---

7 On this discussion, see the article Michael G. Cowie & Cesar Costa Alves de Mattos, *Antitrust Review of Mergers, Acquisitions and Joint Ventures in Brazil*. IBRAC Review. Vol. 8, No. 3, (2001).

8 CADE, *Robert Bosch GmbH, ZF Friedrichshafen AG and Knorr-Bremse Systeme für Commercial Vehicle GmbH*. The Superintendence General in (Merger No. 08700.001204/2013-13) (March 4, 2013).

9 CADE, *Robert Bosch GmbH and Siemens AG*. The Superintendence-General in (Merger No. 08700.008819/2014-43) (Nov. 20, 2014).

groups involved in the transactions met the turnover thresholds, CADE's General-Superintendence dismissed the cases on the grounds that the joint ventures would not be active in Brazil and the transactions could not produce effects in the Brazilian market. CADE should be encouraged to continue to issue consistent dismissal decisions in similar joint venture filings.

Moreover, CADE should address the local nexus issue in cases where the target has minimal or sporadic activities in Brazil either through export sales or local representatives, so that it cannot actually be viewed as an actual competitor by local players or as a relevant supplier by local customers.

This goal might be more difficult to be achieved, however, since CADE has recently refused to dismiss a merger where the target had insignificant sales to Brazil in comparison to its overall global sales. The General Superintendence stated that "the parties intended, through their reasons, to raise the analysis of effects to the category of a requirement for the assessment on the need to file the merger, which would be contradictory". In CADE's view, the effects of the merger could only be analyzed once the merger is filed and duly reviewed, and "a different approach would create legal uncertainty, as the merging parties would be allowed to replace the antitrust authority in the review and analysis of the merits of each merger."

CADE could nevertheless eliminate any legal uncertainty surrounding this issue by publishing a guideline on the meaning of effects (local nexus) under the Antitrust Law. Such guidelines could include, for instance, a minimum value of annual sales on a non-periodic basis, formalizing a reasonable interpretation of Article 2 of the Antitrust Law, whereby, turnover requirements notwithstanding, the Brazilian competition law only applies to acts and transactions that "produce or may produce effects" in the Brazilian territory. In so doing, CADE would align the Brazilian merger filing thresholds with the internationally recommended best practices in this area, and would also eliminate unnecessary burdens on merging parties and its own staff.

III. The Concentration Requirement

Another pivotal controversy existing under the Former Antitrust Law, which the current Antitrust Law has also tried to cope with, concerns the types of transactions that would be subject to mandatory merger control. This effort, however, was only partially successful, since the wording of both the new statute and CADE's subsequent regulations still leave room for debate. The key element to understand such discussions is the notion of concentration.

Article 54 of the Former Antitrust Law established that any act that may limit or harm free competition or result in market dominance should be filed for CADE's approval. Article 54 (3) clarified that acts implying any time of economic concentration would be comprised in the notion of the *chapeau*, including mergers, acquisitions, incorporation of companies or any kind of corporate grouping, provided that a 20% market share threshold or a BRL 400 million turnover threshold was met. Therefore, mergers where only one category among a vast array of acts that could be subject to mandatory filing with CADE.

Additionally, it became widely accepted that concentration could also be found to exist where one of the merging parties acquired dominant or relevant influence over the other party, and not necessarily control. "Dominant influence," which would in practice be tantamount to control, was viewed as the ability of one undertaking to determine on a long lasting and stable basis all the most important commercially sensitive decisions of a previously independent undertaking, such as investment decisions, decisions on output and sales, so that both undertakings would actually perform all their activities as one single economic agent. On the other hand, "relevant influence" related either to contractual structures or shareholding structures that entailed some less decisive level of cooperation among undertakings that remained independent from each other. Such subtle type of influence could exist in several situations, including, *inter alia*, veto powers over important business decisions such as budget or business plans; powers to appoint members of the management team whose position would allow them to influence the strategic commercial behavior of the company or access sensitive commercial information; or a material stake in non-voting stock.

In short, the notion of dominant influence was basically associated with the acquisition of control, while relevant influence would be found in acquisitions of minority shareholdings.

CADE specifically addressed the concept of control in Resolution 15 (1998), which set forth that control means the power to determine the behavior of a firm, either directly or indirectly, internally or externally, *de jure* or *de facto*. This wording is partially in line with the definition of control provided for by Law 6,404 (1964) (the "Brazilian Law of Corporations"), whereby controlling shareholder means the individual or legal entity which, alone or in association with other parties bound by a shareholders' agreement, is (i) entitled to shareholders' rights that permanently ensures the majority of votes in every shareholders' meeting, as well as the ability to appoint the majority of the management members of the controlled company, and (ii) effectively uses such power to conduct and manage the activities of the company.

However, CADE's definition of control was somehow broader and different from the one stemming from said legal provisions, and included inputs from Brazilian legal scholars who distinguished situations of internal and external control (the former being exercised from inside the company by means of its regular decision-making bodies, the latter associated with the abovementioned idea of "dominant influence", being exercised from outside, by any means such as a relevant indebtedness, supply dependence, technology dependence, etc.), and focused on the *de facto* (as opposed to formal) ability to direct a company's most sensitive decisions.[10]

Although CADE's Resolution 15 (1998) defined control in the abovementioned fashion as early as 1998, CADE has not elaborated on the notion of relevant influence under any guideline or precedent for a long time. This situation led to the filing of myriads of acquisitions of minority shareholdings, which were cleared by CADE without any investigation on the powers held by the buyer over the target.

In 2005, after ten years of experience in merger control, one of CADE's Commissioners issued a landmark opinion expressing the understanding that relevant influence may exist where one shareholder has interest to affect the company's decisions, and at the same time has effective powers to do so in a constant and comprehensive manner. Interest would be associated with the overlap between the activities of the shareholder and the target that would facilitate a cooperative behavior, or the existence of contractual relationships between the shareholder and the target. Effective powers could be found, *inter alia*, in the possibility to appoint board members or officers who could guide the company's strategic behavior, or the existence of a shareholders' agreement that would provide the minority

10 *See,* for instance, FABIO KONDER COMPARATO & CALIXTO SALOMÃO FILHO. *Control in Corporations*, Rio de Janeiro: Forense (2005).

shareholder with affirmative voting or vetoing powers over matters relating to the behavior of the target company in the marketplace.[11] Despite the solid grounds of this position, it did not provide sufficient legal certainty for parties to decide not to file certain minority shareholding investments in view of CADE's past precedents.

Against this legal background and CADE's former decisional practice, the Antitrust Law introduced a most welcome development in Articles 88 and 90, which not only clarified that solely acts of "economic concentration" would be subject to merger control, but also addressed the meaning of concentration as follows:

> *"Art. 90. For the purposes of Article 88 of this Law, a concentration act is constituted when:*
>
> *I – two (2) or more previously independent companies merge;*
>
> *II – one (1) or more companies acquire, directly or indirectly, by purchase or exchange of stocks, shares, bonds or securities convertible into stocks or assets, whether tangible or intangible, by contract or by any other means or way, the control or parts of one or more companies;*
>
> *III – one (1) or more companies absorbs one or more companies, or*
>
> *IV – two (2) or more companies enter into an association agreement, consortium or joint venture.*
>
> *Sole Paragraph. The terms described in item IV of the caption, when used for bids promoted by direct and indirect government agencies and for contracts arising therefrom, shall not be deemed concentration acts, for the purposes of Article 88 of this Law."*

Right after the entry into force of the Antitrust Law, CADE issued Resolution 2 (2011), subsequently amended by CADE's Resolution 9 (2014), to clarify when share deals would amount to economic concentration, being subject to mandatory filing provided that the effect test and the turnover thresholds are met.

Pursuant to Resolution 2 (2011), as amended, there is concentration when (i) the deal entails the acquisition of sole or joint control; or (ii) the deal does not entail the acquisition of sole or joint control, but meets any of the following *de minimis* rules:

---

11 Opinion issued by CADE Commissioner Luiz Alberto Esteves Escaloppe *in* CADE, *Flynet S.A. and Ideiasnet S.A.* Reporting Commissioner Luiz Alberto Esteves Escaloppe (Merger No. 08012.010293/2004-48) (July 31, 2007).

"(1) In conglomerate mergers:

(A) Acquisition that directly or indirectly provides buyer with 20% or more of the total capital stock or voting capital stock of the target; or

(B) Acquisition made by an undertaking that already holds 20% or more of the total capital stock or voting capital stock of the target, provided that the directly or indirectly acquired additional interest, from at least one seller individually considered, is equal to or exceeds 20% of the total capital stock or voting capital stock of the target.

(2) In horizontal mergers or vertical mergers:

(A) Acquisition that directly or indirectly provides buyer with 5% or more of the total capital stock or voting capital stock of the target; or

(B) Latest acquisition that individually or added to other acquisitions entails an increase in interest of 5% or more, where the investor already holds 5% or more of the total capital stock or voting capital stock of the target."

Resolution 2 (2011), as amended, also provides that acquisitions of additional shareholdings by the undertaking that enjoys sole control are not subject to mandatory filing.

The rationale behind this regulation is clear and praiseworthy: to provide more legal certainty to merger filings in Brazil firstly by eliminating the broad obligation to file any act that could limit or harm competition, regardless of the size of the shareholding being acquired, and secondly by replacing the debatable notions of dominant influence and relevant influence by an apparently clear-cut "control or *de minimis*" rule.

Despite such apparently clear-cut rules, hot discussions in the Brazilian antitrust practice seem to be far from over in relation to this issue.

The first of them concerns the notion of control itself, which is, as ever, hard to define in clear-cut terms when it comes to borderline cases. In short, although the acquisition of 51% of the voting shares in a company will clearly amount to an acquisition of control and meet the concentration requirement, in a conglomerate merger the acquisition of a 15% shareholding (i.e., of a shareholding bellow the *de minimis* formal threshold of 20%) that grants the buyer veto powers over matters such as budget or business plan is still a controversial issue, because it could in theory be construed, under certain circumstances, an acquisition of joint control. The same would apply to a similar acquisition in companies with a highly dispersed shareholder's basis, for instance. On top of that, unlike CADE's former Resolution 15 (1998), the new regulation does not elaborate on the notion of control, and this will certainly remain a zone prone to ambiguities.

Another controversial issue relates to acquisitions of additional shareholdings by undertakings that enjoy joint control.

Under the original wording of CADE's Resolution 2 (2011), acquisitions of additional shareholdings by the controlling entity amounted to concentration where the shareholding directly or indirectly acquired from at least one seller, individually considered, was equal to or exceeded 20% of the total or voting capital stock of the target. It is worth mentioning that the regulation did not limit this rule to the entity holding sole control. However, the current regulation apparently limits the waiver relative to the filing obligation to acquisitions of additional shareholdings by the undertaking that enjoys sole control.

One believes there is no rationale behind this limitation, which may derive from a mistake in the drafting of Resolution 9 (2014). It seems unreasonable not to treat as concentration the acquisition, by a shareholder holding 60% interest, of an additional 40% interest from a seller that was not party to any shareholders' agreement, and at the same time require the filing of the acquisition by a shareholder that holds 45% interest and belongs to the block of control under a shareholders' agreement of an additional 21% interest from a clearly non-controlling shareholder.

This situation should be viewed as a mere corporate restructuring without change of control, which CADE has acknowledged in a recent precedent that would not amount to concentration,[12] provided that it does not entail the direct or indirect entry of any new shareholder in the target's stock.

Finally, a very controversial aspect of the notion of concentration is the concept of "association agreement", a category that was introduced by article 90 (IV) of the Antitrust Law and needs to be submitted to CADE's prior approval if the effects test and turnover requirements are met. There is not a single clue in the statute itself, however, as for the definition of such association agreements, and CADE has only issued a regulation on that topic recently.[13]

---

12 CADE, *Neoenergia S.A.* and Iberdrola S.A. The Superintendence-General in (Merger No. 08700.009472/2014-56) (Nov. 20, 2014).

13 CADE Resolution 10/2014.

According to the regulation, association agreements are agreements involving some sort of horizontal or vertical cooperation between the parties, or entails some sort of risk sharing, so as to put the parties entering into it in a condition of "interdependency". It also determines that such agreements must be effective for at least 2 years.

Resolution 10/2014 also establishes that a filing is mandatory for all agreements in which the parties are "horizontally related in the object of the agreement" if their aggregated market share in the relevant market affected by the agreement is equivalent or superior to 20%. The same will apply to agreements in which the parties are "vertically related in the object of the agreement" if at least one of them has a market share in one of the relevant markets affected by the agreement equivalent or superior to 30%, and the agreement (i) establishes the sharing of revenues or losses between the parties, or (ii) involves or is able to cause a relation of exclusivity.

For the purposes of the abovementioned regulation, a "party" to such agreement would be the contracting party and any other member of its economic group, as defined by the very broad terms of CADE's regulations (addressed in the following section). Moreover, any agreement of this nature, originally entered into for a term of less than 2 years, must be submitted to CADE's approval if a subsequent renewal causes the 2-year period to be triggered.

Although this is not clearly stated in CADE's regulation, filings of association agreements will necessarily fall under the non-fast track review procedure due to the market shares involved, which is way more time-consuming than a fast track case. Also because of this fact, it would have been desirable for the abovementioned regulation to have defined such agreements in a less broad and all-encompassing fashion.

One believes it would have been preferable to simply define association agreements as contractual arrangements capable of producing a practical result equivalent to full economic concentration, by producing long-lasting commercial or operational arrangements between the parties tantamount to a horizontal or vertical formal merger, or to a formal joint venture between the contracting parties. CADE, however, has chosen a different path, and has decided, in practice, to address its scrutiny to any relevant agreement signed by a party holding a relevant share in a given affected market. This is certainly true when it comes to horizontal agreements, but also in the case of vertical agreements holding a 30% market share, the obligation to file for prior approval is key, although the corresponding regulation also demands exclusivity or sharing of losses and profits. This looks definitively less like merger review and more like a prior mandatory analysis of possible abuses of monopoly power, which is something that other jurisdictions have abandoned a long time ago. Anyways, only time will tell how positively or negatively it will affect the business environment in Brazil or even the activities of the agency itself in the forthcoming years.

IV. The Turnover Requirement

As initially stated, the third and last major point to be addressed in this paper refers to CADE's rules governing the calculation of turnovers to as to determine whether the corresponding thresholds are met or not.

The turnover threshold was undoubtedly improved over time and particularly in the new legislation. The far-reaching original language of the Former Antitrust Law, under which any merger was caught provided that any of the parties had posted in its latest balance sheets a global annual gross turnover of at least BRL 100 million (subsequently raised to BRL 400 million), was adjusted by CADE through reiterated precedents which led to the publication of a binding precedent (*súmula*) in 2005 clarifying that only turnover in Brazil was relevant for filing review. Data from that period shows that this adjustment alone resulted, from 2004 to 2006, in a decrease of 30% to 40% in the global number of cases filed.

The turnover requirements were once again revised by the new Antitrust Law, which originally added to the abovementioned BRL 400 million threshold a new additional threshold of BRL 30 million, to be assessed considering the revenues of "at least one other group involved in the transaction", as has been previously mentioned. It also clarified that both turnover thresholds (BRL 400 million and BRL 30 million) would be calculated considering the revenues of the groups in Brazil only. Even before the new law entered into force, these figures were adjusted to BRL 750 million and BRL 75 million, respectively, by a ministerial ordinance.

The new thresholds achieved the goals of reducing the number of unproblematic transactions being caught and allowing CADE's limited staff to review mergers under a reasonable period of time, what was crucial for the successful implementation of the new suspensory regime. In fact, the volume of merger filings in Brazil dropped significantly under the Antitrust Law.

Notwithstanding the foregoing, the Brazilian turnover thresholds still pose some practical difficulties.

The first of them is to determine which entities should be deemed parties to the same "economic group" of the party directly involved in the merger, for the purposes of turnover calculation. CADE tried to cope with this problem in Resolution 2 (2012), which provides that for turnover calculation purposes, an economic group is comprised of (i) the companies under common control, internal or external, and (ii) the companies in which any of the companies under common control holds directly or indirectly at least 20% of the total or voting capital stock.[14-15]

The new regulation gives room for the interpretation that a group should be comprised of (i) the party directly involved in the transaction ("Merging Party"); (ii) its ultimate controlling entity(ies) ("Parent Company"); (iii) all the other companies directly or indirectly controlled by the Merging Party or the Parent Company ("Companies under Common Control"); and (iv) all the companies in which the Merging Party, the Parent Company or any of the Companies under Common Control holds directly or indirectly at least 20% of the total or voting capital stock ("Subsidiaries").

However, a vast and almost unmanageable interpretation has been adopted by the Brazilian antitrust bar following CADE's informal guidance on the reading on the said rule: the group definition should take into account the Merging Party and all the companies that have either control or an interest of at least 20% in the Merging Party.

Under such interpretation, a Merging Party with five shareholders holding stakes of 20% each and not bound by any shareholders' agreement would belong to five different economic groups, instead of being itself the parent of a more limited corporate group defined by control or 20% interest in a downstream line drawn from the Merging Party. Assuming that each of the 20% shareholder in the merging party is subject to the common control of two shareholders, should one take into account at least ten economic

14 By adopting this broad and somehow confusing wording, CADE departed from a more reasonable group definition applicable under the Old Antitrust Law, pursuant to which group was defined in a straightforward manner as a group of companies subject to common control under CADE Resolution 15/1998.

15 A different and even more controversial guideline applies to the calculation of turnover of investment funds, but it will not be addressed in this article.

groups? How far should one go up from the Merging Party to reach the top of its corporate group?

Similar situations arise on a frequent basis in practice, and if one client happens to ask different practitioners on how to define its corporate group, the client would likely end up receiving different answers. This is certainly a very undesirable situation that deserves further improvement in the corresponding regulation.

Another practical difficulty in turnover calculation refers to groups that buy and/or sell companies in the course of the year preceding the transaction. For instance, company C belongs to group G and is party to a merger in 2014. To assess whether the turnover threshold is met, company C must calculate group G's turnover in 2013. In October 2013, group G's parent company entered into an agreement to acquire target T, but the transaction was only closed in January 2014. Should C take T's 2013 turnover when calculating the group revenue?

One believes the answer to this question is No. When calculating the group turnover, one should take into account only the companies that actually belong to the group (i.e., deals signed and closed) on the last day of the year preceding the transaction whose filing obligation is under assessment. But again, this is a controversial issue that leads to significant debate among members of the Brazilian Bar.

V. Conclusion

As mentioned in the introduction to this paper, the new Brazilian Antitrust Law represented a major and very important improvement in Brazil's merger control regime. However, as may happen to any new statute that comes into force, it opened large room for doubts on its application and interpretation. CADE has been trying hard to fill the gaps with new regulations and clarifications on the more controversial provisions, but a lot remains to be done in this field.

Moreover, it is clear that CADE has tried to be as strict as possible in the establishment and construction of the new filing requirements under its relevant regulations, avoiding the use of broad and open-ended concepts and giving preference to objective criteria such as the 20% interest in the case of group turnover calculation, the 20% and 30% market shares in the case of associative agreements, or the 20% and 5% *de minimis* rule for the filing of minority shareholdings. In some cases, the use of such objective figures comes for the good, but in some cases it may have come for the bad, creating over-encompassing requirements that end up catching more cases than they should, and that nevertheless end up leaving room for uncertainties that call for case law construction or even subsequent clarifications by means of new regulations.

None of these shortcomings outshines, however, the improvements that have already been achieved or the successful efforts towards clarification of the relevant legal standards already accomplished by the Brazilian authorities. Quite to the contrary, they just show that subsequent similar efforts are still needed, and hopefully one will see more action in the regulatory arena in the near future .

* * *

Chapter II

OVERVIEW OF RECENT MERGER CONTROL RULES: MAIN ASPECTS OF CADE RESOLUTION 2

EDUARDO CAMINATI ANDERS[1]

I. Introduction

On the eve of completing three years of the pre-merger review system in Brazil, the adoption of this system effectively represented important progress in the preventive function exercised by the Brazilian Antitrust Authority (CADE).

The discussions on the advantages of the pre-merger review system compared to the *posteriori* system – and vice-versa –, as well as the concern relative to the fact that the pre-merger review system could, because of the lack of CADE's expediency, adversely affect economy or, as stated by some, represent a "bottleneck for the economy", were discontinued during the first weeks of enactment of Law 12,529/11 (Brazilian Antitrust Law).

The first data on CADE's performance in relation to the pre-merger review system – time of review, quality of review and interaction with the merger parties – which, subsequently, in general, were maintained by the authority, confirmed the right choice in the adoption of such system, as well as that CADE has been properly prepared to implement such system.

Despite the significant lack of support by the Federal Government, which, to date, has not complied with the obligation, as set forth in Article

1 This paper counted on valuable collaboration of academic Júlia Merçon Madella Athayde.

121, of Law 12,529/11, to create two hundred positions of Experts in Public Policies and Government Management, the solid performance of the pre-merger review system in Brazil is recognized by the market, legal community and economists acting before the Brazilian Antitrust System (SBDC), as well as by the antitrust authorities of several jurisdictions.

The implementation of the pre-merger review system in Brazil may be largely attributed to CADE's performance in the preparation to operate the new system. Work groups comprised of CADE and the former Economic Law Secretariat (SDE) were created to analyze, adjust and prepare the new procedures, flowcharts and wording of new resolutions and CADE's new internal rules, as well as to address structural matters, such as the structuring of CADE's staff (coordination) and new head office.

CADE's efforts to implement the pre-merger review system include the creation of CADE Resolution 2, of 2012, enacted on May 31, 2012 (CADE Resolution 2), basically together with the enactment of Law 12,529/11.

For the first time in the Brazilian competition scenario, such resolution created important definitions (e.g., economic groups) and rules (e.g., acquisition of ownership interest) that companies use as tools in the complicated task of determining whether their intended mergers require CADE's previous and mandatory review.

The purpose hereof is to identify the main definitions and rules brought forth by CADE Resolution 2. In addition to the main aspects of CADE Resolution 2, this paper also addresses other important and recent rules created by CADE in the context of merger control, such as the definition of association agreements. This paper shall also refer to certain subject matters, all related to merger control, which are included in SBDC's agenda for discussion and may shortly result in new tools for the companies (resolutions and guidelines).

II. General Aspects of CADE Resolution 2

CADE Resolution 2 provides for the submission of merger filings set forth in Article 88 of Law 12,529/11. This resolution was enacted on May 31, 2012 and certain provisions thereof were amended by CADE Resolution 9, of October 1, 2014.

The main issues addressed by CADE Resolution 2 are: (i) definition of the economic group; (ii) transactions eligible for the fast-track procedure; (iii) rules on the acquisition of ownership interest; and (iv) transactions involving the subscription of notes or marketable securities convertible into shares. Each of these four items shall be individually addressed below.

In addition to these items, CADE Resolution 2 clarified to the companies that the merger filing shall be submitted, whenever possible, jointly by the parties to the merger. In addition, the parties shall immediately report to CADE in relation to any subsequent change to the data included in the initial filing.

Such resolution includes two forms to be used in the preparation of the initial filing before CADE: the form to be completed by the parties to the mergers eligible to the fast-track procedure (Exhibit II) and the form to be completed by the parties to the mergers that are not eligible to the fast-track procedure (non-fast-track procedure, Exhibit I).

Though the form for the mergers subject to the fast-track procedure includes several components of information and data on the parties and respective economic groups, merger and involved markets affected, it is significantly simpler than the form for the mergers subject to the non-fast-track procedure. In the non-fast-track procedure, in addition to the information and documents necessary to perform the fast-track procedure, detailed information on the involved markets, such as review of the entry and competition conditions, monopsony power, coordinated power review, is required.

Under the terms of CADE Resolution 2, CADE, and more specifically, the General Superintendence (SG), may request the amendment to the filing in the event any of the items set forth in Exhibits I or II is not completed (forms).

A. Definition of Economic Group

In order to allow the companies to objectively verify the fulfillment of CADE's thresholds, indices set forth in Article 88, of Law 12,529/11 (revenue criteria), CADE created the definition of economic group both for mergers involving companies and mergers involving investment funds.

The reason is clear: if Brazilian Antitrust Law establishes that a merger must be previously approved by CADE, provided that the parties and respective economic groups have registered a specific gross revenue in Brazil in the year before the merger, under the penalty of pecuniary sanction and annulment of the transaction,[2] the parties must clearly identify the respective revenues, as well as the respective economic group's revenue. Accordingly, in order to reduce the scarcity of legal certainty, CADE, through CADE Resolution 2, created, specifically for this purpose – verification of the fulfillment of the revenue thresholds – the definition of the economic group as referred to above.

Accordingly, CADE itself included in such resolution that such definitions of economic group shall solely be applicable for purposes of the revenue calculation in order to verify fulfillment of the objective criteria set forth in Article 88 of Law 12,529/11 (revenue criteria) and shall not bound CADE in its decisions in relation to the request of information and review of the merits of the merges under discussion.[3]

Before addressing the CADE-determined definitions of economic group in CADE Resolution 2, it is necessary to clarify two issues. The first relates to Article 4, caption, of such resolution that considers as "parties" to the merger those entities directly involved in the legal transaction to be notified to CADE and respective economic groups.

The second relates to the revenue criteria set forth in Law 12,529/11 (Article 88), as amended by Ministry of Justice/Ministry of Finance Ordinance 994/2012. In this regard, the merger filling shall be previously submitted to CADE if: (i) at least one of the groups involved in the merger has registered, in the last balance sheet, annual gross revenues in Brazil, equivalent to or greater than BRL 750 million and (ii) at least another economic group involved in the merger has registered, in the last balance sheet, annual gross revenues in Brazil, equivalent to or greater than BRL 75 million.

Therefore, in order to proceed with the verification of the fulfillment of such revenue criteria, CADE created two definitions of economic group, as has been previously mentioned: one for companies and another for investment funds, as described below.

2 *See* Article 88, Paragraph 3, of Law 12,529/11.

3 *See* Article 4, Paragraph 3 of CADE Resolution 2, as amended by CADE Resolution 9.

i. Definition of Economic Group for Companies

As set forth in Article 4, Paragraph 1, of CADE Resolution 2:

> *"Article 4. The parties to the merger are the entities directly involved in the legal transaction subject to the merger review process, as well as the respective economic groups.*
>
> *Paragraph 1 Economic group is, for purposes of calculation of the revenues set forth in Article 88 of Law 12,529/11, on a cumulative basis:*
>
> *I – the companies under common control, in Brazil or abroad; and*
>
> *II – the companies in which any of the companies of item I is the holder, directly or indirectly, of at least twenty percent (20%) of the capital stock or voting capital."*

In other words, Article 4, Paragraph 1, of CADE Resolution 2, sets forth that, for purposes of the revenue calculation, the economic group comprises – in relation to the companies –, on a cumulative basis, all companies under common control, in Brazil or abroad, and the respective companies in which the companies comprising the economic group hold, directly or indirectly, at least 20% of the capital stock or voting capital.

Despite the direct and objective definition (at least the second part), the definition of control is still somewhat uncertain. However, obviously, such uncertainty exceeds the antitrust limits. In fact, not even the Brazilian corporate law doctrine has reached an agreement in relation to the definition of control. However, this fact shall not invalidate or reduce the importance of the definition set forth in CADE Resolution 2. There is no doubt that the adoption of such definition represented a significant advance towards a legal certainty environment. As discussed below, perhaps an aspect to be considered in the future would be the creation of a guideline relating to the definition of control for purposes of antitrust review.

Anyway, the understanding that the definition of control for the purposes of the merger control review shall be construed based on the definition of control set forth in corporate legislation. In this regard, Article 116, of Law 6404, of December 15, 1976 (Law 6,404/76 – Brazilian Law of Corporations) defines controlling shareholder as "the individual or legal entity, or group of persons subject to any voting agreement, or under common control, that: (a) is the holder of the partner's rights that ensure, on a permanent basis, the majority of the votes at the general meeting's resolutions and the power to elect the majority of the company's management members; and (b) effectively uses the power to guide the company's corporate activities and corporate bodies' mergers".

Another aspect challenged upon enactment of CADE Resolution 2, in relation to the definition of economic group for the companies, relates to whether the simple fact of different companies having the same individuals as shareholders would characterize the economic group. However, CADE has already settled such doubt in previous cases.

Indeed, SG, in at least two previous decisions, understood that the economic group would be characterized by the simple fact that different companies have the same individuals as shareholders. Such previous decisions refer to Mergers No. 08700.009881/2012-91[4] and 08700.002561/2013-91,[5] both acknowledged and approved by SG without restrictions on December 18, 2012 and April 1, 2013, respectively.

The first precedent, involving ABN-AMRO Bank N.V. (ABN-AMRO) and Banco CR2 S.A. (CR2), related to the acquisition by ABN-AMRO of one hundred percent of CR2's shares. According to the record, the merging parties requested CADE not review the merger considering that CR2's revenue would not account for at least BRL 75,000,000.00 and, therefore, it would not meet the filing threshold. The main factor was that CR2 had, amongst its shareholders (individuals), five shareholders that were also shareholders of another company, CR2 Empreendimentos Imobiliários S.A.

Based on such request, SG, after reviewing the case, acknowledged the merger filing, based on the following reasons that would support the merger, *in verbis*:

> *"(...)*
>
> *11. In CR2 Empreendimentos Imobiliários Ltda. there is no individual shareholder (or group of shareholders subject to any agreement) that controls the company individually. This means that, obviously, the control is shared, that is, all shareholders, including the common shareholders, are the company's co-controllers. In CR2, two of these shareholders control the company through the shareholders' agreement.*
>
> *12. Considering that the individuals controlling CR2 are, concurrently, co-*

4 ABN-AMRO Bank N.V. and Banco CR2 S.A.

5 CADE, *Dias Branco Administração e Participações Ltda. and Alphaville Urbanismo S.A.* (Merger No. 08012.009773/2006-28) (May 13, 2007).

controllers of CR2 Empreendimentos, both companies are under common control, as prescribed by Paragraph 1, I of Article 4 of CADE Resolution 2/2012, which provides for the following: (...)

15. In other words, the common shareholders in both companies hold, jointly, significant interest, both in CR2 and CR2 Empreendimentos Imobiliários. The significant ownership interest of five shareholders in both companies (more than 20%) indicates, indeed, the potential joint direction of both companies. (...)." (Technical Opinion No. 279 – SG) (emphasis added)

The other precedent refers to the association agreement entered into by Dias Branco Administração e Participações Ltda. ("Dias Branco") and Alphaville Urbanismo S.A. ("Alphaville"). According to the record, the revenues accrued by Dias Branco would be lower than the amounts set forth in Brazilian Antitrust Law, which would make the pre-merger filing mandatory. However, considering the existence of the same shareholder (individual) both in Dias Branco and in another company, M. Dias Branco, which, in turn, registered the revenues that would meet the filing thresholds, the merging parties decided to submit the merger to CADE *ad cautelam*.

In this regard, SG acknowledged such merger and alleged the following:

"(...)

8. Considering that the individual controlling Dias Branco is, concurrently, the controlling of M. Dias Branco, both companies are under common control, as prescribed by Paragraph 1, I and II of Article 4 of CADE Resolution 2/2012, as follows: (...)

9. In this case, the common shareholder to both companies holds significant interest above 20%, both in Dias Branco and M. Dias Branco, therefore, the revenues registered by both companies should be taken into consideration in the measurement of the revenues for purposes of verification of the filing thresholds. In this regard, the group's revenues exceed the legal limit. The objective assumption for acknowledgement of the merger under discussion was, therefore, met. (...)." (Technical Opinion No. 090 – SG) (emphasis added)

Therefore, as discussed, under the terms of CADE Resolution 2, different companies with similar shareholders (individuals) shall be considered as members of the same economic group for purposes of the measurement of revenues.

Another important note in relation to the review criteria to submit a specific merger to the antitrust authority, as prescribed by Article 4, of

CADE Resolution 2, is in the sense that such criteria shall comply with the parameters objectively established in such legal rule.

In other words, once the direct or indirect interest in the capital stock or voting capital accounts for 20%, in a specific company, such company shall be considered a member of the economic group under discussion, for purposes of this antitrust review.[6]

ii. Definition of Economic Group for Investment Funds

In relation to the investment funds, in turn, Article 4, Paragraph 2, of CADE Resolution 2, amended by CADE Resolution 9, sets forth that, for the purposes of the invoicing calculation, the same economic group comprises, on a cumulative basis: (i) the economic group of each shareholder directly or indirectly holding interest equivalent to or greater than 50% of the shares of the fund involved in the merger; (ii) the companies controlled by the fund involved in the merger and (iii) the companies in which such fund directly or indirectly hold interest equivalent to or greater than 20%. According to such rule:

> *"Article 4 (...)*
>
> *Paragraph 2 – In relation to the investment funds, the same economic group, for purposes of the revenue calculation, as provided for in this Article, on a cumulative basis, comprises the following:*
>
> *I – The economic group of each shareholder directly or indirectly holding interest equivalent to or greater than 50% of the shares of the fund involved in the merger by means of individual interest or any type of shareholders' agreement; and*
>
> *II – The companies controlled by the fund involved in the merger and the companies in which such fund directly or indirectly holds interest equivalent to or greater than twenty percent (20%) of the capital stock or voting capital."*

Similarly to the economic group for companies, the definition set forth in Article 4, Paragraph 2, of CADE Resolution 2, amended by CADE Resolution 9, is clear and objective, to the greatest extent possible.

There are challenges on the extension of the term "control" (item II), aligned with the foregoing item relative to the definition of economic group

6 *See* CADE, *BNDES Participações S.A. and Prática Participações S.A.* (Merger No. 08700.007119/2012-70) (September 29, 2012.); and Technical Opinion 198.

for companies, however, these challenges do not reduce the importance of the definitions set forth in CADE Resolution 2, Article 4.

For over fifteen years, CADE has adopted different legal understandings about the definition of economic group involving investment funds. CADE Resolution 2 finally included a clear, objective and institutional definition of how the companies shall define the economic group of an investment fund. And this fact alone, in addition to the significant improvement, significantly reduced the legal uncertainty that has always characterized this matter.

Another aspect that could also result in doubts relates to the extension of item I of such Article 4, by listing the entities that would comprise the same economic group, refers to the *economic group of each shareholder directly or indirectly holding an interest equivalent to or greater than 50% of the shares of the fund involved in the merger.*

However, immediately after the adoption of this wording, through enactment of CADE Resolution 9, on October 1, 2014, which changed the original wording of CADE Resolution 2, SG, by reviewing the merger[7] involving the acquisition of AXT by CAX, which, in turn, was held by Carlyle U.S. Equity Opportunity Fund, L.P., stated, in relation to the definition of economic group involving the investment fund, the following:

> *"(...)*
> *10. Essentially, the definition of group for purposes of the invoicing calculation shall be solely limited to the fund involved in the merger and disregards, for example, the manager of this fund and the other funds under the same management, as well as the related shareholders and companies. Accordingly, for purposes of the revenue calculation, the shareholders of the fund involved in the merger (limited to those shareholders directly or indirectly holding interest equivalent to or greater than 50% of the shares, individually or by means of shareholders' agreement) and the company of the portfolio of the fund involved in the merger (with the same interest percent set forth previously, that is, 20%, in addition to the subsidiaries) shall be considered." (Technical Opinion No. 430 – SG) (emphasis added).*

---

7 CADE, *CAX Holdings, L.L.C., Carlyle U.S. Equity Oportunity Fund, L.P. e AXT Acquisition Holdings Inc.* CADE. (Merger No. 08700.009945/2014-15) (December 15, 2014), not acknowledged by SG (dismissed without merits), according to the decision issued on December 15, 2014.

Therefore, according to SG, at least based on the previous decision, the literal and direct interpretation of the definition of economic group for investment funds shall prevail.

It is also worth mentioning the expression "by means of any type of shareholders' agreement" set forth in item I of Article 4, Paragraph 2, (*50% of the shares of the fund involved in the merger through individual interest or by means of any type of shareholders' agreement*).

Notwithstanding the fact that CADE still has not had the opportunity to review such matter in detail, it does not seem reasonable to consider that, in the absence of a shareholders' agreement, the regulation of a specific fund, which provides for the creation of an investment committee to decide upon material issues, to which each shareholder would indicate a member, could be construed based on the expression "any shareholders' agreement", referred to in item I, as a type of shareholders' agreement and, therefore, it would allow the shareholders of such fund to be considered members of the same economic group.

As has been previously mentioned, CADE has indicated that the guidelines included in CADE Resolution 2 shall be construed on a direct and objective basis.

In this sense, by considering the CADE approach – which solely the future decisions involving the adoption of this definition of economic group set forth in CADE Resolution 2 and, subsequently, as amended by CADE Resolution 9, in last October, shall confirm –, it would be reasonable to assume that, if the regulation of any fund sets forth a qualified quorum to change the manager/administrator, and this quorum, in practice, would attribute a veto power to a specific shareholder in relation to this matter, such power should not be deemed power to control and, as such, with the power to consider such shareholder, under such resolution, as a member of the fund's economic group, as such shareholder should hold at least 50% of the fund shares or be a party to the shareholders' agreement comprising shareholders holding at least 50% of the fund shares.

It is important to mention that the definition of economic group set forth in CADE Resolution 2, of May 31, 2012, was subsequently amended by CADE Resolution 9.

In fact, upon enactment of CADE Resolution 2, the definition of economic group for investment funds set forth in Article 4, Paragraph 2, had the following wording:

> *"Article 4. (...)*
>
> *Paragraph 2 In relation to the investment funds, the members of the same economic group, on a cumulative basis, comprise the following:*
>
> *I – the funds under the same management;*
>
> *II – the manager;*
>
> *III – the shareholders directly or indirectly holding more than 20% of the shares in at least one of the funds referred to in item I; and*
>
> *IV – the companies comprising the fund portfolios in which the direct or indirect interest held by the fund is equivalent to or greater than twenty percent (20%) of the capital stock or voting capital."*

However, after almost two years and a half of the adoption of this definition, CADE changed such definition and excluded the terms "manager" and "funds under the same management". As such, in October 2014, thc original wording of Article 4, Paragraph 2, was changed by means of CADE Resolution 9 to:

> *"Article 4 (...)*
>
> *Paragraph 2 – In relation to the investment funds, the same economic group, for purposes of the invoicing calculation, as provided for in this Article, on a cumulative basis, comprises the following:*
>
> *I – The economic group of each shareholder directly or indirectly holding interest equivalent to or greater than 50% of the shares of the fund involved in the merger by means of individual interest or any type of shareholders' agreement; and*
>
> *II – The companies controlled by the fund involved in the merger and the companies in which such fund directly or indirectly holds interest equivalent to or greater than twenty percent (20%) of the capital stock or voting capital."*

The aforementioned wording represents an improvement of the definition of economic group for investment funds, resulting from CADE's experience accumulated over the first two years and a half of the adoption of such definition.

However, despite the exclusion, exclusively for purposes of the revenue, of the "manager" and the "funds under the same management" in the definition of economic group involving investment funds, CADE included a more comprehensive definition of economic group for investment funds, including the "manager" in the merger filing forms (both in the fast-track procedure and in the non-fast-track procedure).

In fact, by means of CADE Resolution 9, CADE included a comprehensive definition of economic group involving investment funds in item II.5 of the forms set forth in Exhibits I and II of CADE Resolution 2. *In verbis*:

> *"II.5.2. In relation to the investment funds, the members comprising the same economic group for purposes of a response to this item and the other items of this Exhibit, on a cumulative basis, are the following: a) the fund involved in the merger; b) the funds that are under the same management of the fund involved in the merger; c) the manager; d) the shareholders' groups, as defined in item II.5.1., directly or indirectly holding more than 20% of the shares of the fund involved in the merger; e) the companies controlled by the fund involved in the merger and the companies in which such fund directly or indirectly holds interest equivalent to or greater than twenty percent (20%) of the capital stock or voting capital; and f) the companies controlled by the funds under the same management of the fund involved in the merger and the companies in which such funds directly or indirectly hold interest equivalent to or greater than twenty percent (20%)".*

CADE's explanation for the adoption of two different criteria for the definition of economic group involving investment funds – one more limited, exclusively for purposes of the revenue calculation, and another, more comprehensive, for the companies to fulfill the merger filing form – is that, once the jurisdiction thresholds are properly completed (revenue criteria), which is a formal issue, it is important for CADE to adopt a more comprehensive and detailed understanding of the parties to the merger and their respective economic groups – in terms of merits.

In other words, the definition set forth in Article 4, Paragraph 2, of CADE Resolution 2, shall be adopted in the verification of the fulfillment of CADE's thresholds jurisdictions; that is, in order to determine whether a specific merger should be previously submitted to the antitrust authority.

The purpose of the definition set forth in item II.5.2 of CADE forms (Exhibits I and II), in turn, is to increase the information to be provided by the parties to the merger that shall necessarily be analyzed in advance by CADE (disclosure of information). Because such definition is more comprehensive, it allows the antitrust authority to analyze parts of the merger in detail, by providing more concrete elements to review the merits of the antitrust matter.

B. *Hypotheses of Mergers Eligible for the Fast-track Procedure*

CADE Resolution 2 established the "Fast-track Procedure to Review of Merger Filings". CADE shall use such procedure in the cases that have less competition impact for being simpler mergers.

The parties to the merger classified under the fast-track procedure shall complete the simplified form (Exhibit II, of CADE Resolution 2), which, in practice, means the provision of data, information and documents at a volume significantly lower compared to the non-fast-track procedure form (Exhibit I, of CADE Resolution 2).

In addition to the simplified requirement, CADE is likely to review the merger under the fast-track procedure faster. In general, CADE reviews mergers under the fast-track procedure within thirty (30) days from the filing date, and these decisions are generally rendered within less than twenty-one (21) days.[8]

It is worth mentioning that CADE must choose to use the fast-track procedure, which shall consider the suitability and opportunity criteria.[9]

Under the terms of CADE Resolution 2, the following hypotheses of transactions are eligible for the summary procedure:

> *"I – Classic joint ventures or cooperatives: association of two or more separate companies for the creation of a new company, under common control, whose sole and exclusive purpose is the merger in a market whose products/services are not related on a vertical or horizontal basis;*
>
> *II – Substitution of the economic agent: the acquiring company or its group did not operate in the involved market, or in vertically related markets before the merger, as well as in other markets where the target company or its group operated;*
>
> *III – Low market share with horizontal overlap: the merger results in the control of a portion of the relevant market below 20%, at the General Superintendence's*

[8] The average time of CADE's review in the fast-track procedure is of 20.7 days. In the non-fast-track procedure, the average time is of 77.4 days.

[9] *See* Article 7 of CADE Resolution 2, as amended by CADE Resolution 9.

discretion, in order to make clear the lack of importance of the merger in terms of competition;

IV – Low market share with vertical integration: none of the merging parties or their economic groups controls more than 30% of any of the relevant markets that are vertically integrated;

V – Lack of cause relation: horizontal merger resulting in the HHI variation lower than 200 provided that the merger does not result in the control of more than 50% of the relevant market.

VI – Other cases: cases that, although not covered by the categories above, are considered simple, at the General Superintendence's discretion, and do not require a more detailed review."

The hypotheses of transactions eligible for the fast-track procedure originally set forth in Article 8, of CADE Resolution 2, were subsequently amended by CADE Resolution 9, on October 1, 2014.

In essence, CADE increased the market share percentage in the event of vertical integration from 20% to 30% (item IV) and included the event set forth in item V, lack of chain of causation (*horizontal mergers with HHI variation below 200, provided that the merger does not result in the control of more than 50% of the relevant market*).

The changes brought forth by CADE by means of CADE Resolution 9, relate to the purpose of adopting the fast-track procedure. In other words, the cases that do not significantly impact competition may and shall be subject to prompt and simplified review. In this case, the transactions (i) in which none of the merging parties or economic group controls more than 30% of any relevant vertically integrated market or (ii) that result in horizontal mergers with HHI variation below 200 and do not result in the control of more than 50% of the relevant market, do not impact significantly the competition and, as such, should be reviewed by means of a simpler and faster procedure.

C. *Rules on the Acquisition of Ownership Interest*

Law 12,529/11, in compliance with the constitutional rule for defense of free competition, attributed a double function to CADE: repressive and preventive in relation to economic power abuse, in the markets of products and services, regardless of the form and nature of the organization, of the ownership of private or state control, under the legal monopoly regime or not.

The purpose of the provision set forth in Article 88 of Law 12,529/11 is to prevent abuse of economic power by the company exercising such economic power resulting from the merger comprising two or more previously independent companies. In other words, as a result of business integration.

However, by addressing the CADE preventive function, with its objective wording, Law 12,529/11 does not accept the interpretation that CADE should only review mergers that could adversely affect competition. Article 90 of such law expressly defines "concentration acts" (*atos de concentração*) as the legal transaction that complies with any of the provisions set forth in items I to IV. *In verbis*:

> "*(...)*
>
> *I – two (2) or more previously independent companies are merged;*
>
> *II – one (1) or more companies directly or indirectly acquire, by means of purchase or exchange of shares, shares, notes or marketable securities convertible into shares, or tangible or intangible assets, through an agreement or any other means or form, the control or part of one or other companies;*
>
> *III – one (1) or more companies merge into or with another company or companies; or*
>
> *IV – two (2) or more companies enter into an association agreement, consortium or joint venture.*" (emphasis added)

Accordingly, as it refers to a legal transaction, as prescribed in items I to IV, of Article 90, and upon fulfillment of the two jurisdiction thresholds of Article 88 (revenue), such merger shall be analyzed by CADE.

In relation to item II above, specifically in what concerns the purchase of shares, CADE determined, by means of CADE Resolution 2, that the following acquisitions of ownership interest shall be subject to antitrust review:

a. Resulting in the acquisition of single or shared control (Article 9, I, CADE Resolution 2, amended by CADE Resolution 9);
b. Not resulting in the acquisition of individual or shared control (but in the acquisition of "parties", under the terms of Article 90 of such law), however:

(i) In the event the investee is not a competitor and does not operate in a vertically related market,[10] the acquisition grants the purchaser the ownership (direct or indirect) of 20% or more of the investee's capital stock or voting capital (Article 10, I, a, CADE Resolution 2);

(ii) In the event the investee is not a competitor and does not operate in a vertically related market,[11] the acquisition is performed by the holder of 20% or more of the capital stock or voting capital, provided that the ownership interest directly or indirectly acquired, of at least one seller considered exclusively, is equivalent to or greater than 20% of the capital stock or voting capital (Article 10, I, b, CADE Resolution 2);

(iii) In the event the investee is a competitor and operates in a vertically related market,[12] the acquisition grants to the purchaser the ownership (direct or indirect) of 5% or more of the investee's capital stock or voting capital (Article 10, II, a, CADE Resolution 2); and,

(iv) In the event the investee is a competitor and operates in a vertically related market,[13] the last acquisition that, individually or together with other acquisitions, increases the ownership interest by or more than 5%, in relation to those cases that the investor already holds 5% or more of the investee's capital stock or voting capital (Article 10, II, b, CADE Resolution 2).

Therefore, not all acquisitions of ownership interest shall be classified as mergers, although they meet CADE's revenue thresholds. As said, CADE Resolution 2, Articles 9 and 10, provides for the rules that shall be complied in order to determine the acquisitions of ownership interest that shall be analyzed by CADE. Such rules are summarized as follows:

---

10 It is worth mentioning that, under the terms of CADE Resolution 2, Article 10, Sole Paragraph, the following shall be considered for the purposes of verification of the horizontal and/or vertical relationships between the acquiring company and the investee: the activities of the acquiring company and of the other companies comprising its economic group, as set forth in Article 4, of CADE Resolution 2.

11 *See supra* note 10.

12 *See supra* note 10.

13 *See supra* note 10.

Investee/investor	Acquisition of direct or indirect ownership interest in the investee's capital stock/voting capital	Increase of direct or indirect ownership interest in the investee's capital stock/voting capital
Parties are not competitors and/or do not operate in vertically related markets	Mandatory submission if it results in the ownership of 20% or more of the investee's capital stock	Each increase of 20% (acquired from at least one seller considered exclusively)
Parties are competitors and/or operate in vertically related markets	Mandatory submission if it results in the ownership of 5% or more of the investee's capital stock	Each increase of 5% (through one or more mergers)

On the other hand, Article 9, Sole Paragraph, of CADE Resolution 2, expressly sets forth that the acquisitions of ownership interest by the single controller are not subject to mandatory antitrust filing.

Such rule was subsequently included in CADE Resolution 2, by virtue of CADE Resolution 9, of October 1, 2014. The original wording of CADE Resolution 2 did not include such provision and set out that the acquisition by the controller would represent a "concentration act" if the (direct or indirect) ownership interest acquired from at least one seller would be equivalent to or above 20% of the capital stock or voting capital of the company whose ownership interest would be acquired.

Nevertheless, CADE did not classify the acquisition of ownership interest by a single controller, as merger subject to mandatory review, despite the percentage to be acquired by the controller (below or above 20%). CADE's correct understanding is based on the assumption that this type of acquisition of ownership interest (by a single controller) does not affect competition and, therefore, should not be previously approved by the antitrust authority.

In short, according to the table above, the acquisitions of ownership interest below 5% must not be previously submitted to CADE. Ownership interest between 5% and 19.9% shall solely be reported to CADE in the event of the existence of any competition or vertical relation (even if potential) between the purchaser and the investee. And in the event a single controller acquires the ownership interest, such transaction shall not be classified as merger subject to mandatory submission to CADE.

D. *Mergers Involving the Subscription of Notes or Marketable Securities Convertible into Shares*

One matter that was not included in CADE Resolution 2 and was subsequently included in CADE Resolution 9 refers to the mergers involving the subscription of notes or marketable securities convertible into shares. An example that has been frequently used to demonstrate this type of merger, at least before SBDC, is the acquisition of debentures convertible into shares.[14]

In this sense, based on the experience accumulated over the first two years of adoption of Law 12,529/11, CADE regulated the mergers that involve the subscription of notes or marketable securities convertible into shares, specifically the debentures.

CADE Resolution 9, which in this specific case supplemented CADE Resolution 2, established[15] that the subscription of notes or marketable securities convertible into shares (e.g., acquisition of debentures) shall be submitted to CADE[16] provided that:

(i) the future conversion into shares is classified under any event set forth in Articles 9 and 10 of CADE Resolution 2[17] (such events are: a) transaction resulting in the ownership of 20% or more of the investee's capital stock or of 5% or more of the investee's capital stock, in the event of competition and/or b) vertical integration between the acquiring company and the investee); and

(ii) the note or amount entitles the purchaser to the right to appoint managers or oversee corporate bodies or to voting or veto rights on sensitive matters, except for those rights already granted by applicable law.

---

[14] CADE, *Oncoclínicas do Brasil Serviços Médicos S.A and VSAP21 Fundo de Investimento em Participações* (Mergers No. 08700.005472/2012-15) (Aug. 9, 2012); CADE, *BNDES Participações S.A. and Marfrig Alimentos S.A.* (Merger No. 08700.011097/2012-42) (Jan. 14, 2013); CADE, *BNDES Participações S.A. and Sete Brasil Participações S.A.* (Merger No. 08700.005634/2013-04) (July 8, 2013)

[15] *See* Article 11 and Paragraphs of CADE Resolution 2, as amended by CADE Resolution 9.

[16] Upon fulfillment of the revenue criteria (CADE's jurisdiction thresholds).

[17] Under the terms of Article 11, Paragraph 3, of CADE Resolution 2, the number of acquired shares shall be calculated as if the conversion would be exercised on the subscription date.

Therefore, CADE must previously approve the acquisition/subscription of notes or marketable securities convertible into shares,[18] if classified under one of the events set forth in Articles 9 and 10 of CADE Resolution 2 and the note or amount entitles the purchaser to the right to appoint managers or oversee corporate bodies or to voting or veto rights on sensitive matters.[19] In this case, such submission to CADE (acquisition/subscription of notes or marketable securities convertible into shares) excludes the need of another submission to CADE before the respective conversion into shares.[20]

On the other hand, the acquisition/subscription of notes or marketable securities convertible into shares that does not grant to the purchaser the right to appoint managers or oversee corporate bodies or voting or veto rights on sensitive matters, except for those rights already granted by applicable law, shall not be previously submitted to CADE:[21] CADE shall solely approve, in advance, the future and eventual conversion into shares.[22]

Accordingly, CADE duly regulated the submission of transactions involving the subscription of notes or marketable securities convertible into shares, in order to clearly set forth the rule if and when this type of merger must be subject to CADE's prior approval, which reduces the legal uncertainty that has always characterized this matter.

III. Other Important Rules Created by CADE in the Context of the Pre-Merger-Review System

In addition to the rules set forth in CADE Resolution 2, as amended by CADE Resolution 9, CADE regulated other important matters related to the review of merger filings, such as the provisions related to the (i) acquisitions over the stock exchanges and public offers of shares; and (ii) association agreements, through new resolutions and changes to its Internal Rules, as described below.

18 Upon fulfillment of the revenue criteria (CADE's jurisdiction thresholds).

19 Except for those rights already granted by applicable law.

20 *See* Article 11, Paragraph 3, of CADE Resolution 2.

21 Upon fulfillment of the revenue criteria (CADE's jurisdiction thresholds).

22 Upon fulfillment of the revenue criteria (CADE's jurisdiction thresholds) and classification under one of the events set forth in Articles 9 and 10 of CADE Resolution 2.

A. Rules on Acquisitions at Stock Exchanges and in Public Share Offerings

CADE's Internal Rules (RICADE), as prescribed by Article 89 of Law 12,529/11, set forth that CADE does not have to previously approve the relevant subscriptions in public offers of shares[23] or public offer of notes or marketable securities convertible into shares;[24] however no political right related to the shares, notes or amounts shall be exercised before CADE approves the merger.

In this regard, CADE does not have to approve, in advance, all other transactions carried out at stock exchanges or at organized over-the-counter markets.[25] However, the political rights relating to the ownership interest acquired in such mergers shall not be exercised before CADE approves the merger.[26]

In the event the exercise of the political rights relating to the shares acquired in public offers or in other transactions carried out at stock exchanges or organized over-the-counter markets results in the need to fully protect the investment value, CADE may, as requested by the parties, authorize such exercise before issuing the final decision on the merger.[27]

Accordingly, in the event the parties to the potential merger meet the revenue criteria set forth in applicable Law (CADE's jurisdiction thresholds), despite the mandatory submission to CADE, as it relates to an acquisition in the stock exchange, the transaction could be submitted to CADE solely upon publication, and the subscription of shares could be performed regardless of the antitrust approval, provided that the political rights related to the acquired shares are not exercised before the transaction is approved by CADE.

CADE has already reviewed transactions involving the public offer of shares. The main precedents are as follows:

---

[23] *See* Article 109, Paragraphs 1 and 2, of RICADE.

[24] *See* Article 11, Paragraph 3, of CADE Resolution 2, as amended by CADE Resolution 9.

[25] *See* Article 109-A of RICADE.

[26] *See* Article 109, Paragraph 1, RICADE.

[27] *See* Article 109, Paragraph 2, of RICADE.

Suzano Papel-BNDESPAR: the transaction comprised the following: (i) acquisition by BNDESPAR of preferred shares issued by Suzano Papel, by means of public offer; and (ii) conversion of debentures mandatorily convertible into shares. SG approved the transaction, without restrictions, on December 27, 2012.

DASA-Cromossomo Part. II: voluntary public offer of shares for the acquisition of DASA's common shares by CP II. On May 9, 2014, SG challenged the merger before CADE's Administrative Court and recommend that the respective approval should be subject to the execution of an Agreement on Concentration Control (ACC) proposed by the Merging Parties. CADE's Administrative Court approved the merger subject to the execution of the ACC on July 16, 2014.

B. Rules on Association Agreements

Item IV, of Article 90, of Law 12,529/11, provides for the execution of association agreements between companies as a merger subject to mandatory prior approval by CADE.

However, although included in the events of "concentration acts", the term "association agreement" is not set forth in applicable Law. In spite of the increased objective approach of Law 12,529/11, compared to the previous law – Law 8,884/1994 –, in relation to the identification of the transactions that must be reported to CADE, over almost three years of enactment of the new antitrust law, several concerns were raised on the mandatory report to CADE in relation to certain legal transactions, such as certain partnership agreements, technology licensing or supply agreements that could be classified as association agreement.

In order to provide further information to the companies on the types of association agreements that should be previously analyzed by the antitrust authority, CADE enacted Resolution 10 (CADE Resolution 10) on October 29, 2014.

Such resolution, which provides for the association agreements that shall mandatorily be submitted to CADE, as prescribed by item IV, Article 90, of Law 12,529/11, came into effect in January 2015.

In general, CADE Resolution 10 sets forth that the association agreements subject to CADE's previous approval, effective for more than two (2) years, are those agreements in which:[28]

I – the parties are horizontally related to the object of the agreement whenever the sum of the market share in the relevant market affected by the agreement is equivalent to or greater than 20%; or

II – the parties are vertically related to the object of the agreement, whenever at least one of the parties accounts for 30% or more in the relevant market affected by the agreement, provided that at least one of the following conditions is met:

a. the agreement provides for the sharing of revenues or losses between the parties;

b. the agreement provides for exclusivity relationship.

In the event the parties are vertically related to the object of the agreement, in addition to the market share of 30%, at least one of the conditions referred to in item "a" (shared revenues or losses) or "b" (exclusivity) shall be met. This requirement shall not be applicable to those agreements in which the parties are horizontally related to the object of the agreement.

As such resolution came into effect in January 2015, CADE has not yet issued decisions in which it has thoroughly discussed the terms of CADE Resolution 10.[29] Nonetheless, the objective nature introduced by such resolution and CADE's discourse in the sense that this resolution shall be adopted to limit the association agreements that shall be previously approved by the antitrust authority represent a significant progress to eliminate the legal uncertainty that such matter created upon enactment of Law 12,529/11.

---

[28] Article 2, first Paragraph, of CADE Resolution 10.

[29] Although CADE Resolution 10 has already been applied by SG in a recent precedent: CADE, *Sanofi-Aventis Farmacêutica Ltda. and Herbarium Laboratório Botânico Ltda* (Merger No. 08700.001403/2015-85) (March 26, 2015). Merger not acknowledged by SG (dismissed without merits), according to the Technical Opinion 110/2015, of SG, dated March 26, 2015.

Conclusion

CADE has brought forth several improvements in terms of structuring the pre-merger review system. In addition to Law 12,529/11, the resolutions and the adoption of new internal rules, subject to subsequent adjustments, provided companies with important rules and tools for merger control.

When one looks into the future, it is clear that it is necessary to create a guideline on the definition of control over companies in the competition review. As discussed in this paper, in several situations, both companies and the authority are required to identify "control" to apply the rules concerning the pre-merger review system. Albeit being specifically limited to merger control, such definitions, as is the case of the definition of economic group provided for CADE Resolution 2, would result in clarity and objectiveness and would reduce legal uncertainty. The definition of control would certainly be a significant tool to be used together with the tools CADE has recently created.

Another issue that should be further analyzed is gun jumping: its characteristics, identification procedure and extension of fines. CADE is currently addressing this matter and has submitted a draft for a resolution on the gun-jumping review procedure[30] to public consultation and is discussing a guideline related to the characterization of gun jumping.

CADE has undertaken several normative improvements related to the pre-merger review system since the enactment of Law 12,529/11. It is clear that there is still room for improvement. Considering the enthusiasm shown by CADE since the implementation of the pre-merger review system, CADE is expected to have an Olympic performance in the upcoming years.

* * *

30 Public Inquiry No. 06/2014.

CHAPTER III

THE ANTITRUST REVIEW OF MINORITY SHAREHOLDINGS BETWEEN COMPETITORS – THE BRAZILIAN PERSPECTIVE

CAIO MARIO DA SILVA PEREIRA NETO
PAULO LEONARDO CASAGRANDE
FILIPPO MARIA LANCIERI

I. Introduction

Transactions in which companies acquire a minority stake in a counterpart that is active in the same relevant market or in related markets are common in a globalized economy. In general, a minority shareholding is defined as a "situation in which a shareholder holds less than 50% of the voting rights attached to the equity of the target firm"[1] and does not have control of the company in any other way. Therefore, it represents a structural link between companies that may be horizontally or vertically related. One may arguably claim that the larger the minority shareholding and the closer the markets where the linked companies operate, the stronger the competitive concerns related to such equity stake.

1 EUROPEAN COMISSION, WHITE PAPER *Towards more effective EU merger control* (2014), p. 6.

The antitrust review of minority shareholdings among competing companies is a rapidly evolving issue in several competition jurisdictions around the world, and Brazil is no exception. The purpose of this chapter is to present the main aspects of such enforcement area in the country, in view of both regulatory and case law developments under the responsibility of the Administrative Council for Economic Defense ("CADE"), the Brazilian competition watchdog. The next few pages provide an overview of the local treatment given to this increasingly important topic by indicating both the similarities and the peculiarities of the Brazilian experience *vis a vis* the situation of such matter abroad.

This chapter is divided into five sections, the first of which is this short introduction. The second presents a brief overview of academic writings on the matter and the discussions taking place in certain foreign jurisdictions. The third describes the merger control regime applicable to minority shareholdings under the current and the former Brazilian Competition Laws. The fourth reviews the recent Brazilian case law regarding minority shareholding and the fifth concludes this paper with a critical assessment of the treatment CADE has given to such cases.

II. Recent Academic Discussions and Enforcement Cases Abroad

Two important papers dating from 2000 may be deemed as pioneers in the recent academic debate on the antitrust issues that arise from partial ownership. The first was written by Gilo,[2] and the author argued that minority shareholdings between competitors, even when done "solely for investment", could harm competition as companies might compete less aggressively so as not to diminish the value of their investments. Gilo therefore claims that the "solely for investment" antitrust exemption present in Section 7 of the United States' Clayton Act[3] is not completely aligned with sound economic theory.

[2] DAVID GILO, *The Anticompetitive Effect of Passive Investment*, 99 MICH. LAW REV., 1-47 (2000).

[3] Paragraph 7 of the Clayton Antitrust Act established merger control over the acquisition by one corporation of stock of another. Nevertheless, the third paragraph of such section reads that "This section shall not apply to persons purchasing such stock solely for investment and not using the same by voting or otherwise to bring about, or in attempting to bring about, the substantial lessening of competition. Nor shall anything contained in this section prevent

The second paper was penned by Salop and O'Brien,[4] and summarizes possible anticompetitive concerns that may arise from different forms of minority stakes in several degrees of market concentration.[5] In such article, the authors consider two main types of minority stakes. The first, *financial interest*, does not entail the capability of the interest holder of influencing the business policy of the invested company. In some circumstances, these minority stakes may raise concerns of unilateral effects, such as higher incentives for the investing company to increase prices, considering that part of the lost sales may be recouped through profits from the invested company.

On the other hand, there are minority stakes that grant the investing company some type of *corporate control* over the invested company, i.e. the power to influence or determine certain relevant aspects of its activity in the market. This kind of investment may raise concerns of coordinated behavior between the investing and the invested company, either by direct influence in the management of the latter or by information exchange among them, enabled by such structural link.

It is important to stress that Salop and O'Brien did not develop a binary method of analysis, in which one company either has financial interest or limited control over its competitor. On the contrary, the authors' study defends that a number of intermediary tranches exists in both categories, each reflecting the level of influence that the partial ownership conveys to its owner, dividing it into (i) total control (ability to dictate the conducts of the acquired company); (ii) partial control (acquirer influences decision-

---

a corporation engaged in commerce or in any activity affecting commerce from causing the formation of subsidiary corporations for the actual carrying on of their immediate lawful business, or the natural and legitimate branches or extensions thereof, or from owning and holding all or a part of the stock of such subsidiary corporations, when the effect of such formation is not to substantially lessen competition". Therefore, it creates a legal exemption for acquisitions of shareholdings smaller than 10% of total capital that are made "*solely for the purposes of investment*", which are unenforceable under such section. Please refer to *Id.* p. 29-39; and EUROPEAN COMMISSION, Annex To The Commission Staff Working Document Towards More Effective Eu Merger Control 16 (2013).

4 DANIEL P. O'BRIEN & STEVEN C. SALOP, *Competitive effects of partial ownership: financial interest and corporate control*, 67 ANTITRUST LAW J. 559-614 (2000).

5 *Id.* at 568-571; EUROPEAN COMMISSION, *Annex To The Commission Staff Working Document Towards more effective EU merger control* 7 (2013).

making, but does not dictate it); and (iii) silent financial interest (acquirer has no ability to influence competitor's decision-making process).[6] Based on such classification, the authors developed what they refer to as the *Modified Herfindahl–Hirschman Index* ("MHHI"),[7] which basically adds a term to the regular *Herfindahl–Hirschman Index* in order to adjust the market concentration levels according to the degree of relevant influence the partial ownership grants the minority stakeholder.

Such study increased the awareness of potential concerns derived from minority shareholdings, providing a more sophisticated discussion on the matter. In so doing, it also prompted responses by other authors that did not perceive such stakes as posing substantial concerns. A special reference should be made to the paper written by Dubrow in 2001.[8] A corporate lawyer rather than a trained academic economist, Dubrow believed that Salop's and O'Brien's purely theoretical analysis was far from the reality of most markets, in which companies could hardly maximize profits or coordinate actions solely due to partial ownership in a competitor. According to the study, any investigation of minority shareholdings should focus on quantifying *actual* rather than *potential* effects of such structural link, considering all the restraints for unilateral or joint maximization presented in the functioning of real corporations.[9]

More specifically, Dubrow held that a number of real world circumstances prevented the materialization of the theory of harm raised by Salop and O'Brien. In particular, Dubrow claimed that incomplete information, management incentives (managers are rewarded for the performance of their area, rather than for the firm as a whole) and the inability to capture benefits (e.g. easy entry preventing joint-maximization,

6 O'Brien and Salop, *supra* note 4, at 577-584.

7 *Id.* at 594-602. The MHHI builds on the work made by BRESNAHAN and SALOP on the analysis of joint-ventures, *see* Timothy F. Bresnahan & Steven C. Salop, *Quantifying the competitive effects of production joint ventures*, 4 Int. J. Ind. Organ. 155-175 (1986).

8 Jon B. Dubrow, *Challenging the Economic Incentives Analysis of Competitive Effects in Acquisitions of Passive Minority Equity Interests*, 69 Antitrust Law J. 113 (2001).

9 *Id.* at 128-129.

as competitors capture lost sales due to increased prices) diminish actual antitrust concerns associated with partial ownerships.[10]

Such pioneering articles preceded the increasing importance of minority shareholdings between competitors throughout the 2000s both as an academic and a policy issue.[11] Perhaps the most representative enforcement matter were the cases reviewing the minority stake held by Ryanair, a low-cost carrier, in its direct Irish competitor Aer Lingus, both at the European Union[12] and the United Kingdom levels.[13]

Such cases exposed the limitations of the European Commission under the Merger Regulation to review this type of increasingly important transactions involving minority investments,[14] in contrast to

---

10 *Id.* at 131-137. It is important to stress that Salop and O'Brien wrote a reply to Dubrow's arguments in 2001 (*see* Steven C. Salop & Daniel P. O'Brien, *The Competitive Effects of Passive Minority Equity Interests: Reply*, 69 Antitrust Law J. 611–625 (2001).). Nevertheless, one believes that the relevance of Dubrow's criticism of the initial analysis remains.

11 The number of relevant cases somewhat related to involving minority shareholdings has since increased significantly. For examples, please refer to Univision/HBC (United States v. Univision Commc'ns Inc., No. 1:03CV00758 (D.D.C. Mar. 26, 2003)) and The Carlyle Group/ Riverstone/ Kinder Morgan (TC Group, 72 Fed. Reg. 4508) in the United States; and Nordea / Postgirot (Case M. 2567), Allianz / Dresdner (Case M. 2431), Siemens/VA Tech (COMP/M.3653) and Toshiba / Westinghouse (Case M. 4153) in the European Union, among others. For an overview of developments in the field, see also OCDE – Policy Roundtables – Minority Shareholdings (2008).

12 Ryanair first attempted to acquire the control of Aer Lingus in 2006, and such merger was blocked by the Commission (M.4439 Ryanair/Aer Lingus). As Ryanair remained with around 30% of Aer Lingus' capital stock, the invested company required the Commission to order the divestiture, but the authority decided it did not have the powers to review minority shareholdings short of control, which was confirmed by the General Court (case T-411/07 Aer Lingus v Commission [2010] ECR II-3691). Ryanair filed another proposed transaction to purchase the full control of Aer Lingus, and was once again blocked by the Commission in 2013 (M.6663 – Ryanair/Aer Lingus).

13 For the United Kingdom decision on the review of Ryanair's minority shareholding interest in Aer Lingus under UK competition law, please refer to the "*Competition Commission report on the complete acquisition by Ryanair Holdings plc. of a minority shareholding in Aer Lingus Group plc*", dating as of August 28, 2013.

14 As the most recent White Paper published by the Commission to amend the EU Merger Guidelines state: "Now, when the acquisition of a minority

the enforcement regimes of certain Member Countries, such as Germany, Austria and, most notably, the UK, which actually investigated Ryanair's minority stake in Aer Lingus and ordered a partial divestment.[15] Moreover, the competition authorities of other countries, such as the United States, Canada, Japan as well as Brazil, also have powers to review minority shareholdings,[16] whereby the European Commission has initiated public consultation to consider possible legal measures in order to enhance its enforcement powers over this type of transaction.[17]

As will be seen below, such discussions by scholars and enforcement agencies abroad are important as a background for the presentation of the current status of this issue in Brazil, to be addressed in the remaining sections of this article.

III. Criteria for Notification of Minority Shareholdings

CADE has reviewed minority shareholdings both under the former competition law – Law 8,884, enacted in 1994 –, and the current governing legislation, Law 12,529, of 2011.[18]

---

shareholding is unrelated to an acquisition of control, the Commission cannot investigate or intervene against it. The Commission can only intervene against a pre-existing minority shareholding held by one of the merging parties when control is specifically acquired. For example, the Commission can intervene if the undertaking in which one party has a minority stake is a competitor of the other merging undertaking. If the minority shareholding is acquired subsequent to the Commission's investigation, however, the Commission has no competence to deal with possible competition concerns arising from it despite, the fact that the competition concerns arising from the minority shareholding may be similar to those that arise when control is acquired." *See supra* note 1, at 8-9.

15 UK cuts Ryanair stake in Aer Lingus – GCR, GLOBAL COMPETITION REVIEW, August 28, 2013, *available at* http://globalcompetitionreview.com/news/article/34065/uk-cuts-ryanair-stake-aer-lingus/ (last visited Feb 24, 2015).

16 Please refer to, *supra* note 4, at 9, for more information on the matter.

17 *Id.*

18 Please refer to CAIO MARIO DA SILVA PEREIRA NETO & PAULO LEONARDO CASAGRANDE, *Merger Control Under the New Brazilian Competition Law*, 11 ANTITRUST CHRON. (2011), available at https://www.competitionpolicyinternational.com/merger-control-under-the-new-brazilian-competition-law (last visited Mar 3, 2015) for more information on the matter.

Article 54 of Law 8,884/94 established a post merger review regime and provided for a broad definition of '*atos de concentração*' (mergers) that must be submitted to CADE's review. Paragraph Three of the same article had thresholds to identify mergers of mandatory notice: (i) whenever the parties to the merger reached a joint market share of 20% in a given relevant market; or (ii) one of the players involved had gross annual revenues in excess of BRL 400,000,000.00 in Brazil during the preceding year.

As per minority shareholdings, CADE had a specific Precedent (*Súmula 02*) where it determined waivers for the notification of certain types of transactions. According to such Precedent, the acquisition of a minority stake did not trigger mandatory notification if the acquisition was executed by the already controlling shareholder, and the seller did not have the power to: (i) appoint officers; (ii) determine business policies; or (iii) have veto power on corporate decisions. Also, in order not to trigger the notification requirement, the agreement (iv) should not include non-compete clauses effective for more than 5 years and/or territorial scope wider than that of actual activities of the involved undertaking; and (v) should not result in any type of corporate control relationship between the parties, after the merger. If these requirements were not met, the acquisition of a minority shareholding was subject to notification – once either the turnover or the market share thresholds were met. Of course, this still left quite a few grey zones, such as the minimum stake to trigger a notification to CADE, especially considering investment in publicly listed companies.

CADE set the most important precedents on the material criteria for the competitive review of minority shareholdings under such former merger control regime, as will be shown in the next section.

Current Law 12,529/11 sets a more specific definition of "merger", which now explicitly covers transactions where one or more undertakings acquire, directly or indirectly, the control or *parts* of one or more undertakings, among other hypotheses (Art. 90, III). Moreover, Art. 88 of such Law, as updated by Joint Ordinance 994/2012 from the Ministries of Finance and Justice, holds that concentration acts must be reported to CADE only if: (i) one of the economic groups involved earned, in Brazil, gross annual revenues in excess of BRL 750,000,000.00 in the preceding fiscal year; and (ii) another economic group involved earned, in Brazil, gross annual revenues in excess of BRL 75,000,000.00 in the preceding fiscal year.

In order to further specify such legal concepts – especially that of the 'partial acquisition of a company' –, CADE adopted specific provisions under Resolution 02/2012.[19] Such Resolution determines that CADE must review transactions where: (i) one party acquires the sole or joint control of another party (art. 9, I); (ii) one party acquires 20% or more of a company that cannot be considered a competitor and does not perform activities in a vertically related market (art. 10, I, a);[20] and (iii) one party acquires a stake of 5% or more, if the target is a competitor or develops activities in a vertically related market (art. 10, II, a).[21]

Such minimum shareholding thresholds for mandatory notification determined by CADE in its Resolution 2/2012 are fairly low in a comparative perspective: in Germany and Austria, a firm has to purchase 25% of the shares of another company,[22] while in Canada these thresholds range from 20% to 35% of shares, depending on whether the company is publicly listed or not.[23]

Finally, art. 88, Paragraph 7 of Law 12,529/11 also establishes that CADE is entitled to require private parties to submit any transaction for its review, even if the turnover thresholds were not met. In this case, however, the parties are entitled to close the transaction before CADE's final decision, which will implement an *ex post* analysis.

Therefore, it is clear that CADE has broad powers to review cases involving minority shareholdings under the current legal regime, including through the requirement of *ex-post* submission of transactions that do not reach the minimum turnover thresholds.

---

19 Resolution 2 has been updated twice since its initial adoption in May 2012, to better reflect CADE's experience in merger review. The most recent amendment dates back to October 2014.

20 Mergers in which a party that already holds more than 20% of a company that is neither a competitor nor vertically related thereto acquires a stake of 20% or more in the same company are also subject to mandatory notice (art. 10, I, b)).

21 Art. 10, II b) also holds that mergers in which a party that holds 5% or more of a competitor or a vertically related company acquires another stake of 5% or more of said company's capital must be submitted to CADE's review.

22 *See supra* note 4, at 11-14. It is also important to stress that such thresholds are complemented by qualitative threshold regarding the "acquisition of competitively significant influence".

23 *Id.* at 17. Similarly, Canada also has a notification trigger whenever "significant interest" in a company is acquired.

IV. CADE's Relevant Case Law on the Purchase of Minority Stakes

The Brazilian experience analyzing minority shareholdings has increased significantly over the past five years. Four cases are especially noteworthy as the most important rulings of CADE on the matter: (i) Telefonica/TIM, in 2010, complemented by the Telefonica/VIVO decision in 2013; (ii) two mergers that involved the review of the structural link between Amil and the FMG group, in 2012; (iii) DASA/MD1, in 2013; and (iv) CSN/Usiminas, in 2014. All such precedents were adopted under the previous post-merger review system that was in force until May 2012. Nevertheless, as they are fairly recent, they may be deemed important precedents indicating the current view of the authority on the substantive review of partial ownerships.

A. *Telefonica/TIM and Telefônica/Vivo*

The first substantial decision regarding minority shareholding refers to the review of the purchase of a partial stake by Spanish telecom group Telefonica in its Italian counterpart, Telecom Italia.[24] Telefonica was the co-controlling shareholder of Vivo,[25] Brazil's leading mobile services provider, while Telecom Italia controls TIM, another key player in the Brazilian mobile market. Together, both mobile operators accounted for approximately 55% of such relevant market.

In short, Telefonica was the majority shareholder (42.3% of the shares) of Telco, which, by its turn, acquired a 23.74% stake in Telecom Italia, becoming the company's main shareholder, as the remaining 76.26% of shares were diluted in capital markets. Therefore, the transaction enabled Telefonica to influence the business policies of Telecom Italia, and potentially influence the business policies of TIM Brasil, one of its main rivals in the Brazilian mobile market.

[24] CADE, *Telefónica S.A., Assicurazioni Generali S.p.A, Intesa Sanpaolo S.p.A., Sintonia S.A. e Mediobanca – Banca di Credito Finanziario S.P.A.*, Reporting Commissioner Carlos Emmanuel Joppert Ragazzo (Merger 53500.012487/2007), (April 30, 2010).

[25] Telefonica owned 50% of the shares of Brasilcel, which, by its turn, owned 88,9% of Vivo's voting capital. Portugal Telecom owned the remaining 50% of Brasilcel's capital.

The transaction was submitted to both CADE and the telecom regulator ANATEL in 2007. As a condition for its regulatory approval, ANATEL required a series of commitments to ensure the independence of TIM's operations in Brazil.

In turn, CADE performed a comprehensive review of possible antitrust effects arising from minority shareholdings, referring to international scholarship on the matter. It identified four different types of partial shareholding: (i) stakes that ensure parties the control of the acquired company; (ii) stakes that ensure a relevant influence over the business of this acquired company; (iii) stakes that may be considered passive (i.e. with no power to influence business), but that ensure the buying party access to confidential information of the invested company; and (iv) passive investments that do not ensure the buying party any confidential information whatsoever.

Given its abovementioned characteristics, Telefonica's stake was defined as (ii), as it ensured the company a relevant influence in Telecom Italia (and consequently TIM Brasil), but could not guarantee the exercise of sole control.

After a thorough analysis of all markets where the companies operated, CADE concluded that, in general, minority shareholdings among rivals could hardly benefit competition. Moreover, specifically on the merger, CADE also stated that the indirect corporate link between Telefonica and TIM Brasil had a significant risk of harming competition – either by means of coordination between the companies or by means of unilateral action by Telefonica to jointly maximize profits with TIM Brasil. Therefore, CADE concluded that, in order to be approved, the merger required the imposition of additional behavioral remedies that were aimed at ensuring the absolute independence of TIM's operations in Brazil.

The parties then executed a settlement whereby Telefonica agreed not to: (i) exercise any kind of corporate control of TIM's operations in Brazil; (ii) attend any shareholders' meeting relative to discussions on TIM's operations in Brazil; (iii) attend any meeting of the Board of Directors of Telecom Italia where the matters regarding TIM Brasil's operations were discussed (Telefonica's appointed Directors had to execute specific agreements with ANATEL and CADE reinforcing such obligation); (iv) appoint any officers or directors that might qualify as an interlocking directorate; (v) establish any corporate relation between VIVO and TIM

Brazil; and, finally (vi) Telefonica also agreed to establish a wide number of Chinese walls, aimed at preventing the exchange of information between Telefonica and Telecom Italia regarding TIM's operations in Brazil.[26]

In view of the foregoing, though it was deemed a behavioral remedy, CADE's decision in fact prevented Telefonica from exercising any rights related to or have access to any information on TIM's operations in Brazil. In doing so, CADE affirmed that it was effectively changing Telefonica's influence in TIM from relevant influence (ii) to a passive investment (iv).

The 2010 Telefonica/TIM decision was later complemented by CADE's review of a merger in which the Telefonica acquired the remaining 50% of Brasilcel's capital, previously owned by Portugal Telecom.[27] In so doing, Telefonica became the sole controller of Vivo. Thanks to a series of capital injections, Telefonica concurrently increased its interest in Telco to 70% of the company's capital, which could arguably make it the controller of Telco and, therefore, Telecom Italia.

In its review, CADE affirmed that the new corporate structure where Telefonica would be the sole controller of Vivo and *de facto* controlling shareholder of Telecom Italia would harm the Brazilian mobile services market (Vivo and TIM accounted for approximately 55% of the market).[28] Still acknowledging that Telefonica's participation in TIM Brasil should be considered as a *passive investment*, CADE affirmed that the relevant stake the company owned in both competitors was enough to diminish the competitive pressure between both companies by: (i) enabling Telefonica to recoup eventual losses from demand shifts caused by price increases; and (ii) strong signaling the Brazilian telecom market (comprised of four players) that both companies would accept a tacit collusion to increase prices.[29] In CADE's view, Portugal Telecom's position as a co-controller in Vivo was essential to prevent joint-maximization of profits' initiatives, as

26 Please refer to Commissioner's Eduardo Pontual vote in CADE, *Telefônica S.A. and Portugal Telecom SGPS S.A.*, Reporting Commissioner Eduardo Pontual Ribeiro (Merger 53500.021373/2010) (December 10, 2013), at 7.

27 CADE, *Telefônica S.A. and Portugal Telecom SGPS S.A.*, Reporting Commissioner Eduardo Pontual Ribeiro. (Merger 53500.021373/2010) (December 10, 2013).

28 Comissioner Pontual's vote, p. 25.

29 *Id.* at 28-29.

Portugal Telecom would not profit from strategies where Vivo could raise its prices and shift some of its demand to TIM.[30]

As a result, CADE approved the merger, provided Telefonica would: (i) accept a new co-controller in Vivo to replace Portugal Telecom; or (ii) sell its direct or indirect interest in TIM, under a confidential timeline.

B. AMIL/FMG

The second relevant precedent refers to transactions involving the review of a structural link between AMIL and the FMG Group, both companies with important hospital operations in the metropolitan area of Rio de Janeiro.[31] Both AMIL and FMG acquired several hospitals in the region. However, during its review of both mergers, CADE discovered that AMIL held a 10% shareholding in Medise, a company responsible for controlling two of FMG's hospitals in Rio (FMG owned 85% of the shares of Medise, and the remaining 5% was held by a third party). Moreover, the Medise's shareholders' agreement ensured AMIL a series of veto powers in the management of the company, as well as access to certain confidential information of the FMG group.

In its review, CADE reinforced its understanding that there are four main types of minority shareholdings, as described in the Telefonica/TIM decision, and concluded that AMIL's powers over Medise guaranteed the company would have relevant influence over FMG's business. Such reasons backed the consideration of both companies as part of a single economic group for the purpose of assessing potential negative impacts in the relevant markets involved in the transactions. In an important concurring opinion, Commissioner Ricardo Ruiz stressed that fiduciary duties under corporate law were incapable of preventing antitrust risks.[32]

---

30 *Id.* at 33-36.

31 CADE, *Amil Assistência Médica Internacional Ltda. and Casa de Saúde Santa Lúcia S.A.*, Reporting Commissioner Elvino Mendonça (Merger 08012.010094/2008-63) (August 29, 2012); and CADE, *FMG Empreendimentos Hospitalares S.A. ("FMG") e Hospital Fluminense S.A.*, Reporting Commissioner Marcos Paulo Veríssimo (Merger 08012.006653/2010-55) (Aug. 29, 2012).

32 The case also involved certain discussions on potential coordination regarding vertical relations established between AMIL and Medise, but they are not relevant to the discussion hereof.

As a result, CADE concluded that the minority stake could enable coordination between the activities of AMIL and FMG Groups, and in order to approve both mergers, CADE required AMIL to sell its minority stake in Medise. The company then executed a settlement with the authority, whereby it agreed to disinvest its shares within a 90-day period from execution of the settlement.

C. *DASA/MD1*

This decision, adopted by CADE after more than three years of review, referred to the merger between Diagnósticos da America SA (DASA), Latin America's largest diagnostics company, and MD1 Diagnósticos (MD1).[33] MD1 was a large player in the diagnostic testing markets of Rio de Janeiro. The company was property of Mr. and Ms. Bueno, who, at the time, also controlled AMIL, Brazil's largest health insurance company. By means of the merger, in a stock for stock transaction, Mr. and Ms. Bueno acquired 23% of DASA; in October 2012, they sold their controlling stake in AMIL to United Health Group, keeping 10% of its capital. Moreover, Mr. Bueno remained president of AMIL.

The Economic Supervision Office of the Ministry of Finance (SEAE) recommended severe restrictions to the merger in April 2012, just short of blocking it. As the case was sent to CADE's Court, Reporting Commissioner Ricardo Ruiz reviewed SEAE's opinion and made a detailed analysis of the market, requesting a significant amount of information from the parties and other players. It included the evaluation of the diagnostic services markets in Rio de Janeiro and neighboring cities, considering both horizontal issues between DASA and MD1, as well as alleged horizontal and vertical issues with AMIL due to the minority stakes held by Mr. and Ms. Bueno in both this company and DASA.

Notwithstanding such fairly low indirect minority linkages between AMIL and DASA/MD1, CADE concluded that these companies should be considered as part of a single economic group for competition law matters.[34] The merger was approved with negotiated remedies involving i)

---

33 CADE, *Diagnósticos da America SA and MD1 Diagnósticos S.A.*, Reporting Commissioner Ricardo Ruiz (Merger 08012.010038/2010-43) (Oct. 10, 2013). The authors acted as legal counsel to DASA in the matter.

34 CADE, *Aquisição da MD1 pelo Grupo Dasa é aprovada com restrições* (2013), http://www.cade.gov.br/Impressao.aspx?f84cda2ec75db37f8bb888d874d6 (last visited Feb 24, 2015).

the divestment of assets in Rio de Janeiro with combined annual turnover of BRL 110 million, and ii) temporary prohibitions for further acquisitions in the areas of Rio de Janeiro, São Paulo and Curitiba.

D. CSN/Usiminas

Another important precedent on minority shareholdings involved two steelmakers: CSN's acquisition of a 17,42% stake in its rival Usiminas. Together, both companies accounted for approximately 75% of the Brazilian flat steel production capacity, with ArcelorMittal responding for most of the rest, and 50% of the flat steel production in the Southern Cone (Brazil plus Argentina, Chile, Paraguay and Uruguay).[35] CSN bought this stake in the stock exchange hoping to acquire Usiminas' control, an objective that failed after Usiminas' controlling shareholders decided to sell their stake to Ternium/Techint, an Italian-Argentinean group. As a consequence, Usiminas was hostile to CSN, and challenged the acquisition before CADE.

In April 2012, CADE adopted an interim measure to block further purchases by CSN and to suspend its voting rights in Usiminas shareholders' meetings. The Reporting Commissioner conducted a detailed investigation immediately thereafter, and CSN presented a number of legal and economic studies defending that: (i) the stake was insufficient for CSN to influence Usiminas, as the invested company was controlled by Ternium which also held a 30-year shareholders' agreement with another shareholder; (ii) Usiminas was a public company and all information CSN would have access to would also be disclosed under securities regulation; and (iii) the financial results of Usiminas had no effect on CSN's incentives, as the latter was most efficient player in the Brazilian steel market and Usiminas had not distributed profits in the latest years. Finally, CSN also held that any attempt to coordinate its actions with Usiminas would be subject to CADE's strict scrutiny under Brazilian anti-cartel rules.

In its review, CADE reinforced its case law dividing minority shareholdings in the abovementioned four types, depending on the level of corporate influence and access to confidential information that

---

35 CADE, *Companhia Siderúrgica Nacional – CSN, and Usinas Siderúrgicas de Minas Gerais – Usiminas.* Reporting Commissioner Eduardo Pontual Ribeiro. (Merger 08012.009198/2011-21) (April 15, 2014). The authors acted as legal counsel to CSN

resulted from the partial ownership. It then considered CSN's stake a silent financial interest, as CADE's interim measure prevented any management powers in Usiminas. Notwithstanding the specifications of CSN stake in Usiminas, CADE held that the partial ownership could lead to less intense competition in the flat steel market due to potential joint-maximization of profits. As a result, the case was approved conditionally to a negotiated remedy involving the sale of an undisclosed amount of Usiminas's shares within a confidential timeframe, in order to avoid excessive disruptions in the negotiations of both CSN and Usiminas shares in the stock exchange, as both players are important publicly traded companies.

V. CADE's Treatment of Minority Shareholding: the Road Ahead

Initially, it must be stressed that CADE's case law has incorporated the scholarly distinction between *financial interest* and *relevant influence*, which is reflected in its recurrent use of the four types of partial ownership. In so doing, CADE brings some sophistication to the review of partial acquisitions, recognizing a wide spectrum of different types of transactions, which leads to different degrees of concerns. This nuanced approach, at least in theory, aligns CADE with the frontline of antitrust scholarship.

However, a closer look shows that CADE still has room to improve its perspective on minority stakes between competitors. As the precedents presented above demonstrate, CADE still performs a rather formal review on the possible anticompetitive effects of minority shareholdings in general. Indeed, opposite to Dubrow's recommendations, the authority's reviews have only lightly considered actual market specifications that might prevent coordination or joint maximization of profits. CADE has also neglected a proper evaluation of how corporate law may ensure or restrict voting rights and access to information in practice (and not just in theory). Neither has CADE properly evaluated how future enforcement actions, under its own anti-cartel policy, may hinder information exchange or prevent other forms of corporate cooperation.

CADE's case law has also presented a very strong presumption that any minority shareholding between competitors will lead to a joint maximization of profits between the parties involved, despite the actual circumstances of the market where the companies operate.[36]

[36] Relevant examples of such approach are the CADE decisions concerning two

This strong presumption is particularly unaligned with international experience on partial ownership, as shown in Competition Commission's thorough decision in the case Ryanair/Aer Lingus,[37] where the CC expressively held that the strong historical competition between the parties, combined with the uncertainty in the future distribution of profits by Aer Lingus, prevented the authority from simply presuming the adoption of joint-maximization conducts.[38]

Also, it is important to highlight that in accordance with international scholarship on partial ownerships,[39] CADE has shown a clear

---

research and development (R&D) joint ventures among Brazilian pharma companies to develop new kinds of biopharmaceuticals, called Orygen and Bionovis. Notwithstanding the fact that no actual horizontal or vertical overlaps were identified, and the fact that such biopharmaceuticals are new products to be introduced in the Brazilian markets, the authority imposed conditions on both mergers because there was an indirect cross shareholding among the two JVs. CADE required the companies to inform or request authorization for any change in the activities of the JVs within 4 years, due to the possibility of a future overlap between them. CADE, *Biolab Sanus Farmacêutica Ltda., Cristália – Produtos Químicos Farmacêuticos Ltda., Eurofarma Laboratórios Ltda., Libbs Farmacêutica Ltda.*, Reporting Commissioner: Marcos Paulo Veríssimo (Feb. 2, 2013); and CADE, *Aché Laboratórios Farmacêuticos S.A., EMS Participações S.A., Hypermarcas S/A, União Química Farmacêutica Nacional S.A.*, Reporting Commissioner Elvino Carvalho Mendonça (Feb. 2, 2013)

37 Competition Commission, *supra* note 13.

38 *In verbis*, the Competition Commission held that: "7.148 We conclude that Ryanair would not be expected to compete less strongly because of its financial interest in Aer Lingus. In reaching this conclusion, we took into account that the acquisition of its miniroty shareholding in Aer Lingus was part of Ryanair's overall strategy of acquiring the entirety of Aer Lingus. Any incentive to compete less strongly might also be reduced by the uncertainty and indirectness by which Aer Lingus's profits would flow back to Ryanair. (..)7.158 We were not aware of any evidence suggesting that Ryanair and Aer Lingus were coordinating on their core fares or the geographical area of their operations. In general, the relationship between the management of the two companies appeared to be antagonistic, rather than cooperative. We found considerable and sustained evidence of price competition between airlines, and of airlines' fares reacting to each other (and to the presence of the other airline on a route). 7.159 We found it unlikely that Ryanair's minority shareholding in Aer Lingus would lead to coordinated effects" (p. 64-66 of CC in Ryanair/Aer Lingus).

39 Please refer to OCDE – Policy Roundtables – Minority Shareholdings, *supra* note 14.

preference for divestiture decisions. Even in the Telefonica/TIM decision, CADE's behavioral remedy was very extensive and was only short from full divestiture, completely restricting Telefonica from influencing TIM's management in any manner. As seen, such decision was later reviewed by the authority, and CADE finally ordered Telefonica to cease any form of corporate link with TIM Brasil.

Based on the foregoing, minority shareholdings are becoming a topic of growing concern from competition watchdogs around the world. More and more such authorities understand that even passive structural links may, under certain circumstances, diminish competitive pressures.

CADE is not lagging behind in the review of such market structures, as demonstrated by the ever-growing number of important precedents involving minority shareholdings that have been evaluated over the past five years. But there is certainly room for a more nuanced review, separating anticompetitive concerns that may require structural remedies from light discomfort that may be dealt with by behavioral remedies or even no intervention at all.

* * *

Chapter IV

INVESTMENT FUNDS: SALIENT ISSUES IN MERGER FILINGS IN BRAZIL

René Guilherme S. Medrado
Luís Henrique Perroni Fernandes*

I. Introduction

One of the major challenges in antitrust law law is the processing of merger filings (known in Brazil as 'concentration acts') regarding investment funds[1] by the Brazilian antitrust authority, *Conselho Administrativo de Defesa Econômica* ("CADE"). A number of deals have been submitted to

* The authors acknowledge insightful comments received from Alessandro P. Giacaglia, Caio Ferreira Silva, Rodrigo Manso Vieira and Tiago Severo Gomes, on earlier drafts of this article. Errors are to be attributed solely to the authors.

1 Under Brazilian law, an investment fund basically consists of a collective investment vehicle organized as a condominium, providing for the co-ownership of assets by investors. These investment funds can only operate in Brazil upon prior registration with the Brazilian Securities Commission (CVM). Investment funds, along with the securities they issue (*quotas*), and their investors (*quotistas*), are also subject to CVM's oversight. A condominium may be defined as a joint property (in rem) right exercised by two or more persons over a certain asset or pool of assets, each holder (a co-owner or *condômino*) being attributed a pro-rata fraction of such asset. The condominium itself has no legal personality apart from that of its owners.

CADE, especially since Law 12,529 of 2011 came into force, but none of them was found to raise any material competition concerns.

CADE has reviewed several transactions under the aegis of Law 12,529 of 2011,[2] all of which were approved without any restrictions, as further detailed below. Statistic data further point to the proliferation of merger filings involving investment funds that have no impact or relevance whatsoever in the competition environment, which is highly undesirable both from an antitrust policymaking and efficiency standpoints. This scenario suggests that this issue should remain high up on the agenda of the Brazilian antitrust authorities.

Accordingly, local authorities' attention and efforts on this front should rather be focused on devising clear-cut criteria to identify and segregate in an accurate and quick manner the transactions that are eminently financial in essence (and, as such, should not be taken to the antitrust authorities for review or, if so, should be processed under a special, more simplified and fast-tracked proceeding) from those potentially affecting the market (and, thus, relevant from an antitrust perspective). Unlike what happens in other jurisdictions, the fact that prevailing local rules do not provide for safe harbor provisions or express waivers for the duty to submit transactions involving investment funds to antitrust authorities reinforces the need of having the efforts on this space shifted to the evaluation of submission criteria that could tackle antitrust concerns.

This paper therefore, points out certain issues that are noteworthy in the analysis of merger filings involving investment funds in Brazil, although with no intent of exhausting such discussion.

II. Context

A new resolution dealing with merger filings involving investment funds recently came into force. Resolution 9 of 2014 should be interpreted within the context it was conceived. Hence, comments will be made on the evolution of such subject and treatment CADE ultimately conferred to it.

Further to Law 8,884 of 1994 – and given the absence of criteria specifically directed at investment funds, all transactions that achieved the turnover thresholds provided for in Article 54, main section, Paragraph 3, qualified for merger filing. Such scenario translated into a vast number

2 Data updated until October 31, 2014.

of reportable transactions, especially due to vagueness in the law on the annual turnover calculation by the parties.

As a result, the CADE Board was time and again discussing whether there was room for improving the applicability of Article 54, so that "(...) only the transactions in which investment funds served as a vehicle for potential market concentration were eventually submitted to the antitrust authorities (...)".[3]

Such concerns were in keeping with antitrust policy objectives and guidelines – among which, the efficient allocation of scarce public efforts and resources to relevant antitrust cases only.

It can thus be seen that CADE was increasingly aware of the need to segregate transactions merely comparable to financial investments from those that could somehow bring competition concerns. In 2010, CADE Board adopted a methodology to address such aspects,[4] primarily based on the (i) identification of the economic groups involved in the transaction; (ii) participation of pension funds as investors in the transactions submitted to CADE; and (iii) applicability of the turnover criterion established in Article 54, Paragraph 3, of Law 8,884 of 1994.

According to this methodology, transactions involving investment funds would only qualify as concentration acts if both the following criteria were met: (i) if investors had the power to influence the conduct of investment fund managers, and (ii) if the latter held powers to influence the management of the target company.

This criterion focuses on the ability to interfere in decision-making powers. Thus, if investors were unable to interfere in the administration or management of the investment fund, or if the fund managers had no say in the management of target companies comprising their managed portfolios, then the transaction was not reportable to CADE, *regardless of the turnover or market share of market players involved.*

3 Art. 54. The acts, under any manifest form, that may limit or anyhow harm free competition, or result in the domination of a relevant market of goods or services, shall be submitted to CADE.

4 CADE, *Capital Tech Inovação e Investimentos, Huntington Centro de Medicina Reprodutiva.* Reporting Commissioner Olavo Zago Chinaglia. (Merger No. 08012.009529/2010-41) (September 11, 2010),.

Moreover, in determining whether a transaction should be submitted for CADE's review, the aforementioned elements (i.e., the investment fund shareholders' ability to influence investment decisions, and, concurrently, the investment fund's ability to influence the management of the target company) should be accompanied by the following requirements: (i) the fund shareholders having a relevant influence over the fund administration had to meet, individually or in combination, at least one of the criteria established in Article 54, Paragraph 3, of Law 8,884 of 1994, and (ii) the business companies in which the fund exercised a material influence also had to fall under these same requirements.

The heart of the matter was thus the existence of 'material influence', that is, "(...) the possibility of a market player to make use of a minor shareholding, or even of a mere contractual relation, to interfere in the decision-making process of the target company, so affecting its share value and strategies."

As for Brazilian private equity investment funds (*Fundos de Investimento em Participações* – FIPs), which are a constant presence in most corporate transactions involving investment funds, CADE established the possibility of exercise by the FIP of a material influence over target companies as a legal presumption, on the grounds that the exercise of such a degree of influence was expressly required by Article 2 of Ruling No. 391, issued by the Brazilian Securities Commission (CVM),[5] which governs the setting up, management and operation of Brazilian private equity investment funds (FIPs), namely:

> *"Article 2 – The private equity investment fund, which is created as a closed-ended entity, is a pool of resources intended for acquisition of shares, debentures, warrants and other bonds and securities convertible into or exchangeable for shares issued by publicly- or privately-held companies, also participating in the decision-making process of the investees, with an actual influence over their strategic policy and management, especially by designating members to the Board of Directors."*

Another relevant aspect of CADE Board's decision under scrutiny referred to the participation of pension funds (as investors) in the transactions submitted to antitrust review when involving investment

[5] CVM stands for *Comissão de Valores Mobiliários*, the administrative body in Brazil analogous to the Securities Exchange Commission in the U.S.

funds. In this sense, the existence of investment committees empowered to confirm decisions made by pension fund managers would not suffice to determine the possibility of exercise of material influence of pension funds over investment funds.

Another aspect worthy of particular mention is how the turnover criterion under Article 54, Paragraph 3, of Law 8,884 of 1994 should apply. According to the CADE Board decision at stake, (i) the turnover of fund shareholders and respective economic groups exercising a material influence over the fund management should be taken separately, and (ii) the turnover of companies (and respective economic groups) in which the investment fund held a stake should be taken jointly, even if they were not involved in the notified transaction.

A. CADE Resolution 2 of 2014

CADE Resolution 2 of 2012, published in the Federal Register (DOU) on May 31, 2012, offered new perspectives by regulating the notification of mergers referred to in Article 88 of Law 12,529 of 2011 brought new insights into the issue. In general, it has primarily intended to eliminate the analysis of material or significant influence by replacing it with objective criteria along the same lines of Law 12,529 of 2011.

These concerns are clearly consistent with the options adopted by lawmakers in drafting the new antitrust law. After all, the criteria adopted for turnover calculation under Article 88 of Law 12,529 of 2011 tried to escape subjective interpretation as much as possible.

As for the notification of transactions involving investment funds, CADE's commitment to devising objective analytical elements seems to be at the core of CADE Resolution 2 of 2012. It was then decided that the following would be taken into consideration, collectively, in calculating the turnover to be considered for submission purposes: (i) funds under the same management; (ii) the fund manager itself; (iii) the fund shareholders that directly or indirectly held more than 20% of shares in at least one of the funds under the same management; and (iv) the companies pertaining to the investment fund's portfolios, whenever the direct or indirect stake of such investment fund was equal to or greater than 20% of the total or voting capital of those companies.

Despite CADE's efforts to establish objective criteria, CADE Resolution 2 of 2012 received criticism for the reasons outlined above.

B. CADE Resolution 9 of 2014

The discussion that followed CADE Resolution 2 of 2012 clearly contributed to the drafting of CADE Resolution 9 of 2014, which specifically applies to investment funds. The changes introduced by CADE Resolution 9, which entered into force on October 7, 2014, were limited to the definition of economic group, but only in terms of turnover calculation vis-à-vis the objective criteria set out in Article 88 of Law 12,529 of 2011.

CADE established that the following should be taken into consideration, cumulatively: (i) the fund involved in the transaction; (ii) the economic group of each fund shareholder that directly or indirectly holds stake equal to or greater than 50% of the shares in the fund involved in the transaction, whether individually or through any kind of fund shareholders' agreement; (iii) the companies controlled by the fund involved in the transaction and the companies in which the fund directly or indirectly holds stake equal to or greater than 20% of the total or voting capital of those companies.

For the turnover calculation, it is important to stress that CADE no longer considers the funds under the same management and also the fund manager. The rationale seems to be to reduce the number of reportable transactions and instill objective criteria that are easier to apply and closer to market reality.

Also, it must be highlighted that CADE Resolution 9 only reduced the scope of analysis (review of the economic group definition for the purposes of the turnover calculation) with respect to the assessment of whether a transaction is reportable. In contrast, the same resolution increased the amount of information to be provided by the investment funds, once the conclusion on the mandatory reporting of the merger is drawn.

Unlike the previous resolution, CADE Resolution 9 requires information on the economic groups of the fund shareholders (of those holding stake higher than 20% of the fund), and makes clearer that information should also be furnished on the companies controlled by the investment fund involved, or by the investment funds under the same management of the investment fund involved. It also requires the form to contain information on the companies in which such funds hold stakes equal to or higher than 20% of the total or voting capital (item II.5.2).

CADE Resolution 9 distinguishes the information to be provided by the investment funds involved in the transaction from the information to be provided by funds that are only under the same management thereof. For the latter, the resolution limits the information to be provided only to the investment funds and companies that are horizontally or vertically related to the activities related to the object of the transaction. Although it is meritorious to link the scope of the information to be provided to the competition object of the transaction (concept defined below in this paper), it seems that the resolution could have gone farther, as discussed below.

In reality, the dichotomy above still reveals a need for further reassessment, in view of a fine balance to be achieved, considering the increased burden put on the parties on the supply of substantial information and the actual benefits the authority will obtain. In fact, as elaborated below, the efforts to simplify proceedings and the review of cases involving investment funds should also consider the volume and reasonableness of the information to be submitted.

III. Salient Issues

C. Statistics

CADE reviewed 74 mergers involving investment funds under the aegis of Law 12,529 of 2011, all of which were approved were cleared without any restrictions.

It is also important to highlight that such transactions were reviewed in an average period of 22 days. The short time span achieved by CADE for merger review could be explained by the fast-track proceeding (as adopted for all of them) and also by the clear perception that most cases involving investment funds raised no competition concerns.

Such perception is also supported by statistics. Out of the 74 transactions under scrutiny, all of them but one were reviewed only by CADE's General Superintendence. In other words, 98.65% of the cases were not even elevated for review by CADE's Administrative Tribunal.

It is also worth noting that only two investment fund classes engaged in corporate transactions were submitted to CADE's review during the period. In relation to the merger filings involving investment funds, most of them (98%) referred to Brazilian private equity investment funds (FIPs), while the remaining ones consisted of only two merger filings (2.7%) involving to Brazilian real estate investment funds (*Fundos de Investimento Imobiliários* – FIIs).

The chart below better illustrates the foregoing statements:

INVESTMENT FUNDS (Merger filings involving investment funds submitted to CADE since the entering into force of Law 12,529 of 2011)[6]		
Merger filings		74
Types	FIPs	72
	FIIs	2
Processing	Fast track	74
	Ordinary	0
Time of Review		22 days
Body Responsible for Final Decision	General-Superintendence	73
	CADE's Administrative Tribunal	1
Approval	No restrictions	74

D. *Concept of 'Influence' and Resolution 9 of 2014*[6]

The wording of Article 4, Paragraph 2, I, of Resolution 2 of 2012 clearly incorporates, albeit implicitly, the concept of 'influence':

> *"Paragraph 2. As for investment funds, the following are regarded as part of the same economic group, in calculating the turnover under this Article, cumulatively:*
>
> *I – The economic group of each fund shareholder that holds directly or indirectly a stake equal to or above 50% of the shares in the fund involved in the transaction, whether individually or through any type of fund shareholders' agreement; (...)"*

The inclusion in the filing of the economic group of each fund shareholder that holds a stake equal to or above 50% of the shares in the

[6] Data updated to October 2014.

fund involved in the transaction seems to signal a regulatory option to focus on cases where the shareholder either holds or shares *control* over the fund acting individually, as such an ownership stake (i.e., 50% or more of the fund's shares) per se should generally entitle the fund shareholder to controlling interest in the fund it holds (by analogy to the Brazilian Law of Corporations).

Despite the apparent objectivity of the above threshold, it is interesting to note that it goes back, to a certain extent, to the idea of *influence*, even though only when *control* or *co-control* is held to exist. In a way, this regulatory option seems to come to a balance by limiting the reporting interest only to cases where the influence in the investment fund is substantial (thus characterizing the existence of *control or at least shared control*). With respect to portfolio companies, however, the bar has not yet been raised in that the 20% threshold remains valid (which is similar to an affiliate (*coligada*) status under the Brazilian Law of Corporations).[7]

E. Volume of Requested Information in Multi-party Cases

The definition of 'economic group' for the purpose of requesting information and analyzing the merits may lead to situations in which the spectrum of companies to be considered is extremely wide, including some that are not much related to the concentration act under scrutiny. Furthermore, it is worth remembering that the gathering of information takes time, and this usually translates into expenses that are excessively burdensome for the parties, while not actually relevant for CADE's review.

Therefore, besides the probable irrelevance of bulky information provided, the reasonableness of such information vis-à-vis the issue under probe should also be taken into account.

Thus, the major difficulty seems to lie in finding the right balance between two factors: *the certainty and extent of information provided v. the burden of the parties in obtaining it*. The more information an antitrust

7 On this matter, it is worth highlighting that Resolution 9 adopted different criteria regarding the composition of economic groups for, on one hand, the assessment of whether a transaction is reportable, and, on the other hand, the supply of information in the form, once a conclusion is drawn on whether the transaction must be reported.

authority obtains, the more probable it is to render a more accurate decision, which implies the need for greater collection of information by the parties.

When it comes to investment funds, however, such correlation should be examined with caution. The maximum availability of information at the excessive expense of the parties may end up becoming counterproductive – and that would run against the very policy that has been implemented by CADE –, notably given the fact that transactions involving investment funds do not raise substantial competition concerns.

Waivers are not part of the Brazilian antitrust culture, but the statistics discussed above seem to favor a more reasonable treatment to transactions involving investment funds. CADE should assess certain alternatives, particularly those focusing less on the means (information) and more on the purpose (review focused on the 'competition object' of the transaction). For example, the antitrust authority could ask the parties to categorically answer whether they identified any portfolio company that had (horizontal or vertical) relations with the 'competition object' of the transaction under scrutiny. In other words, as transactions involving investment funds are usually unlikely to raise competition concerns, the antitrust authority could focus on obtaining direct answers from the parties about the expected effects of a transaction on their competition object.

This second option – i.e., asking direct questions about the competition object of a transaction – seems to be a reasonable solution that is easy to implement. In this case, a specific filing form would be made available for transactions involving investment funds, which would be in keeping with the quest for more objectivity in cases involving investment funds.

This would help achieve a good balance between *the certainty and extent of information provided v. the burden of the parties in obtaining it*, in that the level of reasonableness of information would be at least similar to what is attained under the erstwhile proceeding but at a lesser expense for the parties, thus contributing positively to improving the business environment in terms of lower transactional costs and greater expeditiousness.[8]

8 Finally, antitrust authorities must also take into consideration that expanding the reach of the information request may result in the fund having to supply information about certain companies that are not under its control, which may pose serious difficulties on obtaining the information, and on checking the reliability of the information in itself.

It should be noted that though still timidly, CADE Resolution 9 has started to walk down such path, when CADE decided to limit the information to be provided by the investment funds/companies under the same management only to the information related to the "object of the transaction". This is exactly the concept of 'competition object' of the transaction advocated in this paper.

F. Types of Funds

The interrelation between investment funds and antitrust law stirs important debates and considerations. Within the context of structured investment funds, it is possible to identify, certain aspects that are more or less relevant from a competition perspective, based on their specificities, and that should be taken into consideration by the antitrust authority. These points are laid out below:

G. Real Estate Investment Funds (FIIs)

FIIs may be defined as closed-end funds (*condominia*) governed by CVM Ruling No. 472 of 2008, as amended, without legal personality and characterized by a pool of assets gathered through the placement of securities via the distribution system for investment in real estate enterprises.

Closed-end funds are funds existing during a predefined duration and shareholders cannot opt in or out at any time. When funding is completed, new shareholders are generally not permitted, as is the case in relation to new investments by the existing shareholders, except as provided for in the FII's organizational documents. Therefore, there are typically defined periods during which the fund is open for funding. As a general rule, FII shareholders are not liable for any legal or contractual obligation attributable to the FII, nor do they hold any real (*in rem*) right in and/or to the real estate and real estate enterprises comprising the fund's portfolio. By contrast, they are generally entitled to distributions of earned profits arising from the FII on a cash basis.

Despite the existence of such specific vehicle (FII), an analysis of statistical data shows that merger filings involving real estate investment funds are normally made via Brazilian private equity investment funds (FIPs).

This fund class enables shareholders/investors to make investments that were otherwise possible only by means of the traditional direct purchase of real estate. It is worth mentioning that in such cases, acquisition of real estate was not reportable to CADE. As these more sophisticated investment vehicles blossomed, reporting to CADE has increasingly turned into a reality in such market.

However, the real estate market is highly dispersed. Most cases involving the real estate market result in fast-track approvals, given the lower market shares held by the plethora of market players usually involved (generally, the municipal area is taken into consideration in terms of geographic market). Such feature, based on the *certainty and extent of information provided v. the burden of the parties in obtaining it* assessment matrix, suggests that the existing regulation should take a more reasonable approach towards FIIs in view of the clear lack of competition concerns.

H. Brazilian Private Equity Investment Funds (FIPs)

The Brazilian Private Equity Investment Fund (FIP), as regulated by CVM Ruling No. 391 of 2003, is intended (according to Article 2 of said Ruling) to primarily invest in bonds and securities either convertible into or exchangeable for shares issued by joint-stock companies, and must necessarily be organized as a closed-end fund (*condominium*). Only qualified investors under applicable regulations are permitted to subscribe for or acquire FIP's quotas, and the minimum amount for subscription is currently set at BRL 100,000.00.

Under CVM Ruling No. 391, the FIP must necessarily participate in the decision-making process of the investee and exercise an actual influence over the investee's strategies and management (including by designating members to the target company's board of directors).

Accordingly, FIPs in fact do (and must) interfere in the decision-making process of the companies in which they invest by operation of law. In principle, this would suggest the existence of competition concerns, once one same fund could hold interest in companies acting in the same industry (or even in the same relevant market).

It is worth noting, however, that, despite such assumption (namely, that FIPs can and must exert influence in investees), all cases involving investment funds (98% of which refer to FIPs) comprised in the above samples have not generated competition concerns. This seems to add further strength to the regulatory authorities' option to pursue a more objective approach in lieu of a primarily subjective analysis based on the 'influence' criterion. Nevertheless, it seems that such option should take a step further by adopting a simplified form for merger filings.

In fact, the existing data seems to suggest that such vehicles have not been used as *longa manus*, or as conduit companies, which could end up serving as a mechanism for exercising a dominant position in specific markets (such as by creating trusts that the antitrust laws are designed to combat), but rather as a special type of investment conduit entailing a set of legal and regulatory features that advocate for its use as the preferred private equity vehicle in Brazil. Among such features, the flexibility and generally favored tax regime accorded to the FIP make it a powerful tool for structuring M&A transactions involving target companies in Brazil.

I. Mutual Venture Capital Fund (FMIEE)

Governed by CVM Ruling No. 209 of 1994 and organized as a closed-end *condominium*, the FMIEE must allocate at least 75% of its portfolio to a diversified portfolio of securities issued by startup companies. Further, according to Article 1, Paragraph 1, of said ruling, a startup company is a company that has annual net revenues, or consolidated annual net revenues, below BRL 150,000,000.00. Paragraph 3 of that same Article prohibits the FMIEE from investing in companies that are controlled by a group of companies, whether *de facto* or *de jure*, posting net assets above BRL 300,000,000.00. For its part, Article 2 establishes that the fund duration is of 10 years, extendable by resolution of the annual shareholders' meeting. Further, FMIEEs will always be organized as closed-end funds, and its shares will be issued at the minimum price of BRL 20,000.00.

It is worth mentioning that 75% of the FMIEE assets must necessarily be invested in a diversified portfolio of securities issued by startup companies and also to the prohibition against investing in groups posting net assets above BRL 300,000,000.00. The rationale is that such requirements will cause investments to be dispersed and also directed at companies of smaller prominence (which generally do not significantly influence the market they act in).

Prima facie, such characteristics are indicators that competition concerns should drift off in these cases as there are legal deterrents to investment concentration in one single asset (company). It is nevertheless necessary to keep in mind, however, that the structure varies from market to market, so CADE could exceptionally see the need for deeper review and thus call for submission of a complete form.

J. Private Equity Fund for Investment in Innovative Startup Companies (FIEEI)

CVM Ruling 415 of 2005 added Chapter XI-A to CVM Ruling 209 of 1994, which specifically regulates FIEEI. According to Article 43-B of those rulings, once the FIEEI is set up and authorized to operate, it should allocate at least 75% of its investments to shares, debentures convertible into shares or warrants issued by innovative startup companies.

Under Paragraph 2 of Article 43-A, innovative startup companies should be organized as corporations and primarily engage in innovations or improvements in the production process or corporate environment that result in new products, processes or services.

It is possible to infer that the innovation factor is highly pro-competitive, and the antitrust authorities should thus look favorably upon it. Such circumstance nevertheless does not dismiss the review of potential market effects, but the very nature of this investment vehicle should be taken into consideration from an antitrust law perspective.

Conclusion

In view of the foregoing, it is possible to conclude that the antitrust review of transactions involving investment funds raises several interesting questions that should be further explored by antitrust authorities and by the society as a whole.

The recent changes CADE has implemented, particularly through improvements vis-à-vis past decisions or, subsequently, by issuance of CADE Resolution 2 of 2012 and 9 of 2014, attest to CADE's efforts to make antitrust review more reasonable and productive specifically with regard to investment funds.

However, a closer look at statistical data and at the most common types of structured investment funds indicates that CADE's review of merger filings could indeed be more flexible. Considering *the certainty and extent of information provided v. the burden of the parties in obtaining it* assessment matrix, there is indeed room for the Brazilian antitrust authorities to be less demanding in terms of the information volume required from investment funds in merger filings.

Thus, this paper suggests the adoption of a simplified form for investment funds focusing on direct questions strictly related to the competition object of notified transactions. Such alternative is justifiable not only because of the negligible competition concerns involved in this type of transaction (thus enabling the antitrust authorities to lower the bar in this regard), but also as a means of lessening the burden of parties in transactions involving investment funds.

* * *

Chapter V

ASSOCIATIVE AGREEMENTS UNDER THE BRAZILIAN ANTITRUST LAW

Fabíola Cammarota de Abreu
Joyce Midori Honda

I. Introduction

As far as the merger control is concerned, one of the most common criticisms to the previous Brazilian antitrust law (Law 8,884/94) referred to the generic provision regulating merger filings. Because of the vague and diffuse concept set forth thereunder, economic agents generally raised questions concerning the obligation to notify the Brazilian Antitrust Authority (CADE) on certain transactions the merging parties believed did not require notification as merger filings.

In this context, in addition to other aspects that raised questions, such as the approval of the antitrust authority after a business transaction had already been entered into, the opportunity came for a broad restructuring of the Brazilian Antitrust System (SBDC), both from the perspective of its institutional design as well as in terms of its scope of operation. Thus, opening a new stage of the Brazilian competition policy, Law 12,529/11 was enacted on November 30, 2011 and became effective on May 30, 2012 (Antitrust Law or Law 12,529/11).[1]

1 Law 12,529/11 was enacted after a substantial legislative process period, which started in 2004.

Among the main innovations introduced by the new law was the establishment of a pre-merger review system for merger filings. This practice led to the modernization of CADE's *modus operandi* to align the Brazilian antitrust policy with international practices. The consequences of the *a priori* system review of merger filings directly affect the subject matter under analysis since the term *associative agreement* has been expressly quoted in the law, specifically in the article that governs merger filings, a scenario that in itself differs from Law 8,884/94.

Despite the fact that Law 12,529/11 has established objective criteria for the notification of mergers, listing the acts that are subject to notification as merger filings, including the associative agreement, the degree of uncertainty was still present. Being aware of such uncertainty and based on former decisions, CADE sought to orient the understanding by showing criteria that would theoretically be capable of clarifying the matter. This scenario did not materialize and there were even cases of divergence among the commissioners themselves. Such scenario of legal insecurity called for a more concrete action, particularly with regard to the pre-merger review requirement and the related risks thereto.

As a result, in February 2014, CADE made a public inquiry on the draft of a resolution covering associative agreements.[2] After receiving several contributions, the resolution became effective in early 2015.[3] Although Resolution 10 is at its initial stage, the preliminary practical experience indicates that, as far as its enforcement is concerned, it is not possible to determine whether it will be successful. This is due to the fact that as it was issued, Resolution 10 may not have the expected impact on the submission of certain contracts for review, particularly those with vertical integration between the parties.

In one's opinion, as a result of the apparently questionable criteria from the economic rationale point-of-view, depending on how Resolution 10 is interpreted, there is a serious risk that any type of contract,[4] most of which are generally used in day-to-day corporate transactions, or

2 Public Consultation 3/2014. Contribution period: February 19, 2014 to April 22, 2014.

3 Resolution 10, in force as from January 5, 2015. This resolution was published in the Brazilian Official Gazette on November 4, 2014.

4 Provided that the turnover thresholds established by the Antitrust Law are verified.

even without any competition relevance, would be subject to notification to CADE; CADE, in turn, could face a flood of minor transactions to be reviewed, having to turn its attention away from the priority matters included in its agenda of challenges and assignments. In addition, if there is no increase in the number of notified transactions, the economic agents might be unaware of the new regulatory framework they are now part of.

In view of the foregoing, it is now time to make some practical considerations on this matter. The assessment of former decisions is a useful method to suggest more effective measures to handle associative agreements. This approach is intended to make the subject matter workable, thus preventing it from being disregarded because the criteria to apply Resolution 10 would still be unclear. At any cost, attempts are being made to prevent Resolution 10 from showing to be innocuous. Based on the foregoing considerations, this paper includes suggestions on the determination of safe harbours, block exemptions and period of inquiries.

For the sake of being didactic, this paper has been structured as follows: the first chapter presents a historic panorama of Law 8,884/94 for the review of supply and distribution contracts within the scope of the previous merger control regime, given the potentially associative nature of these contracts. This assessment covers CADE's former decisions and outlines the interfaces in the realm of anticompetitive conducts. The second chapter covers Law 12,529/11, including associative agreements in the context of the new regime, examining former decisions and detailing the prerequisites of such agreements under the resolution. This chapter represents the core of this paper and addresses the suggested measures for the purposes of making the new resolution more effective. The third chapter provides a short description of a paradoxical situation in the Brazilian regime, where associative agreements may be assessed as mergers or as conducts. The conclusion seeks to summarize the ideas brought forth hereunder, outlining suggested measures in order to grant effectiveness and legal security to this typical institute of the Brazilian antitrust law.

II. Associative Agreements under Law 8,884/94

First, it is necessary to define the subject to be investigated in this paper. To this end, reference will be made to Law 8,884/94 in this paper to bring some insight on how the issue was addressed prior to the creation of the premerger notification system. Much like Law 12,529/11, currently in force,

Law 8,884/94 established two ways to regulate abuses of the economic power, namely: (i) the repressive control, which is an *ex post* repression of conducts regarded as harmful to competition, punishing anticompetitive corporate strategies (Art. 20, items I to IV);[5] and (ii) the preventive control, which is an *ex ante* control of the structures, requiring the approval from the antitrust authority for the implementation of transactions capable of impairing competition (Art. 54).[6]

Regarding the structure control or merger control regime, the opening paragraph of Article 54 required acts that could in any way limit or restrain free competition or result in the control of relevant markets for certain products or services to be filed with CADE. On this matter paragraph three set forth that the acts mentioned in the opening paragraph also include any act intended for any type of economic concentration, whether through merger with or into other companies, organization of companies to control third parties or any other form of corporate grouping in which (i) the resulting market share was equal to or greater than twenty percent (20%); or (ii) any of the parties had posted annual gross revenues equivalent to or greater than four hundred million reais (BRL 400,000,000.00) in its latest balance sheets.

As a result, CADE was questioned, in several occasions, whether it was necessary for the parties to submit a merger for review if such merger did not fall under the cases covered by the opening paragraph of Art. 54, for they could not limit or impair free competition or result in the control of a relevant market, not even potentially. The prevailing understanding at the time was disclosed in the opinion of Commissioner Roberto Pfeiffer, in Merger filing No. 08012.007790/2001-16 (Microtecnica/Magnaghi case), according to which said paragraph three of Art. 54 established a specification of the content of the opening paragraph.

In this context, Pfeiffer concluded that the objective assumptions of notification referred to cases whose impact on the competition environment would presumably be verified:

> *"Thus, the legislator understood that under certain circumstances it was necessary to make it absolutely clear that notifying the act to the antitrust authority for a review of the possible effects it might have on the competition*

5 Corresponding to Article 36 of Law 12,529/11.

6 Corresponding to Articles 88 and 90 of Law 12,529/11.

environment was required. In such cases, the economic agent is not given an option: even if the transaction is regarded as not leading to limitation or impairment of competition or does not imply control of a relevant market, CADE should be notified of the act. It is up to the antitrust authority, rather than to the economic agent, to decide not to oppose to the act, provided that this does not lead to the effects set forth in the opening paragraph hereof".[7]

Thus, if, on the one hand, the objective criteria set forth in paragraph three represented a complement to the generic criteria set forth in the opening paragraph, there were cases where an economic merger filing was established just by meeting the criteria set forth in the opening paragraph, although the objective criteria were not present.[8] Incidentally, in Merger filing No. 08012.003726/2001-66 (NRG/Itiquira case), Pfeiffer clarified that, in addition to the acts already expressly specified in paragraph three, all other acts that would fall within the cases covered by the opening paragraph of Art. 54 should also be notified.[9] The subjectivity of the rule was highly criticized. In fact, and as will be later discussed, supply and distribution contracts would possibly be classified under the opening paragraph of Art. 54, regardless of the objective criteria of paragraph three being met.[10]

---

7 Opinion of Commissioner Roberto Pfeiffer in the Microtecnica/Magnaghi case.

8 In that regard, *see* Fábio Ulhoa Coelho. *Direito antitruste brasileiro: comentários à Lei n. 8,884/94*, 127. São Paulo: Saraiva, 1995, "Note that the aforementioned corporate transactions [merger, consolidation, establishment of parent company or corporate grouping] must be submitted to CADE whenever they can result in limitation or harm to competition, notwithstanding they do not meet the characteristics set forth in Art. 54, paragraph three".

9 To illustrate, Commissioner Roberto Pfeiffer cited the economic cooperation cases, which, as referred by Calixto Salomão Filho when considering antitrust purposes: "may be characterized by uniformity of a certain conduct or by joint implementation of certain activities without the intervention in the autonomy of each of the companies". *See* vote of Commissioner Roberto Pfeiffer *in* CADE, *NRG International Inc. and Itiquira Energética S/A,* Reporting Commissioner Thompson Andrade (Merger Filing 08012.003726/2001-66) (Nov. 8, 2002).

10 There were rare occasions in which a merger filing was submitted exclusively due to the criteria of Art. 54, opening paragraph. CADE acknowledged such fact without examining the objective thresholds established in paragraph three. In that sense, *see* CADE, *Psinet do Brasil Ltda. and Site Internet Ltda.* Reporting Commissioner João Bosco Leopoldino da Fonseca (Merger 08012.009661/99-69) (Feb. 26, 2001). Under such case, there was a possibility of the company "reaching the minimum legal gross revenue or the relevant market share (above 20%) by

As such, two types of criteria established under Law 8,884/94 would apply to determine the mandatory notification, namely: (i) subjective criteria (Art. 54, opening paragraph); and (ii) objective criteria (Art. 54, paragraph three). Based on this perspective, because of the problems inherent to having subjective criteria, the modification of said law seemed to be urgently required.

At the same time, doctrine would bring different approaches for the two criteria. On the one hand, acts of business cooperation were being addressed under Art. 54, opening paragraph (subjective), whereas the economic concentration transactions would be those shown in Art. 54, paragraph three (objective). Such doctrine distinction is developed with the application of two concepts. In the cases of economic concentration, the concept of *dominant influence* is applied: the traditional approach considers dominant influence as the ability to determine all core aspects of the business planning of an economic agent in a decisive and lasting manner, in other words, decisions on research and development, investments, production and sales (Calixto Salomão Filho, 282-283. 2007). Consequently, structural and lasting changes among the economic agents involved in the transaction are indispensable to provide a glimpse of an economic concentration. As a result of the concentration, the agents would start developing all their activities under the structure of a single economic agent with only one main decision-making body.[11]

The opposite would take place in relation to the concept of business cooperation (act), since, in this case, the individuality of the economic agents would subsist, limited only to certain market behaviors (Calixto Salomão Filho, 293-294, 2007). This understanding proved to be outdated, since, among other circumstances, it would be possible to find cases where an economic concentration would be structured in a contractual fashion in relation to the dominant influence.[12]

In practice, in light of the laws effective at the time, any acts meeting the objective criteria (sales revenue or market share), regardless of being

---

the end of the fiscal year". Opinion of Commissioner João Bosco Leopoldino da Fonseca.

11 Calixto Salomão Filho. *Direito concorrencial – as estruturas*. 293-294. Malheiros. São Paulo, 2007.

12 Calixto Salomão Filho. *Direito concorrencial – as estruturas, supra* note 11, at 288

merger filings or business cooperation, were subject to CADE approval. The acts that did not meet the objective criteria but raised doubts about meeting the subjective criteria, would not be filed for lack of legal certainty or, if filed, were not acknowledged, except in rare cases.[13]

A. Supply and Distribution Agreements

It is known that the term *associative agreement* was not used in Law 8,884/94 to address merger filings. In fact, based on a systematic interpretation, it is possible to infer that some types of contracts, considering their specifications, would be classified as business cooperation and may therefore be subject to notification as merger filings. For instance, from this point-of-view, supply and distribution agreements could be classified separately under the opening paragraph or under paragraph three of Art. 54.

Supply and distribution agreements result in a vertical relationship[14] between the parties, thus becoming types of vertical agreements. The existence of vertical restraints is inherent to the nature of such agreements. They are indicated by exclusivity clauses, restrictions on resale prices, minimum volume contracting, territory division, etc.

These agreements specifically have a technical distinction adopted in jurists' opinion. In relation to the supply contract, there is an understanding whereby the supplier is bound, based on a fixed or adjustable price, to deliver the products to the buyer and/or render services periodically. Such a contract may be entered into for a determined or undetermined term, though it is usually a long-term arrangement. The supplier may be bound by mere periodic delivery of things against payment of a price,[15] or act as a fundamental element in the client's production chain and in the development of its business. Thus, there are cases where the relationship

---

13 The antitrust review encompasses the assessment of admissibility and merits. Cases that did not meet the objective thresholds were not acknowledged, usually without reviewing the meeting of the subjective criteria. In rare occasions there was the acknowledgment of cases exclusively due to the subjective criteria. *See supra* note 11.

14 A vertical relationship is verified when companies operate at different levels of the production chain, although there is no effective business relationship among them.

15 Rubens Requião. *Aspectos modernos de direito comercial (estudos e pareceres)*, 129, in Paula A Forgioni. São Paulo: RT, 2007, p. 25.

between the supplier and the customer may be deemed a lasting commercial partnership (Bittar, 2008, p. 40).

In turn, as far as the distribution agreement is concerned, there is a legal instrument making the manufacturer's production flow possible and the reach of its products is broader than if the manufacturer tried to approach end consumers directly. There are narrower relationships between the manufacturer, which is responsible for selling the products at agreed terms, and the distributor, which is responsible for reselling the product at its own risk, also based on conditions agreed upon with the manufacturer (Bittar, 2008, p. 78).

It is therefore clear that both agreements establish a vertical integration. This justifies the understanding on the (potential) restrictive nature covered by the vertical agreement.[16] For competition purposes, however, the technical difference between these agreements and the legal instrument that formalizes/carries the vertical relationship is of little importance. The reason for this relies on the peculiarities of each contract, which will determine the greater or smaller impact caused on the competition in the markets they will affect.

B. Precedents: Supply Agreements

As explained by Commissioner Roberto Pfeiffer, the economic agents are those who will preliminarily review the classification of a possible supply/distribution agreement under the assumptions set forth in Art. 54. Based on said assumption, the review of CADE's precedents in light of Law 8,884/94 is of vital importance.

---

[16] According to PAULA A. FORGIONI (*supra* note 15, at 23), "vertical agreements are those executed among economic agents that are located along the production or distribution chain, that is, an imaginary line that goes from the production of raw materials up to the final distribution of the product or service". Under such perspective, vertical agreements assume a variety of types, which may be grouped according to the similarity of their economic function, namely, enabling production flow (distribution agreements) or the provision of goods or services (supply agreements). The difference between distribution and supply agreements lies in the emphasis of the obligations established and the characteristics of the products sold PAULA A. FORGIONI (*supra* note 15, at 24). Technically speaking, Forgioni noted that the distribution agreements refer to a category to which commercial concession (or distribution agreement *stricto sensu*), franchising, commercial representation, market allocation, etc., belong.

First, it is worth mentioning the opinion of former Commissioner Paulo Furquim in Merger filing No. 08012.011058/2005-74 (Camargo Correa/Holcim case). The case referred to a supply agreement that, according to the case handler, did not fall under the classification established by Law 8,884/94 in Art. 54, paragraph three, as it did not result in economic concentration, transfer of assets or change in the corporate control of companies or relevant assets from a competition standpoint. The case neither fell under the description of the opening paragraph of Article 54. According to the vote, "there is nothing in the supply agreement subject matter of this proceeding that qualifies it as potentially anticompetitive, regardless of the assessment on its merits, for which reason it is not possible to recognize that a filing was required."

Furquim then explained that certain supply agreements may fall under mandatory merger filing, if, for example, (i) the agreement provides for "substantial changes in the control of assets that are relevant to competition, as well as in the incentives for their use"; or (ii) "the agreement contains vertical restraints that are relevant to competition (such as, for example, the transfer of the right of use of relevant assets or exclusivity clauses that restrict the right of use of such assets".

The vote was not followed by CADE's commissioners at the plenary session and the dissenting vote of Commissioner Ricardo Cueva prevailed. According to the Commissioner, the subsumption assessment is "necessarily a casuistic" opinion since it is impossible to establish a typology including all acts that may not, *a priori*, limit or restrain competition or lead to relevant market control".[17] Cueva mentioned a number of acknowledged cases, including the imposition of restrictions, stating that the harmfulness of a supply agreement can only be determined after an analysis of its contents.

At the time, CADE decided on a tight judgement[18] to adopt a conservative position so as not to create a rule that might exclude acts and agreements of its review; such a rule might not accurately separate the cases that would not even have the potential to limit competition (no acknowledgment) from the cases that could theoretically limit competition

17 Review opinion of Commissioner Ricardo Cueva in the Camargo Corrêa/Holcim merger.

18 Four commissioners followed Commissioner Ricardo Cueva, whilst three commissioners followed Commissioner Paulo Furquim.

(acknowledgment),[19] whereby the assessment must be preceded by a case-by-case review. For this purpose, the cases should be filed with CADE.

After that case, CADE's Chairman Arthur Badin made an important contribution to the case law in Merger filing No. 08012.000182/2010-71 (Monsanto/Iharabras case). Badin then stressed that he intended "to provide the market with a clearer sign on the situations in which a notification with CADE is dispensable, because there are no anticompetitive effects arising out of the transaction".[20] Badin remarked that although most of the merger filings related to supply agreements had been approved without restrictions, CADE had seldom assessed and indicated its position on the classification of such transactions as subject to mandatory filing; in most cases, CADE only checked for the presence of one of the objective criteria set forth in paragraph three of Art. 54 to justify the acknowledgment of the transaction.

In Badin's vote, it is worth mentioning the appropriate moment for CADE to overcome the excessive caution in the review of supply agreements, so as to settle something for so long signaled to the economic agents, that is, that most of such agreements do not result in any competition-related concerns. In fact, "in the few cases approved with restrictions, the restrictions were imposed only because of existing exclusivity clauses in the agreement".[21]

Badin's opinion prevailed over Reporting Commissioner Ricardo Ruiz's opinion.[22] According to Badin, the filing with CADE was not required since supply agreements are not capable of limiting or impairing

---

19 Once again, when referring to the "acknowledgement" or "non-acknowledgement" of the merger filing, such terms are used as regards the prerequisite of admissibility that is prior to the judgment on the merits, in other words, whether the merger falls under the legal provision determining mandatory submission of the merger for CADE's review.

20 CADE, *Monsanto do Brasil Ltda. and Iharabras S.A. Indústrias Químicas.*Reporting Commissioner Arthur Badin (Merger 08012.000182/2010-71) (March 23, 2010)

21 Review vote of the former CADE's President, Arthur Badin, *in* CADE, *Monsanto do Brasil Ltda. and Iharabras S.A. Indústrias Químicas, supra* note 20.

22 Commissioner Ricardo Ruiz later adopted the new jurisprudential understanding. *See* CADE, *Bayer S.A.* Reporting Commissioner Ricardo Machado Ruiz. (Merger 08012.007331/2010-23) (August 18, 2010).

free competition and that such agreements do not result in control over products and services if they:

> *"(a) do not imply the transfer of rights over competitively relevant assets, (b) do not contain exclusivity or equivalent clauses of any nature capable of restricting the right to make decisions relative to the assets (products and services), (c) are effective for less than five years (including possible extensions), (d) include the possibility of immediate termination with no burden to the party, (e) do not represent the negotiation of large volumes of products, greater than the percentage established in Art. 54, paragraph three of Law 8,884/94".*[23]

Another important precedent was established with the opinion of former Commissioner Carlos Ragazzo in Merger filing No. 08012. 005367/2010-72 (Monsanto/Dow case). When dealing with a contract for supply of glyphosate (Monsanto and Dow Groups), Ragazzo found out that the contract did not contain any exclusivity clause or the transfer of assets. During the acknowledgment review, Ragazzo pointed out that until that time, CADE had reviewed many contracts of the same nature, which had been filed for merger review only for having fallen under one of the objective criteria for filing, as set forth in paragraph three of Art. 54.

Ragazzo referred to the recent change in CADE's position regarding the need for review/acknowledgment by an antitrust authority of mergers related to supply agreements (Art. 54, opening paragraph).[24] After listing certain examples of cases acknowledged and not acknowledged, Ragazzo mentioned the specifications identified in the abovementioned Badin's vote and stated his understanding that the "supply agreements involving no transfer of assets of any kind nor exclusivity clauses[25]do not provide for the production of anticompetitive effects, as a rule, and, therefore, no filing with CADE is required under the terms of the opening paragraph of Art. 54 of Law 8,884/94". It is noteworthy that Ragazzo disagreed to the time-period criterion (5-year limit) and the requirement for possible immediate termination of the agreement. He justified that the remaining specifications

---

23 Review opinion of former CADE Chairman, Arthur Badin, in the Monsanto/ Iharabras case, *supra* note 20.

24 CADE, *Monsanto do Brasil Ltda. and Dow Agrosciences Industrial Ltda.* Reporting Commissioner Carlos Ragazzo (Merger 08012.005367/2010-72) (June, 30, 2010).

25 Or other provisions with equivalent effects.

sufficed to consider the agreement as not being subject to notification to CADE (for being a mere business contract).

It is also worth mentioning the opinion of former Commissioner Olavo Chinaglia in Merger filing No. 08012.006493/2010-44 (Syngenta/Dow case). The opinion referred to a non-exclusive supply agreement between Syngenta Supply AG and Dow Agrosciences Industrial Ltda. At the time, Chinaglia reviewed the contract terms to determine whether it referred solely to a business relationship, without an exclusivity or non-compete clause, and with no exchange of information other than the information required to comply with the terms of the agreement. Also, the companies should be kept independent, in other words, operating in a competitive environment. Considering the peculiar nature of the supply of technology and industrial patent license, Commissioner Chinaglia pointed out that only in very specific cases (non-competition and/or exclusivity clauses), these types of agreement result in some sort of competition concern.

The Commissioner concluded that the case should not be acknowledged since the agreement did not include any clauses that could lead to anticompetitive effects under the opening paragraph of Art. 54. It is noteworthy that Chinaglia expressly avoided the application of the "relative presumption" covered by paragraph three, since it was not a case of economic concentration materialized by the transfer of equity shares of companies, operational assets, joint ventures or any other kind of partnership grouping.[26]

Regarding the contract term, Chinaglia followed the understanding of Commissioner Ragazzo that time should not be regarded as a requirement for the transaction not to be acknowledged. In his words, the remaining characteristics of the contract ("absence of transfer of rights over competitively relevant assets as well as absence of exclusivity or equivalent clauses of any nature") sufficed for it not to be necessary to submit the merger for CADE's review.[27]

---

[26] Vote of Commissioner Olavo Chinaglia *in* CADE, *Syngenta Supply AG and Dow Agrosciences Industrial Ltda*. Reporting Commissioner Olavo Chinaglia. (Merger 08012.006493/2010-44) (Oct. 22, 2010).

[27] In a previous circumstance, the same Commissioner had already manifested on the incompatibility of certain supply agreements and the concept of economic concentration. *See* CADE, *Monsanto do Brasil Ltda. and Nufarm Indústria Química e Farmacêutica S.A.* Reporting Commissioner Olavo Chinaglia. (Merger

Chinaglia added that if the supply agreement operated in such way as to implement anticompetitive strategies, nothing in the opinion in the Syngenta/Dow case could be invoked as a defense argument in any possible administrative proceeding to repress the abuse of economic power. Chinaglia also concluded that "the existence of an anticompetitive potential does not necessarily imply that such instruments may not be inappropriately used – as in the assumptions of a 'de facto' exclusivity requirement – and that, as a result, the anticompetitive effects are verified and corrected accordingly".[28]

C. Precedents: Distribution Agreements

In what concerns distribution agreements under Law 8,884/94, whenever such agreements include exclusivity clauses,[29] they receive the same treatment given to supply agreements of this nature (in some of the

08012.010018/2008-58) (Jan. 13, 2009). CADE, unanimously, did not acknowledge the transaction, under the vote of Reporting Commissioner Olavo Chinaglia.

28 Vote of Commissioner Olavo Chinaglia *in* CADE, *Syngenta Supply AG and Dow Agrosciences Industrial Ltda*, *supra* note 26.

29 In that sense, the following Merger Filings: CADE, *Bunge Alimentos S.A. and Corn Products Brasil – Ingredientes Industriais Ltda.* Reporting Commissioner (Merger 08012.012506/2007-19) (July 28, 2008); CADE, *Abbott Laboratório do Brasil Ltda and Merck S.A.* Reporting Commissioner Ricardo Villas Bôas Cueva. (Merger 08012.011192/2007-37) (June 02, 2008); CADE, *Basf S/A and Monsanto do Brasil Ltda.*, Reporting Commissioner Fernando de Magalhães Furlan. (08012.006832/2008-78) (Sept. 17, 2008); CADE, *Syngenta Proteção de Cultivos Ltda. and Monsanto do Brasil Ltda.* Reporting Commissioner Olavo Chinaglia. (08012.007238/2008-02) (Oct. 02, 2008); CADE, Bayer S.A. and Monsanto do Brasil Ltda. Reporting Commissioner Paulo Furquim de Azevedo. (08012.006693/2008-82) (Sept. 17, 2008); CADE, Bunge Alimentos S.A. and Corn Products Brasil – Ingredientes Industriais Ltda. Reporting Commissioner Olavo Chinaglia. (08012.001951/2008-34) (Nov. 04, 2008); CADE, *Polibor Ltda., Targa Ltda., Indústria Frontinense de Látex S.A. and Cremer S/A.* Reporting Commissioner Vinicius Marques de Carvalho. (Merger 08012.008755/2009-71) (July 21, 2010); CADE, *Zodiac Produtos Farmacêuticos S/A and Merck Sharp & Dohme Farmacêutica Ltda.* Reporting Commissioner César Costa Alves de Mattos (Merger 08012.000168/2009-34) (May 05, 2009); CADE, *CHR Hansen Indústria e Comércio Ltda. and Laboratórios Pfizer Ltda.* Reporting Commissioner Fernando de Magalhães Furlan. (Merger 08012.003773/2009-67) (Sept. 21, 2010); CADE, Killing S.A Tintas and Adesivos and Henkel Ltda, Reporting Commissioner Olavo Chinaglia. (Merger 08012.009815/2009-73) (March, 03, 2010); and CADE, *Cremer S.A., Embramed Indústria e Comércio de Produtos Hospitalares Ltda.*,

cases, CADE recognized that the distribution agreement "may produce effects similar to those of a merger").[30] Even in relation to non-exclusive distribution, but in which the distribution agreement had been entered into between competitors, an effect similar to a merger was recognized.[31] In other cases, in line with former decisions involving supply agreements, the transactions were acknowledged just for meeting one of the objective criteria for submission.

Therefore, in cases in which the issue of acknowlegment exceeded the mere verification on whether the objective criteria have been met, the specifications of the agreement were taken into account to determine the requirement or waiver of a submission to CADE.

D. *Understanding the Precedents*

After consolidating the initial understanding that the supply/distribution agreements should be submitted to review whenever the objective criteria (sales revenues or market share thresholds) are met, CADE gradually began adopting a stricter standard to distinguish agreements that had no competition implications (in other words, business activities in which the parties remain independent in relation to the control of their respective competitively relevant assets), thus assuming the position of not requiring that a notification should be filed in those cases.[32]

Paraisoplex Ind. e Com. Ltda. and KTorres Beneficiamento de Plásticos Ltda. Reporting Commissioner (08700.010984/2010-90)

30 CADE, *Henkel Ltda.* Reporting Commissioner Olavo Chinaglia. (Merger 08012.009815/2009-73) (March 03, 2010); and CADE, *Syngenta Proteção de Cultivos Ltda & Monsantot do Brasil Ltda.*. Reporting Commissioner Olavo Chinaglia.(Merger 08012.007238/2008-02) (Oct. 02, 2008)

31 Vote of Commissioner Olavo Chinaglia in *Syngenta Proteção de Cultivos Ltda & Monsantot do Brasil, supra* note 30.

32 The (a) supply agreements that meet the definition of merger included (i) the estimates substantial changes in the control of relevant assets for competition, as well as in the incentives for their use; (ii) relevant vertical restraints to competition (e.g. transfer of right to use relevant assets or exclusivity provision restricting the decision right on the use of these assets); and (iii) transfer of rights on production for a long term, so as to imply partial control over the assets. Quite to the contrary, (b) the supply agreements that did not require submission were generally those that (i) did not involve transfer of rights in competitively relevant assets; (ii) did not establish exclusivity provision or equivalents of any kind that were able of

Following this course of evolution, CADE focused its attention on concerns relating to the following peculiarities behind the supply/distribution agreements:[33] (i) no transfer of rights over competitively relevant assets; (ii) no exclusivity or equivalent clauses of any nature; and (iii) sale volumes that do not exceed the percentage established in Art. 54, paragraph three of Law 8,884/94.

The exclusivity clauses then became of greater importance. According to Badin, "in the few cases in which mergers were approved with restrictions, the restriction was imposed only because of an existing exclusivity clause in the contract".[34] Despite the fact that there are other types of vertical restrictions that may be used in supply/distribution agreements (for example, territory division, restrictions on resale prices, matched sales, etc.), the former decisions analysis revealed that the exclusivity agreements represented risks of greater impact on the competition.

In this discussion, a parallel subject worthy of more attention concerns the repressive control when dealing with supply/distribution agreements. In other words, it is possible that the vertical restraints included in these agreements make them more susceptible to typifying violations against competition.

E. *Exclusivity Agreements: Type of Vertical Restraint and Risks of Classifying as Anticompetitive Conduct*

First of all, it is important to define *exclusivity agreements*. In a broad sense, they are agreements whereby "the buyers of certain products or

preventing the decision right on the assets (goods or services); (iii) were effective for less than five years (considering possible extensions); (vi) contemplated the possibility of immediate termination without charge to the requesting party; and (v) did not represent a negotiation exceeding twenty percent (20%) in terms of volume. As noted, the Commissioner Carlos Ragazzo was against the time issue and to the possibility of immediate termination of the agreement, justifying that the other characteristics would suffice to dismiss the notification of supply agreements.

33 The concerns were initiated under the vote of Commissioner Paulo Furquim (Camargo Corrêa/Holcim case, *supra* note 17) and were definitely introduced by the review vote of the former CADE's President, Arthur Badin (Monsanto/Iharabras case, *supra* note 20), having been re-evaluated under the vote of Commissioner Carlos Ragazzo (Monsanto/Dow case, *supra* note) 24.

34 Review vote of the former CADE's Chairman President, Arthur Badin, in Monsanto/Iharabras case, *supra* note 20.

services commit themselves to purchase such products or services on an exclusive basis from a certain seller (or vice-versa), thus being prohibited from selling said items to rival suppliers" (CADE Resolution 20/99). It is a type of vertical restraint imposed by the producers/suppliers of products or services in a certain market (of origin) on vertically related markets – upstream or downstream – along the production chain (target market). It may also be imposed on the supplier by the distributor.

Exclusivity agreements may have a double effect; in other words, they may result in benefits and losses to the market. The benefits or economic efficiencies usually associated with vertical restraints are: (i) reduction of cost distribution, rendering scale economies viable; (ii) facilitating the entry of new economic agents into the distribution market, thanks to the provision of return on an investment made; (iii) restriction to act as free riders; (iv) no concentration of distributors so as not to allow those that are more aggressive ending up by incorporating others, thus causing an undue degree of concentration in the market; and (v) permission to preserve the product image.

Offsetting the economic efficiencies that may result from vertical restrictions, the potential anticompetitive effects, particularly with regard to exclusivity agreements would be associated: (i) with the implementation of collusive conducts, usually leading to the creation of cartels in the market of origin when used as an instrument for division of market for replacement products (collusion); or (ii) with the increased unilateral market power of the company that imposes exclusivity by blocking and/or increasing barriers to the entry into the distribution segment (or supply of inputs). This may result directly from contract clauses, or indirectly by increasing the rivals' costs (exclusion).

As such, the exclusivity agreement and other vertical restraints should be reviewed according to the rule of reason, which establishes that it is necessary to weigh the potential anticompetitive effects of the agreement on a case by case basis, considering possible economic efficiencies in the relevant markets of products or services of the involved parties so that, in the end, it is possible to make a decision on the admissibility thereof from the competition standpoint.

As has been pointed out, exclusivity clauses may be reviewed for antitrust purposes: (i) from the perspective of preventive action – when one or more companies enter into an agreement that implies economic power voluntarily file for the review; (ii) from the perspective of repressive action – when a contract, or even an existing practice among the companies is brought to CADE's knowledge by a third party as a complaint, or when CADE itself starts the proceeding because of the potential unlawfulness of the conduct.[35]

As an example of a case reviewed within the scope of structure control, it is worth mentioning Merger filing No. 08012.008755/2009-71 (Cremer/Targa and Polibor case). After a thorough assessment of the upstream and downstream markets, Commissioner Vinicius de Carvalho referred to several factors in his opinion that would mitigate possible damaging effects to the competition environment, despite the use of an exclusivity clause.

With regard to the repressive analysis, despite the fact that both Law 8,884/94 and Law 12,529/11 do not include an exhaustive list of what constitutes a violation to competition (Art. 21 of Law 8,884/94 and Art. 36, paragraph three of Law 12,529/11), Art. 20 and Art. 36, respectively set forth assumptions to define a violation. According to Art. 20 and Art. 36, regardless of the agent's fault, the violation would be configured in any act intended for or capable of producing (even if not reaching) the following effects: "(i) limit, distort or otherwise restrain free competition or free initiative; (ii) control a relevant market of products or services; (iii) increase profits arbitrarily; or (iv) abusively exercise a dominant position".[36] After checking the assumptions shown in Art. 20/Art. 36, including a market share greater than twenty percent (20%), the economic violation would be configured.

The conclusion is that the exclusivity clauses imposed by an agent holding economic power in a certain market (as a rule, market share greater than twenty percent (20%) means that the agent has market power) could lead to the exclusion of competitors (either because of access limitation or impediment or the difficulties created for the operation, or still as a result of a discrimination among competitors).[37]

---

35 In any case, CADE promotes public interest by protecting free competition and restraining abuses of economic power (and not the private interests).

36 The dominant position is presumed when the company or group of companies controls twenty percent (20%) of the relevant market; however, CADE may modify such percentage for specific sectors of the economy.

37 For examples of cases of unlawful exclusivity agreements, *see* CADE, Reporting Commissioner Fernando de Magalhães Furlan. (AP 08012.008678/2007-98)

III. Associative Agreements under Law 12,529/11

Before analyzing associative agreements per se, it is necessary to put Law 12,529/11 into context regarding structural control. As has been previously mentioned, the new law introduced the premerger review system for reportable acts, resulting in a real change of culture in the Brazilian antitrust system.

The new law established objective criteria for filing for merger review (Art. 88[38]) and defined the transactions that may be classified as mergers (Art. 90[39]). Theoretically, the new system would be a positive advancement,

---

(Sept. 14, 2007); CADE, *Condomíno Shopping Center Iguatemi & Shopping Center Reunidos do Brasil Ltda.* Reporting Commissioner Luís Fernando Rigato Vasconcellos (AP 08012.009991/1998-82) (May 19, 2004); CADE, *Globo Comunicações e Globosat Programadora Ltda.* Reporting Commissioner Paulo Furquim de Azevedo (AP 08012.003048/2001-31) (Nov. 13, 2006); CADE, *Cervejaria Kaiser do Brasil S.A.* the Superintendence-General (AP 08012.003805/2004-10) (Dec. 20, 2008); CADE, *FESEMPRE v. Banco do Brasil S.A.* Reporting Commissioner Marcos Paulo Veríssimo (AP 08700.003070/2010-14) (April 9, 2013).

38 ANTITRUST ACT (Law No. 12,529/11), art. 88. The parties involved in the transaction shall submit the merger filings with CADE if on a cummulative basis:

I – at least one of the groups involved in the transaction has posted annual sales revenue or total business volume in the country in its latest balance sheets, in the year before the transction, equivalent to or higher than seven hundred fifty million reais (BRL750,000,000.00);

I – at least one other group involved in the transaction has posted annual sales revenue or total business volume in the country in its latest balance sheet, in the year before the transaction, equivalent to or higher than seventy-five million reais (BRL75,000,000.00).

39 Art. 90. For the purposes of Art. 88 of this law, mergers are filed when:

I – two (2) or more previously independent companies are merged;

II – one (1) or more companies purchase, either directly or indirectly, by means of a purchase or exchange of shares, units, securities convertible into shares, or tangible or intangible assets, by a contract or otherwise, the control or parts of one or other companies;

III – another company or companies is/are merged into one (1) or more companies; or

IV – two (2) or more companies enter into an associative agreement, establish a consortium or joint venture.

facilitating the identification of mergers subject to mandatory filing with CADE.

In this context, a new concern in the Antitrust Law refers to the possible premature closing of the transaction (*gun jumping*). Acts defined as gun jumping are any acts aimed at the implementation of the transaction before CADE's review. It is a premature integration of the parties' businesses changing the competition conditions among them. This constitutes a serious violation capable of rendering the transaction null and void, with the imposition of a pecuniary fine[40] without limiting the filing of administrative proceedings. In short, the parties exceed their limits and end up by frustrating the competitive conditions among them, either because they do not protect and keep their businesses separately or because of the influence of one party over the other or the exchange of competitively sensitive information.[41]

Based on the foregoing, unlike the previous law, Law 12,529/11 expressly refers to associative agreements as the legal term to define it as a merger filing. However, despite the linguistic innovation, there are no clear and effective limits outlining the concepts behind the term, thus making the decision of whether certain agreements should be notified a very delicate matter, particularly with regard to the *a priori* analysis and the consequences of the filing of the transaction after its implementation.

Thus, in order to regulate Art. 90, IV of the Antitrust Law, CADE conducted a public inquiry concerning the draft of the resolution aimed at establishing the required criteria for the filing of associative agreements (Resolution 10[42]). Nevertheless, as further detailed below, according to the initial indications, the way CADE has regulated the matter leads us to

40 Ranging from BRL 60,000.00 to BRL 60,000,000.00.

41 For correspondent case law, *see:* CADE, *Potióleo S.A. and UTC Óleo e Gás S.A.* Reporting Commissioner Alessandro Serafin Octaviani Luis (Merger 08700.008292/2013-76) (Feb. 11, 2014); CADE, *Aurizônia Petróleo S.A. and UTC Óleo e Gás S.A.* Reporting Commissioner Ana de Oliveira Frazão (Merger 08700.008289/2013-52) (Feb. 11, 2014); CADE, *Fiat S.p.A. and Chrysler Group LLC.* Reporting Commissioner Márcio de Oliveira Júnior (Merger 08700.002285/2014-41) (May 20, 2014); and CADE, Petróleo Brasileiro S.A. and Total E&P do Brasil Ltda., Reporting Commissioner Alessandro Octaviani Luis (Merger 08700.007899/2013-39) (April 09, 2014).

42 Effective as from January 5, 2015.

believe that doubts are still to be expected. The suggested measures and proposals show the path to improve the regulation of associative agreement, making it at least more functional.

A. CADE Precedents under Law 12,529/11

Until the introduction of Resolution 10, the most typical cases involving associative agreements, if they are understood as such, essentially refer to licensing contracts. The assessment on the precedents will be summarized and restricted to certain merger filings of Monsanto group.

For the sake of contextualization, the following cases were assessed: Merger No. 08012.002870/2012-38 (Monsanto/Syngenta case); Merger filing No. 08012.006706/2012-08 (Monsanto/Nidera Sementes case); Merger filing No. 08700.003898/2012-34 (Monsanto/Coodetec case); and Merger filing No. 08700.003937/2012-01 (Monsanto/Don Mario Sementes case). In short, the discussion was raised due to license agreements with no exclusivity clause under which Monsanto granted a non-exclusive license for the production, testing, development and sales of a soybean seed variety in Brazil (Intacta RR2 PROTM, a technology that allows for the increased resistance of the seeds to certain agrochemical products and insects).

The central issue of the discussion relates to the mandatory submission of the merger to CADE's approval. Former Commissioner Marcos Paulo Veríssimo, reporting commissioner in the Monsanto/Syngenta case, understood that the transaction was not subject to mandatory notice. Commissioner Alessandro Octaviani, reporting commissioner of the Monsanto/Nidera, Monsanto/Coodetec and Monsanto/Don Mario cases understood it was a case of acknowledgment and, on the merits, approved the mergers without any restrictions. It so happens that, at the time, Commissioner Ana Frazão and Commissioner Ricardo Ruiz asked to review the records of the case, claiming it was necessary to find out which competitors held the patents covered in the cases and to verify the legal monopoly involved. As a result, after the required diligences, Ana Frazão was favorable to the non-acknowledgment of the mergers, though she changed her opinion after Commissioner Eduardo Pontual's opinion. In the session held on August 28, 2013, Commissioner Eduardo Pontual Ribeiro voted for the acknowledgment of the transactions and, on the merits, for the approval with restrictions regarding contractual clauses that "allowed Monsanto to control the licensees in commercial and corporate decisions unrelated to Monsanto technology seeds". The transactions were finally acknowledged and approved with restrictions,[43] based on the majority of the opinions.

In this context, it is worth mentioning that the transactions involved were discussed for the first time in December 2012 and the decision was only reached on August 28, 2013. In other words, the divergences among commissioners as to the acknowledgment of the license agreement are obvious. In this respect, Commissioner Frazão's considerations are noteworthy. According to Frazão, it is necessary to question to what extent the patent license agreements should be deemed subject to merger filings and then to assess whether their possible effects should be governed by the structure control. Frazão understood that the sheer possibility of anticompetitive effects would not make such agreements become subject to review and such effects could give rise to control by means of conducts and not by structures. Though this rationale seems to bear credibility, Frazão eventually followed Pontual's opinion.[44]

Frazão also explained that the term associative agreement has a broad meaning that makes it different from commutative agreements in which the cooperation is an ancillary obligation. Actually, under the associative agreements, the cooperation is the provision itself, in other words the main obligation. Consequently, the associative agreements are not different from other agreements because of an existing cooperation, but rather and mainly because of the level and type of concentration. According to Frazão, it is only possible to accept that a patent license agreement should be understood as an associative agreement if the cooperation is considered in broader terms. However, as pointed out by Frazão, that is not the purpose of the Antitrust Law. The intention of the new Antitrust Law is not to broaden the concept of associative agreement. If it were so, all long-lasting business contracts would be construed as associative agreements, inevitably leading to legal

43 At the time, Commissioner Vinicius Carvalho, in an opinion covering three mergers, backed the opinion of Commissioner Eduardo Pontual, as did Commissioners Alessandro Octaviani and Ana Frazão.

44 The opinion was changed after Commissioner Frazão learned new facts brought by Commissioner Pontual regarding the contractual clauses (factual assumption). She kept the legal assumptions of her opinion, noting that the existence of anticompetitive effects is not sufficient to determine the obligation to notify an agreement as the prerequisite of concentration should not be neglected.

uncertainty. Based on this reasoning, Frazão found it more coherent to assess patent license agreements without exclusivity clauses from the point of view of conduct control.

It is also necessary to mention the acknowledgment criteria applied by Octaviani in his opinions. Octaviani stated that because of the nature of the agreements (involving technology), there would be a "huge and practically insurmountable asymmetry of information between developers and holders of ultra-specialized technologies (...) and the antitrust authority (...)". Among the acknowledgment criteria outlined by Octaviani was the *ab extra* corporate control, with no ownership interest in the capital of a company by another".[45]

To summarize the understanding of Commissioners Veríssimo, Pontual and Frazão, it is clear that all commissioners agree that the acknowledgment of a patent license agreement with no exclusivity clause is not necessary. Therefore, this means that a traditional patent license agreement should not be submitted to CADE if it does not include exclusivity clauses capable of influencing competitive actions regardless of the parties, and there is no common undertaking, transfer of assets or any other agreement, even if implied, that would result in changes of decision centers or competition restrictions..[46] In fact, the patent license agreement without exclusivity clauses would be interpreted as being pro-competitive if it provides for the sharing of patented technology and makes it possible to enter into contracts with other competitors.[47]

In the case under analysis, Pontual found indications of Monsanto's external influence in licensees' commercial decisions that went beyond the purpose of the contracts. According to Pontual, there was an intricate system of incentives that increased the entry barriers, thus increasing Monsanto's market gains, which justified the need to file for CADE approval.

---

45 LUDMILA SOMENSI. *Conhecimento de Contrato de Licenciamento Sem Cláusula de Exclusividade e (In)Definição de Contrato Associativo*, 289. Revista do IBRAC. Vol. 24, July 2013.

46 Op. cit.

47 As noted by the Commissioners, ensuring patent exclusivity may trigger anticompetitive effects, which, in most cases, will be assessed under behavior control.

It is worth mentioning that these cases were reviewed under Law 8,884/94, although they were decided by CADE after Law 12,529/11 was in force. Such cases nevertheless led to relevant precedents and are being reported for such reason.

An emblematic case under Law 12,529/11, also of interest to Monsanto, was 08700.004957/2013-72 (Monsanto/Bayer case). The case refers to the technology license agreement between Monsanto and Bayer which, after an analysis by CADE's General Superintendency (SG), resulted in the recommendation that the transaction should not be acknowledged.[48] However, Commissioner Eduardo Pontual assigned the case to the Court, having claimed that such technology license transactions may involve issues that would restrain free competition. Commissioner Alessandro Octaviani reported on the case, and, after a detailed assessment decided for the acknowledgment[49]and, on the merits, approved the transaction following adjustments to the contract clauses.[50]

Octaviani sought to describe the "specificities of the contract types listed in item IV of Article 90 of Law 12,529/11" in a non-exhaustive/exclusive manner, namely: "(i) the communion of business interests; and (ii) the exercise of a common undertaking by means of (iii) the coordination of corporate activities such as the due (iv) sharing of risks of this activity".[51]

48 "In view of the foregoing, it is understood that licensing of technology use, provided that they do not bring non-compete agreements, transfer of assets, organization or corporate links of any kind, or any measure that implies modification of the decision-making center or competitive constraint, are not of mandatory notification to CADE under Law No. 12,529/11." On the merits, the technical opinion observed the absence of change in the competitive structure of the market. Technical opinion No. 171 issued by the CADE's General Superintendence.

49 Based on article 90, items II and IV of Law 12,529/11.

50 For example, clauses ruling value sharing, increased incentive, mechanisms for minimum royalty, etc., so as to not allow the exercise of external influence of Monsanto over Bayer.

51 The Commissioner refers to the analysis made by the Commissioner Ana Frazão in previous transactions involving Monsanto. There would be the associative agreements *lato sensu*, being the consortia, joint ventures and associative agreements *stricto sensu* their species. Under that context, as Frazão pointed: "in such agreements, the parties keep their economic and financial independence, do not restructure their management or controlling power and do not necessarily acquire assets and, if they do so, it occurs merely in an instrumental manner. Nevertheless, they jointly become owner of a business power or create a new

According to Octaviani, the foregoing specificities would constitute the theoretical basis for the antitrust review of the associative agreements.

Finally, there is also Merger filing No. 08700.008736/2012-92, whose merging parties were Petrobras Distribuidora S.A. (BR) and the MPEC Consortium (BR/MPEC Consortium case). In short, the merger referred to the partnership between BR and the MPEC Consortium to offer environmental and oil by-products risk management services. The merging parties requested the non-acknowledgment of the transaction, claiming that the partnership agreement did not generate any structural relationship (as classical forms of economic concentrations) since the decision centers of the parties remained unchanged. The parties had only entered into one agreement, which though did not constitute a partnership relation operated as the way for the parties jointly providing the services. CADE's attorney office (ProCADE) decided at the time that the case was subject to mandatory notification based on Art. 88 and Art. 90, item IV of Law 12,529/11. SG accepted this understanding. Among the main reasons for the acknowledgment, ProCADE highlighted the following:

> *"1) it is about the establishment of a relationship between companies which, despite maintaining their legal and economic independence, shall jointly develop an economic activity. It is also noteworthy that the partnership to be established will provide Petrobras with the technical and structural complement (know-how) it requires to exploit this type of economic activity considering the needs of its customer network that buys oil by-products and 2) the contract calls for exclusivity between the parties, preventing them from providing services to third parties that are similar to those covered by the partnership arrangement".*

Also, ProCADE mentioned that this type of association could change market conditions and, as a result, should be subject to antitrust concerns since it would theoretically provide for the sharing of information and/

center of management or decision (…) This is because the common thread of such agreements is precisely the idea of a company or common business goal under which the efforts of the parties are coordinated". With respect to associative agreements *stricto sensu*, it appears that there would be a kind of "qualified" cooperation between the contractors, which would result in some form of common organization. According to the understanding of Commissioner Alessandro Octaviani, this feature would be the common denominator between the associative agreements *strictu sensu* and consortia and joint ventures.

or infrastructure, a fact that might change the behavior of the parties or interfere in the relationship of the parties with third parties.

B. Resolution 10 and Initial Suggestions

As has been previously mentioned, given the environment of legal insecurity, CADE carried out a public inquiry about the draft of a resolution aimed at regulating associative agreements.[52] The antitrust authority received 24 contributions corroborating a proactive participation of the society. Contributions received included, for example, those highlighting the difficulties related to the scope of the concept of associative agreements (54% of the contributions), as well as those related to the increase in the number of notifications considering contracts with no competition impacts (67% of the contributions). It is also noteworthy that 18 criteria were suggested for the qualification of associative agreements.[53]

To summarize, the resolution defined associative agreements as agreements effective for more than two (2) years, either as an initial term or a full term as a result of a renewal of the initial term, in which there is (i) horizontal or (ii) vertical cooperation or (iii) sharing of risk that leads to an interdependence relationship between the parties. The resolution adds (Art. 2, Paragraph One) that (i), (ii) or (iii) apply where there is:

a. an agreement in which the parties are horizontally related in the purpose thereof whenever the resulting market share in the relevant market affected by the agreement is equal to or greater than twenty percent (20%); or

b. an agreement in which the parties are vertically related in the purpose thereof, whenever at least one of the parties holds thirty percent (30%) or more of the relevant market affected by the agreement, and further

---

[52] Public Consultation 03/2014. Contribution period: February 19, 2014 to April 22, 2014.

[53] The main criteria were: (i) undertakings or joint organization / exercise of joint economic activity / sharing of business interests / integrative element (integration of willingness or goods); (ii) autonomous economic activity; (iii) structural changes as a result of the agreement; (iv) agreements which have as target markets in which the parties are horizontally or vertically related; (v) agreements of continued provision / long-term exploitation of economic activity; (vi) sharing of information /good / competitively sensitive rights, among others (source: presentation of CADE – Chairman Vinicius Carvalho, dated September 2014).

provided that the agreement contemplates either (a) the sharing of profits and losses between the parties or (b) an exclusive relationship.[54]

First of all, Resolution 10 includes the term of duration of more than two (2) years. According to CADE precedents, the term of duration that was relevant for the antitrust review was five (5) years[55] or no term at all since other conditions could suffice to conclude that no filing is required irrespective of the term of duration.[56] Therefore, CADE should ideally have kept consistency with past cases by establishing that the term of duration is not relevant or a relevant term of duration is of five (5) years.

Another issue raised by the term of duration refers to when filings must be made. Resolution 10 establishes that if there is a renewal of an agreement with duration of less than two (2) years, the submission must be made when the two-year term is reached or exceed. If the agreement is not being renegotiated, and the parties did not include a provision to regulate the merger filing, when the two-year period is exceed will they need to wait until the transaction is cleared to continue the relationship? It seems to be difficult to reconcile the premerger system with ongoing commercial relations that have different dynamics when compared to mergers or corporate transactions.

Secondly, certain technical terms were used but not defined by Resolution 10, thereby giving grounds to subjectivity. For example, the exact notion of sharing of risks or interdependence relationship or sharing of profits and losses remain unclear. Since items (1) and (2) of paragraph one of Art. 2 list the contracts with a horizontal relationship (item 1) and vertical relationship (item 2), would *sharing of risks* be an additional concept or would it be applicable only to vertical contracts in which there is (a) profits or losses sharing between the parties or (b) an exclusivity relationship (*interdependence relationship*)?

One must nevertheless take into account CADE's efforts to put in place a resolution clarifying the concept of associative agreement. Moreover, when comparing the draft resolution with the final version, CADE has included the market share threshold adding significant criteria to avoid a

---

54 Such agreements shall only be notified if the revenue thresholds are achieved, pursuant to Article 88, items I and II of Law 12,529/11.

55 Badin's opinion in the Monsanto/Iharabras case, *supra* note 20.

56 Ragazzo's opinion in the Monsanto/Dow case, *supra* note 20.

catch-all rule. However, as has been recognized in CADE's precedents, most of the contracts of such nature are not capable of raising antitrust concerns. In this sense, it is important to take due account to CADE's precedents to avoid that the usual day-to-day contracts used by the economic agents, namely commercial contracts with suppliers/distributors could be subject to notification depending on how Resolution 10 is interpreted only because the parties meet the turnover thresholds provided by the law. In cases in which antitrust concerns would effectively happen, CADE would certainly be able to investigate these contracts in an administrative proceeding.

As a matter of fact, the assessment of these types of contract would be better factually and legally supported with the conduct control by verifying the restrictive measures affecting competition (for example, discount policy, exclusivity, etc.). Therefore the assessment theoretically indicates that the new resolution raises questions, particularly when the vertical relationships are reviewed. This is because every associative agreement established between non-competitors (meaning without horizontal relationship) may fall under the definition of vertical agreement, creating a relationship between agents in different levels of the supply chain.

In this scenario and without any intention to exhaust this matter but rather to provide examples of certain day-to-day corporate agreements, it is worth mentioning the following agreements: raw material supply agreements for the pharmaceutical industry; lease of commercial spaces in shopping malls or airports or other properties; purchase agreements with retail suppliers of the food industry, etc.; agreements involving punctual partnerships for marketing purposes, promotion of a certain product, among other contracts covering the flow of production items, outsourcing of a production process, etc.

There is considerable risk that CADE could receive a large number of notifications as a result of the potential need to notify contracts that create vertical relationships but are not associative in nature. Although the requirement of the exclusivity clause has been long established by CADE's case law, the sharing of profits or losses is a rather new concept. Does this concept include agreements that establish a variable compensation system? One should bear in mind that sharing of risks by creating an interdependence relationship means more than sharing profits or losses. As has been established by CADE precedents, the associative nature requires the exercise of a common undertaking with the coordination of corporate activities. If sharing of risks is not seen as a separate prerequisite, and literally it is not, then chances are that the Resolution is taking a step back in terms of avoiding unnecessary notification of agreements that clearly would not have any impacts in the competitive landscape.

Considering this scenario, it would be more conceivable, even if to save public funds, to concentrate the analysis to be made from the perspective of the conducts. On the other hand, one should not neglect the risk of reverse effect, in other words, the very small number of filings involving these types of contract considering the legal insecurity of those involved. Without limiting any of the assumed scenarios, there would be no practical effectiveness for the measure. All this leads to the following conclusion: it would be more logical and less costly with regard to competition to review the vertical contracts, as a rule, under the perspective of the conducts.

In fact, there are commercial contracts that should be subject to antitrust review. As a result, in order to create a filter and provide a consistent guideline for this matter (it is an indispensable measure in light of the premerger review system) CADE could look to foreign jurisdictions and apply parallel review mechanisms.[57] From this perspective, the

[57] In the US, there is no requirement for prior filing of merger agreements. The main criterion used to review agreements among competitors is the *Antitrust Guidelines for Collaboration Among Competitors*. Available at: http://www.ftc.gov/sites/default/files/attachments/press-releases/ftc-doj-issue-antitrust-guidelines-collaborations-among-competitors/ftcdojguidelines.pdf (accessed February 7, 2015). Under such guideline: "A "competitor collaboration" comprises a set of one or more agreements, other than merger agreements, between or among competitors to engage in economic activity, and the economic activity resulting therefrom. "Competitors" encompasses both actual and potential competitors. Competitor collaborations involve one or more business activities, such as research and development ("R&D"), production, marketing, distribution, sales or purchasing. Information sharing and various trade association activities also may take place through competitor collaborations" (underlined in the original). p. 2-3. In the EU, Since the individual notification system for business cooperation contracts was abolished, only the notification of merger filings remained. The orientation is more clear and determines that (i) it is not necessary to make a prior review of contracts of this nature, and (ii) as regards possible contracts entered into either they will be classified as included in the block exemption or may be assessed case by case and, if they are not covered by the benefits of Art. 101(3) they will be considered to be anticompetitive conducts.

establishment of safe harbors or block exemption by contract category[58] would be very helpful.

In this context of suggested measures providing mechanisms to easily detect and submit (or not to submit) associative agreements to CADE review, it would be equally interesting for the antitrust authority to assess the possibility of receiving inquiries on the need to submit. In other words, the possibility of submitting inquiries and not having the cases automatically converted into merger filings is suggested so that society may submit inquiries to CADE on the classification of the contract in the cases of exemption. In practical terms, such inquiry mechanism could be available for one (1) year, during which time the economic agents would proactively contact CADE to request information on the official understanding of the contract relevance for submission purposes. This procedure would effectively create an environment to encourage society to participate and provide for the always-desirable cooperative approach between the authority and the economic agents. Although CADE has recently issued Resolution 12 about the proceeding of inquiries,[59] the relevance of the associative agreement issue call for more flexible criteria to submit inquiries about this matter.

Also, in anticipation of possible questions regarding this mechanism, it is worth mentioning that if the parties were to submit to CADE an inquiry about a materialized contract and, after analyzing the case, CADE concludes that the notification is required, there are legal grounds to authorize the retrospective merger review as it may be understood from Art. 88, paragraph seven of Law 12,529/11.[60] In other words, the authority is free to

---

58 Under the Monsanto/Bayer opinion, Commissioner Alessandro Octaviani stated that "when not expressly provided by law, general hypotheses of exemption under the merger control review (in the context of the antitrust authorities' scrutiny) do not have any discursive legitimacy. It is not allowed to the interpreter to establish what is not yours; it is not allowed to the regulator to remove the protection that the law requires it to materialize". It is worth noting that by suggesting the creation of safe harbours or block exemptions one does not expect to require CADE to exempt transactions whose agents are legally obliged to notify. One is simply suggesting the removal of the existing grey area and interpretation of the concept of associative agreements in such a way that anything that must be notified is absolutely clear.

59 As from March 11, 2015.

60 Article 88, Paragraph Seven of Law No. 12,529/11: "CADE is free to require,

review merger filings as from one (1) year following consummation thereof. Despite this alternative, what is expected from the suggested channel is to extensively increase awareness and accumulate expertise, so that society may be capable of distinguishing contracts that may be classified under the cases of exemption. This would render the economic agents capable of distinguishing contractual arrangements that require notification from those which notification is not mandatory. It is clear that this type of attitude is, at the end, the consequence of an action towards antitrust compliance, meeting the objectives of the Brazilian antitrust system for the promotion and strengthening of the competition defense policy.

After CADE receives several inquiries on this matter, it would even be possible to draw a regulation based on the negative trend, in other words, to establish, to the extent required, which types of vertical contracts would not be subject to mandatory submission. Although it would not be possible to cover an exhaustive list as the authority could neglect situations that result in competition concerns and which may be disguised to avoid filing, at least certain safe harbors could be established, thus reducing legal uncertainty.

A relatively less costly method would be CADE's decision to regulate Resolution 10 through precedents. The problem with this measure is the period of time required to consolidate former decisions. Additionally, agents submitting transactions *ad cautelam* on a very conservative approach may create bad precedents that all others will have to follow. An unforeseeable scenario would prevail, contrary to what is desirable.

Also, considering the current situation, Resolution 10 leads to the conclusion that the review procedure to be adopted would be, as a rule, the non-fast track proceeding since, for horizontal and vertical relations the twenty (20%) and the thirty percent (30%) criteria, respectively, for market share would be exceeded. In fact, it would be possible to adopt the fast-track proceeding for review when there is no causal connection in the realm of horizontal relationships as addressed in Art. 8 of CADE Resolution 2 (list of cases eligible for fast-track proceeding). The assumption that the proceeding is non-fast track corroborates the understanding that Resolution 10 should not aim to review day-to-day contracts with no relevance from

within one (1) year from the respective consummation date, the submission of the mergers that do not comply with the provisions of this article".

the competition standpoint. Furthermore, the return of the market share criterion brings back one of the issues roughly criticized under Law 8,884/94, although one should recognize that any type of qualification and criteria to make the associative agreement concept more tangible is welcome.

IV. Brazil: Control of Conducts x Structures

In comparison with other jurisdictions, there are concerns in our system since business cooperation may be dealt with as mergers subject to structure control or as a violation subject to the conduct control, as already explained.

According to DUTRA (336, 2003), the basic distinction between abusive acts and merger filings is "the implicit unlawfulness of the abusive act, while the merger has a licit purpose and its effects may be harmful to free competition – but is not unlawful in nature". Other differences are determined with regard to the purpose and certainty that the practice brings to the agent: the abusive act with the use of economic power is effectively harmful to free competition, while the merger filing may or may not have harmful effects to free competition. It is based on the exercise of the right of free enterprise (DUTRA, 336. 2003).

According to SALOMÃO FILHO (2347-348, 2008), a careful systematic interpretation is required to distinguish the cases in which a certain economic cooperation will be subject to the scrutiny of the structures from those cases subject to the rule of unlawfulness. It is necessary to identify the main purpose of the agreement.[61] Salomão Filho acknowledges that, in many cases, it is difficult or virtually impossible to determine what the main purpose of the agreement is. For this reason, for competition law purposes, the "effects are then used to replace the intentions" (Calixto Salomão Filho, 349-350. 2007).

This understanding allows us to argue that, in cases where the lawfulness of a supply and distribution agreement is attested in the light of Art. 36 of the Antitrust Law, there will be no penalty to the companies,

---

[61] CALIXTO SALOMÃO FILHO. *Direito Concorrencial: As Estruturas,* 347-348, Malheiros, São Paulo, 2002. In the context of Law No. 8,884/94, Salomão Filho noted: "the illicit of article 21 represent cases in which the restriction of competition is the only purpose of the agreement (...) The two provisions coexist harmoniously with each other, provided it is understood that the hypotheses of article 21 refer to agreements whose sole or core purpose (and not secondary purpose) is such effects".

there being consequently no reason to talk about the nonfulfillment of the duty to file a merger under the structure control since:

> *"Thus, in most cases, there is no unlawfulness. Also, there is no type of restriction to competition or any other risk of market control. Translating into positive terms, this means that many of the collaborations involving the companies, even those involving parties with great market power will not even be classified under the cases set forth in the opening paragraph of Art. 54 . In other words why it is difficult to state, in most cases, that there is the obligation of filing the agreement for review. The filing is advisable to the extent that it prevents the negative consequences of a later dissolution order or a coercive rescission. However, in those cases in which the identification criteria and sanctioning criteria of the market power are coincidental, it does not seem possible to accept the existence of an unfulfilled obligation of submission to a preventive control" (our highlights).*

It is therefore clear that any excesses in structural control could generate negative consequences since they have the potential to inhibit the formation of efficient units for the market, which could be beneficial to consumers (pro-competitive effect).[62] As a result of the unguided application of this type of control, it would be possible to observe two consequences in the structural field:

> *"(...) either this control must be excessively strict, punishing structures that are not necessarily harmful to competition and unnecessarily limiting the corporate free initiative; or else, keeping the same application standards there is a serious risk of a rather reduced practical usefulness, because the indispensable complement is missing.".*[63]

It would be therefore advisable that the antitrust authority improve certain aspects of Resolution 10, particularly in making it clear that the sharing of risks is a necessary prerequisite and the exact meaning of it. Ideally, in the cases where there are still doubts, the filing should occur only in order to prevent the configuration of the illicit acts set forth in Art. 36. If these contracts are not filed for review with CADE, they will only be

---

62 In line with EDUARDO MOLAN GABAN; JULIANA OLIVEIRA DOMINGUES. *Direito Antitruste*. 3rd. ed., Saraiva, São Paulo, 2012.

63 CALIXTO SALOMÃO FILHO. *Direito Concorrencial: As Condutas*. Malheiros, São Paulo: 2003.

subject to future investigation because of the possible configuration of an anticompetitive conduct.

Conclusion

As precedents evolve, CADE's understanding on mandatory notification in cases of associative agreements was being developed. The key elements of these contracts were outlined in the course of time, allowing the parties involved to develop a better understanding of the criteria to notify these type of contracts. However, more specification for full legal security was still missing. With the correct decision to establish steady guidelines, the antitrust authority ruled the matter under Resolution 10. As has been pointed out, despite being a praise-worthy initiative, certain aspects of the resolution could have been addressed to guarantee the effectiveness of its application.

As such, attention is drawn to the portion of the resolution covering vertical cooperation. One believes CADE should establish more effective metrics for the ordinary business contracts of the economic agents, such as typical supply, distribution and technology license agreements that do not result in any anticompetitive concerns. Actions are suggested to increase efficiency and optimize resources, such as the establishment of block exemption, safeguards, inquiry channels, etc., which would be welcome to improve the definition of associative agreements. Since the resolution became effective, only a very limited number of associative agreements were reported. This may indicate certain difficulty to understand the scope of the resolution.

In other words one of the challenges to be faced by CADE will be to make this resolution reach all the transactions it is supposed to reach and, in case it is not reaching, how the authority will deal with possible failures to notify such transactions. With regard to vertical relations, as seen before, it could be more difficult to distinguish daily and ordinary commercial transactions because certain concepts may give rise to doubts in the cold reading of the law. In any event, the economic agents should understand the new regulatory framework they are now subject to and request appropriate clarification when they face a situation in which they do not have full understanding about the rules and how they apply.

Bibliography

ALISON JONES; BRENDA SUFRIN. *EC competition law. Text, cases and materials.* 2. ed. Oxford: Oxford University Press, (2004).

CALIXTO SALOMÃO FILHO. *Direito concorrencial: as estruturas.* São Paulo: Malheiros, (2007).

______. *Direito concorrencial: as condutas.* São Paulo: Malheiros, 2003b.

CARLOS ALBERTO BITTAR. *Contratos Comerciais.* São Paulo: Forense (2008).

CONSELHO ADMINISTRATIVO DE DEFESA ECONÔMICA – CADE, available at http://www.cade.gov.br/

EDUARDO CAMINATI ANDERS; VICENTE BAGNOLI; LEOPOLDO PAGOTTO (coord.). *Comentários à Nova Lei de Defesa da Concorrência.* São Paulo: Método, (2012).

EDUARDO MOLAN GABAN; JULIANA OLIVEIRA DOMINGUES. *Direito antitruste.* 3rd ed. São Paulo: Saraiva, (2012).

EUROPEAN COMMISSION – EC, available at http://ec.europa.eu/.

FÁBIO ULHOA COELHO. *Direito antitruste brasileiro: comentários à Lei n. 8.884/94*, São Paulo: Saraiva, (1995).

FEDERAL TRADE COMMISSION – FTC, available at http://www.ftc.gov/

______. *Antitrust Guidelines for Collaboration Among Competitor.* Available at http://www.ftc.gov/sites/default/files/attachments/press-releases/ftc-doj-issue-antitrust-guidelines-collaborations-among-competitors/ftcdojguidelines.pdf.

______. *Antitrust Guidelines for the Licensing of Intellectual Property.* Available at http://www.ftc.gov/sites/default/files/documents/reports/antitrust-enforcement-and-intellectual-property-rights-promoting-innovation-and-competition-report. s.department-justice-and-federal-trade-commission/p040101promo tinginnovationandcompetitionrpt0704.pdf.

______. *Guidelines on the Applicability of Article 101 of the TFEU to Horizontal Cooperation Agreement.* Available at http://eur-lex.europa.eu/legal-content/EN/TXT/PDF/?uri=CELEX:52011XC0114(04)&from=EN.

JOSÉ INÁCIO FERRAZ DE ALMEIDA PRADO FILHO. *Controle Concorrencial Preventivo de Negócios Jurídicos Verticais: A Experiência Recente do CADE No Controle Estrutural de Contratos de Fornecimento.* In: Revista do IBRAC – Direito da Concorrência, Consumo e Comércio Internacional. 223-270 Vol. 19: (2011).

JOYCE MIDORI HONDA; KARINA SCHULTE. *Contratos de Distribuição e Fornecimento: Uma Análise sobre a Obrigatoriedade de Submissão como*

Atos de Concentração ao CADE. in André Marques Gilberto; Celso Fernandes Campilongo; Juliana Girardelli Vilela (Coord.). Concentração de Empresas no Direito Antitruste Brasileiro – teoria e prática dos atos de concentração. São Paulo: Singular, (2011).

Luciano Sotero Santiago. *Direito da concorrência. Doutrina e jurisprudência*, Salvador: Jus Podivm, (2008).

Ludmila Somensi. *Conhecimento de Contrato de Licenciamento Sem Cláusula de Exclusividade e (In)Definição de Contrato Associativo.* In: Revista do IBRAC - Direito da Concorrência, Consumo e Comércio Internacional. Vol. 24. Jul/2013. 289p.

Pedro Dutra. *Livre concorrência e regulação de mercados: estudos e pareceres.* Rio de Janeiro: Renovar, (2003).

Rubens Requião. *Aspectos modernos de direito comercial (estudos e pareceres).* In: Paula A. Forgioni, Direito concorrencial e restrições verticais. São Paulo: RT, (2007).

Vinicius Marques de Carvalho; Ticiana Nogueira da Cruz Lima. *A Nova Lei de Defesa da Concorrência Brasileira: Comentários sob uma perspectiva histórico-institucional.* In: A Nova Lei do CADE – Publicações da Escola da AGU. Brasília, n. 19 (2012). Available at http://www.agu.gov.br/page/content/detail/id_conteudo/234959.

* * *

Chapter VI

TECHNOLOGY TRANSFER AGREEMENTS AS "ASSOCIATIVE AGREEMENTS" SUBJECT TO MERGER CONTROL IN BRAZIL

Paulo Eduardo Lilla
Erika Vieira Sang

I. Introduction

Technology transfer agreements may be defined as the licensing of technology rights where the licensor authorizes the licensee to exploit the licensed technology rights for the production of goods or services.[1] Such agreements are essential for economic growth and technical development, as they create incentives for innovation and dissemination of goods and services protected by intellectual property rights ("IPRs"), such as patents, trademarks and software, or by confidentiality obligations, such as know-how and trade secrets (i.e. non-patented technology).[2]

---

1 *See* European Commission (EC) Regulation 772 (2004), Paragraph 4. *See also*, European Union, *Treaty for the Functioning of the European Union (TFEU),* art. 101, Paragraph 3.

2 Intellectual property laws grant exclusive rights to holders of patents, copyright, design rights, trademarks and other legally protected rights. Under intellectual property laws, owners of intellectual property are entitled to prevent unauthorized use of the relevant intellectual property and to exploit it, for example, by licensing

Although technology transfer agreements are generally pro-competitive and efficiency enhancing, certain contractual restrictions included in these agreements, such as exclusivity, non-compete covenants, tying arrangements, territorial restrictions, among others, may adversely impact competition in the relevant markets affected by the agreement. The likelihood that such pro-competitive and efficiency-enhancing effects will outweigh any anticompetitive effects due to restrictive provisions contained in technology transfer agreements usually depends on the level of market power of the contractual parties and, thus, on the extent to which those parties face competition from other companies offering substitute technologies or products.

While the US and EU antitrust authorities have substantial experience in dealing with technology transfer agreements, having issued comprehensive guidelines for the assessment of the effects of these agreements to competition, the Brazilian Antitrust Authority (*Conselho Administrativo de Defesa Econômica* – CADE) has assessed only a limited number of cases regarding this matter. The antitrust analysis of said licensing agreements may be *a posteriori*, by means of the investigation of anticompetitive behavior, or it may be *a priori*, in the prior control of structures. It is worth mentioning that most of CADE's decisions in these cases derived from agreements notified under the merger control review procedure.[3]

The new Brazilian antitrust law ("Law 12,529/11" or "Antitrust Law"), which came into effect in May 2012, has raised new discussions on the matter, as it defined the so-called "associative agreements" as a

it to third parties. Technology may be either protected by IPRs (i.e. a patent or software), or by contractual confidentiality obligations (i.e. know-how and trade secrets).

3 Only a few cases involved investigation of licensing abusive conducts, such as CADE, *Koninklijke Philips Eletronics N.V.* Reporting Commissioner Paulo Furquim de Azevedo. (Preliminary Investigation No. 08012.005181/2006-37) (May 22, 2009), in which CADE investigated Philips' licensing practices in Brazil related to CD and DVD technologies. The investigation started after a third party complaint that the company was allegedly abusing its dominant position by collecting excessive royalties from certain Brazilian producers of blank optical discs for the licensing of the corresponding patents. In the end, CADE dismissed the case on the grounds that Philips' royalty charges were legitimate and lawful.

type of reportable transaction under the pre-merger control regime.[4] However, until November 2014, CADE had never defined the concept of "associative agreements", nor set a guidance on which types of agreements must be notified, thereby raising significant doubts and risks, as reportable transactions cannot be effective before CADE approval, under gun jumping fines ranging from BRL 60,000.00 (roughly USD 18,500.00) to BRL 60,000,000.00 (roughly USD 18,000,000.00), and all acts performed to consummate the transaction may be declared void.

In the absence of a clear guidance on the matter, several commercial agreements between parties that met the turnover thresholds provided for in the Antitrust Law were notified to CADE, including technology transfer agreements.

This scenario changed with the approval of CADE Resolution 10/2014, which defines the concept of "associative agreements" and sets out criteria for the notification thereof. However, uncertainty remains with regard to technology transfer agreements, as there is no specific guidance to define in which circumstances this type of agreement should be deemed "associative" and, thus, subject to mandatory notification.

The purpose of this paper is to assess CADE's case law on technology transfer agreements submitted to merger control, and to evaluate in which circumstances these agreements may be deemed "associative agreements" subject to merger control in Brazil, including an assessment on the possible impacts of Resolution 10/2014 on licensing arrangements.

Section 2 focuses on the reasons for antitrust concerns derived from licensing practices, as well as the international experience related to the antitrust analysis of technology transfer agreements. In turn, section 3 brings an assessment of restrictive practices in technology transfer agreements in Brazil, including a regulatory overview of the matter, as well as the Brazilian antitrust practice related with licensing restrictions, including the assessment of CADE's case law on the matter. Section 4 critically assesses the concept of "associative agreements" set out in Resolution 10/2014 and evaluates how the new regulation may affect licensing agreements. Finally, section 5 brings the conclusions drawn in this study.

---

4 *See* ANTITRUST ACT (Act. No. 12,529/11), art. 90, IV.

II. Antitrust Control of Technology Transfer Agreements

There is a general understanding among antitrust agencies worldwide that intellectual property ("IP") laws and antitrust laws share the common purpose of promoting innovation and enhancing consumer welfare. IP laws provide incentives for innovation and its dissemination by establishing enforceable exclusive rights for the creators of new and useful products and cutting-edge technology.[5] The antitrust laws, in turn, promote innovation and consumer welfare by prohibiting certain commercial practices that may harm competition, thereby putting pressure on economic agents to invest in the development of new products and technologies so as to obtain legitimate competitive advantages in the market.[6]

It is therefore crucial to preserve the incentives to innovate, which means that the innovator should not be unreasonably restricted in the exploitation of valuable IPRs. In this regard, the IP and the antitrust laws must protect the legitimate exploitation of IPRs, including the capacity of the innovator to obtain appropriate remuneration by licensing IPRs and technologies to third parties.

In view of the foregoing, antitrust agencies worldwide share the common view that technology transfer agreements are generally favorable to competition, as they usually improve economic efficiency and enable integration of complementary technologies for the development of new products and services, as the IPRs usually constitute important input for innovative activities, thereby spurring innovation and strengthening market competition. In this regard, the US Guidelines for the Licensing of Intellectual Property ("US Guidelines") clarifies that "*this integration* [of complementary technologies] *can lead to more efficient exploitation of the intellectual property, benefiting consumers through the reduction of costs and the introduction of new products*".[7]

---

5 In the absence of IPRs, imitators could free ride on the efforts of innovators and investors without incurring in the respective innovation costs. Therefore, rapid imitation would reduce the commercial value of innovation, thereby chilling the incentives to invest in the development of new products, services and technology, which ultimately would harm consumers.

6 *See Antitrust Guidelines for the Licensing of Intellectual Property* (1995), item 1; and European Union, *The Treaty on the Functioning of the European Union (TFEU)*, (Oct. 26,2012) art. 101 Paragraphs 6-7.

7 US Departament of Justice & Federal Trade Commission, *Antitrust*

Considering the importance of protecting the integrity of the licensed IPR and/or proprietary technology, technology transfer agreements generally contain contractual restrictions imposed by the licensor to limit the use of these "intellectual assets" by the licensee. In fact, most licensors would be reluctant to license their IPRs without imposing obligations on the licensee to ensure the protection of economic value of the licensed technology. Many of these contractual restrictions, such as exclusivity provisions and territorial restraints, may be indispensable to induce licensors to license their technology in the first place and/or to protect the licensees' investments.[8]

In this context, Steve Anderman provides an interesting view on this matter:

> *"In the course of drafting an IP licensing agreement, the parties must inevitably place certain contractual obligations upon each other to achieve the object of their agreement. Many licensees will be reluctant to undertake the risks of investment in manufacture and sale of new product without the protection of an exclusive license that limits direct competition from the licensor and other licensees within the licensed territory. Most licensors will not give an exclusive license without the quid pro quo of a minimum royalties clause. In addition most licensors will not license their IP without the reassurance of obligation undertaken by licensees designed to protect the integrity and value of the IP once it is licensed."*[9]

Guidelines for the Licensing of Intellectual Property (1995), *supra* note 6.

8 *See* US DEPARTAMENT OF JUSTICE & FEDERAL TRADE COMMISSION, *Antitrust Guidelines for the Licensing of Intellectual Property* (1995), item 1; and EUROPEAN UNION, *The Treaty on the Functioning of the European Union (TFEU),* (Oct. 26,2012) art. 101, item 2-3: "Field-of-use, territorial, and other limitations on intellectual property licenses may serve procompetitive ends by allowing the licensor to exploit its property as efficiently and effectively as possible. These various forms of exclusivity can be used to give a licensee an incentive to invest in the commercialization and distribution of products embodying the licensed intellectual property and to develop additional applications for the licensed property. The restrictions may do so, for example, by protecting the licensee against free-riding on the licensee's investments by other licensees or by the licensor. They may also increase the licensor's incentive to license, for example, by protecting the licensor from competition in the licensor's own technology in a market niche that it prefers to keep to itself. These benefits of licensing restrictions apply to patent, copyright, and trade secret licenses, and to know-how agreements."

9 STEVEN ANDERMAN. The new EC competition law framework for technology

However, it is undeniable that certain restrictive provisions may raise competition concerns depending on the level of market power of the parties and also on the extent to which these parties face competition constraints from other companies offering substitute technologies or products.

Based on the US and EU experiences, antitrust issues most commonly arise in cases involving, among others:

(i) Exclusive license and territorial restraints:

Provisions restricting the licensor's right to license others and to make use of the licensed technology. It is unlikely that such provision would raise antitrust concerns, unless the licensor and the licensee are in a horizontal relationship (i.e., competitors in the relevant market affected by the transaction), as the arrangement may result in unlawful market allocation between competitors.

(ii) Exclusive dealing and non-compete clauses:

Restrictions preventing licensees from licensing, selling, distributing, using or even developing competing technologies. This type of restriction could raise antitrust concerns when the licensor holds market power, in which case licensor could have the ability to foreclose access to, or increase competitors' costs of obtaining, important inputs, or facilitate coordination to raise price or reduce output. However, the restriction may have pro-competitive effects by ensuring the protection of the integrity and economic value of the licensed technology, thus stimulating the licensor to transfer its technology.

(iii) Tying arrangements:

Provision whereby a seller forces the buyer to purchase the "tied" product that the buyer did not want as a condition to obtain the "tying" product. In the context of technology transfer agreement, tying occurs when the licensor makes the licensing of one technology (the tying product) conditional upon the licensee obtaining a license for another technology or purchasing a product from the licensor (the tied product). In general, a tying arrangement could be deemed unlawful only if: (i) the seller or licensor has market power in the tying product; (ii) it involves two separate products or

transfer and IP licensing, *in* JOSEF DREXL (Editor). *Research Handbook on Intellectual Property and Competition Law*, 111-112, Cheltenham, UK: Edward Elgar, 2008.

technologies; (iii) the arrangement has an adverse effect on competition in the relevant market for the tied product; and (iv) efficiency justifications for the arrangement do not outweigh the anticompetitive effects;

(iv) Grantbacks:

Provision imposing the obligation, upon licensees, to license any improvements or enhancements made by using the licensed technology to the licensor. The grantback provision is usually pro-competitive, as it may promote the dissemination of technology by ensuring the licensor that it will have a continuing right to make use of its own technology. On the other hand, this type of provision may raise antitrust concerns when it has the potential to discourage innovation promoted by licensees, which generally occurs in the event of an exclusive grantback by which only the licensor has the right to use the improvements;

(v) Cross-licensing and patent pooling:

Cross-licensing and pooling arrangements are agreements of two or more owners of different items of IP or technology to license one another or third parties. These arrangements may provide pro-competitive benefits by integrating complementary technologies, reducing transaction costs, clearing blocking positions, and avoiding costly infringement litigation. Anticompetitive effects may arise when: (i) the arrangements include collective price or output restraints and do not contribute to an efficiency-enhancing integration of economic activity among the participants; (ii) the patent pooling is exclusive, and (ii.a) excluded economic agents cannot compete without access to the technology; and (ii.b) the pool members collectively hold market power; and (iii) the pooling arrangement discourages or deters members from engaging in research and development (e.g. the arrangement contains exclusive grantback provisions).

In order to clarify which licensing practices could be problematic from the antitrust standpoint, the US antitrust authorities – Department of Justice and the Federal Trade Commission – jointly issued the Antitrust Guidelines for the Licensing of Intellectual Property ("the US Guidelines"). The US Guidelines set forth a flexible approach to the economic assessment of technology transfer agreements, expressly to the pro-competitive benefits of licensing. Three basic principles were established: (i) IP is essentially comparable to any other form of property; (i) IPRs are not presumed to create market power; and (iii) IP allows firms to combine complementary factors of production and is generally pro-competitive.

Likewise, the European Commission ("EC") issued the EC Technology Transfer Block Exemption Regulation ("TTBER") and the accompanying Guidelines ("EC Guidelines") in 2004, which are similar to the approach undertaken by the US Guidelines to assess licensing practices, although TTBER and the EC Guidelines reflect policy principles designed to protect the European single market,[10] which reflect a more strict approach in dealing with vertical territorial restraints.[11]

Both the US Guidelines and the EC TTBER and EC Guidelines are similar in the sense that they describe the approach to evaluate licensing practices, recognize that technology licensing is generally pro-pro-competitive, distinguish licensing arrangements between competitors and non-competitors, acknowledge the importance of outweighing efficiencies against possible anticompetitive effects arising out of licensing restrictions, and, more importantly, sets out "safe harbors" with exemptions to licenses when the parties have market share below certain levels in the relevant markets affected by the arrangement, provided that there are no "hardcore" restrictions, which are deemed likely to harm competition.[12]

[10] Competition law in Europe aims at protecting the European single market and eliminating the trade barriers among the Member States. In this regard, Commission Regulation (EU) 316 (March 21, 2014), *on the application of Article 101(3) of the Treaty on the Functioning of European Union to categories of technology transfer agreements,* at Article 26, provides that "*The Union shall adopt measures with the aim of establishing or ensuring the functioning of the internal market, in accordance with the relevant provisions of the Treaties. The internal market shall comprise an area without internal frontiers in which the free movement of goods, persons, services and capital is ensured in accordance with the provisions of the Treaties.*" In this regard, the cornerstones of the single market are often said to be the "four freedoms" – the free movement of people, goods, services and capital. These freedoms, which are enshrined in the TFUE, form the basis of the single market framework.

[11] For a complete assessment of the differences between US and EU antitrust policy for licensing arrangements, *see* Richard Gilbert. Converging Doctrines? US and EU Antitrust Policy for the Licensing of Intellectual Property. University of California, Berkeley, Competition Policy Working Paper. (February, 2004), *available at* SSRN: http://ssrn.com/abstract=527762 or http://dx.doi.org/10.2139/ssrn.527762.

[12] In Europe, for example, technology transfer agreements between competitors that

As per the US and EU experience on the matter, antitrust concerns may either arise from technology transfer agreements between actual or potential competitors (i.e. horizontal relationship) or between parties active in different markets within a given technology supply chain (i.e. vertical relationship), such as when the technology owned by the licensor is input for the production activities carried out by the licensee.

Restrictive clauses included in horizontal technology transfer agreements may be harmful to competition especially when the agreement facilitates market allocation or entails price fixing between the parties. Vertical agreements, in turn, may contain license restrictions with respect to one market that could harm competition in another market by foreclosing access to, or significantly raising the price of, an important input, or by facilitating coordination to increase price or reduce output.[13]

The US and EU authorities may deem some of the licensing restrictions unlawful *per se*. According to the US Guidelines, for instance, naked price-fixing, output restraints, and market allocation among horizontal competitors, as well as certain group boycotts do not require an in-depth investigation on their anticompetitive effects.

The EC TTBER, in turn, provides a list of hardcore restrictions. Under these rules, technology transfer agreements could be considered null and void whenever provisions such as price fixing (including minimum resale price maintenance), limitation of output, market or customers' allocation,[14] among others, are present. However, the EU provides for stricter rules with respect to vertical restraints, especially those related to

---

hold joint market share under 20% or between non-competitors whose individual market share is under 30%, and that do not contain "severely anticompetitive restraints" do not fall under the scope of COMMISSION REGULATION (EU) 316 (March 21, 2014), *supra* note 10, at Article 101(1). The "safety zone" in the US determines that the licensor and its licensees (jointly) must not hold a 20% market share affected by the arrangement. For technology markets in which market data is unavailable, the exemption is applied in case there are at least four independently controlled substitutable technologies to the one that is being licensed.

13 *See* US DEPARTAMENT OF JUSTICE & FEDERAL TRADE COMMISSION, *Antitrust Guidelines for the Licensing of Intellectual Property* (1995), *supra* note 6, at item 3.1.

14 COMMISSION REGULATION (EU) 316 (March 21, 2014), *on the application of Article 101(3) of the Treaty on the Functioning of European Union to categories of technology transfer agreements*, *supra* note 13, at Article 4.1 (c) and 4.2 (b).

territorial restrictions for sales.[15] As already stated, this is consistent with the European policy designed to protect the European single market.

Aside from these exceptions, both the American and the European authorities assess the vast majority of technology transfer agreements under the rule of reason. In this regard, when relying upon the rule of reason, the authority should firstly verify whether the restraints could produce anticompetitive effects in a given relevant market and, if so, evaluate whether there are economic efficiency justifications that could outweigh those anticompetitive effects. This assessment requires a thorough knowledge of the market conditions, such as market concentration, barriers to entry and elasticity of demand and supply.

It should be noted, however, that the assessment of licensing restrictions is usually carried by the US and EU *ex post* under repressive rules, that is, as anticompetitive conducts. In Brazil, however, technology transfer agreements have been scrutinized under merger control review, i.e., as transactions subject to mandatory notification to CADE, as described in further detail below.

III. Antitrust Analysis of Licensing Restrictions in Brazil

Much like the US and EU antitrust authorities, the Brazilian authority – CADE – also recognizes that intellectual property laws and competition laws share common objectives, as they both promote innovation and economic development, thereby increasing social welfare.[16] In this regard,

[15] By establishing exceptions to the hardcore restrictions, the Commission Regulation (EU) 316 (March 21, 2014), *on the application of Article 101(3) of the Treaty on the Functioning of European Union to categories of technology transfer agreements* recognizes situations in which territorial restrictions are indispensable

[16] In CADE, *Fiat Automóveis S.A., Ford Motor Company Brasil Ltda., Volkswagen do Brasil Ltda.*, Reporting Commissioner Carlos Emmanuel Joppert Ragazzo (PI 08012.002673/2007-51) (Feb. 25, 2011), Reporting Commissioner Carlos Ragazzo confirmed this understanding in his opinion, as follows: "However, industrial property is neither absolute, nor immune from antitrust enforcement. Much like industrial property rights, competition law is also protected by the Brazilian Constitution and by federal laws (…) and although it is true that these two bodies of law are generally complementary to each other, the enforcement of an industrial property right, at times, may violate competition law and, thus, such two bodies of law may collide. In this regard, even though the enforcement of industrial property rights is not anticompetitive in any way, and that in most

one should firstly take into account that the Brazilian Constitution protects both IPRs and competition. While the protection of IPRs is a fundamental right ensured by the Constitution, given their importance to technical progress and to the economic development, the protection of free competition and the repression of the abuse of economic power are core constitutional principles of the Brazilian economic order.[17]

Thus, CADE usually takes the foregoing assumptions into account in the antitrust analysis of cases involving the interface between IPRs and competition, especially technology transfer agreements. It is worth mentioning that in such cases, antitrust enforcement analysis may be *a posteriori*, in the repression of anticompetitive practices, or *a priori*, in the prior control of market structures. It is also noteworthy that CADE assessed the vast majority of technology transfer agreements under merger control review.

In this regard, it is unquestionable that the current Antitrust Law has brought significant and beneficial changes to the Brazilian legal system, including the adoption of clearer rules on pre-merger control, which are in line with the best international practices. Certain issues nevertheless remained unclear, such as the concept of "associative agreements" as reportable transactions under the new pre-merger control regime, which may impact technology transfer agreements that could be deemed "associative" in nature, especially in the presence of certain types of contractual restrictions, such as exclusivity and non-compete provisions.

The following subsection provides the legal and regulatory overview for the antitrust analysis of restrictive provisions in technology transfer agreements in Brazil. It first describes the more interventionist approach of the Brazilian Patent and Trademark Office (*Instituto Nacional da Propriedade Industrial* – "INPI") in the assessment of licensing arrangements, followed

---

of the times these rights are incapable of granting market power to the respective holder, they frequently produce anticompetitive effects that effectively imply an unlawful anticompetitive conduct subject to antitrust enforcement, as shown in several cases reviewed in different jurisdictions".

17 Refer to to CF 1988 art. 5, XXIII (protecting copyrights) and XXIII (protecting industrial property rights, like trademarks and patents); CF 1988 art. 170, IV (protecting free competition); and art. 173, Paragraph 4 (dealing with the repression of the abuse of economic power.

by CADE's approach to the review of technology transfer agreement subject to mandatory notification.

A. *Regulatory Aspects of Technology Transfer Agreements*

In Brazil, intellectual property is divided into two categories: (i) industrial property, which includes patents, utility models, trademarks, industrial designs, and geographic indications; and (ii) copyright, which includes literary, scientific and artistic works such as novels, poems, films, musical works, drawings, paintings, photographs and sculptures, architectural designs and also software.[18]

The Brazilian industrial property rules are set forth in Law 9,279/96 ("Industrial Property Law") and INPI, the government agency linked to the Ministry of Development, is the authority responsible for reviewing and granting the registration of trademarks, patents, industrial designs and geographic indications and related matters. INPI is also responsible for the registration of licensing of industrial property, both for national and international licenses, as well as of all agreements involving technology and know-how (and services related thereto), regardless of whether the licensed property may be registered or not.[19]

The Industrial Property Law provides for general provisions on technology transfer agreements, which are further regulated by INPI

---

[18] The protection of copyright (and copyrights license) does not depend on registration, unlike with other industrial property. The rules applicable to copyrights are set forth in SOFTWARE ACT (Act. No. 9,609/98) and in COPYRIGHT ACT (Act. No. 9,610/98). Copyrights in Brazil comprise the economic rights of the author and the author's moral rights. Such moral rights cannot be licensed, transferred or waived. As to the author's economic rights, the protection of copyright lasts for seventy (70) years as from January 1st of the year following the author's death or as from the work's first publication, in case of anonymous or pseudonymous works, audiovisual and photography works.

[19] There is no definition for the concept of "technology" in Brazilian law. INPI and some scholars construe the term "technology" as the set of information or technical knowledge that enables someone to manufacture a product or render a service according to certain specifications/guidelines. Typically, when INPI uses the word technology, it is referring to "unpatented technology", as opposed to the technology that is covered by a patent ("patented technology"). Moreover, it is worth noting that copyright license agreements are not subject to registration with INPI, or with any other governmental body.

Normative Act 135 of 1997. In this regard, technology transfer agreements must be registered with INPI as a condition precedent for: (i) remittance of royalties abroad as payment under the agreement, observing the currency exchange and tax laws;[20] (ii) deductibility of royalty fees incurred by the Brazilian licensee, if any; and (iii) validity of the agreement in relation to third parties.[21]

According to INPI Normative Act 135/97, the following types of technology transfer agreements must be registered, as explained above: (i) patent licensing; (ii) trademark licensing; (iii) supply of technology or know-how; (iv) technical and scientific assistance; and (v) franchise agreements. It is worth mentioning that because software is protected in Brazil as copyright, software licensing agreements do not have to be registered with INPI, unless the relevant agreement entails the transfer of software source code technology.[22]

It is worth mentioning that Brazil used to be far more interventionist in technology transfer agreements than it is today, imposing strict limitations on restrictive provisions included in such agreements. In the 1970s, the former Industrial Property Law (Law 5,772/1971) provided INPI with a broad mandate to "*adopt measures to accelerate and regulate the transfer of technology and to establish better conditions for the negotiation of such agreements and use of patents*" (emphasis added).[23]

Based on this mandate, INPI engaged in an extremely interventionist approach by issuing a set of regulations (the so-called "normative acts") to

---

20 The registration certificate issued by INPI must be registered with the Central Bank of Brazil (BACEN) in order to enable the foreign remittance of royalties and ensure the deductibility of royalty expenses/fees up to the fixed limits imposed by the Brazilian tax authorities. National Treasury Ordinance 436/58 sets out the tax deduction limits, which range from 1% to 5%, depending on the type of agreement and product involved. In case of agreements between controlling and controlled companies, such deductibility limits are the same for the remittance of royalties, according to the INPI's interpretation of Article 50 of Law 8,383/91.

21 *See* Industrial Property Act (Act No. 9.279/1996), at Article 211, and Normative Act 135/1997, at Section 2. It is worth mentioning that government endorsement is not a condition for the license to be valid or even effective between the contracting parties. Nonetheless, the agreement will only become binding upon third parties after the approval is published in INPI's *Official Gazette*.

22 *See* Software Act (Act. No. 9,609/98), art. 11.

23 *See* Article 2, Sole Paragraph, of Law 5,722/71.

limit the parties' will in the negotiation of technology transfer agreements, including the prohibition of certain restrictive provisions deemed to be abusive or anticompetitive. The most significant of these regulations was Normative Act 15/1975, which authorized INPI to limit the amount of royalties that could be remitted abroad by the recipient of the technology, and also defined a list containing mandatory clauses to be included in the agreements and another one with prohibited restrictive clauses, which were deemed to be null and void.[24]

The alleged purpose of such strict approach was to protect national industry by reducing the reliance on foreign technology and leveling the playing field in negotiations between foreign licensors and Brazilian licensees. Therefore, the Brazilian government believed that these policies could protect the balance of payments, avoid tax evasion, increase the quality of the technology transferred to Brazilian companies and, thus, encourage domestic innovation.[25]

However, such strict approach backfired, as it reduced foreign investments in key sectors of the economy and prevented Brazilian companies from obtaining state-of-the-art technology developed in the most industrialized countries.

Given the negative results of such interventionist policy, by the early 1990s, following the opening and deregulation of the Brazilian economy, INPI engaged in a less strict and formalistic approach to the assessment of technology transfer agreements, which resulted in the issuance of Normative Act 120/1993. As a result, INPI began registering technology transfer agreements without interfering in the party's autonomy to negotiate terms

---

[24] This policy was also adopted in other Latin American countries and influenced the international debate on the implementation of the International Code of Conduct for Technology Transfer under the auspices of UNCTAD, which began in 1976 and ended up in 1985.

[25] For a more complete assessment on this matter, *see* JULIANA L. B VIEGAS. Contratos Típicos de Propriedade Industrial: Contratos de Cessão e de Licenciamento de Marcas e Patentes; Licenças Compulsórias, 66, *in* MANOEL J. PEREIRA DOS SANTOS; WILSON PINHEIRO JABUR. *Contratos de Propriedade Industrial e Novas Tecnologias*. São Paulo: Saraiva, 2007; and, LUCIANO BENETTI TIMM. Contrato internacional de transferência de tecnologia no Brasil: interseção da propriedade intelectual com o direito antitruste, 80, *in* LUCIANO BENETTI TIMM; PEDRO PARANAGUÁ. *Propriedade Intelectual, Antitruste e Desenvolvimento: caso da transferência de tecnologia e do software*. Rio de Janeiro: FGV Direito Rio, 2009.

and conditions as they see fit, especially with regard to price, conditions of payments, contractual terms, limitation of use of IPR, among others.

This new policy was later confirmed when the Industrial Property Law was enacted in 1996, which expressly withdrew INPI's power to interfere in private negotiations between the parties, thereby resulting in the progressive entry of new technologies originated from the developed countries. Immediately thereafter, INPI issued Normative Act 135/1997, which is currently in force, to regulate the registration of technology transfer agreements.

Although INPI's authority is currently limited by law to the assessment of the formal aspects and to the validity of the intellectual property rights that are involved in the registration of contracts proceedings, INPI establishes its own interpretation of the applicable laws to interfere in the party's autonomy to freely set out the terms and conditions of technology transfer agreements. Even though INPI is far more flexible than it was in the past, its approach renders the registration proceeding to be slow and bureaucratic.

More importantly, during the registration procedures, INPI frequently raises questions or even objects to the inclusion of restrictive provisions in technology transfer agreements submitted to its assessment, without carrying out a comprehensive economic assessment on the actual or potential effects of such provisions to competition. In this regard, INPI often imposes percentage limits on the remittance of royalties abroad, as well as limits confidentiality provisions, among other restrictions that impair the party's freedom to contract.[26] In other words, INPI seems to

[26] INPI also imposes additional restrictions on the party's autonomy to negotiate licensing of know-how and non-patentable technology. These agreements must specify their purpose and clearly describe the method to be used for the actual transfer of technology. INPI generally limits the duration of these agreements to five (5) years, which term may be extended once for an additional five-year period, at INPI's discretion. This strict time limitation derives from the fact that INPI does not recognize the licensing of know-how and non-patentable technology, but only the actual supply of technology, which means that once the know-how or non-patentable technology is "transferred", the recipient of the technology will usually have the right to freely use the transferred technology after the expiration of the agreement, without further payments to licensor. Technical/scientific services agreements are subject to the additional following rules: (i) price breakdown, per

conceive certain restrictive clauses as *per se* unlawful, without any economic assessment.

However, INPI currently has powers to enforce the laws dealing with industrial property, such as trademarks, patents, designs and the respective licensing agreements. It has neither a mandate nor jurisdiction to assess the competitive effects of technology transfer agreements. Pursuant to the Antitrust Law, CADE is the sole antitrust authority with powers to assess antitrust matters related with licensing and technology transfer agreements, either in the repression of anticompetitive practices or in the context of merger control review.

It is worth mentioning that CADE has a more liberal approach in assessing the economic effects of restrictive clauses included in technology transfer agreements, in a very similar fashion to the US rule of reason. Thus, as a rule, Brazilian Antitrust Law prohibitions are violated only if the arrangements have an appreciable effect on competition that is not outweighed by any positive outcome. By and large, a restrictive provision included in a licensing agreement is unlikely (but not impossible) to be problematic if the parties' combined market share is below certain levels (20%). Additionally, in general, only benefits that consumers may also enjoy are deemed sufficiently important to prevail over occasional competition restrains.[27]

---

professional skill and hourly rate; and (ii) the parties must estimate the annual fee of the agreement based on each professional and hourly fees.

27 With respect to hardcore cartels, however, CADE considers that though the law does not establish a "*per se rule*", it implies that cartels will be strictly scrutinized by noting that these practices entail more anticompetitive effects than pro-competitive benefits (if any) and therefore require "a more judicious application" of the rule of reason. More recently, in the judgement of the SKF case, which involved the practice of resale price maintenance ("RPM"), one of CADE's Tribunal Commissioners concluded that the rule of reason and *per se* prohibition are merely extreme points of the same "scale of presumptions", in which typically more harmful conduct would fall more closely into the *per se* prohibition and the presumption of illegality (such as hardcore cartels and RPM) and other rarely harmful conducts would be closer to the rule of reason and the presumption of legality (such as tying arrangements and exclusivity). *See* opinion issued by Commissioner Marcos Paulo Veríssimo in the Administrative Procedure No. 08012.001271/2001-44, decided by CADE on January 30, 2013.

The following section further addresses how CADE reviews technology transfer agreements in merger control procedures.

B. *Antitrust Analysis of Technology Transfer Agreements Submitted to Merger Control*

The new Antitrust Law, enacted on November 30, 2011 and in force since May 29, 2012, sets forth preventive and repressive mechanisms against violations to the economic order. The most important modification brought forth by the new law was the adoption of a pre-merger control system, thereby incorporating a suspensory obligation prior to closing, which means that reportable transactions may not be consummated prior to CADE's approval.[28]

According to the new Antitrust Law, a merger filing is required in Brazil when the parties meet the turnover thresholds[29] and the transaction amounts to a "concentration". In this regard, "concentration" is usually defined as a long-lasting structural change in the market, which normally

---

28 As a result, parties must keep structures and facilities separate and may not transfer assets, or exercise any type of "influence" over each other. Parties must also refrain from exchanging commercially sensitive information. Failure to comply with this standstill obligation exposes the parties to gun-jumping fines and all acts performed to consummate the transaction may be declared void.

29 Pursuant to ANTITRUST ACT (Act. No. 12,529/11), at Article 88, a merger filing is required when (i) at least one of the "economic groups" involved (seller or buyer) registered gross revenues in Brazil of BRL 750 million (roughly USD 23 million) or more; and (ii) at least one of the other groups involved (seller, buyer or target) registered gross revenues in Brazil of BRL 75 million (roughly USD 230 million) or more. In this regard, for the antitrust thresholds calculation, an economic group exists between various entities when such entities are subject to "common control". Such "common control" is assumed if and when entities in which any of the entities that are subject to common control hold, directly or indirectly, at least a 20% market share. When it comes to investment funds, the following entities are treated as being part of one single economic group for purposes of the turnover calculation: (a) companies of the economic group of each investor/shareholder which directly or indirectly holds at least 50% of the shares of such investment fund (which takes part in the transaction) via individual interest or by means of any type of shareholders' agreement; plus (b) companies controlled by such investment fund (which takes part in the transaction) if such investment fund directly or indirectly holds interest of at least 20% of the corporate or voting capital.

occurs as a result of classic M&A transactions and joint ventures. Therefore, the control of structures is mainly related to the structural changes of a given transaction, and not on the potential anticompetitive effects thereof.

However, the former competition law – Law 8,884/94 –, which remained in effect until May 28, 2012, did not set forth a clear definition of "concentration", but only provided a very broad definition of transactions subject to merger control in its Article 54, as follows: "*Any acts that may limit or otherwise restrain competition, or that result in the control of relevant markets for certain products or services, shall be submitted to CADE for review*". Paragraph Three further clarified that the acts mentioned in the main section of Article 54 also include any action intended to any type of economic concentration, whether through merger with or into other companies, organization of companies to control other companies or any other form of corporate grouping in which (i) the resulting market share is equal to or greater than twenty percent (20%); or (ii) any of the parties had annual gross revenue equivalent to or greater than four hundred million reais (BRL 400,000,000.00) posted in the latest balance sheets.

Thus, the main section of Article 54 provided a broad concept of reportable transactions, assuming that any act must be notified if it may limit or restrain competition in any way, regardless of its contractual form. As a result, the analysis of whether a transaction must be submitted to merger control review relied on its effects and not on its object.[30] Paragraph Three, in turn, provided a general concept of "concentration" by including certain examples of reportable transactions, mostly M&A transactions, which are clear examples of economic concentration, as they usually result in long-standing change to the market structure.

Because of the broad wording of the main section of Article 54, several contractual arrangements that did not fit the ordinary M&A transactions were notified to CADE, such as distribution and supply agreements, common undertakings, cooperation agreements, licensing and technology transfer agreements, among others, whenever the parties met at least one of the thresholds provided in Paragraph Three of the former competition law (i.e., market share of at least 20% or gross revenue equivalent or greater

---

30 *See* Vinicius Marques de Carvalho. "Agreements and Competition Enforcement: The Choice Between Preventive and Repressive Channels", in: Barry Haunk (editor). *International Antitrust Law & Policy*, New York: Fordham University School of Law, 2014.

than BRL 400 million). Such broad wording left the parties with the tough and subjective task of assessing the economic effects of these agreements in advance, in order to verify whether they could be deemed as "*acts that may limit or otherwise restrain competition*" and, thus, subject to mandatory notification.

Technology transfer agreements represented a great number of contractual arrangements notified to CADE for merger review. Most of them were reviewed without thorough discussions on whether they should be acknowledged or not.[31] When assessing the merits of these filings,

---

[31] Merger Filings CADE, *Monsanto do Brasil Ltda, EMBRAPA*. The Superintendence-General (08012.004808/2000-01) (April, 28, 2000); CADE, *Monsanto do Brasil Ltda. E COODETEC*. The Superintendence-General 08012.003711/2000-17) (Aug. 18, 2000); CADE, *Monsanto do Brasil Ltda, Fundação Mato Grosso e Unisoja S.A.* The Superintendence-General (08012.003997/2003-83) (June 3, 2003); CADE, *Monsanto do Brasil Ltda, Agroeste Brasil S.A.* Reporting Commissioner Ricardo Villas Bôas Cueva. (08012.008359/2005-11) (Jan. 10, 2006); CADE, *Monsanto do Brasil Ltda., Agromen Sementes Agrícolas Ltda.* Reporting Commissioner Luís Fernando Rigato Vasconcellos. (08012.009265/2005-69) (May 2, 2006); CADE, *Monsanto do Brasil Ltda., Dow Agrosciences Industrial Ltda.* The Superintendence-General (08012.000766/2006-61), (Feb. 21, 2006); CADE, *Monsanto do Brasil Ltda., Cooperativa Central de Pesquisa Agrícola.* Reporting Commissioner Abraham Benzaquen Sicsú. (08012.008656/2006-47) (Oct., 30, 2006); CADE, *Monsanto do Brasil Ltda., Syngenta Seeds Ltda.* Reporting Commissioner Luis Fernando Schuartz. (08012.000311/2007-26) (July 18, 2007); CADE, *Monsanto do Brasil Ltda.* Reporting Commissioner Luis Fernando Schuartz. (08012.008725/2007-01) (Dec. 07, 2007); CADE, *Monsanto do Brasil Ltda.* Reporting Commissioner Abraham Benzaquem Sicsú. (08012.003296/2007-78) (Jan 15, 2008); CADE, *Monsanto do Brasil Ltda.* Reporting Commissioner Abraham Benzaquem Sicsú. (08012.004091/2007-18) (Dec. 14, 2007); CADE, *Monsanto do Brasil Ltda.* Reporting Commissioner Luiz Carlos Thadeu Delorme Prado. (08012.006198/2008-73) (Aug. 31, 2008); CADE, *Monsanto do Brasil Ltda., Syngenta Seeds Ltda.* Reporting Commissioner Paulo Furquim de Azevedo. (08012.006556/2008-48) (Sept. 17, 2008); CADE, *Monsanto do Brasil Ltda., Melhoramento Agropastoril Ltda.* Reporting Commissioner. (08012.001558/2009-21) (June 05, 2009); CADE, *Monsanto do Brasil Ltda.,, Soytech Seeds Pesquisa em Soja Ltda.* Reporting Commissioner Vinícius Marques de Carvalho (08012.001559/2009-76) (June 5, 2009); CADE, *Monsanto do Brasil Ltda., Wehrtec-Tecnologia Agrícola Ltda.* Reporting Commissioner César Costa Alves de Mattos. (08012.001560/2009-09) (May 22, 2009); CADE, *Dow Agroscience Industrial Ltda., Syngenta Seeds Ltda.* Reporting Commissioner Vinícius Marques de Carvalho. (08012.002976/2009) (Aug. 22, 2009); CADE, *Monsanto do Brasil*

CADE usually recognized that licensing agreements are pro-competitive and efficiency enhancing, as they enable the dissemination of technology and the entry of new competitors in the market.[32]

In fact, between 2000 and 2009, all technology transfer agreements were acknowledged and reviewed on the merits, which means that CADE's case law consolidated the understanding that these types of agreements were subject to mandatory notification when the parties met the thresholds provided for in the former competition law.[33] Moreover, until 2009, all technology transfer agreements that did not contain exclusivity or non-compete provisions were approved without restrictions, whereas the majority of agreements containing these provisions were approved under the condition that such provisions be removed from the agreement or at least amended.[34]

Ltda., BR Genética Ltda. Reporting Commissioner César Costa Alves de Mattos. (08012.004517/2009-97) (Aug. 03, 2009); and CADE, *Monsanto do Brasil Ltda., Instituto Mato-Grossense do Algodão.* Reporting Commissioner Paulo Furquim de Azevedo. (08012.006034/2009-27) (Sept. 30, 2009).

32 In CADE, *Monsanto do Brasil Ltda. E Syngenta Seeds Ltda.* Reporting Commissioner Luis Fernando Schuartz. (08012.000311/2007-26) (July 18, 2007) Reporting Commissioner Abraham Sicsú recognized in his opinion that transactions involving licensing of technology generally are not capable of harming competition, as they enable the licensee to have access to key technology for productive activities, which would not be possible in the absence of the contractual arrangement. He concluded by saying that "*the full social benefit of the technology is given by its diffusion*".

33 For a statistic assessment, *see* Lucas Barrios. *O Contrato Internacional de Transferência de Tecnologia e o Direito da Concorrência no Brasil: análise à luz da recente jurisprudência do CADE*, 133, *in* Revista de Direito da Concorrência, No. 4, November 2014.

34 For example, *see* CADE, *Monsanto do Brasil Ltda., Syngenta Seeds Ltda.* Reporting Commissioner Luis Fernando Schuartz. (08012.000311/2007-26) (July 18, 2007); and CADE, *Monsanto do Brasil Ltda., Brasmax Genética Ltda.* Reporting Commissioner Abraham Benzaquem Sicsú. (08012.003296/2007-78) (Jan. 15, 2008). These cases suggest that the main concern involving exclusivity provisions in licensing agreements is the possible foreclosure of the technology market, thereby preventing licensor's competitors from licensing alternative technology to licensees, which could result in adverse effects to innovation. As a result, licensees would become dependent of that single technology, as they would not have access to alternative technology that could become more efficient along time.

However, this approach changed in 2010, when CADE recognized that technology transfer agreements that did not include restrictive provisions, such as exclusivity and non-compete clauses, should not be deemed "concentrations" subject to merger control review. In the judgment of a merger filing submitted by Monsanto do Brasil Ltda. ("Monsanto") and Ihabrás S.A., CADE recognized that these contracts are merely a means for economic agents to perform their daily commercial activities and that, in principle, do not result in economic concentration because there is no transfer, sharing or assignment of assets.[35]

Following this judgment, CADE attempted to create parameters for the submission of the so-called "associative agreements" when reviewing several supply agreements submitted to merger control. According to the authority, the following agreements would not be subject to merger control: (i) agreements that did not result in the assignment of rights related to competitively relevant assets; (ii) agreements that did not contain exclusivity or similar clauses that could limit the independence of asset-related decision making; and (iii) agreements that did not represent a volume of business above 20% of a given relevant market; (iv) agreements effective for less than 5 years; and (v) possibility of immediate termination by any of the parties without any burden to the party that notifies the other about its intention to terminate the agreement.[36]

---

[35] CADE, *Monsanto do Brasil Ltda., Iharabras S.A Indústrias Químicas.* Reporting Commissioner Ricardo Machado Ruiz. (08012.000182/2010-71) (March 23, 2010).

[36] *See* CADE, *Monsanto do Brasil Ltda.*, Dow Agrosciences Industrial Ltda., Reporting Commissioner Carlos Emmanuel Joppert Ragazzo (08012.005367/2010-72) (June 30, 2010); CADE, *Basf S.A. and Syngenta Crop Protection AG,* Reporting Commissioner Fernando de Magalhães Furlan. (08012.004571/2010-76) (Aug. 31, 2010); CADE, *Pan-American S.A. Indústrias Químicas and Bayer S.A.* Reporting Commissioner Ricardo Machado Ruiz. (08012.007331/2010-23) (Sept. 17, 2010); CADE, *Dow Agrosciences Industrial Ltda. and Syngenta Supply AG.* Reporting Commissioner Olavo Zago Chinaglia. (08012.006493/2010-44) (Nov. 22, 2010); CADE, *Monsanto do Brasil Ltda., Syngenta Proteção de Cultivos Ltda.* Reporting Commissioner Fernando de Magalhães Furlan. (08012.009227/2010-73) (Nov. 26, 2010); CADE, *Monsanto do Brasil Ltda., Iharabras S.A Indústrias Químicas, supra* note 35. CADE, *Monsanto do Brasil Ltda. FTS Sementes S.A.* Reporting Commissioner Olavo Zago Chinaglia. (08012.000344/2010) (March 17, 2010).

Finally, CADE did not acknowledge two merger filings involving technology transfer agreements on the grounds that they could not be deemed as "concentration", as there was no exclusivity or non-compete provisions. In one of these two cases –a merger filing involving a licensing agreement notified by Monsanto and FTS Sementes – former CADE Commissioner Olavo Chinaglia clarified that the agreement was not subject to mandatory notification, because: (i) it did not contain provisions which could give rise to the anticompetitive effects mentioned in the main section of Article 54 of former Law 8,884/94; and (ii) it did not concern an economic concentration resulting from the transfer of share capital, operational assets, joint ventures, or other form of corporate grouping (i.e., transactions mentioned in Paragraph Three of Article 54 of the former law).

Chinaglia then concluded that the agreement refers exclusively to an IP license, comparable, for all purposes, to the sale of a product or the provision of services in the routine activities of the companies involved. In conclusion, he stated "(...) the only possible competitive effect arising out of the notified transaction would be the entry of a new competitor in the market, which could only give rise to concerns of existing rivals".[37]

These cases shed a light on the broad definition of reportable transactions pursuant to Article 54 of former antitrust law and revealed that CADE was aware of the importance of providing legal certainty and predictability as to which types of transactions should be considered as "concentration" subject to mandatory notification, especially with regard to technology transfer agreements.

In order to remedy the uncertainty of the broad wording of the former legislation, the new Antitrust Law brought a clearer and narrower definition of concentration by listing the transactions subject to mandatory notification in its Article 90. According to the aforementioned provision, a concentration occurs whenever: (i) two or more previously independent companies merge; (ii) one or more companies acquire control or parts of one or more companies, directly or indirectly, by the purchase or exchange of stocks, shares, bonds or securities convertible into stocks or assets, whether tangible or intangible, by contract or by any other means;[38] (iii)

37 CADE, *Monsanto do Brasil Ltda. FTS Sementes S.A.* Reporting Commissioner Olavo Zago Chinaglia. (08012.000344/2010) (March 17, 2010).

38 Pursuant to CADE Resolution 02/2012, the acquisition of parts of one or more

one or more companies absorbs one or more companies, and (iv) two or more companies enter into an "associative agreement", joint venture or consortium (except when used for bids promoted by direct and indirect government agencies and for contracts arising therefrom).

Therefore, the new law represented a shift from a subjective criterion to define reportable transactions, i.e., based on their potential anticompetitive effects, to an objective criterion that clearly defines the transactions that fall within the concept of concentration and, thus, subject to mandatory notification.

In any event, although Article 90 of the Antitrust Law has unquestionably improved the concept of concentration, it failed to provide a clear definition of what should be considered as an "associative agreement". As a result, several contractual arrangements, including technology transfer agreements, continued to be submitted to CADE's review without any certainty as to whether or not they should be deemed "associative agreements".

C. *Technology Transfer Agreements and the Concept of "Associative Agreements" as Reportable Transactions under the New Antitrust Law*

As has been previously mentioned, according to Article 90, item IV of the new Antitrust Law, the so-called "associative agreements" are subject to mandatory notification to CADE whenever the parties thereto (and their respective economic groups) meet the turnover thresholds set forth in the law. However, the Antitrust Law did not clearly define what an "association agreement" is, which caused a great deal of uncertainty as to what type of agreements are subject to mandatory notification. The only available

companies is defined as transactions that do not result in the acquisition of control, but meet the "*de minimis*" rules. In relation to non-competing parties: (a) the acquired interest is equal or higher than 20% of the target's share capital; or (b) the purchaser already holds more than 20% of the share capital of the seller and acquires an additional stake of 20% or more of the target's capital. In case of competing parties or parties in vertical relationship: (a) the acquired interest is equal or higher than 5% of the seller's share capital; or (b) the purchaser already holds more than 5% of the share capital of the seller and acquires an additional stake of 5% or more of the seller's capital.

guidance was CADE's case law, which did not provide a clear solution and was inconsistent at times, as described above.

As a result, the absence of a clear definition of "associative agreements" caused several commercial contracts to be notified to CADE since the enactment of the new Antitrust Law, including licensing and technology transfer agreements, mainly when they contained restrictive provisions, such as exclusivity and non-compete clauses.[39]

CADE thoroughly assessed the concept of "associative agreement" in four cases involving non-exclusive licenses to develop, test, produce and market soy seeds containing the patented technology Intacta RR2 PROTM ("Intacta") owned by Monsanto. Although the four[40] licensing agreements

---

[39] Despite the lack of a legal definition of "associative agreements", some Brazilian scholars have already suggested definitions that could be used as a starting point to interpret Article 90, IV, of the Antitrust Law. Vinicius Marcos de Carvalho understands that "associative agreements" should be defined as "(...) long-term agreements in which parties have an incentive to cooperate for the success of their business". Vinicius Marques de Carvalho. Agreements and Competition Enforcement: The Choice Between Preventive and Repressive Channels, 39, *in* Barry Haunk, (editor). *International Antitrust Law & Policy*, New York: Fordham University School of Law, 2014. According to Eduardo Caminati Anders, Leopoldo Pagotto and Vicente Bagnoli, "associative agreements presumes the sharing of information, facilities, research and development, marketing, thereby affecting the behavior of the contracting parties in the market or between the contracting parties and third parties, without any relationship of property or economic reliance". Eduardo Caminati Anders; Leopoldo Pagoto; Vicente Bagnoli (Coord.). *Comentários à Nova Lei de Defesa da Concorrência: Lei n.º12,529, de 30 de novembro de 2011*, 300. Forense, Rio de Janeiro; Método, São Paulo, 2012. Calixto Salomão Filho, "the theory of the organizational agreement begins with the principle that the general theory of the agreements must be divided into two main types: (i) associative agreements and (ii) exchange agreements. Associative agreements have as their nucleus the creation of the organization. Conversely, exchange agreements have as their main purpose the assignment of subjective rights". Calixto Salomão Filho. *O novo Direito societário*, 44-45, Malheiros, São Paulo, 2006.

[40] CADE, Monsanto do Brasil Ltda., Syngenta Proteção de Cultivos Ltda. Reporting Commissioner Marcos Paulo Veríssimo (08012.002870/2012-38) (Dec. 23, 2013); CADE, Monsanto do Brasil Ltda., Nidera Sementes Ltda. Reporting Commissioner (08012.006706/2012-08) (Dec. 23, 2013); CADE, Monsanto do Brasil Ltda., Cooperativa Central de Pesquisa Agrícola. Reporting Commissioner Alessandro Serafin Octaviani Luis (08700.003898/2012-34) (Dec. 23, 2013); CADE, Monsanto

were notified under the former competition law, they were jointly reviewed by CADE after the new Competition Agreement came into effect. These filings resulted in an interesting debate on how "associative agreements" should be defined and also in which circumstances licensing arrangements could be deemed "associative" in nature, even though they had been reviewed under the old rules.

Because the licenses did not contain any exclusivity provision, there were doubts as to whether or not they should be considered "associative agreements", which could either result in the dismissal of the cases or in the assessment of the merits.

In the Merger Filing involving Monsanto and Syngenta Proteção de Cultivos Ltda. ("Syngenta"),[41] Reporting Commissioner Marcos Paulo Veríssimo recognized the pro-competitive nature of technology transfer agreements and sustained that these arrangements should not be subject to mandatory filing, because: (i) potential competition concerns would arise from the abuse of patent right, which the authority may investigate *ex post*, through repressive and investigative tools provided by law, (ii) from the legal standpoint, non-exclusive transfer technology agreements cannot be deemed an "economic concentration", and (iii) requiring the submission of this type of contracts would result in the illegality of several others that CADE has never reviewed.

Commissioner Ana Frazão backed Veríssimo's opinion, claiming that the specifications of non-exclusive technology transfer agreements render them different from "associative agreements", since these arrangements are not aimed at creating a common undertaking or even parallel behavior. Still according to Frazão, mere cooperation or collaboration is not enough to classify it as an "associative agreement", but rather, the level and type of such cooperation/collaboration.

Frazão sustained that non-exclusive licensing agreements could be classified as long-term commutative agreements, as one party simply grants the right to use its IP upon the payment of royalties to the other. According to Frazão, this type of arrangement does not entail joint undertaking, nor

---

do Brasil Ltda., Don Mario Sementes Ltda. Reporting Commissioner Alessandro Serafin Octaviani Luis (08700.003937/2012-01) (Sept. 03, 2013).

41 CADE, Monsanto do Brasil Ltda. Syngenta Proteção de Cultivos Ltda., *supra* note 31.

common organization, as each party performs it individually, at its own risk, with no interference of other parties.[42-43]

However, in the three other Merger Filings,[44] Reporting Commissioner Alessandro Octaviani defended that technology transfer agreements should always be subject to merger control review, since the "first duty of the competition authorities is to protect conditions for competition and that it would be improper to grant mass exemptions from notification of transactions". The Reporting Commissioner also mentioned the asymmetry of information in biotechnology sectors, which would confirm the need for notification to CADE.[45]

After a detailed analysis of the four Merger Filings, Commissioner Eduardo Pontual Ribeiro identified that although none of the technology transfer agreements contained express exclusivity provisions, they should be acknowledged and reviewed by CADE. His reasoning was not based on Commissioner Octaviani's opinion, but on the fact that the agreements contained licensing and royalty restrictions leading to the creation of a "common undertaking" between the contracting parties, thereby conferring "associative" features to the license agreements. The contractual provisions established a compensation mechanism for the licensees based on sales of the Intacta product and on the sales of certified seeds of Monsanto's competitors. If a licensee chooses to expand its production by also using a patent from a competing product, the compensation from what has been produced with Intacta technology would be reduced. Therefore, the

42 Finally, she concluded by stating that despite the fact that such agreement could lead to external control situations, the possibility of exercising such external control – which could entail a modification in the market structure and therefore a concentration – does not necessarily mean that such exercise will indeed take place, and this mere possibility would not be sufficient to entail the obligation of a pre-merger control.

43 Commissioner Ana Frazão later rectified her opinion to add to Commissioner Pontual's prevailing opinion.

44 CADE, Monsanto do Brasil Ltda. and Nidera Sementes Ltda, *supra* note 31.; CADE, Monsanto do Brasil Ltda. Cooperativa Central de Pesquisa Agrícola, *supra* note 40; and, CADE, Monsanto do Brasil Ltda., Don Mario Sementes Ltda, *supra* note 40).

45 Commissioner Octaviani later rectified his opinion to add to Commissioner Pontual's prevailing opinion.

transaction would only be economically attractive if Monsanto's competitor offset the offer by paying for the correspondent profit reduction.

Moreover, Commissioner Eduardo Pontual Ribeiro pointed out that Monsanto's incentive system would have the potential to reduce the interest of licensees using Intacta soybean technologies to develop new technologies. As a result, the licensing restrictions created mechanisms enabling Monsanto to influence the commercial decisions of its licensees, thereby raising significant barriers to entry in the upstream market of the licensed technology for the production of transgenic soybean.

In the end, the four transactions were cleared on the merits, subject to the modification of all clauses that allowed Monsanto to control its licensees' commercial decisions.

This case has shown that even after the new Antitrust Law became effective, CADE's Commissioners continued to divide opinions as to whether or not technology transfer agreements should be deemed "associative agreements" subject to merger control.

In a Merger Filing[46] involving a technology transfer agreement notified under the new competition rules, CADE had another opportunity to evaluate under which circumstances licensing arrangements should be deemed "associative agreements", pursuant to Article 90, item IV, of the Antitrust Law. This case concerned an arrangement whereby Monsanto would license its Intacta technology to Bayer S.A. on a non-exclusive basis, similarly to the four cases mentioned above.

When assessing the filing, the CADE's General Superintendence ("GS"), which is in charge of the initial review of merger cases, decided that the filing should be dismissed without review on the merits, as technology transfer agreements are not reportable under the new Antitrust Law in the absence of provisions that could grant influence to one party over another.

More specifically, the GS concluded that licensing agreements with no exclusivity provision are not subject to mandatory notification, as long as they do not contain: (i) non-compete clauses, or any other provision capable of restricting competition; (ii) clauses that imply transfer of assets; (iii) corporate links of any kind; or (iv) changes in the decision-making

46 CADE, *Monsanto do Brasil Ltda., Bayer S.A.* Reporting Commissioner Alessandro Octaviani Luis. (08700.004957/2013-72) (Jan. 28, 2014).

bodies of the companies involved in the transaction. In addition, the GS made a very clear statement that this type of agreement (not containing restrictive provisions) is only a means of market de-concentration, as it allows the entry of new players in the market through technology dissemination, for which reason such contracts are not included in the list of reportable transactions of Article 90 of the Antitrust Law.

Nevertheless, CADE's Tribunal overruled GS's decision on the grounds that licensing agreements with no exclusivity clauses are still reportable under the new Antitrust Law if "associative" features are embedded in the contract.

After assessing the case, Reporting Commissioner Alessandro Octaviani found that although there is no express exclusivity provision in the licensing agreement, the agreement contained a mechanism for the creation, maintenance and expansion of licensor's control over the licensee, provisions that transcend or denature the characteristic of a typical technology license.[47]

He also found that certain clauses in the license agreement would harm potential market entrants and limit the choices available to growers and others in the industry.[48] In addition, the mechanism for the collection of royalties established profit and risk sharing between licensor and licensee, in such a way that Monsanto could have access to Bayer's sensitive commercial information in order to monitor its accomplishment. Since

---

47 According to Commissioner Octaviani, the form of an arrangement is not relevant for the purposes of antitrust analysis, but its actual effects in a given relevant market. To back this understanding, he concluded the following: "(…) I understand that a decision on whether the present transaction must be acknowledged, as much as any other technology transfer agreement, relies upon a more detailed antitrust evaluation about the actual market under assessment, about the specific contractual arrangement, and thus cannot rely upon fanciful names of agreements that do not match with their stipulated content and, even less, upon "general rules" on alleged harmlessness of certain practices which have no empirical support or subsist a minimally detailed probe". Free translation of excerpts of the opinion issued by the Reporting Commissioner Alessandro Octaviani in CADE, *Monsanto do Brasil Ltda., Bayer S.A., supra* note 46.

48 The agreement contained terms of use, distribution and indemnification that Bayer must impose on the users of Monsanto's technology. The Reporting Commissioner believed such terms constituted unlawful barriers to entry in the market.

every agent that acts or may act in Intacta soybean's production chain is registered, Monsanto could map out the commercial relationship between them and have access to information that lacked any direct relation with the production and sale of Intacta soybean.

Finally, Commissioner Octaviani concluded that the licensing arrangement was subject to mandatory filing because certain clauses transformed it into an "associative agreement" by providing: (i) common commercial interests; (ii) profit and risk sharing; and (iii) coordination of the parties' activities by means of a common undertaking. He also considered that the agreement could be deemed as an acquisition of control, as its provisions would allow Monsanto to exercise external control over Bayer's strategic activities. As a result, the provisions contained in the licensing agreement could increase the licensor's control over the licensee and improperly raise the market power Monsanto already had in the transgenic soy market.

CADE's Tribunal cleared the transaction on the merits, subject to the exclusion of all clauses that provided for Monsanto's external control of over Bayer, including the rights of first refusal granted to Monsanto in the event of Bayer's potential acquisition of related companies in the soybean market.

Moreover, because of the very specific features of biotechnology markets and also of Monsanto's licensing arrangements – which transcend a typical technology transfer agreement –, the Monsanto cases may not serve as a reliable precedent to evaluate the circumstances under which a license agreement could be deemed "associative agreement" subject to merger control.

In practical terms, the uncertainty surrounding this matter remained unchanged after the new Antitrust Law came into effect, as the absence of a clear definition of "associative agreements" prevents economic agents from evaluating which types of agreements should be notified. The issue is even worse when it comes to technology transfer agreements, as the presence of contractual restrictions is generally necessary to protect the economic value of the licensed IP and also to stimulate the transfer of technology in the first place.

CADE Resolution 10/2014, which provides for the definition of "associative agreements" and clarifies the criteria for their notification to CADE, was supposedly a solution for this issue, though its broad and confusing terms have failed to provide a clear guidance, as shown below.

D. *CADE Resolution 10/2014 Regulating the Notification of "Associative Agreements" and Its Impact on Technology Transfer Agreements*

In order to clarify the concept of "associative agreements" and also define criteria for the notification of these arrangements, CADE approved Resolution 10, of November 4, 2014, which came into effect on January 15, 2015 ("Resolution 10/2014"). As shown below, the wording of Resolution 10/2014 seems to have incorporated the concepts and tests relied upon by CADE to define "associative agreements" in the merger control case regarding the licensing agreement entered into by Monsanto and Bayer.[49]

According to Article 2 of Resolution 10/2014, "associative agreements" are defined as any contract: (i) whose term exceeds two (2) years; and (ii) in which there is horizontal or vertical cooperation, or a sharing of risks that results in an interdependence relationship between the contracting parties (i.e., entities directly involved in the transaction and their respective economic groups).

In addition, the new regulation clarifies, in Paragraph One, that the horizontal or vertical cooperation or sharing of risk resulting in an interdependence relationship will be presumed in agreements in which the contracting parties or their economic groups:

(i) are horizontally related in the object of the agreement whenever the combined market shares in the relevant market affected by the agreement is equal to or higher than 20%; or

(vi) are vertically related in the object of the agreement whenever one of the parties has at least 30% of market share in a vertically related market affected by the agreement and at least one of the following conditions is present: (ii.1) the agreement sets forth a sharing of profits or of losses between the parties; or (ii.2) an exclusivity relationship arises out of the agreement.

Finally, with regard to agreements executed for less than two years, Resolution 10/2014 clarifies in Paragraph Three of Article 2 that once the

[49] *See* CADE, *Monsanto do Brasil Ltda., Bayer S.A., supra* note 46.

turnover thresholds are met, it must be submitted to CADE when, upon its renewal, the two-year term is reached or exceeded.

Although CADE issued Resolution 10/2014 to bring a solution to the uncertainty caused by the lack of a clear definition of "associative agreements", its wording is vague, incomplete and confusing with regard to specific concepts, such as "*sharing of risks*", "*sharing of profits and losses*", "*interdependence relationship*", "*exclusivity relationship*", which could give rise to doubts as to whether or not a given agreement should be notified.

Therefore, as long as CADE does not issue any decision in which is provides clear definitions of such terms, or any regulations or an amendment to Resolution 10/2014, legal uncertainty as to the notification of "associative agreements" will remain.

In any case, the positive side of the new regulation is the market share ceilings, which, much like the US and EU guidelines and regulations, serve the purpose of safe harbors, thereby providing greater legal certainty to the general public by exempting a great number of agreements that are incapable of raising competition concerns from mandatory notification.

In relation to technology transfer agreements, Resolution 10/2014 did not bring any rules or exemptions to deal with the specific features of these agreements. Thus, a possible means to interpret the provisions of the Resolution 10/2014 is by relying upon the US and EU guidelines on IP licensing and technology transfer agreements, which CADE has done so far with respect to other matters. These guidelines may shed a light on how CADE should assess licensing arrangements that could potentially be deemed "associative agreements", within the meaning of the new regulation.

Therefore, in assessing a given licensing agreement to verify whether or not it must be notified to CADE, the very first step is checking if the turnover thresholds of the Antitrust Law are met and if the arrangement has at least a two-year term. If that is the case, the second step is verifying whether the parties are horizontally or vertically related in the object of the agreement, i.e., whether the agreement is entered by competitors in the same relevant market, or by non-competitors active in different levels of a given production chain. The distinction between horizontal agreements (between competitors) and vertical agreements (between non-competitors) is crucial to assess the market share ceilings provided for in the Resolution 10/2014.

E. *Review of Horizontal Licensing Agreements*

As may be observed in the practice of the antitrust authorities in the US and the EU, identifying the nature of the relationship between the parties as horizontal or vertical in licensing agreements is usually more complex than in other cases. This is so because the parties can be competitors and non-competitors at the same time, depending on the relevant markets affected by the agreement, and in each case one should consider: (i) relevant markets for the products affected by the arrangements;[50] (ii) markets for technology;[51] (ii) or markets for research and development (innovation markets).[52] Therefore, the parties may be competitors in the relevant product market, but may not compete in the technology market, and vice-versa, which renders the definition of the relationship as horizontal or vertical a tougher task for the parties.

In this respect, the foreign experience may be used to facilitate the assessment on the nature of the parties' relationship. According to the US Guidelines, when assessing a licensing agreement, the authorities will treat

50 A restraint in a licensing agreement may have competitive effects in markets for final or intermediate products covered by the licensed technology, or it may have effects upstream, in markets for products that are used as inputs, along with the intellectual property, to the production of other products. *See* US DEPARTAMENT OF JUSTICE & FEDERAL TRADE COMMISSION, *Antitrust Guidelines for the Licensing of Intellectual Property* (1995), *supra* note 6, at. item 3.2.1.

51 Technology markets consist of the licensed technology and its close substitutes, i.e., the technologies or products that are close enough substitutes significantly to constrain the exercise of market power with respect to the intellectual property that is licensed. When rights to IP are marketed separately from the products in which they are used, the authorities may rely on technology markets to assess the competitive effects of a licensing arrangement. . *See* US DEPARTAMENT OF JUSTICE & FEDERAL TRADE COMMISSION, *Antitrust Guidelines for the Licensing of Intellectual Property* (1995), *supra* note 6, at. Item 3.2.2.

52 An innovation market consists of the research and development directed to specific new or improved products or processes, and the close substitutes for that research and development. The close substitutes are research and development efforts, technologies, and goods that significantly constrain the exercise of market power with respect to the relevant research and development, for example by limiting the ability and incentive of a hypothetical monopolist to retard the pace of research and development. *See* US DEPARTAMENT OF JUSTICE & FEDERAL TRADE COMMISSION, *Antitrust Guidelines for the Licensing of Intellectual Property* (1995), *supra* note 6, at. Item 3.2.3.

the relationship between a licensor and its licensees as horizontal when they would have been actual or potential competitors in a given relevant market in the absence of the license agreement.[53] In other words, if the agreement did not exist, the question to be made is whether or not the licensee would be able to compete against licensor in the relevant market affected by the agreement without infringing the IPRs or technology owned by licensor.[54]

In general, cross-licensing is a good example of technology arrangement in which the parties may be horizontally related in the object of the agreement. Thus, one should evaluate if the combined market share of the parties and/or of their respective economic groups reaches the limit of 20%, in which case prior notification will be mandatory.

It is worth noting that Resolution 10/2014 does not require the presence of restrictive provisions in the agreement to be deemed a horizontal "associative agreement". Therefore, a simple license agreement between competitors without any exclusive dealing or non-compete provision, would be deemed as "associative agreement" subject to mandatory notification to CADE, only because the parties' combined market share reaches or exceeds 20%.

This means that irrespective of the existence of "horizontal cooperation" or "sharing of risks that result in an interdependence relationship between the contracting parties", the wording of the Resolution 10/2014 suggests that a mere license agreement that does not necessarily entail modifications in the market structure will require a filing with CADE.[55]

---

53 *See* US Department of Justice & Federal Trade Commission, *Antitrust Guidelines for the Licensing of Intellectual Property* (1995), *supra* note, at. Item 3.3

54 This criterion to identify horizontal relations may be difficult to analyze, especially if the parties have chosen the license as an alternative for a lawsuit for infringement of IPR. The infringement proceeding is precisely the result of an uncertainty as to whether or not the possibility exists to legally compete with the licensor, i.e., without infringing licensor's IPRs. Relevant points to assist in the definition of a relationship as horizontal include checking: (i) if the licensee has the technical capacity and the necessary means to enter the market without the licensing agreement; (ii) if evidence has been produced that the licensee had any intention of entering the relevant market in the absence of the licensing agreement of the case; and (iii) if the licensee could have been prevented from entering the relevant market by the licensor that owns the IPR.

55 It is worth mentioning that such filing would probably have to be submitted under

In fact, in the absence of any licensing restriction, a technology transfer agreement between competitors is unlikely to raise any competition concerns and therefore should not be deemed "associative" in nature.

For instance, a cross-license agreement between competitors whereby either party licenses its patent to the other, should be presumably pro-competitive and efficiency-enhancing in the absence of any contractual restrictions, especially when the arrangement entails the licensing of blocking patents. In this respect, a patent "blocks" another when the second cannot be used without infringing the first patent. A good example is an improvement on a patented machine that may be blocked by the patent on the machine. Therefore, a cross-licensing between the two patent holders may serve the purpose of clearing the blocking relationship between the parties, thereby promoting the development of incremental innovation and avoiding possible infringement litigation costs.[56]

However, until CADE clarifies this issue by means of an amendment to Resolution 10/2014 or the interpretation of its provisions, any licensing agreement between competitors with a combined market share of at least 20%, which exceeds a two-year term will be subject to mandatory notification, as long as the parties involved meet the turnover thresholds.

F. *Assessing Vertical Licensing Agreements*

The identification of a vertical relation is usually easier to assess, as most licensing agreements are vertical in nature. According to the US Guidelines, an IP or technology license will be vertical when complementary production factors are combined by parties that are not competitors, such

---

the ordinary filing form, which requires a large amount of detailed information from the parties. This is so because CADE Resolution 02/2012 determines that horizontal transactions that result in total market share above 20% are not eligible to fast-track proceeding and, thus, must be submitted under the ordinary proceeding.

56 Suppose Company A obtains a patent on an improvement of Company B's patented invention, then Company A will not be able to use such improvement without infringing Company B's patent. Company B also would not be able to use the improvement without infringing A's patent. Therefore, in many instances, owners of blocking patents cross license each other and that is an ordinary type of arrangement in the day-to-day business of companies active in innovation and technology markets.

as, for instance: (i) when the primary business of the licensor is limited to research and development activities and the licensee, as manufacturer, acquires the license to use the technology developed by the licensor; (ii) when the licensor is component manufacturer owning IPRs in a product that the licensee manufactures by combining the component with other inputs; or (iii) when the licensor manufactures a product and the licensee distributes and sells the product.

In such cases, one should check if at least one of the parties (and/or its respective economic group) has a market share of at least 30% of the relevant market affected by the agreement, as established in Resolution 10/2014. If such market share threshold is reached, the next step will be checking whether the licensing agreement: (a) entails the sharing of profits or losses between the contracting parties; or (b) results in an exclusivity relationship.

As regards the first condition, because Resolution 10/2014 is silent as to the definition of the concept of "sharing of profits and losses", one could initially infer that all licensing agreements presume the sharing of profits, since royalties are normally calculated on the net sales revenues of the licensee in the commercial exploitation of the products embodying the licensed IP or technology. It is undeniable that any royalty payment scheme is actually a means by which licensee shares the economic gains arising out of the use of the licensed IP or technology with licensor.

However, this interpretation is incorrect and should not prevail, as the mere payment of royalties based on the licensee's net sales is not sufficient to infer the presence of "sharing of profits". The concept of "sharing of profits and losses" should be construed as a business model entailing actual "*vertical cooperation*" or the "*sharing of risks resulting in an interdependence relationship between the contracting parties*", as per the wording of Resolution 10/2014.

Therefore, a simple vertical licensing agreement (without any contractual restrictions) containing a royalty payment scheme based on the licensee's net revenues does not require any cooperation between licensor and licensee, or involves any risk sharing, as there is no interdependence relationship between the contracting parties. Under this type of agreement, the licensee relies on the licensed technology to perform its day-to-day business, thereby assuming all risks involved in its activities.

Moreover, as can be observed in the Monsanto/Bayer case, CADE considered the sharing of profits and losses in the context of risk sharing between the contracting parties, as well as common commercial interests and coordination of the parties' activities by means of a common undertaking.[57] These features, which are present in "associative agreements" according with CADE's case law, go far beyond those of a typical licensing arrangement.

In relation to exclusivity relationship (i.e., the second condition), as has been mentioned above, exclusivity clauses are quite common in technology transfer agreements. However, Resolution 10/2014 neither clarifies the concept of "exclusivity relationship", nor defines which types of exclusivity should be taken into account in the assessment of vertical arrangements.

As has been referred to in section 2, a licensing agreement may involve two different types of exclusivity. First, the licensor may grant one or more *exclusive licenses*, which restrict the right of the licensor to license others and possibly also to use the technology itself. In general, an exclusive license may raise antitrust concerns only if the licensor and its licensees are in a horizontal relationship, as the arrangement may give rise to unlawful market allocation between competitors.[58]

The second form of exclusivity – exclusive dealing – arises when a license prevents or restrains the licensee from licensing, selling, distributing, using or even developing competing technologies. Exclusivity may be achieved by an explicit provision in the licensing arrangement or by other provisions such as compensation terms or other economic incentives, such as those observed in the Monsanto cases. This type of restraint may result in anticompetitive effects by foreclosing access to, or increasing competitors' costs of obtaining, important inputs, or facilitate coordination to raise price or reduce output, though they also may have pro-competitive

---

57 *See* CADE, *Monsanto do Brasil Ltda., Bayer S.A., supra* note 6, at 46, opinion of the Reporting Commissioner Alessandro Octaviani Luis.

58 *See* US Departament of Justice & Federal Trade Commission, *Antitrust Guidelines for the Licensing of Intellectual Property* (1995), *supra* note 6, at. Item 4.1.2. On the same token, according with the EC Regulation on Technology Transfer Agreement, an exclusive vertical licensing arrangement is presumably pro-competitive: "(...) exclusive licensing agreements between non-competing undertakings often fall outside the scope of Article 101(1)."

effects.[59] As showed above, most of the antitrust issues CADE raised when reviewing technology transfer agreements were related to exclusive dealing provisions.

In the absence of a clear definition of "exclusivity relationship" in Resolution 10/2014, both types of exclusivity included in a vertical licensing arrangement must be taken into account when evaluating whether or not the agreement is subject to mandatory notification, at least until CADE clarifies how such "exclusivity relationship" should be interpreted.

Therefore, based on the current wording of Resolution 10/2014, even an exclusive trademark license agreement, which is a trivial commercial arrangement generally incapable of raising any competition concerns, would be reportable whenever the other thresholds are met. However, such an exclusive license agreement should never be deemed "associative", as it does not entail any vertical cooperation or the sharing of risks resulting in an interdependence relationship between the parties.

As such, when it comes to licensing arrangements, CADE should limit the concept of "exclusivity relationship" to license agreements containing exclusive dealing provisions, as this type of restriction included in a vertical arrangement is susceptible of producing anticompetitive effects when any of the parties hold market power, which in itself could justify its inclusion under the concept of "associative agreement".

G. Dealing with Contract Renewal and Agreements with Indefinite Term

Resolution 10/2014 clarifies that agreements with a term of less than two years are subject to mandatory notification when they are renewed for a term that reaches or exceeds two (2) years.[60] However, the new regulation is

---

59 For example, a technology transfer agreement that prevents the licensee from dealing with other technologies may encourage the licensee to develop and market the licensed technology or specialized applications of that technology.

60 In CADE, *Monsanto do Brasil Ltda., Iharabras S.A Indústrias Químicas, supra* note 35, former CADE Chairman Arthur Badin, fixed a five-year term for supply agreements (along with other conditions, detailed in footnote 65) as a parameter for evaluation of necessity of submission of such contracts. This term was based on CADE's Binding Precedent No. 5, which establishes that non-compete clauses of up to 5 (five) years are licit for the protection of the business that was sold. He believed it to be a safe parallel for comparison since it was based on retrictive clauses.

silent as to the moment in which a filing must be submitted in these cases, if upon the execution of the initial agreement that may be renewed for a term exceeding two years, or only at the time of the effective renewal.

To be on the safe side until CADE clarifies this issue, the parties may choose to notify when the initial agreement is executed. In this case, however, the parties would face the risk of CADE dismissing the filing on the grounds that notification should occur at the time of renewal, in which case the parties would have to notify again later on, bearing with double the cost of the filing. On the other hand, if the parties choose to notify by the time of renewal, then they would run the risk of gun jumping, as the agreement would be effective by the time of notification and the new suspensory regime prohibits the consummation of transactions prior to CADE's approval.

This demonstrates another flaw and inconsistency of Resolution 10/2014 in relation to the Antitrust Law: though the wording of the resolution seems to require the notification only upon renewal, the notification of an agreement in full force and effect would be incompatible with the suspensory regime provided by the Antitrust Law, unless in the presence of a clear legal exception.

Finally, the Resolution is also silent as to whether or not agreements executed for an indefinite term are subject to mandatory notification. Whether an indefinite term agreement could be deemed economic concentration is questionable, as the parties have the right terminate the arrangement without cause upon prior notice and most of the times without significant costs. The possibility of an immediate termination without burden to the parties is incompatible with the idea of a long-lasting change in the market structure.

On the other hand, one could argue that an agreement executed for an indefinite term should only be notified at the time it reaches or exceeds two years. However, in order to be on the safe side, it is recommendable to notify the agreement upon its execution.

In any case, CADE should also clarify this point so as to avoid uncertainty and unpredictability.

Conclusion

One of the main goals of the new Antitrust Law was to remedy the uncertainty of the broad wording of Article 54 of the previous competition law regime – Law 8,884/94 – by defining a clear concept of economic concentration by means of a list of transactions subject to mandatory notification included in Article 90 of the new law.

However, though Article 90 of the Antitrust Law has unquestionably improved the definition of "concentration" when compared to the old competition regime, it failed to provide a clear definition of what should be considered as an "associative agreement". As a result, the absence of a clear definition of "associative agreements" caused several commercial contracts to be notified to CADE since the enactment of the new Antitrust Law, including licensing and technology transfer agreements, mainly when they contained restrictive provisions, such as exclusivity and non-compete provisions.

In order to clarify the concept of "associative agreements" and define criteria for the notification of these arrangements, CADE approved Resolution 10/2014. Nevertheless, although CADE issued Resolution 10/2014 to settle the uncertainty caused by the lack of a clear definition of "associative agreements", its wording is vague, incomplete and confusing with regard to specific concepts. Moreover, the new regulation did not establish any rules or exemptions to deal with the specific features of technology transfer agreements.

In fact, the wording of Resolution 10/2014 seems to have incorporated the concepts and tests CADE relied upon to define "associative agreements" in the merger control case regarding the licensing agreement entered into by Monsanto and Bayer, which contains very specific provisions to deal with specific features of the transgenic soybean market. Therefore, CADE relied on a very specific and exceptional case to design rules and concepts applicable to "associative agreements" in general.

In view of the foregoing, although Resolution 10/2014 represents progress in terms of criteria to notify the so-called "associative agreements", creating market share ceilings that will certainly reduce the number of agreements subject to prior notification to CADE, its application to licensing agreements may raise doubts and uncertainties for the contracting parties. In addition, it may unreasonably increase bureaucracy, especially considering that international technology transfer agreements must also be registered with INPI in order to enable the remittance of royalties abroad and tax deductions.

There is no doubt that, in the ideal world, licensing agreements should only be reviewed *a posteriori*, in the antitrust enforcement against anticompetitive behaviors, similarly to the approach undertaken in the US and EU. This is so because the prior control of market structures does not enable an evaluation of the actual effects of such agreements in a given relevant market, or because the agreements present peculiar characteristics that make them be presumably pro-competitive and beneficial to innovation and technical development.

In any case, CADE should take action to improve the concept of "associative agreements" and the criteria to notify such arrangements on the short run, and also develop specific criteria and analytic tools that meet the specific features of licensing agreements, as these arrangements are quite relevant for economic growth and for the competitiveness of Brazilian companies in international markets.

Until CADE clarifies the vague terms used in Resolution 10/2014, legal uncertainty will remain and the general public will continue to have doubts to evaluate whether or not a given commercial agreement should be deemed an "associative agreement" subject to pre-merger control. Consequently, unnecessary filings will continue to be notified to CADE, thus increasing costs for both the government and the economic agents.

Bibliography

ABA Section of Antitrust Law. *Intellectual Property and Antitrust Handbook*. ABA Publishing, 2007.

Alden F. Abbott. Intellectual Property Licensing and Antitrust Policy: A Comparative Perspective. *Law and Policy International Business*, v. 34, n.º 4, 2003.

Calixto Salomão Filho. *Direito concorrencial: as condutas*. São Paulo: Malheiros (2003).

______. *Direito concorrencial: as estruturas*. São Paulo: Malheiros (2007).

______. *O novo direito societário* ("The New Corporate Law"), São Paulo: Malheiros (2006).

CARL SHAPIRO. Navigating the Patent Thicket: Cross Licenses, Patent Pools, and Standard-Setting, in: JAFFE, Adam B.; JOSH LERNER; SCOTT STERN (Ed.). *Innovation Policy and the Economy*, v. 1. Cambridge, MA: The MIT Press (2001).

EDUARDO CAMINATI ANDERS; VICENTE BAGNOLI; LEOPOLDO PAGOTTO (coord.). *Comentários à Nova Lei de Defesa da Concorrência*. Método: São Paulo, 2012.

EDUARDO MOLAN GABAN; JULIANA OLIVEIRA DOMINGUES. *Direito Antitruste*. 3. ed. São Paulo: Saraiva (2012).

EUROPEAN COMMISSION. *Commission Notice: Guidelines on the Application of Article 81 of the EC Treaty to Technology Transfer Agreements* (OJ C 101, 27.4.2004). Avaliable at http://eur-lex.europa.eu/LexUriServ/LexUriServ.do?uri=OJ:C:2004:101:0002:0042:EN:PDF.

HERBERT J. HOVENKAMP. Antitrust and Innovation: Where We Are and Where We Should Be Going, in: *Antitrust Law Journal*, v. 77, Issue 3 (2011).

______. *Federal Antitrust Policy: The Law of Competition and its Practice*, Third Edition, Saint Paul, Minn.: Thomson West, (2005).

JULIANA L. B VIEGAS. Contratos Típicos de Propriedade Industrial: Contratos de Cessão e de Licenciamento de Marcas e Patentes; Licenças Compulsórias, in MANOEL J. PEREIRA DOS SANTOS; WILSON PINHEIRO JABUR. *Contratos de Propriedade Industrial e Novas Tecnologias*. São Paulo: Saraiva, 2007 (Série GVlaw).

LAWRENCE A. SULLIVAN; WARREN S. GRIMES. *The Law of Antitrust: An Integrated Handbook*, Saint Paul, Minn.: West Group, (2000).

LOUIS KAPLOW. A Note on Antitrust Issues in the Licensing of Intellectual Property. *Harvard Law School John M. Olin Center for Law, Economics and Business Discussion Paper Series*. Paper 217, (1997). Available at http://lsr.nellco.org/cgi/viewcontent.cgi?article=1005&context=harvard_olin.

LUCAS BARRIOS. *O Contrato Internacional de Transferência de Tecnologia e o Direito da Concorrência no Brasil: análise à luz da recente jurisprudência do CADE*, in: Revista de Direito da Concorrência, No. 4, November 2014.

LUCIANO BENETTI TIMM. Contrato internacional de transferência de tecnologia no Brasil: interseção da propriedade intelectual com o direito antitruste, in: LUCIANO BENETTI TIMM. Pedro Paranaguá. *Propriedade Intelectual, Antitruste e Desenvolvimento: caso da transferência de tecnologia e do software*. Rio de Janeiro: FGV Direito Rio, 2009.

LUDMILA SOMENSI. *Conhecimento de Contrato de Licenciamento Sem Cláusula de Exclusividade e (In)Definição de Contrato Associativo*. In: Revista do

IBRAC – Direito da Concorrência, Consumo e Comércio Internacional. Vol. 24. (2013).

Mark A. Lemley. *A New Balance Between IP and Antitrust*. John M. Olin Program in Law and Economics Stanford Law School. Working Paper n. 340, April, (2007), available at http://ssrn.com/abstract=980045

Richard Gilbert. *Converging Doctrines? US and EU Antitrust Policy for the Licensing of Intellectual Property* (February (2004). Available at http://ssrn.com/abstract=527762 or http://dx.doi.org/10.2139/ssrn.527762.

Rudolph J. R. Peritz. Competition Policy and Its Implications for Intellectual Property in the United States, in: Steven D. Anderman (Ed.). *The Interface Between Intellectual Property and Competition Policy*, Cambridge University Press, (2007).

Steven Anderman. "The new EC competition law framework for technology transfer and IP licensing", in: Josef Drexl, (Editor). *Research Handbook on Intellectual Property and Competition Law*, Cheltenham, UK: Edward Elgar, 2008.

U.S. Department Of Justice & Federal Trade Commission. *Antitrust Guidelines for the Licensing of Intellectual Property*, 1995.

Vinicius Marques de Carvalho. "Agreements and Competition Enforcement: The Choice Between Preventive and Repressive Channels", in: Barry Haunk (editor). *International Antitrust Law & Policy*, New York: Fordham University School of Law, 2014.

* * *

Chapter VII

REMEDIES IN MERGER CASES: BRAZIL'S RECENT EXPERIENCE

Marcio Dias Soares
Renata Fonseca Zuccolo
João Marcelo Lima

I. Introduction

Brazil became a suspensory jurisdiction on May 29, 2012, when the new Brazilian Antitrust Law[1] introduced a premerger control regime in the country. With this new regime, timing became crucial for the notifying parties, as the closing of transactions subject to mandatory filing in Brazil now depends upon obtaining the necessary antitrust approval from the Brazilian antitrust authority (Administrative Council for Economic Defense or CADE).

Along with this new reality, experience shows a more rigorous and sophisticated approach being taken by CADE, in particular in the context of merger review cases. Complex transactions have faced in-depth investigations that usually involve substantial market tests in the form of both RFIs and discussions with customers and competitors – with a preference to the former –, specific economic analysis led by CADE's Chief Economist team,[2] and, when appropriate, coordination

1 Law 12,529, dated November 30, 2011.

2 CADE is comprised of two divisions: (i) the General Superintendence ("GS"); and

with foreign antitrust authorities, in particular from Europe and the United States.

Such more sophisticated approach has also been seen in the context of remedies negotiations. Since the entering into force of the new Brazilian Antitrust Law, experience shows that remedies negotiations have become more complex in Brazil, with the notifying parties being required to carefully assess the most appropriate stage of the process to approach the authority with a remedy proposal, taking into consideration several variables that come into play – including, but not limited to timing constraints relative to the notified transaction, types of remedies appropriate to address the concerns expressed by the authority, and with whom to start the negotiation (i.e. with the General Superintendent or with the Tribunal directly?). All these variables may change from one transaction to another, and deserve a very careful look already at an early stage of the process, as this can well determine the best way to handle the case with CADE.

The lack of a formal procedure in the regulation or guidelines for negotiations of remedies may indeed create uncertainties, but experience shows that, in general, CADE is prepared to move quickly and engage in a constructive dialogue towards a negotiated outcome. To date, the Brazilian antitrust authority has blocked only one transaction under the new Brazilian premerger control regime, i.e., since May 2012.[3]

At the same time, experience shows a growing preference for structural remedies, many times coupled with behavioral commitments, rather than simple standalone behavioral remedies. There is also a growing trend towards enhancing enforcement mechanisms, with CADE determining the use of monitoring and divestiture trustees – influenced in particular by the European Commission's practice in that respect –, as well as provisions regulating the situations under which CADE may determine that the notified transaction shall be unwound.

(ii) the Tribunal. There is also an Economic Department, led by a Chief Economist, which is responsible for carrying out economic market tests upon request by the GS and/or the Tribunal.

3 Rejection of Braskem deal shows need for companies to address Brazil regulator's concerns (Nov. 13, 2014), *available at*: http://www.mlex.com/Brazil/Content.aspx?ID=610218.

The purpose of this paper is to review the recent decisional practice regarding remedies negotiations in light of the applicable legal framework in Brazil, discussing specific trends that may be inferred from such cases.

II. Legal Framework Applicable to the Negotiation of Remedies in Brazil

As mentioned above, CADE is comprised of two divisions: (i) the GS, and (ii) the Tribunal. The GS, which comprises a General Superintendent and two Deputy Superintendents who coordinate and oversee the work done by case handlers organized in review units, is responsible for the initial review of merger cases and can issue final clearance decisions in relation to transactions that do not raise competition concerns. Whenever the GS concludes that a notified transaction gives rise to competition concerns and cannot be cleared without remedies, the GS must issue a non-binding opinion putting forward the results of its review and indicating the competition concerns that justify the matter being presented to the Tribunal for final decision. The Tribunal is comprised of seven commissioners (one of whom acts as chairman) and it is responsible for issuing final decisions on merger review cases and antitrust investigations.

Merger cases that require remedies have to be necessarily submitted to the Tribunal for a final review and decision. Remedies must be negotiated and approved under a merger control agreement (named ACC). Notifying parties, however, have the right to either negotiate the remedy package in advance with the GS or wait for the matter to be sent to the Tribunal and initiate the negotiation with the Commissioners directly.

There is no specific deadline for the notifying parties to initiate the remedies negotiation at the GS level. From a procedural standpoint, the notifying parties have the right to approach the GS with a remedy proposal since the beginning of the process – including during pre-notification talks – until a later stage before the case is ready to be sent onto the Tribunal. In practice, though, notifying parties tend to prefer to wait until the GS reaches its first conclusions – generally around day 90 of the formal review period – to initiate discussions about possible remedies with the GS.

In the event the notifying parties decide to initiate the remedy discussions at the Tribunal level only, the remedy proposal must be presented to the Tribunal within 30 calendar days, counted as from the date on which the GS issued its non-binding opinion sending the matter to the Tribunal for final decision.[4]

Experience shows that the first option (i.e., initiating the negotiation with the GS) tends to be more effective in terms of timing, especially due to the fact that the GS team is already acquainted with the matter when the remedies discussion starts, as such team is initially in charge of reviewing the case. If the notifying parties leave the entire discussion to the Tribunal, a new negotiation team is formed and they naturally require time to become acquainted with the transaction. The type of remedies that the notifying parties intend to offer may also influence the decision between having the negotiation with the GS or letting the matter go to the Tribunal and starting the negotiation at the level of the Tribunal directly.

Unlike other major jurisdictions, such the European Union[5] and the United States,[6] there are no specific regulations or guidelines dealing with

---

4 Article 125 of CADE Resolution No. 1, dated May 29, 2012.

5 In the European Union, the "Commission Notice on remedies acceptable under Council Regulation (EEC) No 139/2004 and under Commission Regulation (EC) No 802/2004" provides a wide array of possible remedies to be implemented in order to address specific antitrust concerns. Such remedies may be classified as follows:

Divestiture of a business to a suitable purchaser: The divested activities must consist of a viable business that, if managed by a suitable purchaser, can compete effectively with the merged entity on a lasting basis and that is divested as a going concern, i.e., without being threatened by bankruptcy and liquidation in the foreseeable future. The business has to include all the assets and personnel which contribute to its current operation or which are necessary to ensure its viability and competitiveness.

Removal of links with competitors: This may include, for example, the termination of distribution agreements with competitors or any other type of agreement resulting in the coordination of certain commercial behaviour, as long as it is ensured that the product of the competitor will also be distributed in the future and exercise effective competitive pressure on the parties.

Other remedies: The Commission recognizes that despite the divestiture of a business and the removal of links with competitors being the preferred remedies, they are not the only possible ways of eliminating certain competition concerns. Access remedies and the termination or alteration of long-term exclusive contracts are cited as examples. The Commission refers to "Access Remedies" as those "foreseeing the granting of access to key infrastructure, networks, key technology, including patents, know-how or other intellectual property rights, and essential

negotiations of remedies in Brazil.[7] There is only one provision in CADE's internal regulation dealing with the matter, but such provision is limited to basic procedural steps and does not discuss substance to any extent. In view of the lack of specific regulation or guidelines, when engaging in remedy discussions, both CADE and the notifying parties tend to rely on past remedy packages that have been accepted by CADE[8] and international experience.[9]

III. Recent Experience: Cases of Remedies under the New Brazilian Premerger Control Regime

The table below provides a list of the matters reviewed under the new Brazilian premerger control regime (up to February 2015) where the

inputs". This access is normally granted to third parties on a non-discriminatory and transparent basis.

6 In the United States, although the matter is not regulated to the extent it is in the European Union, the relevant authorities have published guidelines that aid the notifying parties in negotiating remedies. The Federal Trade Commission (FTC), for example, issued a statement in 2012 aiming to answer frequently asked questions in merger negotiations (*see* Negotiating Merger Remedies: Statement of the Bureau of Competition of the FTC (Jan. 2012), *available at*: http://www.ftc.gov/system/files/attachments/negotiating-merger-remedies/merger-remediesstmt.pdf). Apart from providing information on how remedy packages should be put together to raise the least opposition from the FTC as possible, the document is clear in indicating the agency's preference for structural remedies: "the Commission prefers structural relief in the form of a divestiture to remedy the anticompetitive effects of an unlawful horizontal merger". However, since each merger case is unique, the document alerts that the fact that "the Commission has accepted a particular provision in the past will not on that basis alone be persuasive that the same provision should be accepted in a new matter".

7 That being said, CADE is expected to issue specific guidelines for remedies negotiations in the near future.

8 Since the previous Brazilian Antitrust Law (Law 8,884, dated June 11, 1994), CADE has always published a non-confidential version of the remedy packages accepted in merger cases. This provides notifying parties with a good sense of the types of commitments CADE has previously accepted and help them prepare the appropriate remedies proposal for their particular case.

9 For example, in CADE, *Braskem S.A. and Solvay S.A* (Merger No. 08700.000436/2014-27) (Nov. 6, 2014), Reporting Commissioner Gilvandro Araújo mentioned an OECD recommendation to reinforce the importance of structural remedies in Brazil.

notifying parties had to negotiate remedies in order to obtain the necessary CADE clearance.[10] The table also provides specific information on whether the remedies were negotiated directly with the Tribunal and how long the review period took at the Tribunal.

Merger No.	Review Period at the Tribunal	Was the Deadline Extended?[11]	Merger Clearance Date	Remedies Negotiated Directly with the GS
08700.006437/2012-13 (WP Roaming III S.r.l and Syniverse Holdings, Inc.)	Less than one month	No.	May 22, 2013	Yes.
08700.009882/2012-35 (Munksjö AB and Ahlstrom Corporation)	Less than one month	No.	May 22, 2013	Yes.
08700.005447/2013-12 (Anhanguera Educacional Participação S.A.; Kroton Educacional S.A.)	Approximately five months and a half	Yes.	May 14, 2014	No.
08700.009198/2013-34 (Estácio/TCA)	Approximately two months and a half	No.	May 14, 2014	No.
08700.002372/2014-07 (Cromossomo Participações II S.A. e Diagnósticos da América S.A. Grupo Edson Bueno) [12]	Approximately two months	No.	July 16, 2014	Yes.

10 Cases concerning gun jumping and non-compete clauses are not contemplated in the table above.

11 CADE has up to 240 calendar days to review the notified transaction and issue a final decision. This formal review period may be extended only once, either for additional 60 calendar days, at the request of the notifying parties, or for additional 90 calendar days, by a unilateral decision issued by the Tribunal.

12 The commitments in this case were merely to extend the remedies that had been previously agreed upon in the context of a previous merger case to certain individuals For this reason, this matter will not be discussed in this paper.

Merger No.	Review Period at the Tribunal	Was the Deadline Extended?[11]	Merger Clearance Date	Remedies Negotiated Directly with the GS
08700.010688/2013-83 (Forte Empreendimentos e Participações Ltda.; JBS S.A.; Rodopa Indústria and Comércio de Alimentos Ltda.)	Approximately three months	Yes.	August 20, 2014	No.
08700.000658/2014-40 (Minerva S.A. and BRF S.A.)	Approximately two months and a half	No.	August 20, 2014	No.
08700.009924/2013-19 (INNOVA S.A.; Lírio Albino Parisotto; Petróleo Brasileiro S.A.; Videolar S.A.)	Approximately six months	Yes.	October 2, 2014	No.
08700.007621/2014-42 (Holcim and Lafarge)	Less than one month	No.	December 11, 2014	Yes.
08700.004185/2014-50 (Continental Aktiengesellschaft and Veyance Technologies Inc.)	Approximately two months	Yes.	January 29, 2015	No.
08700.005719/2014-65 (América Latina Logística S.A. and Rumo Logística Operadora Multimodal S.A)	Approximately two months	No.	February 11, 2015	No.
08700.008607/2014-66 (GlaxoSmithKline PLC. and Novartis AG)	Less than one month	No.	February 25, 2015	Yes.

Under the previous Brazilian Antitrust Law, CADE reviewed a number of complex transactions and imposed a wide array of remedies. An example of a case in which CADE negotiated a combination of structural and behavioral remedies is the Sadia/Perdigão[13] case, while

13 CADE, *Perdigão S/A and Sadia S.A* (Merger No. 08012.004423/2009-18) (July 13, 2011).

the Tim/Telefónica[14] case is considered an important case in which behavioral commitments prevailed in the context of minority acquisitions. Amongst cases involving behavioral commitments, there have been agreements not to acquire other companies,[15] to take no actions to oppose new entrants[16] and to address problems with essential facilities in regulated industries.[17]

The experience under the new Brazilian premerger control regime reveals CADE's tendency to prefer structural remedies, sometimes combined with behavioral commitments, as opposed to purely behavioral remedies. This, however, does not mean CADE will not regard standalone behavioral remedies as sufficient to address competitive concerns identified in connection with a given transaction. In three recent cases, CADE only required behavioral remedies: the Innova/Videolar, Estácio/TCA and ALL/ Rumo cases.[18]

---

14 CADE, *Mediobanca – Banca di Credito Finanziario S.p.A; Intensa Sanpaolo S.p.A; Sintonia S/A; Assicurazioni Generali S.p.A; Telefónica S.A.* (Merger No. 53500.012487/2007) (April 28, 2010).

15 CADE, *BDO Auditores Independentes; BDO Consultores Ltda.; KPMG Risk Advisory Services Ltda.* (Merger No. 08012.002689/2011-41) (October 9, 2013).

16 CADE, *Quattor Participações S.A; Petrobras Química S.A; Petróleo Brasileiro S.A and Braskem S.A.* (Merger No. 08012.001205/2010-65) (February 23, 2011).

17 CADE, *Telecomunicações Ltda. and Net Serviços de Comunicações S.A.* (Merger No. 53500.001477/2008) (April 7, 2010). CADE, *Petróleo Brasileiro S/A and Refinaria de Petróleo Ipiranga S.A.* (Merger No. 08012.002820/2007-93) (December 17, 2008). Another interesting case in relation to behavioral commitments is the Oxiteno/American Chemical case (CADE, *Oxiteno S.A. Indústria e Comércio and American Chemical I.C.S.A.* (Merger No. 08700.004083/2012-72) (November 20, 2013). In this case, CADE was mainly concerned that post-merger Oxiteno could abuse its dominant position in the downstream market by foreclosing the access of its competitors to an input called ethoxylated lauric alcohol, that was only produced by Oxiteno in Brazil. This is a commodity product and prices are benchmarked internationally. The Tribunal was actually not concerned with a potential exclusionary strategy by Oxiteno, given that competitors could import this product with a higher price and the level of capacity of Oxiteno would not make such strategy economically viable. It seems that the main goal of the commitments was to give the market a guarantee that Oxiteno would not discriminate against competitors in the downstream market.

18 CADE, *Innova S.A., Videolar S.A. and others.* (Merger No. 08700.009924/2013-19) (October 2, 2014); CADE, *Estácio Participações S.A.and TCA Investimento em Participações Ltda.* (Merger No. 08700.009198/2013-34) (May 14, 2014); and

A. Recent Behavioral Cases

Innova/Videolar Case. Videolar and Innova notified CADE, on November 11, 2013, of the proposed acquisition of Innova's assets by Videolar. Both companies were active in the polystyrene market. The GS challenged the transaction before the Tribunal arguing that entry was unlikely, and that the fact that only one independent rival would remain active in the Brazilian market (besides the merged entity) would not be enough to maintain the competitiveness of the market.[19] The notifying parties engaged in remedies negotiations directly with the Tribunal, and after discussions that lasted for approximately six months, they obtained CADE's approval on October 2, 2014, conditioned upon the following behavioral commitments: *(i)* the parties were prohibited from acquiring or leasing polyethylene plants in Brazil for five years; *(ii)* the parties committed to maintain minimum production levels; *(iii)* the parties agreed to adopt compliance programs for the development of rules to help prevent antitrust violations; *(iv)* the parties agreed to allow CADE to request technical cooperation or hold inspections in any premises; and *(v)* the parties committed to submit to CADE a plan for the effective transfer of efficiency gains to polyethylene consumers.[20]

Estácio/TCA Case. The proposed acquisition of distance-learning company Uniseb by private education company Estácio Participações was filed with CADE on October 14, 2013. The relevant market definition used by CADE to review mergers concerning the distance-learning sector in Brazil segregated in different relevant markets each course per municipality. Based on that approach, CADE identified competition concerns in relation to 20 courses in 9 cities. In order to address the competition concerns raised by CADE, the parties committed to limit the number of student enrollments in the affected locations during four academic semesters, allowing only one school within to group to offer new enrollments in those cities for the problematic courses. Reporting Commissioner Ana Frazão stated at the hearing that such commitment was enough to solve the competition problems identified by CADE during the review, since it created incentives

---

CADE, *América Latina Logística S.A. and Rumo Logística Operadora Multimodal S.A.*, (Merger No. 08700.005719/2014-65) (February 11, 2015).

19 CADE proposes to block Innova Sale to Videolar (Apr. 3, 2014), *available at*: http://www.mlex.com/Brazil/Content.aspx?ID=521364.

20 Innova's aquisition by Videolar approved with restrictions (Oct. 2, 2014), *available at*: http://www.mlex.com/Brazil/Content.aspx?ID=594870.

for third parties to absorb the excess demand not captured by the merged entity in each specific course/city.[21]

ALL/Rumo Case. This case concerned the merger between two logistics operators active in Brazil. The GS issued an opinion recommending the requirement of remedies to the Tribunal as a condition for clearance due to the fact that the proposed transaction could potentially increase the risk of market foreclosure, facilitate access to competitors' privileged information, and favor bundling. The Tribunal took sixty-five days to further review the case and conclude remedy negotiations with the parties. CADE's Chairman Vinicius Marques de Carvalho noted that CADE's decision to require only behavioral remedies was the result of a trade-off analysis that took into account all efficiencies arising from the proposed transaction. According to Reporting Commissioner Gilvandro Vasconcelos Coelho de Araujo:

> *"The best option for the case is the application of mechanisms that will safeguard the efficiencies resulting from eventual implementation of the announced investment plan and, simultaneously, create a disincentive structure against anticompetitive conducts by the new company. Therefore, the measures adopted should be structured based on three complementary logics: transparency, guaranteed access and equality"*.[22]

The behavioral remedies implemented included the new company having to guarantee access to Rumo's competitors to its terminals in the port of Santos, the obligation to meet objective standards for pricing the services provided to competitors, a limitation on the use of logistical assets by companies related to the controlling group and the total separation of the contracts for the provision of each service by merged entity.

B. Recent Structural Cases

WP Roaming/Syniverse matter.[23] This case concerned the proposed acquisition by Syniverse of its rival, MACH, the two largest providers of data

[21] Acquisition of Uniseb by Estacio gets Brazilian antitrust approval with restrictions (May 14, 2014), *available at*: http://www.mlex.com/Brazil/Content.aspx?ID=536498.

[22] CADE approves ALL/Rumo deal with restrictions (Feb. 12, 2015), *available at*: http://www.cade.gov.br/Default.aspx?5aed3ccd27fc13101a27380c2727.

[23] CADE, *WP Roaming III S.à.r.l and Syniverse Holdings, Inc.* (Merger No. 08700.006437/2012-13) (May 22, 2013).

clearance and financial clearance services to mobile operators in Brazil and worldwide. This was the first case in which CADE requested a waiver to the notifying parties to speak to foreign authorities, and in effect coordinated both the review and the remedies negotiations entirely with the European Commission. In view of the dynamics of the markets concerned, and the lack of local assets, the remedy package negotiated with CADE included the creation of a new global player by means of divestments of certain assets, including IP and customer contracts, located abroad. The notifying parties managed to create a single remedy package that addressed the concerns raised by both CADE and the European Commission, thereby avoiding different sets of commitments in Brazil and Europe. The remedy packages and the implementation procedures were virtually the same, both in Brazil and Europe, with CADE making use of trustees and other mechanisms (e.g. suitable buyer requirements and prior approval) to ensure the fulfillment of all the commitments undertaken by the notifying parties.

Munksjö/Ahlstrom Case.[24] This case concerned the combination of Munksjö's and Ahlstrom's label and processing businesses, originating a global leader in specialty paper. Following an in-depth investigation, which was fully coordinated with the European Commission, based on waivers granted by the notifying parties, the GS concluded that the proposed transaction would lead to high concentration levels in the pre-impregnated decorative paper market and in the heavy-weight abrasive paper backings market, since the entry of new players in the market capable of exercising countervailing power over the merged entity was allegedly not likely and foreseeable. After intensive negotiations with both CADE and the European Commission, the notifying parties reached a remedy package that envisaged the divestment of operational assets located outside Brazil that were considered by CADE as sufficient to address the competitive concerns identified in Brazil. Also in this case, the notifying parties managed to create a single remedy package that addressed the concerns raised by both CADE and the European Commission, thereby avoiding having different sets of commitments in Brazil and Europe. Again, the remedy packages and the implementation procedures were virtually the same, both in Brazil and Europe, and included the use of trustees and other mechanisms to ensure the fulfillment of all the commitments undertaken by the notifying parties.

---

[24] CADE, *Munksjö AB and Ahlstrom Corporation* (Merger No. 08700.009882/2012-35) (May 22, 2013).

Anhanguera Educacional/Kroton Case.[25] The merger between education companies Anhanguera Educacional and Kroton created the largest private education group in the world. The proposed merger resulted in overlaps in over 400 relevant markets, with CADE raising concerns in relation to 171 courses in 55 different cities. In order to address the competition concerns CADE raised, the parties offered a remedy package that combined both structural and behavioral commitments, that included, among other things: *(i)* divestment of certain universities; *(ii)* commitments to reduce the number of new enrollments for a certain time period in order to keep part of the demand available for a new entrant; *(iii)* commitment to increase the quality of the courses offered by the remaining universities; and *(iv)* commitment to submit to CADE's prior approval the acquisition of competitors that meet certain criteria but would otherwise not be caught by the premerger control regime in Brazil for a certain time period.

Forte/JBS/Rodopa Case.[26] This case concerned a purely domestic transaction in the meat sector, more specifically the leasing of three cattle slaughtering units by the Brazilian meat company JBS. Remedies in this case were initially negotiated with the GS, which raised concerns over the elimination of a relevant competitor in a market formed in its majority by small players, whose capability of acting as effective rivals was unlikely. The Tribunal agreed with the GS' concerns and, in order to address such concerns, negotiated with the notifying parties a remedy package that included the sale of assets in certain Brazilian states, as well as certain behavioral commitments.[27]

Minerva/BRF Case.[28] This case also concerned the meat industry in Brazil. Both the GS and the Tribunal raised concerns in relation to the minority stake acquired by BRF in Minerva. In order to address such concerns, the notifying parties agreed to divest certain assets, thereby

25 CADE, *Anhanguera Educacional Participação S.A. and Kroton Educacional S.A.* (Merger No. 08700.005447/2013-12) (May 14, 2014).

26 CADE, *Forte Empreendimentos e Participações Ltda.; JBS S.A.; Rodopa Indústria and Comércio de Alimentos Ltda.* (Merger No. 08700.010688/2013-83) (August 20, 2014).

27 CADE imposes remedies in JBS-Rodopa deal (Aug. 20, 2014), *available at*: http://www.mlex.com/Brazil/Content.aspx?ID=578719.

28 CADE, *Minerva S.A. and BRF S.A.* (Merger No. 08700.000658/2014-40) (August 20, 2014).

reducing the merged entity's share in the production of processed foods market.[29]

Veyance/Continental Case.[30] This foreign-to-foreign transaction concerned the global acquisition of Veyance, a rubber and plastics manufacturer, by car parts manufacturer Continental. The GS expressed concerns over the notified transaction, in particular in relation to the markets for heavyweight steel conveyor belts (used in mining, steel, and construction sectors) and air springs (used as parts of the suspension system of heavy load vehicles). During the review period, CADE requested waivers to speak to various foreign antitrust authorities, including in the United States and Canada. To mitigate the competition concerns raised by CADE, the notifying parties agreed to divest a steel belt factory in São Paulo and a manufacturing facility in San Luis Potosi, Mexico, that makes air springs. According to the Reporting Commissioner Ana Frazão: "The divestment will allow the entry of a major player able to compete effectively in the market and challenge any abuse of a dominant position".[31] In relation to the air springs market, the remedy negotiated with CADE was the nearly the same as the one negotiated by the parties with the US Department of Justice (DOJ).[32] The parties were required to include certain provisions in the Brazilian remedy package to assist coordination between the agencies, thereby minimizing the costs with the monitoring of the remedy. Again, CADE used monitoring trustees, buyer requirements and approval and other mechanisms that are typically viewed in remedy packages in the United States and Europe in this case.

Holcim/Lafarge Case.[33] The merger of cement companies Lafarge and Holcim was filed with CADE on September 12, 2014, after pre-notification

---

29 CADE applies restrictions in BRF-Minerva deal (Aug. 20, 2014), *available at*: http://www.mlex.com/Brazil/Content.aspx?ID=578679.

30 CADE, *Continental Aktiengesellschaft and Veyance Technologies Inc.* (Merger No. 08700.004185/2014-50) (January 29, 2015).

31 CADE clears Continental/Veyance after 10 months of talks (Jan. 30, 2015), *available at*: http://globalcompetitionreview.com/news/article/37872/cade-clears-continentalveyance-10-months-talks/.

32 According to CADE, in order to ensure the divested business' feasibility, the agreement executed with CADE not only covered the manufacturing facility, but it also included intangible assets, such as brands, customer contracts, software, etc.

33 CADE, *Holcim Ltd. and Lafarge S.A.* (Merger No. 08700.007621/2014-42) (December 11, 2014).

talks. When notifying the merger, the parties were allegedly already aware of the complexities there of and decided to negotiate remedies from the outset.[34] The Brazilian divestment package aimed at eliminating the concerns raised by CADE included the sale of three integrated cement plants, two cement grinding stations, two ready-mix concrete plans and several distribution agreements. Once again, CADE used monitoring trustees, buyer requirements and approval and other mechanisms typically found in remedy packages in the United States and Europe in this case. The GS agreed with the remedies proposal presented by the notifying parties and referred the case – along with the remedy proposal – to the Tribunal for clearance conditioned upon the execution of the ACC. During the hearing session, Reporting Commissioner Gilvandro Vasconcelos Coelho de Araújo mentioned that: "The previous dialogue in this case provided for a quick and serious review".[35]

GlaxoSmithKline/ Novartis Case.[36] The proposed joint venture between GSK and Novartis was notified to CADE on October 13, 2015. As a result of this transaction, GSK and Novartis became entitled to 63.5% and 35.5% of the joint venture's shares, respectively. The joint venture was created with the purpose of commercializing over-the-counter health care products. The notifying parties negotiated remedies directly with the GS, which referred the case to the Tribunal attaching the remedy proposal for final review and clearance.[37] According to the GS:

The proposed remedy is sufficient to eliminate potential competition concerns resulting from the transaction in the market for antismoking products, as the proposed package eliminates the horizontal overlaps created by the deal and contemplates necessary conditions for the potential buyer to use the divested assets, becoming an effective competitor.

---

34 Holcim and Lafarge announce a list of proposed asset disposals as part of their planned merger (July 7, 2014), *available at*: http://www.lafarge.com/wps/portal/5_7_1-CFDet?WCM_GLOBAL_CONTEXT=/wps/wcm/connect/Lafarge.com/AllPR/2014/PR20140707/MainEN

35 Brazilian regulator approves Holcim-Lafarge proposal to divest assets (Dec. 10, 2014), *available at*: http://www.mlex.com/Brazil/Content.aspx?ID=618768

36 Merger No. 08700.008607/2014-66, Parties: CADE, *GlaxoSmithKline PLC. and Novartis AG.* (Merger No. 08700.008607/2014-66) (February 25, 2015).

37 *See* GS Order No. 181/2015.

When the case reached the Tribunal, Reporting Commissioner Márcio de Oliveira Junior stated that further review was unnecessary and immediately included the transaction in the agenda for final hearing.[38] The review period at the Tribunal lasted only 14 days, and the transaction was cleared, subject to remedies, on February 25, 2015. The remedy package negotiated with CADE included both structural and behavioral commitments: the structural remedy concerned the sale of antismoking assets related to Niquitin brand tablets and patches, whilst the behavioral remedies included physical and electronic barriers between the companies, compliance training and monitoring mechanisms to prevent the undue sharing of information related to the joint venture with Novartis, monitoring by an external counsel of all meetings in which representatives of Novartis take part, and a prohibition on Novartis representatives in the joint venture also being employed by Novartis.

Conclusion

The analysis of CADE's recent cases in which remedies were required shows how the new reality revolving Brazil's premerger control system has affected remedies negotiations in Brazil. CADE is clearly moving towards the international practice on the matter, becoming more sophisticated and strict when it comes to remedies.

Although there is space for purely behavioral commitments, CADE has a clear tendency to prefer structural remedies. This requires the notifying parties to very carefully assess the dynamics of the markets concerned and the specific concerns raised by CADE in relation to the given transaction before deciding what set of remedies to offer, as this decision can impact significantly the timing and, in some cases, the final outcome of the case.

The notifying parties should also very carefully assess the most appropriate stage of the process to approach the authority with a remedy proposal, taking into consideration several variables that come into play – including, but not limited to timing constraints relative to the notified transaction, types of remedies appropriate to address the concerns expressed by the authority, and with whom to start the negotiation

[38] CADE councilor says further investigation unnecessary on Novartis-Glaxo deal; sets decision for next week (Feb. 19, 2015), *available at*: http://www.mlex.com/Brazil/Content.aspx?ID=647932.

(i.e. with the GS or with the Tribunal directly). All these variables may change from one transaction to another, and deserve a very careful look already at an early stage of the process, as this may well determine the best way to handle the case with CADE.

Bibliography

ACQUISITION OF UNISEB by Estacio gets Brazilian antitrust approval with restrictions (May 14, 2014), available at: http://www.mlex.com/Brazil/Content.aspx?ID=536498.

BRAZILIAN REGULATOR approves Holcim-Lafarge proposal to divest assets (Dec. 10, 2014), available at: http://www.mlex.com/Brazil/Content.aspx?ID=618768.

CADE applies restrictions in BRF-Minerva deal (Aug. 20, 2014), available at: http://www.mlex.com/Brazil/Content.aspx?ID=578679.

CADE approves ALL/Rumo deal with restrictions (Feb. 12, 2015), available at: http://www.cade.gov.br/Default.aspx?5aed3ccd27fc13101a27380c2727.

CADE clears Continental/Veyance after 10 months of talks (Jan. 30, 2015), available at: http://globalcompetitionreview.com/news/article/37872/cade-clears-continentalveyance-10-months-talks/.

CADE councilor says further investigation unnecessary on Novartis-Glaxo deal; sets decision for next week (Feb. 19, 2015), available at: http://www.mlex.com/Brazil/ Content.aspx?ID=647932.

CADE imposes remedies in JBS-Rodopa deal (Aug. 20, 2014), available at: http://www.mlex.com/Brazil/Content.aspx?ID=578719.

CADE proposes to block Innova Sale to Videolar (Apr. 3, 2014), available at: http://www.mlex.com/Brazil/Content.aspx?ID=521364.

CADE, *América Latina Logística S.A. and Rumo Logística Operadora Multimodal S.A.* (Merger No. 08700.005719/2014-65) (February 11, 2015).

CADE, *Anhanguera Educacional Participação S.A. and Kroton Educacional S.A.* (Merger No. 08700.005447/2013-12) (May 14, 2014).

CADE, *BDO Auditores Independentes; BDO Consultores Ltda.; KPMG Risk Advisory Services Ltda.* (Merger No. 08012.002689/2011-41) (October 9, 2013).

CADE, *Braskem S.A. and Solvay S.A.* (Merger No. 08700.000436/2014-27) (November 12, 2014).

CADE, *Continental Aktiengesellschaft and Veyance Technologies Inc.* (Merger No. 08700.004185/2014-50) (January 29, 2015).

CADE, *Estácio Participações S.A. and TCA Investimento em Participações Ltda.* (Merger No. 08700.009198/2013-34) (May 14, 2014).

CADE, *Forte Empreendimentos e Participações Ltda.; JBS S.A.; Rodopa Indústria and Comércio de Alimentos Ltda.* (Merger No. 08700.010688/2013-83) (August 20, 2014).

CADE, *GlaxoSmithKline PLC. and Novartis AG.* (Merger No. 08700.008607/2014-66) (February 25, 2015).

CADE, *Holcim Ltd. and Lafarge S.A.* (Merger No. 08700.007621/2014-42) (December 11, 2014).

CADE, *Innova S.A., Videolar S.A. and others.* (Merger No. 08700.009924/2013-19) (October 2, 2014).

CADE, *Mediobanca – Banca di Credito Finanziario S.p.A; Intensa Sanpaolo S.p.A; Sintonia S/A; Assicurazioni Generali S.p.A; Telefónica S.A.* (Merger No. 53500.012487/2007) (April 28, 2010).

CADE, *Minerva S.A. and BRF S.A.* (Merger No. 08700.000658/2014-40) (August 20, 2014).

CADE, *Munksjö AB and Ahlstrom Corporation* (Merger No. 08700.009882/2012-35) (May 22, 2013).

CADE, *Oxiteno S.A. Indústria e Comércio and American Chemical I.C.S.A.* (Merger No. 08700.004083/2012-72) (November 20, 2013).

CADE, *Perdigão S/A and Sadia S.A.* (Merger No. 08012.004423/2009-18) (July 13, 2011).

CADE, *Petróleo Brasileiro S/A and Refinaria de Petróleo Ipiranga S.A.* (Merger No. 08012.002820/2007-93) (December 17, 2008).

CADE, *Quattor Participações S.A; Petrobras Química S.A; Petróleo Brasileiro S.A and Braskem S.A.S.* (Merger No. 08012.001205/2010-65) (February 23, 2011).

CADE, *Telecomunicações Ltda. and Net Serviços de Comunicações S.A.* (Merger No. 53500.001477/2008) (April 7, 2010).

CADE, *WP Roaming III S.r.l and Syniverse Holdings, Inc.* (Merger No. 08700.006437/2012-13) (May 22, 2013).

Cesar Mattos. Remédios em atos de concentração: a experiência internacional e o Brasil. In: Amanda Flávio Oliveira; Ricardo Machado Ruiz (orgs.). *Remédios Antitruste.* 61-99. São Paulo: Singular, 2001.

European Commission. Commission Notice on remedies acceptable under Council Regulation (EEC) No. 139/2004 and under Commission Regulation (EC) No. 802/2004.

Holcim and Lafarge announce a list of proposed asset disposals as part of their planned merger (July 7, 2014), available at: http://www.lafarge.com/wps/portal/5_7_1-CFDet?WCM_GLOBAL_CONTEXT=/wps/wcm/connect/Lafarge.com/AllPR/2014/PR20140707/MainEN.

Innova's aquisition by Videolar approved with restrictions (Oct. 2, 2014), available at: http://www.mlex.com/Brazil/Content.aspx?ID=594870.

Rejection of Braskem deal shows need for companies to address Brazil regulator's concerns (Nov.13, 2014), available at: http://www.mlex.com/Brazil/Content.aspx?ID=610218.

* * *

Chapter VIII

GUN JUMPING: CADE'S EXPERIENCE UNDER THE NEW ANTITRUST LAW

BARBARA ROSENBERG
GUILHERME MORGULIS
MARCOS EXPOSTO
SANDRA TEREPINS

I. Introduction

Since June 2012,[1] companies doing business in Brazil have faced a new regulatory regime for merger control that has substantially changed the way mergers and aquisitions must be structured. Law 12,529 (2011) – the Brazilian Antitrust Law – introduced a suspensory merger control system, according to which parties to a transaction which qualifies as a 'concentration' under Brazilian law are prevented from closing the deal before it is cleared by the Brazilian Antitrust Authority (CADE). Before the enactment of the law, the previous merger control system set out in Law 8,884 (1994) did not provide for a standstill obligation, but rather allowed parties to close reportable transactions prior to clearance by Brazilian competition authorities, as long as such transaction was notified within 15 business days from the execution date of the first binding document,[2] and

1 The Brazilian Antitrust Law (Law 12,529/11) only came into force on May 29, 2012 (see Article 128).

2 *See* Article 54, Paragraph Four (Law 8,884/94) and CADE's Internal Regulations, Article 98 (Resolution 45/2007).

as long as – in exceptional circumstances – no action had been taken by the authority to withhold closing prior to antitrust clearance.

This means that the business community was required to adapt (and has been adapting) to a system in which special consideration must be given to the limits of premerger coordination, or, in other words, to what conduct may be understood as unlawful in view of the standstill obligation prior to clearance by antitrust authorities. However, in order to comply with such obligation, one must first know what such 'unlawful conduct' is and what are the penalties for violating merger control rules.

This Article seeks to provide guidance on this issue by analyzing CADE's rules and decisional practice in cases involving issues related to unlawful premerger coordination (gun jumping). Based on such purpose, the following sections will describe: (1) the existing rules to which the parties to a transaction are subject in the premerger control context; (2) the decisional practice[3] with respect to the conducts that CADE has considered unlawful; (3) the decisional practice with respect to the conducts that CADE has considered lawful; and (4) the penalties parties are subject to for infringing merger control rules.

II. Legal Framework

This section describes the existing merger control rules applicable to reportable transactions in Brazil, especially in connection with the conduct that is expected from parties to a transaction prior to CADE's clearance decision. Parties' obligations in a premerger context are twofold. First, parties must hold their activities and assets separate until CADE issues a final clearance decision. Second, parties must submit the transaction for the authority's review.[4]

3 CADE's decisions are not precedents under Brazilian law. In any event, public authorities have the duty to provide equal treatment to such decisions in similar situations (Brazilian Constitution of 1988 Article 37) and must refrain from using new interpretations of the law in a retroactive fashion (Article 2, XIII, of Law 9,784/1999).

4 According to Law 12,529/11, Articles 2, 88, 90, all transactions that are 'concentrations', meet the jurisdictional thresholds and have effects in Brazil must be mandatorily notified to CADE. Still, there are no statutory deadlines to file a transaction under Law 12,529/11. According to CADE Regulation 1/2012, merging parties are only required to file a transaction prior to closing and,

Failure to comply with either one of these obligations is subject to the same penalties under Brazilian law.[5] Still, the rationale behind each violation is different. Presuming private agents do not have the intent of violating merger control rules, one that violates the standstill obligation probably failed to adequaly determine the limits of coordination and information exchange before CADE's clearance, while one that closes a transaction without even submitting it to CADE failed to assess whether the transaction was reportable.

This paper focuses on the first set of rules and seeks to provide clarity on CADE's understanding towards the limits of premerger coordination.[6] In this regard, one should note that the Brazilian Antitrust Law does not provide for a clear definition on the types of conduct that should be understood as violations of the premerger control rules. Pursuant to Article 88, Paragraphs Two, Three and Four of Law 12,529/11, parties must not close ("consummate")[7] a transaction and must refrain from modifying

preferably, after the execution of a binding document/agreement. This means that, in addition to the obligations to hold their activities separate and independent before a transaction is cleared by CADE, parties must also (and rather obsviously) submit a transaction to CADE before consummating it.

5 *See* section G below.

6 Cases in which the parties have failed to notify a transaction will be addressed only to the extent in which CADE's decision also provides guidance with respect to the limits of premerger coordination.

7 There are exceptions to the rules that forbid the consummation of a transaction prior to CADE's clearance. Pursuant to Article 109, caption and Paragraph One and 109-A of CADE Regulation 1/2012, acquisitions of shares, debentures or other stocks in public offerings or in the stock exchange may be consummated prior to CADE's approval, but parties must nonetheless refrain from exercising any political (voting) rights resulting from such acquisitions. In other words, parties may move forward with the transaction and closing is allowed, but the purchaser is prohibited from exercising any rights associated with the acquired shareholdings (e.g. vote and attend meetings) until CADE issues a final clearance decision. Before such decision, parties may request authorization to use the acquired rights exclusively with the purpose of protecting the value of their investment. CADE's understands that to request such exceptional exercise of voting rights, parties most not only prove that they need to protect the value of their investment, but also that no anticompetitive effects would result from exercising voting rights in connection with such protection. *See*, in this sense, CADE's Technical Opinion No. 174/2014 issued by the Superintendence General

the competitive conditions among them until CADE's clearance decision becomes final.[8]

CADE's Internal Regulations[9] provide further guidance on the meaning of such rules and establish that parties must maintain their structure and the competitive conditions among them unaltered, which means that they must refrain from: (1) transferring any assets from one to the other; (2) exerting influence over one another; and (3) exchanging information that is sensitive from a competition standpoint, except if such information is strictly necessary to execute a formal binding agreement with respect to the transaction and is not used for any other purposes.

However, such guidance is hardly sufficient to provide legal certainty on what is expected from parties that have entered into a reportable transaction, before it is cleared by CADE. First, because the list of unlawful practices provided in CADE's Internal Regulations is not exaustive. Second, because the list includes broad and open-ended terms, such as "influence" and "information 'strictly necessary to execute an agreement", which have not been defined anywhere else. Moreover, the statute does not address the issue of whether, under Brazilian law, closing parts of a deal that do not affect the Brazilian market (e.g. transfering control over foreign facilities that do not sell products to customers in Brazil) would be acceptable (even though CADE representatives have informally indicated that it would not be).[10]

Therefore, one may expect CADE's decisional practice to solve these and other loose ends. The existing cases that provide guidance with respect to the lawfulness of certain premerger conducts are described in the following sections.

---

on June 20, 2014, CADE, *Companhia Brasileira de Cartuchos – CBC/Forjas Taurus.* (Merger No. 08700.003843/2014-96) (Jan. 26, 2015).

8 *See* Article 88, Paragraphs Two, Three and Four, of Law12,529/11.

9 *See* Article 108, caption and Paragraph Two of CADE's Regulation 1/2012.

10 Merger notifications in Brazil are reviewed by CADE's Superintendence General, which may either clear a case or present an opposition before CADE's Court. The Superintendence General's clearance decision can be appealed by interested third parties and by regulatory agencies. Moreover, CADE's Court may also require that a transaction be assigned to a Tribunal member for further analysis. A clearance decision will become final once it can no longer be appealed or referred to CADE's Court. See Article 132, of CADE Regulation 1/2012.

III. Unlawful Conduct

Considering CADE's decisions in *OGX/Petrobras,*[11] *Petrobras/Total,*[12] *UTC/ Aurizônia*[13] and *UTC/Potióleo*[14] one may note that CADE has already provided indication on several types of conducts which qualify as violations to premerger control rules. In *UTC/Aurizônia* and in *UTC/Potióleo*, for example, CADE explicitly stated that making the payment of the transaction price prior to regulatory clearance, even if only partially,[15] violates merger control rules. Furthermore, a violation also takes place if the transaction documents establish clauses that modify the 'decision-making flow' or grant rights to the purchaser ("create new legal positions") to the acquiror.[16]

It was in *Petrobras/Total*, however, that CADE put together a list of actions (also non-exhaustive) which, pursuant to the law, existing regulations and its decisional practice, would result in noncompliance with merger control rules. The acts that may be construed as illegal pre-merger coordination before CADE's approval according to this case include: (1) payment of the purchase price, even if only partially; (2) early transfers of assets; (3) transfers of enjoyment rights over assets, including cost or profit sharing,[17] (4) any type of influence of one party over another; (5) exchange of information between the parties other than that strictly necessary for the execution of the transaction documents; (6) anticipation of the effects of the deal; and (7) transfer of stock that confers voting rights to the acquirer.[18]

---

11 CADE, *OGX Petróleo e Gás– OGX/Petroleo Brasileiro – Petrobras.* Reporting Commissioner Ana de Oliveira Frazão (Merger No. 08700.005775/2013-19) (Aug. 28, 2013).

12 CADE, *Petrobras/Total E&P do Brasil.* Reporting Commissioner Alessandro Octaviani Luis (Merger No. 08700.007899/2013-39) (April 9, 2014).

13 CADE, *UTC Óleo e Gás/Aurizônia Petróleo.* Reporting Commissioner Ana de Oliveira Frazão (Merger No.. 08700.008292/2013-76) (Feb. 5, 2014).

14 CADE, *UTC Óleo e Gás/Potióleo.* Reporting Commissioner Alessandro Octaviani Luis. (Merger No. 08700.008292/2013-76) (Feb. 5, 2014).

15 *See* Commissioner Ana Frazão's opinion in *UTC/ Aurizônia, supra* note 14, at Paragraph 21(a).

16 *See* Commissioner Octaviani's opinions in *UTC/Potióleo*, supra note 14, Paragraphs 27-29.

17 *See*, with respect to cost of profit sharing, e.g., CADE, Technical Opinion 273/2013, Paragraph 13(ii), issued by the Superintendence General in *UTC/Potióleo, supra* note 14.

18 *See* Commissioner Octaviani's opinions in *Petrobras/Total, supra* note 12, Paragraph Seventy-nine.

All of these conducts, if verified, would allow CADE to presume that a violation of premerger control rules took place. However, as described below, CADE's decisional practice indicates that such presumption is rebuttable, meaning that parties will not be subject to penalties for gun jumping if they are able to prove that, even if the any of the actions above were provided for in the transaction documents, they have not been effectively implemented.

IV. Lawful Conduct And The Use of Screens

There are a number of cases in which CADE has expressly reviewed the existence of gun jumping, but which have not resulted in a positive finding of a violation. Even if only to a limited extent, these cases point to examples of behavior that would likely not qualify as a violation of merger control rules, but that could nonetheless be construed by CADE as *prima facie* indication that merger control rules may have been violated.

Therefore, this section provides guidance on both: (1) the conducts which have been considered lawful by the authorities; and (2) the circumstances that could trigger a gun-jumping investigation by CADE.

A. Transactions That Were Filed Before The Authority Long After Being Executed

CADE's decisional practice indicates that transactions reported to the authorities long after definititve documents have been executed tend to be subject to a gun-jumping invetigation (i.e. an investigation for violation of Article 88, Paragraph Three, of Law 12,529 (2011). That was the case, for example, of the first gun-jumping case CADE ever investigated: *OGX/Petrobras*. According to CADE's Superintendence-General,[19] the investigation into the possible existence of a violation to premerger control rules in *OGX/Petrobras* started because the agreement had been executed

[19] There are two decision-making bodies within CADE,: the Superintendence General and the Board (Court). The Superintendence General has powers to clear transactions, but only the Court may impose restrictions, whether by referral of a case by the Superintendence General, or by assuming jurisdiction over a transaction that was previously cleared by the Superintendence General. Moreover, only the Court may impose penalties for infringing competition law. Therefore, in cases where the Superintendence General finds that premerger control rules have been violated, it must necessarily refer such case to the Court.

seven months before the transaction was submitted to CADE and because such agreement contained provisions that indicated the transaction had already been consummated.[20]

The long period between executing a transaction and filing it with CADE also triggered gun-jumping investigations in several other cases. In *Petrobras/Total*, CADE's Superintendence-General also made a point in arguing that both the execution of the agreement approximately five months before the transaction was filed and the existence of clauses which raised doubts in connection with the consummation of the transaction could be considered as evidence that premerger control rules had been violated.[21] Similarly, in *Fiat/Chrysler*,[22] CADE's Superintendence-General stated that information provided by the parties in the sense that the transaction had been concluded in January 21, 2014, but only submitted to the authority on May 17, 2014 was prima facie evidence of a violation of Article 88, Paragraph Three, of Law 12,529/11.[23]

Furthermore, in *Sé Supermercados/Novasoc*,[24] the parties submitted the merger before CADE on January 24, 2014, while the agreement had been executed on August 18, 2012. In order to explain such a long period between the execution of the merger and its submission to CADE, the parties stated that the apparent delay to file the transaction was due to possible changes to the merger structure (i.e. the company that would directly buy the shares involved).

In *Ouro Preto/ EP Energy*[25] CADE also investigated whether the fact that the agreement had been executed in July 2013, but only filed before

---

[20] *See* CADE, Technical Opinion 205/2013, Paragraph Fifteen, issued by the Superintendence General in *OGX/Petrobras*, *supra* note 11.

[21] *See* CADE, Technical Opinion 271/2013, Paragraph Twenty-Three, issued by the Superintendence General in *Petrobras/Total*, *supra* note 12.

[22] CADE, *Fiat/Chrysler Group.* Reporting Commissioner Márcio de Oliveira Júnior (Merger No. 08700.002285/2014-41) (May 14, 2014).

[23] *See* CADE, Technical Opinion No. 99/2014, Paragraph Nine, issued by the Superintendence General in *Fiat/Chrysler*, *supra* note 22.

[24] CADE, *Sé Supermercados/Novasoc Comercial.* Superintendence General (Merger No. 08700.000580/2014-63) (April 8, 2014). *See* CADE, Technical Opinon No. 107/2014, Paragraph Fourteen, issued by the Superintendence General.

[25] CADE, *Ouro Preto Óleo e Gás/EP Energy do Brasil/EP Energy Pescada.* Superintendence General. (Merger No. 08700.003723/2014-99) (May 27, 2014). *See*

the authorities in February 2014, could indicate that premeger control rules had been violated. The parties explained that right after the agreement was executed, the seller's economic group seeked to change the warranties associated with the transaction and that such change required regulatory approval from other agencies. Only after this issue was solved did the parties file the merger before CADE. Considering such explanations and the fact that the agreement did not contain any clauses which could be associated with gun jumping, the Superintendence-General concluded that there had been no transfer of assets, transfer of rights of enjoyment, influence over the target, payment of the purchase price or transfer of shares with associated voting rights.

Also in the *Petrobras/BP Energy I and II* cases,[26] the transaction agreements had been executed on March 18, 2013, but the parties filed the merger only in August 2014. The parties clarified that they had suspended negotiations while waiting for CADE's final decision with respect to the reportability of mergers involving the acquisition or assignment of rights in oil exploration blocks[27] – which, in the end, were deemed 'concentrations'. Such explanation was implicitly accepted by CADE.

The fact that mergers were filed long after the transaction agreements had been executed was not considered to be conclusive evidence of a violation to premerger control rules in any of the cases described above. There are no statutory deadlines for merger filings under Brazilian Antitrust Law, as long as clearance is obtained prior to the consummation of the transaction. Therefore, the length of the period between execution of transaction agreements and merger notifications has only been used by the authority as a screen for cases that may require investigation of a violation to the standstill statutory obligation. In any event, CADE's decisional

the Technical Opinion No. 166/2014, Paragraph Four-Eight, issued by the Superintendence General.

26 CADE, *Petrobras/BP Energy do Brasil I.* Superintendence General (Merger No. 08700.006248/2014-02) (Oct 24, 2014); and CADE, *Petrobras/BP Energy do Brasil II.* Superintendence General (Merger No. 08700.006249/2014-57) (Oct. 24, 2014). *See* Technical Opinion 356/2014, Paragraphs Five and Six, and Technical Opinion No. 357/2014, Paragraphs Five and Six, issued by the Superintendence General.

27 CADE, *Instituto Brasileiro de Petróleo, Gás e Biocombustíveis – IBP.* Reporting Commissioner Eduardo Pontual Ribeiro. (Inquiry No. 08700.000207/2014-02) (Apr. 2, 2014).

practice shows that reasonable justification for an apparently late filing, coupled with the absence of any further evidence of a violation, has been considered sufficient for CADE not to pursue further scrutiny on parties' premerger behavior.

B. *Interpretation of Exceptions to The Standstill Obligation by Using Analogy*

In *CBC/Taurus,*[28] CBC increased its shareholding in Taurus by means of acquisitions in the stock exchange and, subsequently, also increased its shareholdings by exercising preemption rights in connection with a capital stock increase by Taurus. Both steps were notified to CADE, but consummated prior to a final clearance decision. At that moment, CADE's regulations did not explicitly allow for acquisitions of shares or bonds in the stock exchange to be consummated before CADE's approval. This raised the question of whether CBC could have effectively increased its shareholding in Taurus without violating premerger control rules.

CADE's Superintendence-General and the Federal Prosecution Office at CADE agreed that the acquisition as it was structured did not result in a violation,[29] since a different conduct could not be reasonably expected from CBC. Such reasoning considered that Taurus, as a listed company, had to follow specific procedures in the context of a capital stock increase, which prevented its shareholders (including CBC) from knowing beforehand the shareholding owned after the increase (as not every shareholder exercises its preemption rights) and which provided for immediate liquidation and payment of the shares purchased in the stock exchange. Moreover, requiring that private businesses obtain prior CADE clearance before acquiring shares in the stock exchange could ultimately make any such transactions impossible from a business standpoint (given that the review may take up to 330 days).

According to the Federal Prosecution Office at CADE, this was the same rationale that had lead CADE to establish an exception to the standstill obligation for acquisitions of shares and bonds in public offerings

---

28 CADE, *Companhia Brasileira de Cartuchos – CBC/Forjas Taurus.* Superintendence General, *supra* note 7.

29 *See* the Federal Public Prosecutors Office at CADE's Opinion 297/2014, §2.3, and the Technical Opinion 338/2014, Paragraphs Twenty-Eight to Thirty-Four, issued by the Superintendence General in *CBC/Taurus, supra* note 7.

and that, by analogy, should be replicated in acquisitions of shares in the stock exchange. In such transactions, gun jumping was considered to take place only when political rights associated with the acquired interest are exercised.[30] In other words, early payment of the acquired shares would not violate the Law – i.e. could not be seen as a gun-jumping conduct – as long as the political rights associated with the shares were not exercised.

CBC/Taurus does not provide specific guidance with respect to permitted conduct in a premerger control context. Still, the case is particularly important as it shows the authority is open to expand its understanding towards lawful premerger conduct and even amend regulations taking into consideration the experience it has developed in specific cases.

C. Costumary Practices in Specific Industries

In *OGX/Petrobras*, Reporting Commissioner Ana Frazão recommended that the Superintendence-General initiate proceedings to investigate the existence of transactions in which the parties had adopted a similar behavior to that of OGX and Petrobras.[31] According to Commissioner Frazão, there was some level of regulatory uncertainty which lead the companies in the oil and gas industry to erroneously interpret antitrust law and refrain from notifing mergers involving the assignment of rights associated with concession contracts for exploring oil fields (which, according to the authority, are reportable).

This finding is of particular importance, since it indicates that CADE is willing to investigate if established common business practices violate premerger control rules.

D. Contractual Provisions And The Need For A De Facto Infringement

CADE's decisional practice indicates that the review of the transaction documents plays a central role in the analysis of possible violations to the standstill obligation. First, because if no other elements indicate that gun jumping has taken place, the authorities will initially only screen for possible

---

30 This rule was later incorporated to CADE's Internal Regulation as Article 109-A of CADE's Regulation No. 1/2012.

31 *See* Reporting Commissioner Frazão's opinion, in *OGX/Petrobras*, *supra* note 11, at Paragraph Ninety-five.

violations in the transaction documents which have been submitted along with the merger filing. This was the case, for example, in *OGX/Petrobras*, *UTC/Potióleo*, *UTC/Aurizônia* and *Petrobras/Total*.[32]

Still, the existence of contractual provisions that raise questions as to the parties' lawful behavior before a clearance decision is not sufficient evidence of a violation. In *Petrobras/Total*,[33] the Superintendence General found that the transaction agreement had clauses that provided for immediate rights and liabilities that could be construed to represent the early consummation of the deal – or of a relevant part thereof – before the merger was submitted to the antitrust authorities. Such provisions included: (1) determining that the agreement would be effective from a date preceding the agreement itself; (2) cost sharing prior to CADE's approval; (3) allowing access, by the acquirer, to sensitive information on the target; and (4) influence, by the acquirer, on the target prior to antitrust approval, by means of participation in an operational committee.

In order to assess whether such provisions had in fact been implemented, CADE's Court requested that the parties present further information on the actual consummation of the deal. Based on the information provided, CADE ruled that no violation of Article 88, Paragraph Three had taken place. Basically, CADE concluded that (1) the acquirer could not have had any influence over the target, as the operational committee which would allow him to do so had not been created; (2) payment had not been (and would not be) performed until a final clearance decision by CADE; (3) the lack of an explicit antitrust approval clause would not be sufficient to lead to a gun-jumping violation, especially as there were other conditions for closing which had not been complied with at that moment; and (4) even if the transaction agreement allowed for certain exchanges of sensitive information, the only data the acquiror effectively had access to

---

32 In *Petrobras/Total, UTC/Aurizônia* and *UTC/Potióleo*, the Superintendence General indicated that the absence of a contractual arrangement in connection with merger control review proceedings could reinforce a conclusion that a violation of Article 88, Paragraph Three took place. See Technical Opinion No. 271/2013, Paragraph Twenty-Six, Technical Opinion No. 274/2013, Paragraph Fourteen and Technical Opinion No. 273/2013, Paragraph Fourteen, issued by the Superintendence General in *Petrobras/Total (supra* note 12), *UTC/Aurizônia (supra* note 13) and *UTC/Potióleo (supra* note 14), respectively.

33 *See* CADE's Technical Opinion No. 271/2013, Paragraphs Twenty-Three to Twenty-Seven, issued by the Superintendence General.

was inherent to the due diligence process.[34] As such, CADE concluded that there was not sufficient evidence of a violation.

Furthermore, the review of the transaction agreements was explicitly used as a screen to conclude gun jumping did not take place in *Petroleo Brasileiro/ONGC Campos*,[35] *Petroleo Brasileiro/BC-10 Petroleo*,[36] *OGX/ExxonMobil*,[37] *Maersk Oil Brasil/BP Energy*[38] and *BP Energy/GDF Suez*.[39] In these cases, the Superintendence General simply stated that the transaction agreements submitted to the authorities did not include clauses that would grant the acquirer any immediate rights or liabilities before CADE's approval, as otherwise verified in previous occasions. In *Cambuhy Investimentos/Eneva*,[40] the Superintendence General concluded that the transaction was different from others in the oil and gas industry in which CADE found that gun jumping took place, since it referred to the acquisition of shares in a company that had interests in exploration blocks, while the gun jumping cases involded the assignment of rights (*see* section III above).

The assessment of the existence of gun jumping based on facts and not contractual provisions was also performed in *Sé Supermercados/Novasoc Comercial*. In this case, the parties submitted evidence to CADE showing that, even though the transaction was filed long after the execution of a binding agreement, (1) no measure had been taken to implement the

34 Note that the exchange of information *after* the execution of the transaction documents was not considered a violation of premerger control rules. This clears a previously existing gap in CADE's regulation (Article 108, Paragraph One, of CADE's Regulation 1/2012) and permits that the "information strictly necessary to execute the agreement" be lawfully exchanged both before and after the execution of the transaction documents.

35 CADE, *ONGC Campos/Petrobras*. Superintendence General (Merger No. 08700.009365/2013-47) (Nov. 19, 2013).

36 CADE, *BC-10 Petróleo/Petrobras*. Superintendence General (Merger No. 08700.009364/2013-00) (Nov. 19, 2013).

37 CADE, *OGX/ExxonMobil Exploração Brasil*. Superintendence General (Merger No. 08700.009624/2013-30) (Nov. 20, 2013).

38 CADE, *Maersk Oil Brasil/BP Energy do Brasil*. Superintendence General (Merger No. 08700.002883/2014-10) (May 2, 2014).

39 CADE, *BP Energy do Brasil/GDF Suez/Petrobras* Superintendence General (Merger No. 08700.010416/2014-64) (Dec. 23, 2014).

40 CADE, *Cambuhy Investimentos/Eneva/DD Brasil Holdings/OGX*. Superintendence General (Merger No. 08700.010029/2013-47) (Dec. 2, 2013).

transaction; (2) no payment or transfer of shares had taken place; (3) the acquiring group already held external control over the target and, as such, the agreement hich formalized the transaction did not alter governance or management rules; and (4) no information which was otherwise not already available to the acquiring party was exchanged. Also, the parties presented bank statements to the Superintendence General in order to prove that payment of the transaction price was still pending. In addition, CADE formally asked individual sellers whether they had already received payment or transferred their shares to the acquirer and checked public trade registries to assess if any corporate acts relating to the transfer of shares had been executed. Upon having concluded that none of the above had taken place, the Superintendence General found that there was no evidence of violation of the premerger control rules.

In a similar fashion, the Superintendence General requested the parties to the *Petrobras/BP Energy I and II* cases to submit clarifications with respect to two clauses in the transaction agreement which established that the acquirer would share the costs related to the target assets and should be consulted with respect to any decisions in connection with the target assets during an "intermediate period" (which dated between the agreement's effectiveness date and the approval by the National Oil Agency (ANP), or the competent regulatory agency). In response, the parties submitted: (1) the minutes of a Technical Subcommittee Meeting that took place after the agreement was executed, when the parties limited their discussions to technical aspects of the assets and supposedly only exchanged the same information which was required to support the acquiror's decision to invest in the target assets and which were not sensitive from a competition standpoint; (2) records of votes of the target's management body (operational committee), demonstrating that only the parties which formed the exploration block before the merger had exercised voting rights; and (3) an independent audit company report supporting that the acquiror had not performed payment before CADE's clearance decision. The Superintendence General also issued an information request to a member of the exploration block – which was not involved in the transaction – confirming that the acquiror had not participated of the decision-making process of the Technical Subcommittee and that the acquirer had no exercised voting rights in the operational committee. This company also confirmed that the acquirer had not borne any costs or expenses associated with the blocks or had participated of turnover or profits. Based on such evidence, the Superintendence General concluded that the parties had not taken any action resulting from the transaction which pointed to the transfer of assets or its enjoyment, the possibility of influencing BP Energy in the management of the exploration blocks, exchange of sensitive information or any payments.

Considering the foregoing cases, one may conclude that the analysis of contractual provisions may be sufficient for CADE not to pursue a gun-jumping investigation while reviewing a merger filing. Moreover, even if there are clauses which raise doubts as to the early consummation of a deal, CADE has indicated that parties may present evidence rebutting that any such clauses are *per se* violations or evidence that such clauses have not been *de facto* implemented. The same reasoning is also applicable when, regardless of the existence of contractual provisions or formal registration of the transfer of assets, the parties to a transaction *de facto* perform any consummation acts before CADE's approval. In *Goiás Verde/Brasfrigo*,[41] the Superintendence General indicated that a gun-jumping violation had taken place, since, in addition to performing the payment of the purchase price, the parties had also transferred certain assets and brands, even if such transfer had not yet been registered with the applicable authorities.

E. *Integration Planning*

The Brazilian Antitrust Law and CADE's regulations do not provide any type of guidance on the actions that may be undertaken in the context of planning the integration of merging parties' activities, prior to CADE's decision. So far, this issue has only been analyzed in *Rumo/All*,[42] in which the creation of a transition committee was the object of gun-jumping claims filed by interested third parties.[43] Such committee comprised independent

---

41 *See* CADE, Technical Opinion 86/2015, Paragraphs 9-11, issued by the Superintendence General in CADE, *Goiás Verde Alimentos/Brasfrigo Alimentos.* (Merger No. 08700.010394/2014-32), which is currently pending a final decision by CADE's Court.

42 *See* CADE, *Rumo Logística Operadora Multimodal/ALL – América Latina Logística* Reporting Commissioner Gilvandro Vasconcelos Coelho de Araújo (Merger No. 08700.005719/2017-65) (Feb. 11, 2015).

43 Subject to a discretionary decision by CADE, interested third parties may intervene in a merger case if they request to participate in the proceeding within 15 days from the publication of the case notice in the Federal Register (DOU). See Articles 44 and 118 of CADE's Regulation 1/2012. In such discretionary

members from the parties, who left their prior attributions and were dedicated exclusively to the evaluation of deal efficiencies and investment opportunities in a post merger context.

In his opinion, Reporting Commissioner Gilvandro Araujo acknowledged that creating a transition committee and using clean teams would be a lawful practice, especially as such teams usually help ensure that: (1) any exchange of information which is sensitive from a competition standpoint be limited to specific individuals, who are then responsible for keeping such information confidential; and (2) there would be no influence of one party to the deal over another. Commissioner Araujo also made a point that the acquiror's unilateral plans for the integration cannot be reasonably assumed to influence the activities of the target company.[44]

F. Comment

So far, publicly available information indicates that, in the majority of cases, CADE has pursued parties for failure to notify and for illegal premerger coordination in deals in the oil & gas industry, which is likely a consequence of Commissioner Ana Frazão's opinion in *OGX/Petrobras* metioned above, which recommended that mergers in the oil & gas industry be subject to special scrutiny with respect to violations of the standstill obligation.

Moreover, the records of the cases in which gun-jumping concerns have arisen reveal that CADE is more likely to investigate the issue if, for any reason, circumstances indicate that a violation is likely to have taken place (e.g. when contractual provisions point towards such direction or if the deal is notified several months after a final agreement was executed). Still, a positive finding of a violation may be rebutted in the context of a *de facto* analysis or if CADE deems that, from a policy standpoint, penalizing certain types of actions might prevent certain types of transactions from even taking place.

decision, the CADE must analyze if the interested third party (1) has a claim that is under CADE's jurisdiction, (2) has a legitimate interest in the outcome of the case and (3) is well placed to effectively contribute in the fact-finding phase of the proceeding (see the Federal Prosecution Office at CADE Opinion 143/2014 in *Araucania Participações/CTIS Tecnologia*. Superintendence General (Merger No. 08700.002772/2014-04) (May 2, 2014).

44 *See* Commissioner Gilvandro Araujo's opinion in *Rumo/ALL*, *supra* note 42, in Paragraphs Seventy-Seven to Ninety-One.

G. *Penalties For Gun Jumping And Interim Measures*

Law 12,529/11 provides that the failure to notify a merger or the early consummation thereof prior to CADE's approval subjects parties to fines ranging from BRL 60,000.00 to BRL 60,000,000.00.[45] Furthermore, if CADE finds such violations have occurred, (*i*) all acts performed by the parties may be declared void, which would require parties to wind-up the transaction, and (*ii*) parties may be subject to investigations of anticompetitive behavior. Moreover, even if there are no mandatory rules on who should file a merger notification, all merging parties are statutorily liable for ensuring that a reportable deal is filed and that premerger control rules are complied with. The details on the nature and extent to which such penalties may affect parties is described in the following subsections.

V. Statute of Limitations

There are no cases in which CADE analyzed the statute of limitations applicable to the penalties associated with gun jumping. In any event, Article 1 of Law 9,873/99 and Article 46 of Law 12,529/11 provide that the investigation of anticompetitive conducts or of the violation of other legal provisions of such laws will be time-barred within five years, from the date on which the violation took place (or ceased, in the event it is a continuous conduct). These time limits may be presumed to be applicable to gun-jumping fines, but not to the possibility of having the deal annulled.

This is because even though there are no clear legal provisions on the issue, the fact that a merger may be declared void (null), could make CADE more prone to interpreting that there is no statutory limitation period for the authorities to request that any consummation acts be undone and or to review the possible anticompetitive effects of the deal, as was CADE's decisional practice under Law 8,884/94.[46]

---

45 *See* Article 88, Paragraphs Three and Four, of Law 12,529/11 and Article 108, Paragraph Two, of CADE Regulation 1/2012.

46 Under Law 8,884/94, CADE understood that there was no limitation period applicable to the review of a merger on the merits, which meant that the statute of limitations should only apply to the penalties for late filing. *See, e.g,* CADE, *DR Empresas de Distribuição e Recepção de TV/Antenas Comunitárias Brasileiras.* Reporting Commissioner Carlos Emmanuel Joppert Ragazzo. (Merger No. 53500.028086/2006) (Aug. 31, 2011).

H. *Criteria Affecting the Range of the Fines*

According to Article 45 of the Brazilian Antitrust Law and to Article 112, Paragraph One, of CADE Regulation No. 1/2012, the following criteria should be taken into consideration for the calculation of the fines: (1) seriousness of the infraction; (2) good faith and intention of the parties; (3) the benefits accrued by the parties as a result of the violation; (4) the consummation of the violation; (5) the degree of damage or danger to competition represented by the violation; (6) the negative economic effects of the violation; (7) the financial status of the nonperforming parties; (8) the existence of prior violations by the same parties; (9) the size of the parties; and (10) the price of the merger.

CADE's decisional practice indicates that gun jumping will always be deemed a serious violation.[47] It also indicates that the good faith of the parties and the benefits accrued should be assessed considering the specific circumstances involving the violation of premerger control rules (*e.g.* if there were reasonable doubts, in the parties' views, as to the actual need for the merger to be submitted to CADE ,[48] if the merger was voluntarily filed before CADE[49] and if there was an actual change in the parties' behavior, in addition to the payment of the transaction price).[50]

A similar reasoning also applies to the review on the consummation of the merger. When reviewing this criteria, CADE may reduce the fine if there is no "modification in the physical structures and competitive conditions between the parties, no transfer of assets or even a change in their business relations."[51] CADE reviews the negative effects of the deal over the market and the harm or danger to competition, in turn, by taking

47 *See* Commissioner Frazão's opinion in *OGX/Petrobras, supra* note 11, in Paragraph Sixty-Four.

48 *See* Commissioner Frazão's opinion in *OGX/Petrobras, supra* note 11, in Paragraphs Sixty-Five to Sixty-Nine.

49 *See* Commissioner Márcio de Oliveira Júnior's opinion in *Fiat/Chrysler, supra* note 23, in Paragraph Fifty-Two.

50 *See* Commissioner Frazão's opinion in *UTC/Aurizônia, supra* note 13, in Paragraph Thirty-Four.

51 *See* Commissioner Frazão's opinion in *UTC/Aurizônia, supra* note 13, in Paragraph Thirty-Five to Thirty-Seven.

into consideration the analysis of the competitive effects of the deal and of the status of the acquired assets (operational or not-operational).[52]

The economic status of the parties was only reviewed in one case (*OGX/Petrobras*), in which OGX successfully showed the authorities, by means of its consolidated cash flow financial statements, to be under sufficient financial distress to reduce the company's fine.[53] Ultimately, the transaction value[54] and the size of the parties[55] are criteria used to assess the percentage the fine represents in the parties annual profits, turnover or in the value of the deal. In the interest of clarity, the criteria used to calculate the fine in the cases where CADE found that merger control rules had been violated is summarized in the table below.

Case	Criteria	Settlement/ Fine
OGX/Petrobras	1. Good faith, intent and benefit from the violation (-): regulatory uncertainty indicated that the parties acted in good faith and with no intention to benefit from the violation. 2. Size of the parties (+): measured in terms of turn-over. 3. Consummation of the violation (+): acknowledged by the parties. 4. Competition concerns (-): not relevant. 5. Financial status of the parties (-): the fact that OGX was in financial distress was recognized in order to re-duce the fine. 6. Seriousness of the violation (+): gun jumping would always be serious.	BRL 3 million (settlement) [56]

[52] *See* Commissioner Frazão's opinion in *OGX/Petrobras*, *supra* note 11, in Paragraph Seventy-Two. Note that gun-jumping violations may take place even in if the target assets are not yet operational.

[53] *See* Commissioner Frazão's opinion in *OGX/Petrobras*, *supra* note 11, in Paragraph Seventy-Three to Seventy-Four.

[54] *See* Commissioner Frazão's opinion in *UTC/Aurizônia*, *supra* note 13, in Paragraph Fourty-Two to Fourty-Four.

[55] See Commissioner Márcio de Oliveira Júnior's opinion in *Fiat/Chrysler*, Paragraphs Fifty-Three to Fifty-Four, *supra* note 22.

[56] In *OGX/Petrobras* (*supra* note 11), the parties settled to pay a substantially higher fine than in other cases as a result of the high value of the deal.

Case	Criteria	Settlement/ Fine
UTC/Aurizônia	1. Seriousness of the violation (+): gun jumping would always be serious. 2. Good faith, intent and benefit from the violation (-): buyer already held control over the target, which meant that there was no antitrust risk in connection with access to information. 3. Consummation of the violation (-): there were no changes to the commercial behavior of the target and parties remained completely independent. 4. Size of the parties (+): measured in terms of turnover. 5. Competition concerns (-): not relevant. 6. Size of the transaction (-): small transaction in comparison to OGX/Petrobras.	BRL 60,000 (settlement)
UTC/Potióleo	1. Size of the transaction (-): small transaction in comparison to OGX/Petrobras.	BRL 60,000 (settlement)
Fiat/Chrysler	1. Competition concerns (-): not relevant. 2. Good faith and intent (-): no intent to prevent antitrust analysis, since the transaction was of no concerns from an antitrust standpoint. Moreover, the parties voluntarily submitted the transaction. 3. Seriousness of the violation (+): gun jumping would always be serious. 4. Size of the parties (+): measured in terms of turnover and profit margins. 5. Financial status of the parties: not relevant for purposes of fine calculations	BRL 600,000 (settlement)[57]

I. *Acts Subject to Annulment*

The Brazilian Antitrust Law provides that all acts consummated before CADE's clearance may be declared void (Article 88, Paragraph Three). Still, experience shows that CADE will not make use of such provision in all cases. In *OGX/Petrobras* and *UTC/Aurizônia*, for example, CADE considered that there was no need for a merger to be declared void if the following conditions are cumulatively present: (1) the merger does not give rise to competition concerns; (2) the target assets are not operational or their governance structure has not been affected by the infringement;

57 In Fiat/Chr*ysler* (*supra* note 22), the parties settled to pay a fine for having failed to notify the merger before it was consummated. In all other cases, the merger had not been fully implemented before CADE's decision.

and (3) only acts which are merely related to the day-to-day operational activities of the target have been performed or the payment of the price is the only forbidden conduct undertaken by the parties prior to regulatory clearance.[58]

Such conditions should not be construed as the only case in which CADE will not seek to void the merger as a whole or specific acts consummated in advance by the parties. However, it is the only guidance with respect to which circumstances need to be present, in the context of settlement negotiations, to ensure that a deal is in a safe harbor against a decision of the authority to wind-up all consummation acts already performed.

J. Ancillary Impacts of Gun-Jumping Investigations

The negative effects of gun-jumping investigations are not limited to the possibility that fines or other penalties be imposed. In several cases, the Superintendence General has indicated that all cases in which there is a finding of violation to the standstill obligation necessarily need to be sent to CADE's Court for a final decision.[59-60] This proceeding may ultimately delay clearance even for fast-track cases, especially if the assigned reporting commissioner deems that further review is necessary before issuing a final decision.

Moreover, the Brazilian Antitrust Law also provides that, irrespective of the imposition of fines or of the annulment of any acts performed by the parties to a transaction prior to CADE' clearance,[61] a gun-jumping violation may also constitute anticompetitive conuduct (i.e. a cartel). So far, there are no cases in which CADE has pursued both gun-jumping and cartel investigations under Law 12,529/11. In any event, under Law 8,884/94, there is at least one case in which the authority has found two companies guilty of an antitrust law violation due to the integration of their

---

58 *See* Commissioner Frazão's opinion in *OGX/Petrobras (supra* note 11), in Paragraph Fifty-Nine, and in *UTC/Aurizônia, supra* note 13, in Paragraph Thirty.

59 *See*, e.g. Technical Opinion 86/2015, issued by the Superintendence General in *Goiás Verde/Brasfrigo, supra* note 41, in Paragraph Twelve.

60 CADE conducted public consultations with respect to the applicable proceeding to gun jumping and failure to notify investigations and CADE is expected to issue new regulations on the issue still in 2015.

61 *See* Article 88, Paragraph Three, of Law 12,529/11.

activities prior to regulatory clearance by the Brazilian Telecommunications Agency (ANATEL), which already had pre-merger review powers in the telecommunications prior to the current Antitrust Law.[62] In this particular case, the parties to the transaction started offering the same products, for the same price, even after ANATEL had blocked the deal, with harmful effects to consumers.[63] This case is indicative that CADE, as a matter of policy, may be more willing to pursue cartel investigations against premerger coordination with apparent anticompetitive effects or that clearly violates an administrative decision (*e.g.* an order to hold activities separate).

K. Interim Measures in Gun-Jumping Investigations

It should be noted, finally, that CADE's Internal Regulations establish that, in the context of a gun-jumping investigation, the authority may seek any judicial or administrative measures deemed necessary to void the acts which have already been consummated and to ensure that the effects of the deal remain suspended until a final decision is issued by the authority. So far, publicly-available information indicates that CADE has deemed such interim measures necessary in only one case.[64] After a positive finding of a violation of the standstill obligation, CADE executed an agreement to preserve the reversibility of the merger whereby Goiás Verde Alimentos acquired Brasfrigo Alimentos, which even provided for the termination

---

62 According to Commissioner Luis Fernando Rigato Vasconcellos opinion, in CADE, *DR Empresa de Distribuição e Recepção de TV and Antenas Comunitárias Brasileiras* (Administrative Proceeding No. 53500.003888/2001) (Aug 25, 2012), on pages 3-4,: "before any ANATEL decision with respect to the transfer of BTV's quotas to DR-NET (pages 105-115), the investigated companies, in an "extra-oficial" fashion, started to coordinate their activities, in a clear collusive behavior between competitiors, with the purpose of acting as a single entity," seeking to circumvent possible restrictions by ANATEL and allow for the market to be dominated by a single company".

63 *See* Commissioner Luis Fernando Rigato Vasconcellos opinion, in CADE, *DR Empresa de Distribuição e Recepção de TV and Antenas Comunitárias Brasileiras, supra* note 62, in pages 5 and 10, in Administrative Proceeding No. 53500.003888/2001 (*DR Empresa de Distribuição e Recepção de TV and Antenas Comunitárias Brasileiras*).

64 *See* CADE's Press Release (Feb 2, 2015) "CADE signs reversibility agreement for the acquisition of Brasfrigo by Goiás Verde", *available at* http://www.cade.gov.br/Default.aspx?df53a3758c81979c69d668fc55fc, in connection with CADE, *Goiás Verde Alimentos/Brasfrigo Alimentos, supra* note 41.

of certain agreements executed after the merger was consummated.[65] According to public information, such agreement "establishes conditions that ensure the reversibility of the transaction and partially mitigates the impacts derived from its anticipated closing until the agency's final decision".

VI. Summary of Conclusions

So far, CADE's Court has decided five cases in which gun-jumping issues have been investigated. In four of them, CADE's Court found that the parties had violated the standstill obligation. In all such cases, parties settled to pay fines and CADE did not declare any of the mergers null or void. As also described above, and even though these cases do not necessarily consolidate CADE's opinion, one could presume that: (1) CADE is likely to push for high fines in gun-jumping investigations depending on the size of the deal[66] and the parties' turnover or profit margins,[67] and (2) the authorities will assess the actual need to require parties to wind-up a merger before defining penalties on a case-by-case basis.

Furthermore, CADE's decisional practice also provides certain guidance with respect to the conducts which may be deemed unlawful under premerger coordination rules. As seen above, for example, certain contractual provisions, such as clauses that grant any level of influence over the target before CADE's approval or which establish the exchange of information which is sensitive from a competition standpoint, may be presumed unlawful. Still, in order for there to be a violation, there must be a nexus or link between the transaction and such influence or access to information. This means that, if the acquiring party does not exercise any rights other than those it already had prior to the merger or does not access

65 *See* Technical Opinion No. 86/2015, Paragraphs 7-8, issued by the Superintendence General in *Goiás* Verde/*Brasfrigo* (*supra* note 41). The information on the types of terminated agreements is currently not available in the public version of the case records.

66 *See*, e.g., Commissioner Octaviani's opinion in *Potióleo/UTC, supra* note 14, in Paragraph Thirty-Two.

67 *See*, e.g., Commissioner Oliveira Júnior's opinion in *Fiat/Chrysler, supra* note 22, in Paragraphs Fifty-Three to Fifty-Four.

any information than it already needed to conduct a due diligence over the target, before CADE's decision becomes final, no violation will take place.[68]

In the interest of clarity, and taking into consideration the descriptive purpose hereof, the table below contains a comprehensive list of CADE's decisions on gun-jumping issues thus far and of the merger control rules with respect to the conduct which is allowed for in a premerger control context.

Acts	CADE's Decisional Practice and Rules
Transfer of assets, including stocks and shares	Considered gun jumping, if performed before CADE's decision becomes final.
Transfer of rights of enjoyment, including with respect to stocks and shares	Considered gun jumping, if transferred before CADE's decision becomes final.
Influence from one party over the other	Generally considered gun jumping, as provided for under CADE's regulations. There are no precedents which exhaustively define the meaning of "influence" and most analysis are held confidential (*see* the Federal Prosecution Office Opinion No. 182/2013 in *OGX/Petrobras*). Establishing the participation of the acquiror in management bodies is not a violation, if such management body is yet to be organized (*Petrobras/Total*) or if it only deals with merely technical issues (*see Petrobras/BP Energy I and II*).
Closing (consummation)	Early closing violates merger control rules, even if the target assets are not currently operational (*see OGX/Petrobras*). Early closing violates merger control rules, even if the acquiror already holds control over the target. The fact that the acquirer is already the manager/controlling shareholder or operator of the target company/assets is only considered for purposes of reducing applicable fines (*see UTC/Aurizônia*; *Fiat/Chrysler*).
Effective date of the transaction agreement	Clauses that establish that an agreement becomes effective on a date preceeding CADE's clearance decision may be understood to qualify as gun jumping.

68 See Commissioner Frazão's opinion in *UTC/Aurizônia, supra* note 13, in Paragraph Twenty-Nine.

Acts	CADE's Decisional Practice and Rules
Cost or profit sharing	Sharing costs or profits before CADE's clearance violates merger control rules. Contractual clauses that establish cost or profit sharing starting on a specific date preceeding CADE's clearance do not violate merger control rules, if such obligations are nonetheless to be implemented after clearance (*see Petrobras/Total*).
Payment	Early payment, even if only partial or in installments, is a violation of merger control rules (*see Petrobras/Total*; *UTC/Potióleo*; *UTC/Aurizônia*).
Access to, or exchange of, information	Information exchange which is necessary for the execution of the transaction documents and for due diligence is lawful. Access to, or exchange of, information after the execution of the agreement is not a violation, if such information is the same as the one necessary to evaluate the target and execute a final binding agreement (*see Petrobras/Total*). Negotiations to amend contractual provisions of an agreement which is subject to merger review is not a violation (*see Sé Supermercados/Novasoc*). Acquirer's attendance at meetings involving the targets' internal affairs is lawful if such meetings are held by bodies with no decision-making powers and if no information other than that which the acquiror already had access to in the context of the due diligence is exchanged (*see Petrobras/BP Energy*).
Absence of contractual provisions regulating merger notifications to antitrust authorities	Absence of provisions regulating merger notifications is not gun jumping, if there are still other conditions for closing which have not been fulfilled. Example: clearance by other regualtory agencies (see *Petrobras/Total*). Even if it is not a violation, such absence may still give rise to further investigations by CADE (*see*, e.g., *UTC/Potióleo*).
Date of the merger filing	As long as it is takes place prior to the consummation of the deal, the merger may be filed at any time. Still, a long period between the execution of the transaction agreements and actual filing may support further investigations by CADE on the existence of gun jumping (*see OGX/Petrobras*; *Petrobras/Total*; *Ouro Preto/EP*; *Fiat/Chrysler*; *Petrobras/BP Energy;* and Sé Supermercados/Novasoc).

Acts	CADE's Decisional Practice and Rules
Transactions in the stock exchange and public offerings	Closing is allowed in such transactions, as long as no political rights are exercised until the final decision by the authority (*see* CADE's Internal Regulations; and *CBC/Taurus*).

Finally, as far as future developments related to this matter are concerned, CADE is expected to issue guidelines for the review of gun-jumping cases, establishing a specific procedure for the review of gun-jumping violations and providing further guidance on what types of conduct are permissible prior to regulatory clearance. These documents will be very welcome advances in CADE's case law on gun jumping, as they will organize and consolidate the authority's opinion on an issue that has impacts on the business community's day-to-day activities. Also, issuing formal guidelines brings more transparency and speed to the investigation of gun-jumping matters, providing parties with greater predictability of the outcome of any such investigations.

* * *

Chapter IX

ANTI-CARTEL ENFORCEMENT IN BRAZIL: STATUS QUO & TRENDS

Ana Paula Martinez
Mariana Tavares de Araujo

Hardcore cartel prosecution has quickly evolved in Brazil over the past decades. From 1994 to 2003, Brazil's antitrust authorities focused primarily on merger reviews, and substantial resources were devoted to the review of competitively innocuous mergers. In 2003, the antitrust authorities established a hierarchy of antitrust enforcement that placed anti-cartel enforcement as top priority. From 2003 to 2008, Brazil's antitrust authorities implemented the leniency program and built a network with criminal prosecutors that allowed them to tap into sophisticated investigative techniques and secure criminal sanctions, including jail sentences for cartelists. Following that, CADE concluded the first high profile cartel cases and spent significant resources on public outreach on harmful effects of cartels. A more recent phase began in May 2012, when the current antitrust law entered into force and introduced key legal changes, including revised administrative and criminal sanctions to cartel conduct.

This article provides an overview of anti-cartel enforcement in Brazil and discusses current trends.

I. Overview of the Anti-cartel Enforcement

A. Administrative Enforcement

At the administrative level, antitrust law and practice in Brazil is governed by the recently enacted Law 12,529/11, which entered into force on May 29, 2012 and replaced Law 8,884/94.[1] The new antitrust law has consolidated the investigative, prosecutorial and adjudicative functions into one independent agency: the Brazilian Antitrust Authority – CADE. CADE's structure includes a Court comprised of six Commissioners and a Chairman; a Directorate-General for Competition – DG; and an Economics Department. The DG is the chief investigative body in matters related to anticompetitive practices. CADE's Tribunal is responsible for adjudicating the cases investigated by the DG – all decisions are subject to judicial review. There are also two independent offices within CADE: CADE's Legal Services, which represents CADE in court and may render opinions in all cases pending before CADE; and the Federal Prosecution Office, which may also render legal opinions in connection with cases pending before CADE.

In Brazil, the Anglo-American concept of binding judicial precedent (i.e., *stare decisis*) is virtually non-existent, which means that CADE's Commissioners are under no obligation to follow past decisions in future cases. Under CADE's internal regulations, legal certainty is only achieved if CADE rules in the same way at least ten times, after which they codify a given statement via the issuance of a binding statement. To date, CADE has issued nine binding statements, all related to merger review but one.[2]

1 Prior to Law 12,529/11, there were three competition agencies in Brazil: the Secretariat of Economic Monitoring of the Ministry of Finance/SEAE, the Secretariat of Economic Law of the Ministry of Justice/SDE, and the Administrative Council for Economic Defense/CADE. SDE was the chief investigative body in matters related to anticompetitive practices, and issued non-binding opinions in connection with merger cases. SEAE also issued non-binding opinions related to merger cases and issued opinions in connection with anticompetitive investigations. CADE was structured solely as an administrative court, which made final rulings in connection with both merger reviews and anticompetitive practices.

2 Binding Statement No. 7, whereby it is an antitrust violation for a physicians' cooperative with monopoly power to prevent affiliated physicians from being affiliated with other physicians' cooperatives and medical insurance plans.

Article 36 of Law 12,529/11 sets forth the basic framework for anticompetitive conduct in Brazil. Article 36 addresses all types of anticompetitive conduct other than mergers. The law did not change the definition or the types of anticompetitive conduct that could be prosecuted in Brazil under the previous law. The law prohibits acts '*whose object or effect is to*' (i) limit, restrain or, in any way, adversely affect open competition or free enterprise; (ii) control a relevant market of a certain good or service; (iii) increase profits on a discretionary basis; or (iv) engage in abuse of monopoly power. However, Article 36 specifically excludes the achievement of market control by means of '*competitive efficiency*' from potential violations. Under Article 2 of the law, practices that take place outside the Brazilian territory are subject to CADE's jurisdiction, provided they produce actual or potential effects in Brazil.

The law was broadly drafted to apply to all forms of agreements and exchange of sensitive commercial information, formal and informal, tacit or implied. Cartels, as an administrative offense, may be sanctioned by CADE – fines[3] against the companies may range from 0.1 to 20 % of the company's or group of companies' pre-tax turnover in the economic sector affected by the conduct, in the year prior to the beginning of the investigation. To date, CADE has not issued secondary legislation clarifying in which cases the agency will resort to the group's sales instead of taking into account only the turnover of the defendant. CADE's Resolution No. 3/2012 lists 144 'fields of activities' to be considered for the purposes of calculating the fine under the new law. CADE may resort to the total turnover, whenever information on sales derived from the relevant 'sector of activity' is unavailable. Moreover, the fine may be no less than the amount of harm resulting from the conduct. CADE has seldom resorted to this provision when determining fines and, when it has, the fine imposed was less than the equivalent to the maximum percentage of the defendant's turnover allowed by the law.

Officers and directors[4] liable for unlawful corporate conduct may be fined an amount ranging from 1 to 20% of corporate fines; unlike the

[3] Individuals and companies may also be fined (a) for refusing or delaying the provision of information, or for providing misleading information; (b) for obstructing an on-site inspection; or (c) for failing to appear or failing to cooperate when summoned to provide oral clarification.

[4] Under Article 32 of the law, directors and officers may be held jointly and severally liable with the company for anticompetitive practices perpetrated by the company. Con-

previous law, CADE must currently determine fault or negligence by the directors and officers in order to find a violation. Other individuals, business associations and other entities that do not engage in commercial activities may be fined from approximately BRL 50,000.00 to BRL 2 billion.[5]

According to Article 45 of Brazil's antitrust law, the following shall be taken into account by CADE when setting fines: (i) level of seriousness of the infringement; (ii) good faith of the defendant; (iii) gain obtained or aimed by the defendant; (iv) whether the conduct has been consummated or not; (v) level of actual or potential harm to competition, Brazilian economy, consumers or third parties in general; (vi) detrimental economic effects caused by the conduct in the market; (vii) economic situation of the defendant; and (viii) recidivism. Finally, fines must be doubled if the defendant was already sanctioned by CADE for antitrust offenses in the last five years,.

Apart from fines, CADE may also: (i) order the publication of the decision in a major newspaper, at the wrongdoer's expense; (ii) debar wrongdoers from participating in public procurement procedures and obtaining funds from public financial institutions for up to five years; (iii) include the wrongdoer's name in the Brazilian Consumer Protection List; (iv) recommend tax authorities to block the wrongdoer from obtaining tax benefits; (v) recommend the intellectual property authorities to grant compulsory licences on patents held by the wrongdoer; and (vi) prohibit individuals from exercising market activities on his/her behalf or representing companies for five years.[6] As for structural remedies, under the law, CADE may order a corporate spin-off, transfer of control, sale of assets or any measure deemed necessary to cease the detrimental effects associated with the wrongful conduct.

---

sidering the strict sanctions that have been imposed to legal entities by CADE to date, this provision has nearly been forgotten as virtually no individual would be in a position to be held liable for the sanctions imposed against the company.

5 Approximately USD 17,482.00 to USD 699,300,000.00 (exchange rate of USD 1.00 = BRL 2.86).

6 The idea behind this provision was to deal with situations in which CADE debarred wrongdoers from participating in public procurement procedures and from obtaining funds from public financial institutions for up to five years. To avoid this penalty, the parties simply set up a new company and resumed activities in the same sector without being subject to the restrictions imposed by CADE's decision.

The law also includes a broad provision allowing CADE to impose any '*sanctions necessary to terminate harmful anticompetitive effects*', whereby CADE may prohibit or require a specific conduct from the wrongdoer. Given the quasi-criminal nature of the sanctions available to the antitrust authorities, CADE's wide-ranging enforcement of such provision may prompt judicial appeals.

As for law enforcement, the prosecution of cartels has been a top priority in Brazil since 2003. Approximately fifty leniency agreements have since been signed, the majority with alleged members of international cartels, and more than 400 search warrants have been served since 2003.

As a result of the use of more aggressive investigative tools, CADE has been imposing extremely high fines on both companies and individuals found liable for hardcore cartel conduct. The record fine imposed by CADE in connection with a cartel case was of roughly USD 1 billion, in 2014. The level of fines imposed is considerably higher when the case is supported by direct evidence (average of 15% of the annual gross sales of the defendant in cases with direct evidence, as opposed to an average of 1% of the annual gross sales of the defendant in cases without direct evidence). The table below provides a summary of the main cartel cases sanctioned by CADE and the duration of the investigation:

Case	Filing of the Investigation – Adjudication	Fines (USD)[7]	% of the Total Turnover[8]
Marine Hose	2007-2015	5 million	Not available
Hospitals	2000-2015	3.8 million	Not available
Metal Detector Security Doors	2008-2014	4.4 million	Not available
Cement	2006-2014	1.08 billion	15-20% (30-40%)[9]
LPG Distribution	1997-2014	3.7 million	Not available

7 Exchange rate of USD 1.00 = BRL 2.86.

8 Under the previous antitrust law, fines for corporations for anticompetitive conduct ranged from 1 to 30% of a company's pre-tax sales in the year preceding the filing of the proceedings.

9 The fine of one of the defendants was doubled for recidivism.

Case	Filing of the Investigation – Adjudication	Fines (USD)[7]	% of the Total Turnover[8]
Air Freight	2007-2014	29 million	Not available
Copyright Collection	2010-2013	12.6 million	Not available
Air Cargo	2006-2013	100 million	Not available
Hydrogen Peroxide	2004-2012	47 million	Not available
Industrial Gases	2003-2010	800 million	25% (50%)[10]
Steel Bars	2000-2005	120 million	7%
Crushed Rock	2002-2005	21 million	15-20%
Flat Steel	1996-1999	19 million	1%
Security Services	2003-2007	15 million	15-20%
Vitamins	1999-2007	5.7 million	20%
Sand Extractors	2006-2008	1.0 million	10-22.5%

In addition to the cases described above, there are over one hundred ongoing cartel investigations pending before CADE, including cases involving markets such as TFT-LCD, CDT, CPT, air freight forwarders, DRAM, ODD, underground cables, underwater cables, polymers, salt and silicate, capacitors, several auto-parts cases, most of them initiated through leniency filings.

Brazil's Settlement Program for cartel investigations was introduced in 2007, through an amendment to the previous antitrust law.[11] In March 2013, CADE introduced revised requirements for settlements, according to which all defendants in cartel cases must now acknowledge their

10 The fine of one of the defendants was doubled for recidivism.

11 The 2007 Settlement Regulation also included rules on settlements for other types of anticompetitive conduct, which had been in place since 1994.

involvement in the activity under investigation.[12] The provision does not refer to a 'confession' and the requirement 'to acknowledge participation' may allow for certain flexibility with respect to its terms, compared to a strict 'confession' requirement.[13] Also, under the current rules, meaningful cooperation is mandatory in all cartel cases; and the assessment on whether the parties have or not fulfilled the settlement conditions will only take place when CADE issues a final ruling on the case.[14]

Settlement proposals may be accepted at any stage of the investigation, even after DG has concluded its investigation and while CADE's Court reviews the case. Defendants may only try to settle once ("one-shot game"). The negotiation process may be confidential at CADE's discretion. A scale of discounts is applicable to the settling sum defendants that wishing to settle must pay.[15]

---

12 Until March 2013, such requirement only applied to cases initiated through a leniency agreement.

13 This may also prevent individuals from settling with CADE, since 'acknowledging participation' in connection with the administrative investigation may compromise their respective defense in parallel criminal investigations and may result in conflict of interest between the company and its employees, should the company choose to settle the case with CADE, even if individuals decide otherwise. This situation is specific to Brazil, where it is possible to have parallel enforcement initiatives taken by administrative and criminal authorities against the same individuals, for the same facts.

14 Cooperation may include submitting documents and information in the possession, custody or control of the settling party; using the settling party's best efforts to secure the cooperation of current and former employees; and appearing for interviews, court appearances and trials.

15 Reductions may vary between (i) 30% and 50% for the first party to propose the settlement; (i) 25% to 40% for the second in; and (iii) up to 25% to the other parties that follow. For settlement proposals submitted after the DG has concluded the investigation, reductions are limited to 15%. Theoretically based on the fine that would apply to the parties under investigation for cartel, such discounts are supposed to vary according to (i) the order in which the parties come forward; and (ii) the extent and usefulness of what the parties provide in cooperation with the authorities. Since CADE is yet to issue sentencing guidelines, and case law for hardcore cartel cases is still limited, these standards may be of little help. In practice, CADE has required defendants to pay amounts ranging from 5 to 15% of the sales generated by the party in the year prior to the investigation, in order to settle a case.

The table below provides a summary of the main cartel cases settled by CADE and the duration of the investigation:

Case	Filing of the Investigation –Settlement	Settlement (USD)[16]
CRT (CPT and CDT)	2009-2015	14.4 million
Medical and Hospital Services	2000-2015	1.4 million
DRAM	2010-2014/2015	945,000
Air and Maritime Freight	2009-2014/2015	8.5 million
IT Services	2012-2014	400,000
Coatings and Composites Resins	2014	12.4 million
LCD	2008-2014	15 million
LPG Distribution	2005-2013/2014	9.7 million
Laundry Services	2008-2014	1 million
Ambulances	2005-2014	12.5 million
Underground/ Underwater Cables	2010-2013	480,000
Air Cargo	2006-2013	5.7 million
Marine Hose	2007-2008/2013	10 million
IT Services	2005-2011	16 million
Compressors	2009-2009	35 million
Plastic Bags	2006-2008	8 million
Cement	2006-2007	15.5 million

Finally, Brazil has been increasing its cooperation with foreign antitrust agencies in cartel cases. Brazil's antitrust authorities have

16 Exchange rate of USD 1.00 = BRL 2.86.

executed cooperation agreements with the U.S. Department of Justice, the European Commission, Argentina, Canada, Chile, China, Equator, France, Peru, Portugal and Russia.[17] The Brazilian authorities have requested the assistance of foreign authorities in several occasions to conduct an investigation and, more recently, with the increasing number of dawn raids, foreign authorities and injured third parties have become interested in evidence seized in Brazil.

B. Criminal Enforcement

Apart from being an administrative offense, cartel is also a crime in Brazil, punishable by criminal fine and imprisonment from two to five years. According to Brazil's Economic Crimes Law (Law 8,137/90), this penalty may be increased by one-third to one-half if the crime causes serious damage to consumers, is committed by a public servant or relates to a market essential to life or health. Also, Law 8,666/93 specifically targets fraudulent bidding practices, punishable by criminal fine and imprisonment from two to four years.

Brazilian Federal and State Prosecutors are in charge of criminal enforcement in Brazil, and act independently from the administrative authorities. Also, the Police (local or the Federal Police) may start investigations of cartel conduct and report the results of their investigation to the prosecutors, who may or may not file criminal charges against the reported individuals.

The administrative authorities (former SDE and current DG) have set a framework for the relationship with the criminal authorities, which reduces legal uncertainty and creates a healthy competition among the different criminal enforcement authorities. Each one of the 26 Brazilian States has a State Prosecution Office. Early in its efforts to increase cooperation, SDE established a relationship with prosecutors in São Paulo and encouraged the creation of a special unit within the Prosecution Office of the State of São Paulo – named *GEDEC* – to investigate cartels and cooperate with the competition agencies in joint criminal and administrative investigations. The cooperation experience with São Paulo was used as a reference point

[16] In February 2009, Brazil's administrative and criminal authorities launched the first simultaneous dawn raid in connection with an international cartel investigation, together with the U.S. Department of Justice and the European Commission.

to foster relationships with other prosecutors. In December 2007, the Federal Police established an "*Intelligence Center for Cartel Investigations*" to advance cooperation efforts in joint criminal and administrative investigations of cartels. Along the same line, the Prosecution Offices of the States of Paraíba, Rio de Janeiro, Santa Catarina, Amazonas, Minas Gerais, Rio Grande do Norte and Piauí have organized special anti-cartel units, with the support of the Brazilian Ministry of Justice. In October 2009, the Ministry of Justice launched the National Anti-Cartel Strategy, a permanent forum comprised of both criminal and administrative antitrust authorities to discuss the implementation of the country's criminal anti-cartel laws. In November 2013, CADE executed a cooperation agreement with the Federal Police setting the framework for cooperation under the new antitrust law.

II. Trends

C. *Increased Criminal Prosecution*

More than 350 executives are facing criminal proceedings in Brazil for alleged cartel offenses and there is a final criminal decision sentencing 19 executives to pay a criminal fine for cartel offenses.[18] In 2014, a criminal court sentenced one defendant in an international cartel case to serve 10 years and 3 months in prison, and also determined the payment of damages in the amount of approximately USD 130 million.[19] Even though the maximum statutory prison term for cartel offenses is of 5 years, the judge found the defendant guilty on multiple counts (collusion and criminal conspiracy). Another 21 executives were sentenced to serve jail terms of two and a half to five years and three months for cartel offenses.

Though there are appeals pending review against such judicial decisions, the decisions indicate that an earlier trend of settling criminal cases under specific conditions[20] (*e.g.*, payment of a criminal fine and

18 Foreign executives may also be subject to Brazil's criminal system.

19 Exchange rate of USD 1.00 = BRL 2.86.

20 The ability to settle a criminal investigation for cartel conduct is disputable following the introduction of changes to Brazil's Economic Crimes Law, which became effective in May 2012. The new antitrust law modified the criminal sanctions applicable to anticompetitive conduct. The previous provision of the Economic Crimes Law sets forth jail terms of two to five years *or* the payment

appearance every other month before a judge to state that the person is not involved in cartel conduct) seem to have been overturned. These decisions also reveal that criminal courts now regard cartel conduct as a serious violation that justifies the imposition of jail sentences.

D. *Imposition of Non-pecuniary Sanctions*

In most cartel cases adjudicated in recent years, in addition to fines, CADE had been primarily ordering companies to publish the guilty verdicts in a major newspaper. More recently, CADE has also recommended that tax authorities prohibit wrongdoers from obtaining tax benefits and determined the inclusion of the companies' names in the Brazilian Consumer Protection List.

In 2014, CADE's Court delivered a final ruling on the cement cartel investigation, which had been in progress since 2006. In January, the Reporting Commissioner had recommended that the six companies, six individuals and three industry associations be found guilty of collusion. The judgment came to an end in May and sanctions included a record fine of over USD 1 billion, plus other ancillary sanctions, such as the divestiture of assets and a ban on carrying out transactions in the cement and concrete industry for five years, subject to certain conditions. It was the first time that CADE resorted to structural sanctions, which is relatively unusual in cartel cases. The judgment reasoning and the Commissioners' further public declarations suggest that this case may not have been an outlier and that CADE would consider adopting structural remedies and M&A bans in cartel investigations, particularly in markets in which the alleged conspiracy reportedly went on for a long period of time.

Furthermore, during its last adjudication session in 2014, CADE issued guilty verdicts in connection with three bid-rigging cartel investigations in the markets for metal detector security doors; orthopedic orthotics and prosthesis products; and painting and plumbing materials. In all such cases, apart from the imposition of fines, defendants were also

of a criminal fine. The new law determines that anticompetitive behavior may be punished with a jail term of two to five years *plus* the payment of a criminal fine. Since the minimum criminal sanction is now a two-year jail sentence (and not a fine), some prosecutors understand that individuals are no longer allowed to settle criminal investigations. Such provisions only apply to acts perpetrated on or after May 29, 2012.

debarred from public procurement for a five-year period. CADE had previously imposed this sanction on very few occasions (*e.g.*, cartel on security services adjudicated in 2007).

CADE's rulings in these cases indicate that high fines against companies and decisions in newspapers are no longer the only tool it will resort to in order to severely punish cartel conduct.

E. *Increased Number of Settlements and Interface With Leniency*

Notwithstanding the pros and cons of settling, the fact is that since 2013, CADE has executed approximately sixty settlements, mostly in connection to cartel investigations. From December 2014 to February 2015 alone, the Court approved thirteen settlements with defendants in domestic and international cartel cases.[21]

The current enforcement practice shows that CADE has been open to negotiate settlements at all stages of the proceedings. Accordingly, three of the aforementioned settlements were entered into only a few months after dawn raids had been conducted in connection with the case.[22] Conversely, in 2014, CADE also settled a cartel investigation after it had already been reviewed by all advisory bodies (the DG, CADE's Legal Services and the Federal Prosecution Office), which had recommended the defendants to be found guilty.

On the interface of settlements with leniency, even after the 2013 regulation, the "umbrella" provision, which shields all employees and former employees of the settling cartel participant from administrative liability, even if they are not a party to the settlement with CADE, is still only available for settlements and not for leniency agreements, which may discourage filings for leniency. On the other hand, there is still one major advantage of leniency over settlements for individuals: while leniency applicants address administrative and criminal liabilities together (therefore being entitled to criminal immunity), defendants interested in settling an

---

21 International cartel cases include DRAM, products for the transmission and distribution of electric energy, and air and maritime cargo freight CDT, and CPT.

22 Settlements in the coatings and composites resins investigation in December 2014 (See Cases No. 08700.004496/2014-19, 08700.004627/2014-68 and 08700.005159/2014-49).

ongoing case must deal with the administrative and criminal investigations separately, and criminal immunity is no longer available.

F. *Increased Private Damage Claims*

Private antitrust enforcement in Brazil has been on the rise over the past five years. This may be due to such reasons as the global trend of antitrust authorities encouraging damage litigation by potential injured parties; the growing number of infringement decisions issued by CADE;[23] and the increasing general awareness of antitrust law in Brazil. In Brazil, cartel members, with no exception to the leniency applicant, are jointly and severally liable for damages caused by their illegal antitrust activity, *i.e.*, each cartel member may be held liable for the entire cartel-related damage.[24] Such joint and severally liability has not significantly deterred parties from applying for leniency till recent years. Said scenario began changing in 2010, when CADE sent a copy of its decision finding a cartel violation in the market for industrial and hospital gases to potentially injured parties for the first time, so that such parties could seek damages from the relevant wrongdoers.[25] Said ruling may have tipped the scale for private claims in

[23] As it would be expected, follow-on litigation depends on the strength of CADE's case. CADE's decisions lack collateral estoppel effect, and even after a final ruling has been issued by the agency, all the evidence of the administrative investigation may be re-examined by the judicial courts, which could potentially lead to two opposite conclusions (administrative and judicial) regarding the same facts. In the generic drugs cartel case, for example, CADE found the companies guilty of price-fixing, and the alleged injured parties sought redress in court. The judge, however, concluded that there was no antitrust violation and therefore did not award any compensation to the plaintiffs. In any case, one should take the latter as an exception as, in average, judicial courts confirm over 70% of CADE's decisions.

[24] Pursuant to Article 47 of Brazil's antitrust law, victims of anticompetitive conduct may recover the losses they sustained as a result of a violation, apart from an order to cease the illegal conduct. A general provision in the Brazil Civil Code also establishes that any party who causes losses to third parties must indemnify those that suffer damages (Article 927). Plaintiffs may seek compensation for pecuniary damages (actual damages and lost earnings) and pain and suffering. Under recent case law, companies are also entitled to pain and suffering, usually derived from reputation losses in the market.

[25] *See* CADE, *Industrial and Hospital Gases Cartel Case*. (Case No. 08012.009888/2003-70) (September 1, 2010). Even before 2010, the local State Prosecution Offices representing alleged victims of cartels spontaneously filed few collective damages

Brazil, with a potential adverse effect for leniency. For example, in 2013, the state of São Paulo had already filed a civil claim against a leniency applicant to recover overspent money due to the existence of an alleged bid rigging in connection with the construction and maintenance of São Paulo's subway (the judge later required the government to amend the claim to also include the other co-conspirators). Brazil's Congress must therefore pass new legislation excluding the leniency applicant from joint and several liability with its co-conspirators to preserve the incentives for companies to come forward and self-report antitrust offenses.

Another important aspect regarding the interplay between cartel investigations and private claims is related to the level of protection offered by CADE to documents submitted by leniency applicants. The risk of premature disclosure of leniency documents, especially in view of cross-jurisdictional cases,[26] and the rise of private antitrust enforcement, may deter a cartel member from applying for leniency in Brazil. Even though CADE has been adopting a number of measures to ensure that leniency documents and the identity of the leniency applicant remain confidential throughout the investigation, it is still unclear how it will treat leniency documents following the adjudication of the case. A 2013 incident involving the leakage of the identity of a leniency applicant at an early stage of an investigation on an alleged bid rigging in connection with the construction and maintenance of São Paulo's subway cast doubts on the ability of the authorities involved to comply with the confidentiality assurances given to the leniency applicant.

---

lawsuits, most of which – if not all – in connection with regional fuel retail cartel cases that were initially investigated by the same prosecutors. Relevant case law includes two investigations by the State Prosecution Office in Rio Grande do Sul. Defendants in the Guaporé investigation were sentenced to two-and-a-half years of jail time for fixing fuel prices. After the conclusion of the criminal investigation, the State Prosecution Office filed for individual and collective damages and the parties were sentenced to compensate consumers that had been injured by the cartel and to pay collective pain and suffering for "*harming society, by having abused local consumers that were affected in their vulnerability*." Likewise, in Santa Maria, after retailers were also sentenced to serve jail time, prosecutors filed for individual and collective redress, both granted by the courts.

[26] Brazil's legal system allows defendants to have access to all the leniency documents since the very beginning of the investigation, which may interfere with the course of foreign investigations.

G. Recurrent Use of Borrowed Evidence

The reforms that extended CADE's investigative tools have not eliminated the antitrust authority's need to use borrowed evidence when conducting some of its investigations. Indeed, Brazilian courts have consistently allowed administrative authorities to borrow evidence gathered in criminal proceedings, as long as the original diligence was authorized by a judge and due process of law are respected. According to the case law of Brazilian higher courts, the evidence may be shared with other authorities even if the original proceeding – in which the evidence was gathered – has different defendants.

In the end of 2014, CADE convicted a fuel distributor for influencing its retailers to standardize their commercial practices in two cities of the State of São Paulo, and did so relying on borrowed evidence from labor proceedings.[27] More cases where the authority uses evidence gathered on other instances are likely, including the major investigation of alleged bid rigging in the construction industry, which included dawn raids that did not count on CADE's active participation.

However, relying on other authorities for evidence also exposes CADE to occasional flaws in wiretappings and dawn raids. For instance, the defense of individuals under investigation in criminal proceedings related to the alleged bid rigging in the construction industry has focused on attempting to have the evidence declared illegal. If that happens to be the outcome, part of the borrowed material will not be available to the antitrust authority. In this sense, in May 2014, a federal judge nullified the fines of over half a billion reais CADE had imposed on an industrial gas manufacturer (Air Products) in 2010 sustaining that the supporting evidence, which had been borrowed by the criminal authorities, was illegally obtained.

27 CADE, *Shell Brasil Ltda. (currently Raízen Combustíveis S/A).* (Case No. 08012.011042/2005-61) (November 12, 2014). Earlier in that year, the authority imposed sanctions against pharmaceutical laboratory Merck S/A for having met with the country's largest pharmaceutical companies to prevent distributors from working with generic products. In such case, CADE decided for the admissibility of evidence borrowed from other of its proceedings, in which Merck was not the defendant, reversing the Reporting Commissioner's decision on the issue. CADE, *Merck S/A.* (Case No. 08012.005928/2013-12) (August 6, 2014).

H. *Need for Increased Cooperation with Anticorruption Authorities*

The fight against corruption has been on the rise in Brazil, specially following the enactment of Brazil's Clean Companies Law in 2013 (Law 12,846/13) and the recent so-called Car Wash investigation.[28] Given that some cartel cases, in particular those involving bid rigging, also encompass corrupt practices, it is crucial for CADE and the anticorruption authorities to closely cooperate to ensure consistency and preserve the incentives for the leniency program. Article 87 of Brazil's antitrust law determines that successful fulfillment of a leniency agreement insulates cooperating parties from criminal liability for cartel offenses under Brazil's Economic Crimes Law (Law 8,137/90) and for other criminal offenses perpetrated in connection with the antitrust violation, such as fraudulent bidding practices (Law 8,666/93) and conspiracy to commit crimes (Article 288 of Brazil's Criminal Code).[29] Although the law generally refers to "*crimes directly related to the cartel activity, such as the ones listed in Law 8,666/93 and Article 288 of Brazil's Civil Code*", some prosecutors have already stated that a leniency letter signed with CADE may only protect leniency recipients from criminal conviction regarding the offenses explicitly mentioned by the law. It is therefore necessary for the criminal authorities to align with CADE on what should be the approach for a given corruption case in order to preserve the incentives for leniency and reduce legal uncertainty.

The same concern applies to other corrupt practices that could potentially amount to an administrative offense perpetrated in connection with the antitrust violation. The only difference being that there is no provision in Brazil's antitrust law on the possibility of obtaining immunity for such offenses as a result of a leniency letter executed with CADE. For example, if a cartel participant bribes a public official to direct contracts to the designated winning bidders in connection with a bid-rigging arrangement, the company would also be subject to a fine of up to 20% of the company's gross sales in the year prior to the initiation of the investigation

[28] The so-called investigation is directed to uncover alleged corrupt practices and cartel affecting the state-owned oil company Petrobras. More than 13 whistle-blowers have already signed leniency agreements with the criminal authorities.

[29] A grant of leniency under the previous antitrust law extended to criminal liability under the Federal Economic Crimes Law but not to other possible crimes under other criminal statutes, such as fraud in public procurement. The new antitrust law broadens the leniency grant to increase incentives for leniency.

under Brazil's Clean Companies Law (Law 12,846/13), apart from other sanctions that may be imposed by CADE. A leniency applicant would have to engage into discussions with both CADE and the highest authority of the specific government entity under whose jurisdiction the alleged corruption practice took place (at the Executive, Legislative or Judicial Branches), to try to ensure a more lenient treatment. According to Brazil's Clean Companies Law, self-disclosure of corrupt practices and illegal conduct in public tenders by corporations may result in a reduction of up to two-thirds of the applicable fine and immunity against other sanctions. Unlike CADE's leniency program, the Clean Companies Law does not extend the benefits of its whistleblowers' program to the individuals involved, who may still be held liable under Brazil's Criminal Code and other laws.

Conclusion

Administrative and criminal prosecution against hardcore cartels have been on the rise since 2003, when the first dawn raids were conducted and the first leniency agreement was executed. Since then, Brazilian antitrust authorities have lived up to their promise to increase enforcement and step up sanctions against cartels. In the coming years, more individuals are expected to be sentenced to serve jail time for engaging in cartel conduct, and CADE is expected to impose ever-higher fines and other severe ancillary sanctions against corporations and individuals, contributing to the attractiveness of Brazil's leniency program.

The accomplishments of Brazil's anti-cartel enforcement program show that Brazil's antitrust authorities have scored more hits than misses in this process. Nevertheless, it is still a work in progress and in order to ensure continuous development, CADE needs to be ready to deal with many complex issues, some of which may depend on additional changes to relevant laws and current policies.

* * *

Chapter X

CARTEL PUNISHMENT IN BRAZIL: FACTS AND TRENDS

Mauro Grinberg
Marcela Abras Lorenzetti

The behavior and attitudes of the Brazilian Antitrust Authority (*Conselho Administrativo de Defesa Econômica* – CADE) have been closely observed since the new Brazilian Antitrust Law came into force on May 29, 2012. The purpose of such assessment is to attempt to identify the trends to be followed, if any, by means of the facts. Though some trends clearly reveal themselves, in many ways, one is still in the dark.

The research described in the table below includes twenty-three CADE convictions between May 29, 2012 and December 31, 2014. One will certainly have the opportunity to constantly update such research, as CADE's work will continue. Such twenty-three decisions were assessed from different perspectives, as will be seen below.

I. Types of Cartel

This category includes more accusations than cases, because there are more than one type of cartel in some cases:

Price Fixing:	11
Bid Rigging:	3
Publication of information:	3
Market Allocation:	2
Collective Negotiation:	2
Anticompetitive Boycott:	2

Overview:

Price fixing is certainly the star of the accusations, which may be explained by the comparative easiness to investigate. In fact, price fixing normally leaves traces that can be found, more than it happens in other violations. Besides, the consequences are very easy to spot.

General expectations would raise bid rigging and market allocation as very important, although probably more difficult to investigate. In most cases the agreement is oral and the consequences are more difficult to spot.

Publication of information shows a primary mistake of the parties, making the investigation also primary. In fact, publication of information which should be kept confidential is public and the evidence is catchable at first sight. The clearest example can be the notice of new prices to be practiced within a short period of time. This can be a signal to all competitors to practice the same prices; it may even be a perfect violation, with no need of talks among competitors.

II. Sectors

Sales:	10
Service:	5
Industry:	4
Health:	3
Entertainment:	1

Overview:

(i) Sales and services tend to be easier to investigate than industry, which is much more sophisticated than sales and is often global. We do not see, under this perspective, the trend toward the choice of big cases in order to have important examples. Changing this trend to industry will certainly show an evolution, if and when it happens. In fact, investigating, for example, gas stations, is not that difficult, not only because there is an obligation to have billboards with the prices but also because the players are usually more informal in their contacts. Moreover, they usually happen in smaller communities, where people tend to meet easily. Investigating industry, however, needs more skills because usually we deal with very sophisticated schemes, in which it is easier to hide strong evidence.

(ii) The healthcare industry, which used to "lead" the cartel practices, is apparently attempting to comply with the antitrust rules.

III. Activities

The range of activities in this category is highly diversified, and thus it is very difficult to find profiles:

Gas stations	5
Hospitals	2
Airlines	2
Cement	1
Pharmaceuticals	1
Domestic gas	1
Construction products	1
Garbage collection	1
Blood collection	1
Orthopedic products	1
Bakeries	1
Fire extinguishers	1
Law bookstores	1
Revolving doors	1
Drugstores	1
Driving schools	1
Copyright entities	1

Overview:

(i) As easy as they may be to prosecute, as the contacts are local, it turns out that gas stations, which are frequently undisguised and limited, are the current scapegoat. They are important for the communities; however, from a broad national perspective, it is necessary to question whether the type of efforts that they demand make gas stations a valid choice when compared to the big global cases, considering the scarce resources which the authority can dispose of. The size of the agency, considering the huge tasks they face, is very small. The extensive range of activities demonstrates that the agency does not choose specific cases and handles cases as they are brought to light, either through self-incriminations or accusations.

IV. Geographic Scope

The focus of this paper is not the specific relevant market, but the types of cartel and the scope thereof (in fact, this is the most dramatic category in which to attempt to find trends):

Local	16
National	5
International	2

Overview:

(i) The vast majority of the cases are local, which means that they refer to a specific city or community. For example, the bakeries case is limited to a part of Brasilia. In another example, gas station cases refer either to medium-sized or small cities, none of which are related to one of the large-sized Brazilian cities. Though relevant for the communities, these cases take up the scarce resources of the agency, which could be better used in national and international cases.

(ii) The very limited number of international cases reveals that CADE seldom interacts with other agencies globally, which sounds strange, due to the knowledge that the country has afforded in the recent years throughout the international antitrust community. Such knowledge will, at some point, enable the agency to interact with their counterparts and open investigations referring to global cases, which are comparatively few so far.

V. Fines

CADE-imposed fines range from 0.1% to 20% of the merging party's sales in the year prior to the filing of the case, applied to the class of products to which the product of the relevant market belongs. In certain cases, the relevant markets coincides with the basis for the fine; in other cases, the basis for the fine is much higher and, in order not to be unfair, the authorities may lower the percentage of the fine. However, the data is not precise, as in many cases the percentage of the fine is not publicly available:

Not available	12
15%	5
15% and 20%	1
15% and 17%	1
13% and 15%	1
10%	1
Fixed sums (low sales)	2

Overview:

(i) Considering the range from 0,1% to 20%, the majority of decisions at 15% and 20% can be understood as an abandonment of any proportionality consideration . A proportionality consideration should consider the whole spectrum; however, the lowest fines are around 10% and not near the minimum legal level.

(ii) The low incomes of the parties can lead to a question and a remark. The question is: why to prosecute, for antitrust issues, small companies to which this idea is still unclear. The remark is: the use of this method is not provided by the law. The law of course does not distinguish between small and big companies, national or multinational, etc. But, considering that the agency´s resources are scarce, they could be better used in cases that can bring higher benefits for the economy. In this sense, auto parts is more important than gas stations (regardless the importance of the latter for the communities in which they are) because the benefit for the economy is higher.

(iii) Finally, it is possible to repeat here the same remark above mentioned regarding the use of the scarce resources of the antitrust authorities.

This research is currently in progress and will be update it in order to try to extract facts and find trends in the cartel deterrence in Brazil.

* * *

VI. CADE's Decisions under Law 12,529/11

II. Cartel Cases

DATE (YYYY. MM.DD)	FILE	DEFENDANTS	MARKET	CON-DUCT	FIELD OF ACTIVITY	FINE	IMPORTANT ISSUES
2013.05.22	08012.0040392001-68[1]	Bakeries in a district of Brasília	Sales	Price Fixing	Not available	Fixed sums arising out of low sales. Individuals: 10% of fine applied to the company.	No need to define relevant market in hardcore cartels.
2014.02.02	08012.001794/2004-33[2]	Fire extinguisher companies in Brasília	Sales	Publication of price lists	Not available	15% of income of reference company.	
2013.06.19	08012.004573/2004-17[3] and 08012.00.7149/2009-391[4]	Gas stations (local market)	Gas stations	Price Fixing	Not available	15% of the company's sales. Individuals: 15% or 17% of fine applied to the company.	Relevant market: area of influence.
2014.11.26	08700.008551/2013-69[5]	Hospital in Brasília	Health	Collective negotiations	Not available	Not available	In the healthcare industry, hospitals and clinics have high negotiation powers with health insurance companies. There is almost no asymmetry in negotiations between these agents.

1 CADE, *Bakeries in a section of Brasília*. Reporting Commissioner Ana de Oliveira Frazão (08012.004039/2001-68) (May 22, 2013).

2 CADE, *Fire extinguishers companies in Brasília*. Reporting Commissioner Ricardo Machado Ruiz (08012.001794/2004-33) (Feb. 2, 2014).

3 CADE, *Gas stations*. Reporting Commissioner Ana de Oliveira Frazão (08012.004573/2004-17) (Jun. 19, 2013).

4 CADE, *Hospital in Brasília*. Reporting Commissioner Ana de Oliveira Frazão (08012.007149/2009-39) (Jun. 19, 2013).

5 CADE, *Law bookstores in Brasília*. Reporting Commissioner Gilvandro Vasconcelos Coelho de Araújo (08700.008551/2013-69) (Nov. 26, 2014).

DATE (YYYY. MM.DD)	FILE	DEFENDANTS	MARKET	CON-DUCT	FIELD OF ACTIVITY	FINE	IMPORTANT ISSUES
2013.12.04	08012.012420/1999-61[6]	Law bookstores in Brasília	Sales	Anti-competitive Boycott	Not available	Fixed sums arising out of low sales.	Inelastic market
2013.10.23	08012.011668/2007-30[7]	Gas stations (local market)	Gas stations	Price Fixing	Production, transportation and distribution of fuels	13% and 15% for companies. Individuals: 13% and 15% of the fine applied to the company.	Tape recording used as evidence. No need to define relevant market, market share e effects in hardcore cartels. The potential damages arise directly from the proof of conduct. Cartels are a violation per se.
2014.19.02	08012.010362/2007-66[8]	Aircargo companies	Transportation services	Bid rigging	Air transport	Not available	
2014.12.10	08012.009611/2008-51[9]	Manufacturers of revolving doors and metal detectors	Public bids	Bid rigging Market allocation	Not available	Not available	
2014.10.12	08012.008507/2004-16[10]	Manufacturers of orthopedic products	Public bids	Bid rigging Publication of price lists	Not available	Not available	

6 CADE, *Gas stations*. Reporting Commissioner Ana de Oliveira Frazão (08012.012420/1999-61) (Dec. 4, 2013).

7 CADE, *Gas stations*. Reporting Commissioner Ana de Oliveira Frazão (08012.011668/2007-30) (Oct. 23, 2013).

8 CADE, *Aircargo companies*. Reporting Commissioner Márcio de Oliveira Júnior (08012.010362/2007-66) (Feb. 19, 2014).

9 CADE, *Manufacturers of revolving doors and metal detectors*. Reporting Commissioner Gilvandro Vasconcelos Coelho de Araújo (08012.009611/2008-51) (Dec. 10, 2014).

10 CADE, *Manufacturers of orthopedic products. Gilvandro Vasconcelos Coelho de Araújo*. Reporting Commissioner (08012.008507/2004-16) (Oct. 12, 2014).

DATE (YYYY.MM.DD)	FILE	DEFENDANTS	MARKET	CONDUCT	FIELD OF ACTIVITY	FINE	IMPORTANT ISSUES
2014.12.10	08012.006199/2009-07[11]	Improvement retailers (local market)	Public bids	Bid rigging	Not available	Not available	
2014.10.12	08012.005004/2004-99[12]	Entities for blood collection and maintenance	Health	Publication of doctor's fees.	Not available	10% of income.	In order to avoid anticompetitive measures, the use of compensatory power and price schedules for physicians must be limited to individuals and small companies.
2014.10.29	08012.001020/2003-21[13]	Hospitals (local market)	Health	Collective negotiations	Not available	Not available	
2013.03.06	08012.001003/2000-41[14]	Gas stations (local market)	Gas stations	Price Fixing	Production, transportation and distribution of fuels.	15% of the company's sales. Individuals: 15% or 17% of fine applied to the company.	Tape recording used as evidence.
2014.02.05	08012.011853/2008-13[15]	Garbage collection companies	Services Public bids	Bid rigging	Not available	15% of the company's sales. Individuals: 10% of fine applied to the companies.	Tape recording used as evidence.
2014.05.28	08012.011142/2006-79[16]	Cement companies (national level)	Industry	Price Fixing Market allocation	Not available	15% to 20% of the company's sales. Individuals: 1% of fine applied to the company.	Some companies had to disinvest in order to lower market share.

11 CADE, *Construction products retailers*. Reporting Commissioner Márcio de Oliveira Júnior (08012.006199/2009-07) (Dec. 10, 2014).

12 CADE, *Entities for blood collection and maintenance*. Reporting Commissioner Ana de Oliveira Frazão (08012.005004/2004-99) (Oct. 12, 2014).

13 CADE, *Hospitals*. Reporting Commissioner Márcio de Oliveira Júnior (08012.001020/2003-21) (Oct. 29, 2014).

14 CADE, *Gas stations*. Reporting Commissioner Ana de Oliveira Frazão (08012.001003/2000-41) (March 6, 2013).

15 CADE, *Garbage collection companies*. Reporting Commissioner Eduardo Pontual Ribeiro (08012.011853/2008-13) (Feb., 5, 2013).

16 CADE, *Cement companies*. Reporting Commissioner Luis Fernando Schuartz (08012.011142/2006-79) (May 28, 2013).

DATE (YYYY. MM.DD)	FILE	DEFENDANTS	MARKET	CONDUCT	FIELD OF ACTIVITY	FINE	IMPORTANT ISSUES
2013.08.28	08012.011027/2006-02[17]	Airline companies	Transportation services	Price Fixing	Air transport: passengers and cargo.	Not available	Because of the complaints of companies that carried both passengers and cargo, instead of cargo only companies, CADE decided that it is necessary to determine proportionality and reasonability according to the percentage of the company's sales, and not by the field of activity.
2014.02.19	08012.010215/2007-96[18]	Gas stations (local market)	Gas stations	Price Fixing	Not available	15% or 17% of the company's sales. Individuals: 8%, 10%, 12.5% or 15% of fine applied to the companies.	Tape recording used as evidence. The field of activity applied was "retail". CADE stated that "fuel production, transportation and distribution" is above the field of activity of gas stations and should not be used as basis for the application of the fine. This is contrary to previous CADE understandings.
2014.08.06	08012.005928/2003-12[19]	Pharmaceutical company	Industry	Anti-competitive Boycott (distributors of generic drugs)	Not available	Not available	The alleged cartel practice resulted in the conviction of many other companies. This company was left aside and convicted individually.
2014.10.01	08012.004472/2000-12[20]	Gas stations (local market)	Gas stations	Price Fixing	Fuel production, transportation and distribution	15% of the company's sales. Individuals: 15% of fine applied to the companies.	

17 CADE, *Airline companies*. Reporting Commissioner Ana de Oliveira Frazão (08012.011027/2006-02) (Aug. 28, 2013).

18 CADE, *Gas stations*. Reporting Commissioner Eduardo Pontual Ribeiro (08012.010215/2007-96) (Feb., 19, 2014).

19 CADE, *Pharmaceutical company*. Reporting Commissioner Ana de Oliveira Frazão (08012.005928/2003-12) (Aug., 6, 2014).

20 CADE, *Gas stations*. Reporting Commissioner Ana de Oliveira Frazão (08012.004472/2000-12) (Oct. 1, 2014).

DATE (YYYY. MM.DD)	FILE	DEFENDANTS	MARKET	CON-DUCT	FIELD OF ACTIVITY	FINE	IMPORTANT ISSUES
2014.02.19	08012.004365/2010-66[21]	Drugstores (local market)	Sales	Publication of discount schedule.	Not available	Not available	Despite low sales of the companies, the percentage of the fine was not decreased.
2013.03.20	08012.003745/2010-83[22]	Copyright entities	Entertainment	Price Fixing Anti-competitive Boycott	Not available	Not available	
2014.08.20	08000.009354/1997-82[23]	Distributors of domestic gas	Services	Price Fixing	Not available	Not available	The Brazilian Oil Agency (ANP) took chance of the conduct to avoid free riders.
2014.04.06	08012.003873/2009-93[24]	Driving schools	Services	Price Fixing	Not available	Not available	Applied fines had to keep relation to the fines paid on plea agreements, meaning that the fines should be lower to those who collaborated with CADE.

21 CADE, *Drugstores*. Reporting Commissioner Ricardo Machado Ruiz (08012.004365/2010-66) (Feb. 19, 2014).

22 CADE, *Copyright entities*. Reporting Commissioner Elvino de Carvalho Mendonça (08012.003745/2010-83) (March 20, 2013).

23 CADE, *Distributors of domestic gas*. Reporting Commissioner Eduardo Pontual Ribeiro (08000.009354/1997-82) (Aug. 20, 2014).

24 CADE, *Driving schools*. Reporting Commissioner Eduardo Pontual Ribeiro (08012.003873/2009-93) (April 6, 2014).

Chapter XI

CARTEL SETTLEMENTS IN BRAZIL: RECENT DEVELOPMENTS AND UPCOMING CHALLENGES

Leonardo Maniglia Duarte
Rodrigo Alves dos Santos

I. Introduction

A strong settlement policy may be an effective tool for efficient competition law enforcement and cartel deterrence. Experience in several jurisdictions has shown that negotiated resolutions in cartel investigations may present benefits for the investigated parties, for the antitrust authorities and for society as a whole.

Under the Brazilian Antitrust Law, parties investigated may benefit from deductions in the amount of the fine and, in addition, may avoid costs related to lengthy investigations. For the antitrust authorities and society as a whole, a settlement may be a cost-efficient resolution to an investigation and, therefore, may enable the antitrust authorities to relocate their scarce resources to other cases. A settlement may also be a way of obtaining evidence to build a stronger case and help secure the conviction and punishment of other investigated parties, making the investigations easier and shorter and even strengthening the deterrent effect of cartel prosecution.

Another important advantage presented by a negotiated solution for the antitrust authorities in Brazil is to avoid having their decisions challenged in court by the settling parties. Court challenges may absorb significant public resources, as judicial proceedings in Brazil may last for many years and delay enforcement of the decision by the antitrust authorities. Additionally, a settlement may also allow the antitrust authorities to quickly collect monetary contributions that could otherwise take years of litigation to be finally collected through the imposition of fines.

In certain cases, the authorities may also be able to extract certain commitments from the settling defendants that go well beyond what they could obtain through litigation, which may improve competition in the affected markets – i.e. by correcting market or regulatory failures – and benefit society in ways that could not be achieved in a decision of conviction.

Therefore, it is not without reason that several jurisdictions around the world have decided to include cartel settlement policies in their competition enforcement tool kit, and are constantly seeking to improve the applicable rules to build a system with the right incentives to encourage defendants to settle and cooperate with the investigations, while also avoiding fostering sub-optimal punishment and deterrence or discouraging applications for leniency, which still remain the most effective tool to uncover and dismantle cartels. Finding the optimal balance between these goals is essential to implement a successful cartel settlement system.

The Brazilian experience presents a very interesting example of developments seeking this balance and the interaction and conflicts between a settlement policy and a leniency program in an emerging economy with a still-young tradition in competition enforcement.

There is little doubt that the Brazilian antitrust settlement policy has been successfully improved in recent years. Nevertheless, in spite of all the significant progress and success in this area, some controversial issues have not yet been properly addressed by the applicable rules or by case law, which may prevent the antitrust settlement system in Brazil from achieving its full potential and curb its effectiveness.

The purpose of this paper is to present an overview of recent developments in the Brazilian antitrust settlement system with focus on settlements in cartel cases, pointing out the most controversial aspects surrounding this subject under the current legal framework and case law. This paper will also discuss proposals to improve the current system and bring more transparency and predictability to the negotiation process, so as to establish the right incentives to encourage both defendants and authorities to seek a negotiated resolution whenever possible.

This paper will be divided into the following sections: (i) Brief comments on the development of settlements under Brazilian Competition Law; (ii) Negotiating cartel settlements under the current legal framework; (iii) Final remarks.

A. *Brief Comments on the Development of Settlements under Brazilian Competition Law*

So as to better understand the path and the foundations that led to the legal framework currently in place for the negotiation and execution of antitrust settlements, it will be useful to briefly review how this negotiating instrument was introduced and developed in Brazil.

1. The early years of enforcement of the 1994 Antitrust Law

It is fair to state that the first effective competition legislation enacted in Brazil was the 1994 Antitrust Law, following the opening of the Brazilian economy in the late 1980s/early 1990s.[1] As in many jurisdictions with a young tradition in competition law, enforcement in the early years of the 1994 Antitrust Law was mainly focused on merger control.

Investigations of anticompetitive conducts were limited and usually derived from complaints lodged by third parties, with rare efforts from the authorities to detect possible violations and seek evidence. The lack of better investigation tools and scant experience in this area limited the authorities' ability to effectively detect and prosecute anticompetitive practices, particularly cartels, which, by their very nature, are usually quite difficult to uncover.

In this context, even though the 1994 Antitrust Law provided for the possibility of executing settlements in cartel investigations, inspired by the U.S.' consent decrees,[2] this instrument was barely used during the first

---

[1] Note, however, that Brazil has had other laws dealing with competition matters before, such as: Law 2,919/1914; Decree-Law 22,626/1933; Decree-Law 431/1938; Decree-Law 869/1938; Decree-Law 4,599/1942; Decree-Law 7,666/1945; Brazilian Constitution of 1946; Law 1,521/1951; Law 4,137/1962; Brazilian Constitution of 1967; Brazilian Constitution of 1988; Law 8,137/1990; Law 8,158/1991; Law 8,666/1993.

[2] Eros Roberto Grau, and Paula A. Forgioni, *O Estado a Empresa e o Contrato.* 233. São Paulo: Editora Malheiros, 2005.

years of enforcement of the 1994 Act, with just a few agreements executed between the years of 1995 and 2000.[3]

2. *The 2000 Amendments to the 1994 Antitrust Law: the leniency program and the prohibition on settling in cartel cases*

In 2000, the 1994 Antitrust Law was amended to introduce the leniency program and the possibility of making dawn raids with court authorization, which equipped the antitrust authorities with more effective tools of investigation.[4] Nevertheless, the same amendment prohibited the execution of settlements in cartel cases, on the assumption that this restriction would boost the leniency program and encourage violators to apply for leniency rather than trying to settle in ongoing investigations afterwards.

In spite of the amendments to the 1994 Antitrust Law in 2000, it was only in 2003 that the antitrust authorities began to make effective use of the new tools of investigation, with the first dawn raid operations[5] and the execution of the first leniency agreement,[6] which took the authorities' capabilities to detect and successfully prosecute cartels to the next level. As from 2003, the fight against cartels became a top priority in Brazil. The antitrust authorities executed 8 leniency agreements and carried out several dawn raids between 2003 and 2007.[7-8]

---

3 Only 18 cases were identified during this period. For more information in this regard, please refer to: PEREIRA, Guilherme Teixeira. *Política de Combate a Cartel no Brasil: Análise Jurídica do Acordo de Leniência e do Termo de Compromisso de Cessação de Prática*, 53, 2011. *Available at* http://bibliotecadigital.fgv.br/dspace/bitstream/handle/10438/8518/disserta%E7%E3o%20de%20mestrado%20-%20vers%E3o%20final%20banca%20examinadora.pdf?sequence=1.

4 Law 10,149/2000.

5 CADE, *Mineradora Pedrix Ltda.* Reporting Commissioner Luiz Carlos Delorme Prado (Administrative Proceeding No. 08012.002127/2002-14) (Aug. 21, 2006)

6 CADE, *Surveillance Services Cartel.* Reporting Commissioner Abraham Benzaquen Sicsú (Administrative Proceeding No. 08012.001826/2003-10) (Sept. 11, 2007).

7 For additional information in this regard, see the presentation made by the Superintendent-General of CADE at IBRAC's International Seminar on Competition Policy in 2014. *Available at* http://www.ibrac.org.br/Uploads/Eventos/20SeminarioConcorrencia/PALESTRAS/%C3%9Altimo%20Painel.pdf.

8 For additional information, see the competition enforcement annual report issued by the extinct Antitrust Division of the Secretariat of Economic Law – SDE in 2007. *Available at* http://portal.mj.gov.br/services/DocumentManagement/

Cartel cases have also become more complex – frequently involving leniency agreements, dawn raids and international/multijurisdictional investigations – and based on direct evidence of violation, increasing the chances of conviction and leaving the defendants with less room to question the existence of the conduct. As a result, defendants started to become more inclined to challenge the legality and validity of the evidence, at both the administrative and judicial levels.

In view of the fact that a negotiated resolution was no longer an option for cartel cases since the 2000 amendments, and that only the first-in could benefit from a leniency agreement, defendants had no alternative but to litigate, even if a negotiated resolution presented a more favorable outcome for both defendants and authorities. This situation led to a substantial increase in the number of lawsuits filed by defendants to question the authorities' decisions, increasing litigation costs for all parties and the duration of the investigations, preventing antitrust authorities from allocating their limited resources to new investigations and, consequently, limiting the effectiveness of competition enforcement and cartel deterrence.[9] The lack of a settlement option also prevented the authorities from benefiting from possible cooperation, which could help to secure the conviction of other defendants.

3. *The 2007 Amendments to the 1994 Antitrust Law: the reinstatement of a cartel settlement policy*

The need to have negotiated resolutions in cartel cases became clear and, as a result, the 1994 Antitrust Law was amended again in 2007 to reinstate a settlement policy in cartel investigations, with some adjustments to make it compatible with the leniency program.[10] In order to preserve the leniency program and avoid the possibility of placing a settling defendant in a more favorable position than through a leniency applicant, the 2007

FileDownload.EZTSvc.asp?DocumentID=%7B543BCEB7-954A-4AEB-85F2-7D9CB082221A%7D&ServiceInstUID=%7B2E2554E0-F695-4B62-A40E-4B56390F180A%7Dh.

9 Paulo Furquim de Azevedo, and Alexandre Lauri Henriksen. *Cartel Deterence and Settlements: The Brazilian Experience*, 5-6. *Available at* http://bibliotecadigital.fgv.br/dspace/bitstream/handle/10438/6896/TD%20265%20%20Paulo%20Furquim%20de%20Azevedo.pdf?sequence=1&isAllowed=y

10 Law 11,482/2007.

amendment required that settlements in cartel cases should necessarily be conditional upon payment of a monetary contribution, which could not be less than the minimum fine provided by law in case of a conviction.

In addition, the Administrative Council of Economic Defense – CADE amended its Bylaws in 2007 to regulate the new settlement procedure, and included the additional requirement that the defendants should necessarily plead guilty in order to settle in investigations involving leniency agreements.[11]

Another innovation introduced by CADE in the 2007 amendment to its Bylaws was to allow the submission of a settlement proposal only once ("one-shot only"), in order to encourage defendants to submit their best offer at first, rather than submitting less attractive proposals during the course of the investigation and their best offer only at the end, when a final decision was about to be rendered.

Following the 2007 amendments to the 1994 Antitrust Law and the CADE Bylaws, an impressive number of settlement agreements were negotiated in cartel investigations. Between the years 2007 and 2010, 21 settlements were executed, which was more than the total number of agreements executed before 2007.[12] In this initial period, negotiations were carried out separately by each CADE commissioner and his or her respective staff, not always followed the same negotiation standards and criteria. In addition, the fact-finding authority at the time, the Secretariat of Economic Defense of the Ministry of Justice – SDE/MJ, did not participate in the negotiations, which limited the possibilities of extracting more effective cooperation from the defendants settling.

Therefore, it proved necessary to create more effective mechanisms and procedures within CADE for purposes of ensuring consistency in negotiations and improving knowledge management on this matter, in order to capture, develop, share and effectively use the knowledge and experience acquired in the negotiations.[13] In 2009, CADE again amended its Bylaws

---

11 CADE Regulation 46/2007.

12 Carlos Emmanuel Joppert Ragazzo. *O CADE e as Soluções Negociadas*. Conjuntura Econômica 60-62. 2010. Available at: http://works.bepress.com/carlos_ragazzo/9.

13 Breno Zaban Carneiro. *Negociando com a Administração: Experiências Concretas na Superação dos Obstáculos à Negociação de Particulares com o Estado*, 18, available

to create the "negotiation commissions", entrusted with the attribution of carrying out negotiations of settlements under the supervision of the CADE commissioners in charge of reporting the case.[14]

CADE also created a working group to train negotiators to make up the negotiation commissions, to ensure retaining and sharing knowledge and experiences obtained in previous negotiations, and to study more effective negotiating techniques based on the best international practices, including training negotiators abroad and exchanging experiences with antitrust authorities from other jurisdictions.[15-16] As a result, CADE started to develop a staff progressively more knowledgeable and experienced in this area.[17]

4. The 2011 Antitrust Law: restructuring the antitrust settlement policy

In 2011, The Brazilian Congress approved a new Antitrust Law (the "2011 Antitrust Law"), which came into force in 2012. The 2011 Antitrust Law made significant changes in the Brazilian Competition System's institutional framework[18] and also a pre-merger review system, but made

at: http://repositorio.fjp.mg.gov.br/consad/bitstream/123456789/607/1/C4_TP_NEGOCIANDO%20COM%20A%20ADMINISTRA%C3%87%C3%83O%20EXPERI%C3%8ANCIAS.pdf.

14 CADE Regulation No. 51/2009.

15 Carlos Emmanuel Joppert Ragazzo. "O CADE e as Soluções Negociadas" Conjuntura Econômica 60-62. 2010. *Available at* http://works.bepress.com/carlos_ragazzo/9.

16 For instance, the participation of Brazilian authorities in the discussions regarding cartel settlements carried out by the ICN cartel working group and by the OEDC Competition Committee in 2008.

17 André Marques Gilberto. *O Processo Antitruste Sancionador – Aspectos Processuais na Repressão das Infrações à Concorrência no Brasil.* 292. São Paulo: Lex Editora, 2010.

18 Under the 1994 Antitrust Law, the Brazilian Competition System was composed of three competition enforcement agencies: the Secretariat of Economic Law – SDE, the Secretariat of Economic Monitoring – SEAE, and the Administrative Council of Economic Defense – CADE. SDE, through its Antitrust Division, used to be the chief investigative agency for anticompetitive investigations and also issued non-binding opinions in merger cases. SEAE was primarily in charge of reviewing merger cases and issuing non-binding opinions. CADE worked as the decision-making authority in charge of rendering final decisions in both anticompetitive investigations and merger cases. The 2011 Antitrust Law restructured the

few changes to the rules for anticompetitive investigations and settlements provided under the 1994 Antitrust Law, as amended in 2007, delegating to CADE powers to establish complementary rules for settlement agreements through regulations.

When the 2011 Antitrust Law came into force in 2012, CADE enacted its new Bylaws under the new law and established rules for the negotiation and execution of antitrust settlements very similar to those provided by its previous Bylaws, as amended in 2009. The new Bylaws provided for adjustments to adapt the procedures to the new institutional framework established by the 2011 Antitrust Law.

In 2013, CADE amended its Bylaws to establish new paradigms, incentives and goals for the negotiation and execution of antitrust settlements. CADE also reorganized its internal procedures for the management of cartel cases seeking more effectiveness and celerity for cartel investigations.[19] Based on the knowledge and experience gathered in settlement negotiations since 2007 and on the best international practices on this matter, CADE identified the need to design a system with the right incentives to pursue the following goals:

(i) Extract more cooperation from the settling defendants to strengthen the evidence against other defendants and increase the chances of conviction, rewarding defendants that cooperate more with larger discounts in the monetary contribution and leaving behind the pay-to-go settlement model that prevailed under the previous rules, in which little or even no cooperation was required from the settling defendants, even in cases that were still at the fact-finding stage;

Brazilian Competition System to concentrate all competition enforcement functions held by the three previous agencies on CADE, leaving the SEAE in charge of competition advocacy. The Superintendent-General's Office was created within CADE as an investigative unit in charge of investigating anticompetitive practices and reviewing and clearing merger notifications. CADE's Administrative Court remained as the decision-making authority in charge of rendering final decisions in anticompetitive investigations and merger filings which cannot be unconditionally cleared by the SG-CADE.

19 Carlos Emmanuel Joppert Ragazzo and Diogo Thomson Andrade. *Beyond Detection: The Management of Cartel Cases*. Competition Policy International (2012). *Available at*: http://works.bepress.com/carlos_ragazzo/14.

(ii) Encourage defendants to settle sooner rather than later, rewarding defendants that settle first and at the early stages of the investigation with larger discounts in the monetary contribution, considering that the sooner a settlement is executed, the more the authority can benefit from cooperation and save its resources for other investigations;

(iii) Preserve and foster the Leniency Program and ensure that a settlement does not present a more favorable outcome for defendants than a leniency agreement, with mandatory acknowledgment of participation in the conduct under investigation in cartel cases and payment of monetary contributions high enough to ensure deterrence;

(iv) Promote public perception of deterrence through the requirement of monetary contributions high enough to ensure dissuasion and disclosing to the public the terms of the agreements and benefits to competition and to society as a result of the settlements;

(v) Create two different procedures and incentive packages for the negotiation of settlements according to the stage of the investigation: (i) negotiation with SG-CADE before the end of the investigatory stage, when cooperation is more useful and a settlement tends to be more desirable for the authorities; and (ii) negotiation with the CADE commissioner selected to report the case, when the fact-finding stage has already ended, and the case is at the CADE Administrative Court for judgment, in which case execution of a settlement usually becomes less attractive for the authorities.

The 2013 amendments to the CADE Bylaws established the legal framework currently in force for the negotiation and execution of antitrust settlements in Brazil, following the guiding principles described above. The applicable rules, requirements and procedures for negotiating an antitrust settlement in Brazil, plus the most controversial issues arising in the negotiations and in the most recent case law on this matter, will be discussed in greater detail in the following section.

B. *Negotiating Cartel Settlements within the Current Legal Framework*

As mentioned before, the current rules regarding the negotiation and execution of settlement agreements with CADE are established in Law 12,529/11 (the "2011 Antitrust Law"), and in CADE Regulation No. 1/2012, as amended ("CADE Bylaws").

1. Steps and procedures to propose and negotiate a settlement

According to the 2011 Antitrust Law, any defendant in an antitrust investigation may propose a settlement agreement to CADE before a final decision is rendered. The defendant, however, has only one opportunity to do so in the same investigation, so as to create a strong incentive for defendants to be efficient when proposing and negotiating a settlement.[20] The CADE Bylaws set out detailed rules governing the proposal and negotiation of settlement agreements.

The 2011 Antitrust Law and CADE Bylaws established two different procedures for the negotiation of settlements, according to the stage of the investigation. If the case is still at the fact-finding stage at SG-CADE, the settlement should be proposed to and negotiated with SG-CADE. The applicable rules also allow SG-CADE to take the initiative and propose a settlement to the defendants.[21] If the defendants do not accept SG-CADE's proposal, they may still propose a settlement before a final decision is rendered.

If the fact-finding period is over and SG-CADE has already concluded its opinion and forwarded the case to the CADE Administrative Court for judgment, the settlement should be proposed and negotiated with the CADE Commissioner randomly selected to report the case. In both situations, a negotiation commission will be appointed to carry out the negotiations, under the supervision of either the Superintendent-General or the Commissioner.

The first step when a defendant decides to propose and initiate a negotiation is to contact the authorities and obtain a marker to ensure its place in line, considering that the current system awards larger discounts in the monetary contributions to settle for the defendants who come in first. It is possible to contact the authorities to confirm if there are other negotiations in progress and what would be the best place in line available at the moment.

---

20 Perpaolo Bottini, Ricardo Inglez, and Fernanda Ayres Delloso. *A nova dinâmica dos acordos de cessação de práticas anticoncorrenciais no Brasil*, published in the Revista do IBRAC, vol. 23 (2013).

21 To the best of the authors' knowledge, SG-CADE has not made use of this provision up to the date on which this paper was written.

The authorities usually provide a written marker to secure the applicant's place in line and grant it a 5-day period to formally propose negotiations, which may be very useful when the applicant still needs additional time to make a decision on starting a negotiation, but wishes to secure the best position in line available as soon as possible. Unfortunately, there is as yet no regulation on how to obtain a marker to negotiate a settlement, and the provision of clear guidelines on this matter by CADE would certainly be a welcome improvement.

With the submission of the formal request to negotiate, SG-CADE or the Commissioner will issue a decision to appoint the members of the negotiation commission and determine the start of the negotiation period. At SG-CADE, the negotiation period may be determined by the Superintendent-General, and suspended at its discretion. In practice, SG-CADE has been establishing a 30-day initial period and extending it for additional 30-days periods if necessary, at SG-CADE's discretion. At the Administrative Court, there is a 30-day initial period for negotiations, which may be extended for additional 30-day periods, or suspended at the Commissioner's discretion.

When the negotiation period is concluded, the authorities will grant a 10-day period for the settling defendant to submit its settlement proposal. In practice, the settling defendant usually submits a draft settlement proposal to the authorities in advance, allowing them to confirm that all terms are in line with the understandings reached during the negotiation, before a final proposal is formally submitted. It is also common for the Superintendent General or the Reporting Commissioner to discuss the terms of a draft proposal in advance with the other members of the CADE Administrative Court to confirm that the proposed terms are acceptable. This interaction with the CADE Administrative Court has proved to be extremely useful, considering that the Administrative Court can only accept or reject a settlement proposal, and cannot propose any amendments to it.

The CADE Bylaws state that the authorities may allow interested third parties to comment on the settlement proposal submitted by a settling defendant, who will have 10 days to make any amendments if any comment is presented.

Once the settling defendant submits its final proposal, SG-CADE will issue its opinion, recommending approval or rejection of the proposal, and submit it to the CADE Administrative Court for approval. If the negotiation is conducted by the Reporting Commissioner, he or she will submit the settlement proposal to the Administrative Court with his or her vote to approve or reject it.

After the parties execute a settlement agreement, CADE will declare suspension of the investigation with respect to the settling defendant until the date of the fulfillment of all the conditions and performance of the obligations set out in the agreement. Once the conditions established in the settlement are fulfilled, the administrative proceedings will be ended with respect to the defendant who executed the settlement.

However, if the settling party does not comply with the provisions of the settlement, CADE may impose the applicable penalties and resume the investigations against the settling defendant. In addition, CADE may also adopt other administrative and legal measures to enforce the terms of the agreement.

2. Confidentiality and guarantees if an agreement is not reached

The CADE Bylaws ensure that a proposal to initiate negotiations to settle will not be considered as any form of confession or acknowledgment of any illicit conduct under investigation. At CADE's discretion, the negotiation process and the proposal to settle may be treated as confidential and disclosed only when submitted to the CADE Administrative Court for approval. Although confidentiality is not a guarantee, as a rule CADE has been granting confidential treatment to negotiations until their submission to the CADE Administrative Court for approval.

The settlement agreement will necessarily become public after its approval by the Administrative Court, and CADE usually releases public statements to disclose the terms of the agreements, the amount of the monetary contributions collected, and the benefits for competition resulting from the settlement, so as to increase the public perception of deterrence. The information and documents submitted as part of the defendant's cooperation may be treated as confidential and disclosed only to the other defendants for the specific purposes of exercising their right of defense.

According to the rules provided by the CADE Bylaws for the negotiation of leniency agreements, all information and documents presented by the leniency applicant during the negotiation will be either returned or destroyed and may not be used by the authorities if an agreement is not reached. CADE has been extending the same guarantees to settlement negotiations, although the CADE Bylaws are silent on this matter.

Considering that these guarantees are not expressly provided for under the CADE Bylaws, it is usually advisable to obtain a written statement from the authorities confirming that they will be extended to the settlement negotiation. Although CADE has been accommodating this frequent concern of defendants during the negotiations, it is important that CADE should include this guarantee explicitly in its Bylaws, so that defendants can feel more comfortable to fully cooperate and share information and documents with the authorities without any reservations.

3. Mandatory requirements in a settlement agreement

According to the 2011 Antitrust Law, all settlement agreements must state: (i) the commitments to be undertaken by the settling party in order to cease the anticompetitive conduct or its effects, plus other commitments that CADE considers suitable; (ii) the fine to be imposed in case of noncompliance with the agreement; and (iii) the compensation to be paid to the Fund for Defense of Diffuse Rights (*Fundo de Defesa de Direitos Difusos* – "FDD"),[22] when applicable.

In cases involving the investigation of concerted practices between competitors, the Antitrust Law states that payment of a monetary contribution is mandatory, and the amount may not be less than the minimum fine set by law.[23] According to the law, payment of a monetary contribution in cases other than cartel investigations is not strictly mandatory, but may be required when applicable, at CADE's discretion. In practice, CADE has also been imposing this payment as a condition for

22 The Fund for Defense of Diffuse Rights financially supports projects to repair damages to the environment, free competition, consumer rights and the historical, cultural and artistic heritage.

23 As provided for by Article 37 of the 2011 Antitrust Law, anticompetitive conducts subject offenders to fines of 0.1% to 20% of the annual gross revenues registered by the company, economic group or conglomerate in the year before filing the Administrative Proceeding, in the business activity where the conduct occurred.

settling in practically all recent cases involving non-cartel violations (i.e. unilateral conduct and abuse of dominance) for deterrence purposes.[24]

The CADE Bylaws also require that settling defendants acknowledge their participation in the conduct under investigation and cooperate with the investigations in cases involving cartels.

4. Negotiating a settlement

As mentioned before, antirust settlements are negotiated with a negotiation commission consisting of at least 3 members of CADE's staff, under the supervision and instruction of either the Superintendent-General or the Reporting-Commissioner, depending on whether the case is at SG-CADE or at the Administrative Court. As a rule, the officials involved in the investigations and who are familiar with the details of the cases are invited to be part of the negotiation commissions. CADE has invested in negotiation skills training to prepare its staff for this task, and developed negotiation procedures to ensure that negations move quickly and efficiently.

In this context, CADE has been dividing the negotiation procedures into three steps in order to separately discuss the three main commitments required from defendants in a cartel settlement: (i) cooperation; (ii) acknowledgment of participation in the conduct; and (iii) monetary contributions. The purpose of this division is to avoid discussion of one commitment contaminating discussions of the others, compromising the negotiations.

The order of discussions is also important to allow the authority to assess how effective and useful the cooperation the defendant has to offer is. This aspect may affect negotiation of the requirements that follow, considering that the more a defendant cooperates with investigations, the better its discount in the monetary contribution should be. In principle, strong cooperation may also put a defendant in a better position to negotiate

---

[24] In this regard, *see*, for example, CADE, Reporting Commissioner Márcio de Oliveira Júnior (Settlement Agreement No. 08700.004410/2014-58) (May 27, 2014). CADE, Reporting Commissioner Olavo Zago Chinaglia (Settlement Agreement No. 08700.004379/2010-21) (Aug. 25, 2010).

the scope of acknowledgment of participation in the conduct. Each of these main topics of the negotiation will be described in greater detail below.

C. *Cooperation with the Investigations*

The first step of a settlement negotiation is to discuss what the defendant has to offer in terms of cooperation and what the authorities expect in this regard. Within the current legal framework, a cartel settlement will only be attractive for the authorities if the defendant settling is willing and able to cooperate with the investigations. The type and extent of cooperation, however, may vary from one case to another and may not necessarily be limited to the provision of direct evidence to confirm the existence of the cartel and participation of other defendants. Cooperation may also involve technical assistance regarding the markets under investigation, assistance in the analysis of documents and associated evidence, among others. As a rule, CADE requires the settling defendants to provide a summary of the conduct and also documents to support the facts declared by the defendants.

The level of cooperation will be considered by CADE in setting the monetary contribution to settle, which is calculated based on the amount of the expected fine that could be imposed on the defendant in case of conviction, minus a discount for settling. If an agreement is reached and a settlement is executed, CADE usually requires the settling party to agree to provide additional cooperation until the investigation is ended, if necessary.

In certain cases, CADE may waive the defendant settling from the obligation to cooperate, particularly if the defendant has no valuable cooperation to offer or if the case is already at an advanced stage, with sufficient evidence to support a decision. In the absence of valuable cooperation, a settling defendant may receive a smaller deduction from the monetary contribution.

a. Acknowledgement of participation in the conduct

The second step of the negotiation is to discuss the extent and scope of acknowledgment of participation in the conduct under investigation. As discussed before, this requirement has been made mandatory in cartel settlements, to preserve the leniency program and deterrence. This mandatory commitment may play a key role in a defendant's decision to settle, considering that a settlement agreement does not shield defendants against possible civil claims for damages[25] or any individuals involved against criminal prosecution,[26] taking into account that practicing a cartel is also considered a crime under applicable Brazilian law. Therefore, it is advisable to make a careful risk assessment of possible civil claims for damages and criminal prosecution before entering into a settlement negotiation.

The lack of criminal immunity for individuals who decide to settle has been considered a major barrier that may prevent individuals from engaging in settlement negotiations, particularly at the present time, when there seems to be a trend towards intensifying criminal prosecution for anticompetitive practices.[27] This factor may also prevent companies from entering into negotiations seeking to preserve their executives and employees, or make it very difficult to convince individuals to cooperate and join the agreements.[28]

Nevertheless, the antitrust authorities do not seem to be supportive towards an amendment to the 2011 Antitrust Law to create criminal immunity for settlements. A possible concern is that the extension of this benefit to settlements might weaken the leniency program.

---

25 Antitrust lawsuits for damages are not yet very common in Brazil, considering that the Brazilian legal framework does not offer the necessary tools and incentives for private parties to build a successful case and to encourage them to seek compensation before the courts of law. A high level of burden of proof is imposed on the plaintiffs (who need to demonstrate the damages actually suffered as a result of the conduct). In addition, there are no treble damages or punitive damages in Brazil (compensation must be proportional to the actual damages suffered). Only a few lawsuits for antitrust damages have been filed in Brazil and in none of them has a final decision been rendered so far. In this regard, *see* LEONARDO MANIGLIA Duarte, LÍVIA GANDARA, and GEORGE CAROLL. *Private Antitrust Enforcement in Brazil*. Robins, Kaplan, Miller & Ciresi L.L.P. Antitrust Bulletin – Fall 2012 | Vol. 4, No. 2. *Available at* http://www.robinskaplan.com/resources/newsletters/~/media/013947DD3E0A44F396EEFAD7B2438C44.ashx

26 Although criminal prosecution for a cartel is still not very common in Brazil, the Public Prosecutors have recently become more active, filing criminal charges against individuals in certain cases.

27 PERPAOLO BOTTINI, RICARDO INGLEZ, and FERNANDA AYRES DELLOSO. *A nova dinâmica dos acordos de cessação de práticas anticoncorrenciais no Brasil*, *supra* note 20, at 9.

28 BRIAN BYRNE, and, CARVALHAES AMADEU RIBEIRO. *Three Proposals To Improve Brazil's Cartel Settlement Process*. 6-7. ABA/IBRAC's Antitrust in the Americas Conference, São Paulo, Brazil, 2013.

These risks may be mitigated depending on the extent and scope of acknowledgment of participation that the defendant is able to negotiate with CADE. There have been cases in which CADE has accepted generic descriptions for purposes of acknowledgement of participation in the settlement agreement disclosed to the public, leaving the specific details of the conduct to the confidential "summary of conduct" submitted by the settling defendant for cooperation purposes, which is usually treated as confidential and available to CADE and the other defendants only for purposes of exercising their right of defense.[29] Therefore, a successful negotiation of the extent, scope and confidentiality of this requirement is crucial for mitigating possible risks for the settling defendants.

The approach of accepting a generic and less detailed acknowledgement of participation in the conduct as part of the settlement agreement to be made available to the public fully meets the legal requirement on this matter and, at the same time, mitigates the level of exposure of defendants to possible risks arising from this acknowledgment. This approach benefits not only the defendants, but also the authorities with an additional incentive to encourage defendants to settle, and increase the attractiveness of the settlement policy. In this context, it would be a significant improvement if CADE were to amend its Bylaws to expressly provide for this possibility, so as to afford defendants greater predictability and attractiveness when considering the possibility of settling.[30]

It would also bring more comfort to defendants to have clear rules addressing the possibility of acknowledging participation only in part of the conduct, considering that there are cases involving a variety of different conduct, timeframes and geographic regions, not always related to all the defendants. In fact, it is unreasonable and unfair to require a defendant to admit participation in all the conduct under investigation when there is no evidence in the case files that such defendant would have participated in all of them. Therefore, it is advisable for the CADE Bylaws to lay down clear rules allowing a partial admission of participation, which should be limited to the extent of the evidence against the defendant settling in the case files.

---

29 Alberto Afonso Monteiro. *Settlements in Cartel Cases: Recent Developments and Proposals for Improvement,* 17. *Available at* http://www.veirano.com.br/upload/content_attachments/95/Compromisso_de_cessacao_em_casos_de_cartel_avancos_recentes_e_propostas_de_aperfeicoamento_2013_original.pdf.

30 *Idem.*

b. Monetary contribution

Discussions regarding the monetary contribution are left to the end of the negotiation, not only because it is usually the toughest topic to be negotiated, but also because setting the amount of the contribution will be affected by the extent and value of the cooperation provided. Although the 2011 Antitrust Law states that the monetary contribution may not be less than the minimum fine set by law,[31] monetary contributions in cartel cases have been set at levels far beyond the minimum amount.

The criteria established by the CADE Bylaws for setting monetary contributions take into consideration the amount of the "expected fine" that could be imposed in case of conviction, minus a discount for settling. According to the CADE Bylaws, for settlements negotiated with SG-CADE, the amount of the contribution must take into account the degree of the defendant's cooperation with the investigations and the point at which the defendant makes the proposal, observing, whenever possible, the following levels of discounts:

(i) Reduction from 30% to 50% of the expected fine for the first defendant to propose a settlement agreement;

(ii) Reduction from 25% to 40% of the expected fine for the second defendant to propose a settlement agreement;

(iii) Reduction up to 25% of the expected fine for other defendants that propose a settlement agreement.

For settlements negotiated when the case is already at the CADE Administrative Court, however, the amount of the contribution should take into consideration the status of the investigation, and the maximum discount applicable is 15% of the expected fine only.

If the authorities consider that the settling defendant has provided strong cooperation, they usually grant the maximum discount allowed (i.e. 50% for the first to settle, 40% for the second to settle and 25% for the third to settle while the case is still at SG-CADE). Nevertheless, it is not possible to receive a higher percentage discount than the percentage granted to

---

31 As stated by Article 37 of the Antitrust Law, anticompetitive conducts subject offenders to fines of 0.1% to 20% of the annual gross revenues registered by the company, economic group or conglomerate in the year before filing the Administrative Proceeding, in the business activity in which the conduct occurred.

other defendants in previous settlements reached in the same investigation. As discussed above, these provisions seek to encourage defendants to settle sooner rather than latter and when the case is still at the fact-finding stage before SG-CADE, when cooperation is more useful for the authorities.

One of the most challenging topics when negotiating a settlement is to reach a common understanding on what should be the "expected fine" in case of conviction, which results from the lack of clear guidelines for setting fines under the 2011 Antitrust Law. The estimate of the expected fine requires the definition of: (i) the relevant revenues to be considered as the basic amount for calculating the fine, which, according to the Antitrust Law, should be the revenues registered by the company or group in the "business activity in which the violation occurred"; and (ii) the percentage fine to be applied, which, according to the Antitrust Law, may vary from 0.1% to 20% of the relevant revenues.

The definition of "business activity in which the violation occurred" has been the source of debates and disagreements between antitrust authorities, legal practitioners and academics since enactment of the 2011 Antitrust Law. It is undoubtedly one of the most controversial issues regarding setting fines and negotiating settlements in Brazil nowadays. Some hold that this legal concept should be interpreted to encompass only the products and services affected by the conducts under investigation or the relevant markets affected, while others, including the authorities, defend a broader interpretation to include other products and services that may be considered part of the same activity.

In this regard, CADE has enacted CADE Regulation No. 3/2012 to establish a list of "business activities" for purposes of setting of fines, which was based on the National Classification of Economic Activities – CNAE. The CNAE was inspired by the United Nations International Standard Industrial Classification of All Economic Activities – ISIC.[32]

---

[32] Some academics sustain that CADE Regulation No. 3/2012 is illegal, based on the argument that it would exceed CADE's normative powers, considering that the Antitrust Law did not delegate to CADE specific powers to enact rules on setting fines. In this regard, please refer to Sérgio Varella Bruna's presentation at the IBRAC International Seminar on Competition Policy in 2012. *Available at:* http://www.ibrac.org.br/Uploads/Eventos/18SeminarioConcorrencia/PALESTRAS/Sergio%20Varella%20Bruna.pdf

The problem is that most of the categories of business activities on this list are overly vague and wide-ranging, and frequently end up capturing revenues derived from the sale of products and services not even slightly affected by the alleged violations, leading to the setting of fines that may be disproportional to the anticompetitive effects potentially produced by the conduct under investigation.[33]

Although the CADE Administrative Court has in some cases already expressed the understanding that CADE Regulation No. 3/2012 could be applied with shades of proportionality in the light of the specific circumstances of each case, there are still many uncertainties on this matter, limiting predictability and transparency in the negotiation of monetary contributions and making settlements less attractive for defendants.

For instance, in the air freight cartel investigation, the CADE Administrative Court concluded that only billing from air cargo transportation should be considered for calculating all the fines / monetary contributions levied on the defendants, even though CADE Regulation No. 3/2012 defines "Air Transportation – passengers and cargo" as one selfsame "business activity".[34]

Following the same approach, in the settlement agreements executed in the investigation of a cartel in a tender for procurement of ambulances, the CADE Administrative Court concluded that it would not be reasonable and proportional to set the expected fine on the basis of the total billing of the economic group, based on the classification of business activity as provided by CADE Regulation No. 3/2012, considering as a parameter the amount of the contract related to the tender, taking into account that the scope of the investigation was limited to just one tender.[35] A similar understanding was also applied by the CADE Administrative Court in the settlement agreement executed in the investigation of a cartel in tenders for providing laundry services to public hospitals in the State of Rio de Janeiro, in which the CADE Administrative Court also applied a more flexible approach for reasons of proportionality.[36]

---

33 Alberto Afonso Monteiro. *Settlements in Cartel Cases: Rece nt Developments and Proposals for Improvement, supra* note 33, at 15.

34 Administrative Proceeding No. 08012.011037/2006-02

35 Administrative Proceeding No. 08012.003931/2005-58

36 CADE, Reporting Commissioner Márcio de Oliveira Júnior (Administrative Proceeding No. 08012.008850/2008-94) (May 2, 2014).

Based on these precedents, there is still a significant level of uncertainty on how to define the "business activity in which the violation occurred" for purposes of setting fines, which may have the undesirable effect of leading to fines or monetary contributions that are unreasonable and disproportional to any potential effects caused by the conduct under investigation in the affected relevant markets.

The most suitable solution for this problem would be to interpret the legal concept of "business activity in which the violation occurred" as the product(s) or service(s) potentially affected by the conduct under investigation, following the best international practices on this matter.[37-38-39] CADE could easily settle this highly controversial issue by regulation to amend or replace CADE Regulation No. 3/2012 or even through case law, with more conclusive and clear rules or guidelines for setting fines.

The list of business activities provided by CADE Regulation No. 3/2012 may even be considered as an initial parameter or starting point for a definition of the business activity in which the violation occurred, but never as a strict listing to be applied mechanically and automatically, without taking into consideration the peculiarities of each case. Otherwise, it will inevitably end up taking in separate business activities that may not be even remotely related to or affected by a given conduct.

In the context of a negotiation of a settlement, in which there is usually no final assessment of the scope of the conduct under investigation and of the level of participation of each defendant, it is essential for the definition of the relevant revenues to serve as the basis for calculating the expected fine to take into consideration the scope of the accusations and evidence against the settling defendant and the business activities that may actually have been affected by the conduct defined in such accusations.

Although it is important to preserve the amount of the expected fine that might be imposed in case of conviction as a parameter to set

---

37 For instance, the European Commission guidelines on the method of setting fines imposed pursuant to Article 23(2)(a) of Regulation (EC) No. 1/2003 (*Commission Guidelines on fines*), Official Journal C 210 of 1.9.2006, and the United States Sentencing Commission Guidelines Manual § 8C4.1 (November 1, 2014).

38 Alberto Afonso Monteiro. *Settlements in Cartel Cases: Recent Developments and Proposals for Improvement, supra* note 33, at 15.

39 Brian Byrne, and Carvalhaes Amadeu Ribeiro. *Three Proposals To Improve Brazil's Cartel Settlement Process, supra* note 28, at 14.

the amount of the contribution, so as to ensure deterrence, it is equally important to avoid setting contributions that may be disproportional to the potential negative economic effects derived from the conduct and possible advantage gained or pursued by the violator. If CADE does not adopt a proportional approach in setting fines and monetary contributions, there is a risk that defendants may be discouraged to settle, with convicted defendants ending up challenging CADE's decision before the courts of law, which may ultimately decide what should be the best interpretation for the legal concept of business activity.

Another troublesome aspect in discussing the "expected fine" with the authorities is to determine the percentage of the fine that might be imposed on the settling defendant in the event of conviction. In the most recent decisions in settlement cases, CADE has applied a standard percentage of 15% to estimate the expected fine, considering that fines in recent cases of cartels have been mostly set around this percentage. The automatic application of a percentage of 15% in each and every case involving an accusation of a cartel, on the sole argument of its involving a violation considered to be grave, fails to take into account other criteria for weighting the penalties provided for by the Antitrust Law, and minimizes the importance of the constitutional principle of individualization of the penalty.

In addition to the seriousness of the violation, the 2011 Antitrust Law also determines that weighting the penalty should take into account, among other criteria, the good faith of the offender, possible negative economic effects produced on the market and the advantage gained or pursued by the offender. It is essential for all aggravating and attenuating circumstances covered under the Antitrust Law should be duly considered when setting the expected fine, at the risk of reaching an amount that would be excessive and disproportional.

The peculiarities of each defendant in an investigation may justify the application of different criteria in setting the fine for each defendant, and must be analyzed on a case-by-case basis, out of respect for the constitutional principle of individualization of the penalty and the weighting criteria for penalties provided by law.[40]

---

40 Another interesting argument to question the standard 15% fine is the fact that the 2011 Antitrust Law amended the range for the application of fines from 1% to 30%

In spite of all these arguments, CADE has been insisting on adopting the 15% standard percentage to estimate the expected fine in most cartel cases. Like the dispute regarding definition of the legal concept of "business activity in which the violation occurred", poor predictability and transparency regarding the definition of the percentage of the expected fine also derives from the lack of clear and consistent guidelines for setting fines for anticompetitive violations.

CADE, however, has been more open to adopting a flexible approach for the definition of the relevant revenues in certain cases, which is usually more effective in terms of reducing the amount of monetary contributions. It is important to note that CADE has also required the application of a duration adjustment to increase the amount of monetary contributions in cases of cartels that lasted for longer periods, usually adding 1.5% to the amount of the estimated fine per year of duration of the cartel. The enactment of guidelines to bring more predictability and transparency to the rules for setting fines would be a major improvement.

D. *Other Commitments that May be Required in a Settlement*

In addition to the mandatory commitments required by the Antitrust Law, settling defendants may also be required to undertake other obligations in order to settle, such as refraining from challenging the use of documents obtained either from the leniency applicant or by dawn raids before the courts of law, and implementing or improving compliance programs. In principle, CADE may impose or the settling party may propose different obligations depending on the specificities of each case.

In certain cases, particularly in cases of unilateral conduct, the authorities may try to obtain certain commitments from the settling defendants to improve competition in situations of market or regulatory failures, reduce barriers to entry for new competitors, and create better

(under the 1994 Antitrust Law) to 0.1% to 20%. Therefore, the level of 15% applied by CADE to cases of cartels, under the guidance of the previous law, would be equivalent to approximately 10% under the new law. To maintain proportionality with the levels of fines that were being applied when the previous law was in effect, considering that CADE applied a rate at a percentage corresponding to 50% of the maximum rate provided for in law (15%, considering the maximum rate of 30%), the proportional rate corresponding to 50% of the maximum stated in the new law would be 10%.

conditions for the development of competition in ways which could not be achieved in a decision of conviction.[41]

A desirable improvement to be considered in the regulation of settlement negotiation would be to provide incentives to encourage settling defendants to propose these types of commitments to settle, by granting additional discounts in the monetary contributions in exchange for the implementation of measures which could have the effect of correcting market or regulation flaws or in some way improving competition in the affected markets.

II. Final Remarks

It is undisputable that the antitrust settlement policy in Brazil has undergone considerable progress since enactment of the 1994 Antitrust Law. The current rules provided by the 2011 Antitrust Law and CADE Bylaws, as amended in 2013, made considerable improvements in terms of predictability and transparency, and took the Brazilian antitrust settlement system to the next level, making it better aligned with the best international practices.

The current system seems to have achieved a good balance between creating incentives to encourage defendants to settle – and to do that sooner rather than later –, while, at the same time, also preserving the attractiveness of the leniency program and the deterrent effect of negotiated resolutions. The success of the settlement policy is borne out by the number of agreements executed in cartel cases since the current rules came into force in 2013: 6 in 2013, 22 in 2014, and 6 in just the first two months of 2015.

In spite of all developments so far, there are still many gray areas that need to be clarified by CADE so as to have more transparency and predictability in the negotiation process and provide the settling defendants with a clear picture of the possible outcomes in a settlement negotiation.

41 Administrative Proceeding No. 08012.002474/2008-24. Under the agreement, AmBev agreed to stop using 630-ml returnable bottles with beer of any current of future mark, and to discontinue the line of differentiated bottles, considering that this practice was allegedly increasing rivals' costs as an abrupt departure from the returnable bottle system in place in Brazil for many years, in which all brewers used the same standard 600 ml returnable bottles.

These improvements are key to ensuring the attractiveness of the settlement policy for defendants, and consequently allow the authorities to use settlements as an effective tool for cartel enforcement and deterrence. In this context, the upcoming challenges that CADE still has to face to improve the Brazilian antitrust settlement system may be summarized as follows:

1. **Markers:** establish clear rules and procedures on how defendants can obtain a marker to secure their places in line to negotiate settlements.

2. **Confidentiality**: establish clear rules and guidelines on the situations in which confidentiality may not be granted in a settlement negotiation, and treat these situations as exceptions and confidentiality as the rule. It is also important to ensure the maximum degree of confidentiality possible for the information and documents provided by the settling defendant in cooperation, limiting access to such information and documents to other defendants and for defense purposes only. The greater the level of confidentiality granted by the authority, the better the chances that defendants will fully cooperate.

3. **Guarantees if an agreement is not reached**: establish clear rules to expressly extend the same guarantees provided for the negotiation of leniency agreements to the negotiation of settlements regarding the use of information and documents provided in the negotiation, so as to ensure that all information or documents presented during the negotiation will be either returned or destroyed, and will not be used by the authorities if an agreement is not reached. These guarantees are essential to provide the defendants with the necessary comfort to cooperate and share information and documents without reservations.

4. **Scope of Acknowledgment:** provide clear rules and guidelines for the extent and scope of acknowledgment of participation in the conduct, and allow generic and less-detailed acknowledgement of participation in the settlement agreement to be made available to the public, leaving the details of the facts in the confidential version of the history of conduct to be made available only to the other defendants for defense purposes. This approach is consistent with the legal requirement on this matter and, at the same time, mitigates the level of exposure of defendants to possible risks arising from this acknowledgment, benefiting not only the defendants, but also the authorities with an additional incentive to encourage defendants to settle and fully cooperate. It is also recommendable to have clear rules on the possibility of acknowledging participation in only part of the conduct,

which should be limited to the extent of evidence against the settling defendant in the case files.

5. **Mitigating the risk of criminal prosecution for settling individuals:** a conclusive solution for this concern seems to require amendments to the applicable legislation, to allow the public prosecutors to refrain from criminally prosecuting individuals who decide to settle, or to reinstate the possibility of executing agreements in criminal lawsuits for cartel violations, which was no longer a possibility for cartel violators after the increase in the criminal penalty for cartels introduced by the 2011 Antitrust Law.[42] Therefore, although CADE seems to have little room to solve this concern by itself, it may try to join forces with the public prosecutors to find a reasonable solution to mitigate this risk and encourage individuals to settle.

6. **Setting fines:** It is of the utmost importance for CADE to establish clear rules and guidelines for setting fines for anticompetitive practices in order to improve consistency and predictability not only in the settlement negotiations, but also – and perhaps more important – for setting fines in decisions of conviction. The legal concept of "business activity in which the violation occurred" should be interpreted as the product(s) or service(s) potentially affected by the conduct under investigation, following the best international practices on this matter and in accordance to the principles of proportionality and reasonableness established by the Brazilian Constitution and applicable legislation. CADE should also provide clear rules for defining the percentage of the fine and take into consideration all mitigating and aggravating circumstances in this decision, as opposed to applying a standard percentage for certain practices (i.e. 15% in all cartel cases) regardless of the particularities of each defendant's situation. It is also advisable to establish clear rules for the application of duration adjustments as an aggravating factor.

7. **Extra discounts in the monetary contribution for measures that may improve competition:** provide incentives to encourage settling defendants to propose or accept commitments that may have the effect of correcting market or regulation flaws or in any way improving competition in the affected markets.

---

42 Brian Byrne, and Carvalhaes Amadeu Ribeiro. *Three Proposals To Improve Brazil's Cartel Settlement Process, supra* note 28, at 14.

8. **Tailor-made rules and procedures for settlements in unilateral conduct investigations:** although a detailed analysis of the negotiation of settlements in cases involving unilateral conduct exceeds the scope of this paper, it is worth noting that the 2011 Antitrust Law does not lay down specific rules and requirements for the negotiation of settlements involving unilateral conduct, which presents different challenges and concerns and should therefore be treated differently than cartel cases, with tailor-made incentives to encourage the defendants to settle and cooperate in helping to improve competition in the affected markets. Therefore, it would be an improvement if CADE were to establish specific procedures, incentives and discounts to encourage settlements in these types of investigation.

These proposals would certainly add more predictability and transparency to the negotiation of settlements, and substantially improve the already-successful system implemented by CADE. The recent progress achieved so far in this and other areas of competition enforcement in Brazil is remarkable and demonstrates that CADE has what it takes and is on the right path to facing these challenges and improving even further the legal framework for the negotiation of settlements.

Bibliography

ALBERTO AFONSO MONTEIRO. *Settlements in Cartel Cases: Recent Developments and Proposals for Improvement*. Available at: http://www.veirano.com.br/upload/content_attachments/95/Compromisso_de_cessacao_em_casos_de_cartel_avancos_recentes_e_propostas_de_aperfeicoamento_2013_original.pdf.

ANA PAULA MARTINEZ. *Repressão a Cartéis: Interface Entre Direito Administrativo e Criminal.* São Paulo: Singular, 2013.

ANDRÉ MARQUES GILBERTO. *O Processo Antitruste Sancionador – Aspectos Processuais na Repressão das Infrações à Concorrência no Brasil.* São Paulo: Lex Editora, 2010.

BRENO ZABAN CARNEIRO. *Negociando com a Administração: Experiências Concretas na Superação dos Obstáculos à Negociação de Particulares com o Estado. Available at* http://repositorio.fjp.mg.gov.br/consad/bitstream/123456789/607/1/C4_TP_NEGOCIANDO%20COM%20A%20ADMINISTRA%C3%87%C3%83O%20EXPERI%C3%8ANCIAS.pdf.

BRIAN BYRNE, and CARVALHAES AMADEU RIBEIRO. *Three Proposals To Improve Brazil's Cartel Settlement Process.* ABA/IBRAC's Antitrust in the Americas Conference, São Paulo, Brazil, 2013.

CARLA LOBÃO. *Compromisso de Cessação de Prática: Uma Abordagem Crítica sobre o Instituto.* Revista do IBRAC – Direito da Concorrência, Consumo e Comércio Internacional, vol. 8, January 2001.

CARLOS EMMANUEL JOPPERT RAGAZZO. *O CADE e as Soluções Negociadas.* Conjuntura Econômica 2010: *Available at* http://works.bepress.com/carlos_ragazzo/9.

CARLOS EMMANUEL JOPPERT RAGAZZO, and DIOGO THOMSON ANDRADE. *Beyond Detection: The Management of Cartel Cases.* Competition Policy International (2012). *Available at* http://works.bepress.com/carlos_ragazzo/14.

CÉSAR MATTOS. *O Compromisso de Cessação de Práticas Anticompetitivas no CADE: Uma Abordagem de Teoria dos Jogos*, Revista do IBRAC – Direito da Concorrência, Consumo e Comércio Internacional, vol. 4, January 1997.

DANILO FERRAZ CÓRDOVA, and MARIANA REBUZZI SARCINELLI LOPES. *Política de Combate aos Cartéis: Os Acordos de Leniência, O Termo de Compromisso de Cessação e a Lei 11.482/2007.* Revista do IBRAC – Direito da Concorrência, Consumo e Comércio Internacional, vol. 15, p. 45, January 2007.

EUROPEAN COMMISSION. *Guidelines on the method of setting fines imposed pursuant to Article 23(2)(a) of Regulation No 1/200. Available at* http://eur-lex.europa.eu/legal-content/EN/TXT/PDF/?uri=CELEX:52006XC0901(01)&from=EN.

GUILHERME TEIXEIRA PEREIRA. *Política de Combate a Cartel no Brasil: Análise Jurídica do Acordo de Leniência e do Termo de Compromisso de Cessação de Prática*, 2011. *Available at* http://bibliotecadigital.fgv.br/dspace/bitstream/handle/10438/8518/disserta%E7%E3o%20de%20mestrado%20-%20vers%E3o%20final%20banca%20examinadora.pdf?sequence=1.

INTERNATIONAL COMPETITION NETWORK. Cartel Working Group. *Cartel Settlements: Report to the ICN Annual Conference, Kyoto, Japan, April 2008.* Available at: http://www.internationalcompetitionnetwork.org/uploads/library/doc347.pdf.

LEONARDO CANABRAVA TURRA. *Do Compromisso de Cessação de Prática no Sistema Brasileiro de Defesa da Concorrência: Considerações sobre a sua Natureza Jurídica, Compulsoriedade de Celebração pela Administração Pública e Questões de Direito Intertemporal.* Revista do IBRAC – Direito da Concorrência, Consumo e Comércio Internacional, vol. 13, 2006.

LEONARDO MANIGLIA DUARTE, LÍVIA GANDARA, and GEORGE CAROLL. *Private Antitrust Enforcement in Brazil.* Robins, Kaplan, Miller & Ciresi L.L.P. Antitrust Bulletin – Fall 2012 | Vol. 4, No. 2. *Available at* http://www.

robinskaplan.com/resources/newsletters/~/media/013947DD3E0A44F396EEFAD7B2438C44.ashx.

MASSIMO MOTTA, and AURORA ASCIONE. *Settlements in cartel cases*, "Settlements in cartel cases", European Competition Law Annual 2008: Antitrust settlements under EC Competition Law, Oxford: Hart Publishing, p. 67-83 (2010). *Available at* http://www.barcelonagse.eu/tmp/pdf/motta_settlementscartels.pdf.

ORGANISATION FOR ECONOMIC CO-OPERATION AND DEVELOPMENT – OECD. *Policy Roundtables: Experience with Direct Settlements in Cartel Cases - 2008. Available at* http://www.oecd.org/competition/cartels/44178372.pdf.

PAULO FURQUIM DE AZEVEDO, and ALEXANDRE LAURI HENRIKSEN. *Cartel Deterence and Settlements: The Brazilian Experience. Available at* http://bibliotecadigital.fgv.br/dspace/bitstream/handle/10438/6896/TD%20265%20%20Paulo%20Furquim%20de%20Azevedo.pdf?sequence=1&isAllowed=y.

PIERPAOLO BOTTINI, RICARDO INGLEZ, and FERNANDA AYRES DELLOSO. *A nova dinâmica dos acordos de cessação de práticas anticoncorrenciais no Brasil*, Revista do IBRAC, vol. 23 (2013).

RICHARD WHISH. *Competition Law*. 6. ed. Oxford: Oxford University Press, 2008.

ROBERTO EROS GRAU, and PAULA A. FORGIONI, *O Estado a Empresa e o Contrato*. São Paulo: Malheiros, 2005.

UNITED STATES SENTENCING COMMISSION. Guidelines Manual, §3E1.1 (Nov. 2014). *Available at* http://www.ussc.gov/sites/default/files/pdf/guidelines-manual/2014/GLMFull.pdf.

* * *

Chapter XII

LENIENCY AGREEMENTS IN BRAZIL

Marcelo Calliari
Daniel Andreoli
Marcio Bueno

I. Introduction

Over recent years, Brazil has become one of the most active jurisdictions in respect to anti-cartel investigations.

After a transition period when the Brazilian Antitrust Authority (*Conselho Administrativo de Defesa Econômica* "CADE") has clearly prioritized the implementation of a pre-merger review system that was introduced in 2012 as a consequence of the enactment of the New Antitrust Law (the Federal Act 12,529/11) and also the restructuring of the previous agencies into a single one – CADE the federal enforcer has now been able to resume the intense level of anti-cartel enforcement. In fact, several new cartel investigations have been initiated by CADE's Superintendence General ("CADE's SG") from 2014 and onwards. Simultaneously, the Tribunal, the decision-making body within CADE, has been able to conclude landmark cases including the *Cement* case[1] in which companies and individuals were severely punished with fines exceeding US$1billion and also with unprecedented divestment remedies. There were also two

1 *CADE fines cement cartel in BLR 3.1 billion. Avaliable at:* http://www.cade.gov.br/Default.aspx?71c455a47c9166ad78c596a1b69f.

important international cartel investigations (the *Air Cargo*[2] and the *Marine Hose*[3] cases) that were brought to an end by the Tribunal.

It is fair to attribute a great part of the level of anti-cartel enforcement activity in Brazil to the undisputed success of the country's leniency program. Although, it initially faced doubts from some local practitioners, the Brazilian authority was able to put in place a system that provides the necessary assurances to companies and individuals and therefore has been able to attract an increasing number of applications for immunity.

As a result of the dawn raid revolution,[4] the threat to cartelists became much more credible. This is probably one of the reasons that have lead companies to take benefit of the Leniency Program also incorporated into the former Brazilian Antitrust Law (the Federal Act 8,884/94) by the amendment of 2000, contracting the first impression that it would never work in Brazil due to a wrongly expected cultural repression.

The first Leniency Agreement was entered into with a Brazilian company that was part of a regional bid-rigging cartel among security companies in the State of Rio Grande do Sul. While the second was also related to a domestic cartel, it was entered into by a subsidiary of a German multinational group.

After these first agreements involving domestic cartels, there was a significant wave of agreements related to international cartel investigations,

---

2 *CADE Imposed a BRL 300 million fine against International Air Cargo Cartel. Avaliable at:* http://www.cade.gov.br/Default.aspx?9f9263b64ec358db2e1b2d0452f7.

3 Administrative Procedure 08012.010932/2007 – "CADE condemns companies and individuals for involvement in marine hoses' cartel". *Avaliable at:* http://www.cade.gov.br/Default.aspx?2b1eec3cd54ba161b582d56ec083

4 The success in obtaining astonishingly strong evidence of hardcore cartel violations in its very first dawn raid (Crushed Rock case) in 2003, search and seizure operations became intensively used and a key aspect of anti-cartel enforcement in Brazil. Several dawn raids were carried out in the following years and in many cases hard copies and electronic files reflecting communication among competitors were unveiled. Therefore, the following cartel investigations initiated by the Brazilian authorities were no longer based on circumstantial evidence but on direct proof of the anticompetitive agreement. As a consequence, the cases became much more solid and the level of the fines imposed on companies and individuals were increasingly higher (reaching the upper end of the percentage of annual turnover spectrum set forth by the law).

including the *GIS*, *Air Cargo*, *Marine Hose*, *Freight Forwarder*, *Compressors* and *CRT Glass*.

With the enactment of the new Competition Act in 2011 and the new regulations issued by CADE, there were some improvements to the Brazilian Leniency Program. Notably, the former prohibition for "ringleaders" to apply for leniency was dropped and the requirement that all individuals (employees and former employees) should execute the Agreement simultaneously with the corporate entity to be protected has been relaxed – the new rules now allow for later amendments to the Agreement to incorporate individuals into the Leniency protection.

While these new improvements into the Program have attracted more applications for Leniency in Brazil, it seems that CADE has been more selective in respect to the acceptance of new Agreements.

This is a recent and important trend. In fact, it seems that CADE has been raising the threshold in terms of the identification of effects in the Brazilian market when dealing with international cartels and also for supporting documentary evidence. When faced with applications for Leniency based on material considered insufficient to prove the communication among the competitors and effects into the domestic market CADE has opted to reject the execution of an Agreement and the initiation of an investigation of the reported violation. In these cases to provide minimum comfort to companies that in good faith have decided to approach the Brazilian authority to report violations, CADE has been issuing letters to the applicants on these cases confirming that the evidence provided was deemed insufficient for the initiation of a new investigation.

The Leniency Program has clearly matured over the years and is now considered a central aspect of the Brazilian Competition Policy, attracting the interest from both domestic and international applicants. Over the course of the years several new investigations have been launched based as a direct consequence of the success of the program.

II. The Brazilian Leniency Program

The central objective of the Brazilian Leniency Program is to receive self-reports from companies that have taken part in antitrust offenses that CADE is not aware of. Therefore, whenever the Leniency Applicants are unveiling information to the authority about a new cartel, they will receive the most benefit.

As part of the system, the Leniency Program provides benefit only to the first Applicant and CADE accepts oral applications and uses a marker to formalize the approach by the companies.

The application for Leniency must include the information about the products affected, a very simple description of the conduct, the time period and the name of the participants. It should be addressed to the Office of the Superintendent General who will then check the availability of a marker.

Sometimes CADE's SG will be able to respond immediately whether the requested marker is available (if not, that would mean that someone else has come in first); while on occasions they will need more time to confirm the availability (normally no more than a couple of days, unless there is a more complex issue of related markets).

If the marker is available, the applying company/individual must be identified and a date will be set, usually within a couple of days at the most, for a meeting so that further detail about the conduct can be provided to CADE and a written version of the marker is received.

If the marker is not available, the authorities will say so and generally no identification will have to be provided. Still, follow-up comers will be offered to receive "Sub-Markers" that will hold their place in the line which will allow them to proceed with the Leniency negotiations in case the first in line fails to perfect the original "Marker" and execute the Agreement with CADE.

The "Sub-Markers" are also used as a reference of order of arrival if an investigation is launched and companies opt to propose a Settlement Agreement, because this other program of the Brazilian authority also favors companies to reaching out to the authority as early as possible by granting greater level of discounts to the first companies to apply for Settlement.

According to CADE, over 40 leniency agreements have been executed and several more are under negotiation.[5]

5 *Avaliable at:* http://www.cade.gov.br/Default.aspx?2303050b110f11293f0057.

A. Full Leniency

To be eligible for Full Leniency, the applicant (company or individual) must be the first in and must confess to the violation, and bring sufficient information to the authority before CADE has any knowledge about the anti-competitive practice.

Other companies of the applicant's economic group are also protected by the leniency agreement. Another peculiarity of the Brazilian Antitrust Law is that the corporate immunity is not immediately extended to the employees (or former employees) that participated in the cartel. This means that individuals are also obliged to sign the leniency agreement and to abide by the same obligations as the company. Formerly, individuals would only be allowed to join the leniency application during the course of the negotiations but not after its signature. The new rules, however, allow the Agreement to be amended for the inclusion of current and former employees.

Another requirement of the Leniency Program is the obligation that the company and individuals cease their participation in the conduct by the time of the application. There is controversy whether this also prevent the applicants to continue to have contacts and meetings with the other cartelists with the objective of collecting additional evidence in the benefit of the investigation.

Once the Leniency Agreement is signed the must continue to collaborate and to bring additional information throughout the investigation, and has to abide by confidentiality rules.

The former legislation prevented the ring-leader to benefit from the Leniency Agreement. However, the new Brazilian Antitrust Law (Federal Act 12,529/11) has dropped that requirement and there is no further restrictions in respect to the role that the company or individual played in the conduct.

With respect to individuals, the Leniency Program grants not only administrative but also criminal immunity.

B. Partial Leniency

In case the applicant is the first one to seek Leniency, but in case CADE already has information about the conduct which is been reported, only Partial Leniency will be available. The benefit in this case will be a reduction of the administrative fine from one to two thirds. All the other terms and conditions will continue to apply to this case, including full criminal immunity for the individuals.

C. *Leniency Plus*

The Brazilian Leniency Program also contains a 'leniency plus' provision, by which any co-participant in a cartel who comes forward with evidence regarding another collusive conduct still unknown to the CADE will be granted a reduction of one-third on the penalties imposed in the original investigation. Additionally, said co-participant also enjoys full amnesty for the second practice (for which it was the first-in).

III. Practical Aspects of the Leniency Negotiations

Leniency negotiations in Brazil have substantially evolved over time as both the Authority and the private bar learn with the practice and with the exchange of best practices with the international peers. Below some of the current practicalities are described and explained.

A. *The History of Conduct*

The main contribution of the leniency applicant to CADE is the information and documents incorporated into the document named History of Conduct. The Brazilian authority requires that the History of Conduct should present a complete and comprehensive account of the antitrust violation which is being reported.

The typical structure of the History of Conduct includes an executive summary and the following sections:

a) Summary description of the conduct;

b) Identification of the signatories of the leniency agreement;

c) Identification of the other participants of the conduct;

d) Period (start and end dates) of the conduct;

e) Detailed report of the conduct;

f) Description of the affected market;

g) Identification of the competitors and customers;

h) Explanation of the effects of the conduct in the Brazilian territory; and,

i) Description of the documentary evidence produced.

Such structure and items can and frequently are adapted to the individual case but reflects the general expectation of CADE in respect to what information and documents should be provided by the applicant during the negotiations to qualify for the execution of the Leniency Agreement.

To be able to produce a consistent and solid History of Conduct, parties are expected to make a sufficiently deep internal investigation by means of interviews and review of documents. The information and material collected is then used to enable the applicant to explain with satisfactory detail the reported conduct so CADE can be used it as the starting point of its investigation against the co-participants in the cartel.

In terms of electronic files, CADE has significantly increased the forensic requirements for the collection, processing and identification of the evidence that is used to support the History of Conduct. A table with electronic properties and identification of each document is expected to be produced by the applicant.

B. Criminal Immunity Negotiations

While the Brazilian Antitrust Law provides for automatic criminal immunity for the individuals who execute the leniency agreement with CADE, it has been common practice in many cases to invite Public (Federal and State) Prosecutors to co-sign the leniency agreements. The objective to this is to address the concern raised by some scholars and practitioners with the alleged unconstitutionality of the provision that prevents the criminal prosecution of the leniency applicants as it would violate the full independence granted to the Public Prosecutors. By having them to jointly sign the leniency agreements can serve as a safeguard against such allegations and provide additional protection to the individuals.

C. Confidentiality and Access to Files

One of the key principles of a leniency program is confidentiality. This is important to protect the applicant for leniency in respect to exposures in other jurisdictions and specially in respect to private damages actions.

According to the Brazilian Antitrust Law, the identity as well as all of the evidence produced by the applicant for leniency should remain confidential throughout the course of CADE's investigation up to the final decision (when the names and material will be disclosed).

Public Prosecutors involved in the negotiations for criminal immunity and in parallel investigations as well as the Judiciary in connection with requests for search and seizure warrants based on leniency materials should also observe strict confidentiality.

On the other hand, in respect to the defendants in an investigation, it is not possible to withhold any information or documents. As a matter of due process of law, they must have the right to access all the relevant documents used in the proceedings against them. According to explicit instructions given by CADE, defendants should only use the leniency information and material for the purpose of their defense in Brazil and these could not be used in other forums.

Lately, third parties such as customers have tried to obtain access to the files of the investigations originated by leniency agreements but CADE has consistently refused that recognizing granting access to evidence brought by the leniency applicant that could be used against it on private litigation will mean a strong disincentive for the newcomers and undermine the whole program.

D. Continuous Cooperation

As mentioned above, the contribution of the leniency signatory should continue throughout the investigation and until the final decision by CADE's Tribunal. While making the witness available for depositions is the most common follow-on cooperation that has been required from the applicants in the course of the proceedings, it is also possible that the assistance in respect to technical information as well as the production of additional evidence or even further internal investigation is demanded by the Authority as it makes the case against the defendants.

IV. Recent and Future Trends

According to our experience on recent negotiations, it seems that CADE has been re-adjusting the threshold for the acceptance of leniency applications. In practice, it seems that the Authority has been raising the bar in terms of both the quality of evidence of the conduct which should be produced by the applicant as well as the level of impact in the Brazilian territory when dealing with international cartels without any local activity.

It seems that the aim of CADE's SG while been more rigorous and selective as described above is to be able to launch stronger cases with a high rate of success in terms of conviction before the Tribunal and also in terms of the judicial review of its decisions.

While it is reasonable to allocate its limited resources on cases that have solid basis for enforcement, it is certainly important for CADE to take into consideration the evolving nature of anticompetitive arrangements. As business understands that the Authority is more vigilant, it is expected that new ways of communication are used to avoid detection and therefore finding the "smoking gun" or the "hot document" will become rarer.

The continued adjustment of the thresholds may be one of the most important challenges for the Brazilian Leniency Program going forward.

* * *

Chapter XIII

UNILATERAL CONDUCT LAW AND PRACTICE IN BRAZIL

Ricardo Botelho
Aurélio Santos

I. Introduction

This paper provides an overview of the scope and application of unilateral conduct laws in Brazil. For its purposes, unilateral conduct laws refer to the rules prohibiting dominant firms from misusing their market power to distort competition.[1]

The intent is to present a practical description of the elements and current legal standards governing application of unilateral conduct laws by the Brazilian Antitrust Authority (CADE). The assessment will focus on the main exclusionary conducts: exclusive dealing, conditional rebates, tying and bundling, predatory pricing and refusal-to-deal.[2]

Section B describes the scope and elements of Brazilian unilateral conduct rules. Section C summarizes the current legal standards applicable

1 In such context, unilateral conduct is also commonly referred as monopolization or abuse of dominance practices.

2 It is outside the scope of the analysis of exploitative abuses (such as excessive pricing or exploitative discriminatory pricing), as well as other anticompetitive practices not typically analyzed under the unilateral exclusionary conduct rules (resale price maintenance, sham litigation and others).

to main practices, based on legislation, existing guidelines and case law. Section D comments on the legal consequences of infringement, followed by Section E with conclusions.

A. *Scope and Elements of Applicable Law*

(i) *Law and Guidelines*

Law 12,529, dated November 30, 2011 (Brazilian Antitrust Law) establishes the substantive provisions governing unilateral conducts in Article 36. Different from other competition systems, Article 36 does not expressly set forth different material rules for unilateral conducts as opposed to anticompetitive horizontal or vertical agreements. According to the wording of Article 36, "regardless of the intent, any act that has the object or otherwise is able to produce the following effects, even if such effects are not achieved, shall constitute a violation". The specified effects are: "(1) to limit, hinder or in any way restrain competition or free enterprise, (2) to dominate a relevant product or service market, (3) to arbitrarily increase profits, and (4) to abuse monopoly power".

Paragraph 1 makes it clear that amassing market power "by means of natural process based on superior efficiency in relation to competitors" does not represent a violation of Article 36. Paragraph 3 establishes a non-exhaustive list of conducts that may constitute violation if the requirements of the caption of Article 36 are met.[3]

Reference enforcement guidelines (Guidelines) applicable to unilateral conducts as well as to other anticompetitive practices were established in the annexes of CADE's Resolution 20, dated June 28, 1999.[4] The Guidelines consist of the basic analytic framework for anticompetitive

---

3 The list includes various types of horizontal and vertical agreements as well as unilateral conducts. It mentions, for example, collusion among competitors, resale price maintenance and other restrictions affecting sales to third parties. As to unilateral conduct, the list specifies various actions to exclude or hinder new entrants or existing rivals, including refusals-to-deal and limitations on access to inputs or distribution channels, tying, predatory pricing, imposition of unreasonable contractual conditions and others.

4 Although part of Resolution 20 was expressly revoked, the annexes with the framework for analysis of anticompetitive conduct remain in force.

practices in general for orientation of enforcement[5]–they are not binding to CADE. Annex I contains definitions for anticompetitive practices, classified into horizontal and vertical categories. Annex II outlines the "basic criteria for the analysis of restrictive practices", describing the specific steps to be followed.[6]

(ii) *Foundation on the Brazilian Constitution*

The repression of unilateral conducts is explicitly based on Brazil's Constitution. Its Article 173, Paragraph 4, which is also the constitutional basis for national competition policy, states that "the law shall repress the abuse of economic power that aims at the dominance of markets, the elimination of competition, and the arbitrary increase of profits". Unilateral conducts policy, thus, occupies a central role in the wording of the constitutional provisions of Brazilian antitrust system. In addition, the Constitution also determines that the economic order is founded on the principle of free enterprise as well as on the respect of the value of human work, and must follow certain principles, including "free competition", "private property", "social role of property", and "consumer protection". The enforcement of one of these principles shall not contradict or deny the application of the others. Where there is an apparent clash of two principles in a concrete case, a rule of proportionality (rule of reason) must guide the result.[7]

5 The Guidelines refer to Articles 20 and 21 of the former Brazilian antitrust law (Law 8,884/94), which have practically identical wording as Article 36 of the Brazilian Antitrust Law.

6 These steps include: (1) confirmation if there is sufficient evidentiary basis that the investigated practice has occurred, (2) analysis of the existence of a dominant position, which involves defining the relevant market in both product and geographic dimensions, determining market shares and levels of concentration, and analyzing barriers to entry, and (3) assessment of the economic efficiencies likely to result from the practice against the actual or potential harm to competition.

7 Such rule of proportionality could be divided into three successive rules: (1) capability (or aptitude): the measure (decision, conduct, etc.) is capable of achieving a certain result, (2) necessity: achieving the intended result is not objectively possible without the adopted measure, and (3) strict proportionality: the restriction to the effectiveness of one or more of the considered principles is not disproportionate in view of the relevance of the ultimate goal of the principle (or principles) pursued by the adopted measure.

(iii) *Objectives of Unilateral Conduct Rules*

The Constitution and the Brazilian Antitrust Law do not establish specific objectives for the unilateral conduct policy. In practice, unilateral conduct enforcement by CADE pursues typical Brazilian Antitrust Law goals such as ensuring an effective competitive process, promoting consumer welfare, maximizing efficiency, and ensuring economic freedom.[8]

(iv) *Framework for the Assessment of Unilateral Conducts*

Based on the provisions of Article 36,[9] CADE's case law has consistently acknowledged a general framework for the assessment of unilateral conducts based on the necessary assessment of specific, actual or potential effects of the investigated conduct – an 'effects-based' approach[10]–, which is also reflected in the provisions of the Guidelines. According to this approach, anticompetitive effects must always be balanced by efficiencies and other justifications and defenses in order to establish the net effects to consumer welfare resulting from the conduct under investigation.[11]

---

8 International Competition Network, ICN Report on the Objectives of Unilateral Conduct Laws, Assessment of Dominance/Substantial Market Power, and State Created Monopolies (2007) [hereinafter ICN Report on Objectives and Dominance], *available at* http://internationalcompetitionnetwork.org/uploads/library/doc353.pdf.

9 As well as on identical provisions of Articles 20 and 21 of the former Brazilian antitrust law, substituted by Article 36.

10 According to ICN, "effects-based approach requires a careful and often more complex analysis of the potential effects of a particular behavior [than form-based approach], generating fact-driven outcomes. (...) The effects-based approach allows for an analysis of the circumstances in the particular case, and is therefore particularly suitable where neither economic theory nor empirical research predicts ex-ante a procompetitive or exclusionary explanation for a certain type of conduct with a high degree of certainty. Several alternative economic tests for an effects-based approach can be distinguished; the major alternatives include the consumer welfare balancing test, the profit sacrifice test, the no economic sense test, and the as efficient competitor test". International Competition Network, *Unilateral Conduct Workbook Chapter 1: The Objectives and Principles of Unilateral Conduct Laws* (2012) [hereinafter *ICN* Unilateral Conduct Workbook], at 11 and 14, *available at* http://www.internationalcompetitionnetwork.org/uploads/library/doc827.pdf.

11 Damien Geradin, Caio Mario da S. P. Neto, *For a Rigorous 'Effects-Based' Analysis of Vertical Restraints Adopted by Dominant Firms: An Analysis of the EU and Brazilian Competition Law*, June 2012, *available at* ssrn.com/abstract=2173735.

A unilateral conduct in violation of Article 36 will only exist when the justifications and defenses are not sufficient to outweigh the anticompetitive effects.

The general framework consists of three main steps, analyzed in detail below:[12]

(1) assessing whether the investigated company holds *dominant position* in the relevant market,

(2) evaluating (*actual or potential*) *negative effects* to competition arising from the conduct, and

(3) balancing negative effects with *justifications and defenses* (efficiencies) in order to assess the net effects of the conduct.

Pursuant to this framework, CADE does not admit, in principle, a merely formal ('form-based') approach[13] or even a 'per se' illegality approach to unilateral conducts. In both cases ('form-based' and 'per se' illegality approaches), a practice may constitute an infringement regardless of any case-specific qualitative or quantitative analysis of actual or potential effects. The 'form-based' approach is different from the mere 'per se' illegality in the sense that it still allows the investigated company to put forward justifications and defenses that may outweigh the competition concerns derived from the conduct, as well as to claim the absence of dominant position. In the case of 'per se' illegality, no justification or defense is allowed, as the conduct represents, in itself (or 'per se'), a violation of Brazilian Antitrust Law.[14]

---

12 Paulo Furquim de Azevedo, *Restrições Verticais e Defesa da Concorrência: a experiência brasileira*, Textos para Discussão da Escola de Economia de São Paulo da Fundação Getulio Vargas, July 2010, at 9-10, *available at* http://bibliotecadigital.fgv.br/dspace/bitstream/handle/10438/6895/TD%20264%20-%20Paulo%20Furquim%20de%20Azevedo.pdf?sequence=1&isAllowed=y .

13 According to ICN, "this [the formalistic, bright-line] approach tends to be based on the presumption that a particular conduct leads to anticompetitive or procompetitive effects. It allows little or no room for an agency or court to take into account the actual market effects of the prohibited conduct in the particular circumstances". *See* ICN Unilateral Conduct Workbook, *supra* note 10, at 11.

14 On the distinction between 'form-based' and 'per se' approaches in the context of European unilateral conduct rules, *see* Richard Whish, *Intel v Commission: Keep Calm and Carry on!*, Journal of Economic Competition Law & Practice, Vol. 6, 2015, at 1-2, *available at* http://jeclap.oxfordjournals.org/content/6/1/1.

Consequently, as the second step is a necessary requirement for finding a violation of Article 36, it is correct to state that CADE does not admit a 'form-based' approach to unilateral conduct. Although the general wording of Article 36 does not exclude, in principle, a formal approach to certain anticompetitive practices,[15] CADE has consistently reaffirmed that the analysis of unilateral conducts always requires examination of actual or potential negative effects to competition deriving from the investigated conduct.[16] In addition, given that the first and third steps are likewise necessary requisites for finding a violation of Article 36, thus CADE does not admit also 'per se' illegalities in the application of unilateral conduct rules. Indeed, CADE has consistently acknowledged that 'per se' analysis of unilateral conduct is incompatible with the Brazilian Antitrust Law.[17]

full.pdf+html. *See also* WOUTER P. J. WILS, *The judgment of the EU General Court in Intel and the so-called 'more economic approach' to abuse of dominance*, WORLD COMPETITION: LAW AND ECONOMICS REVIEW, Vol. 37, No. 4, Sep. 2014, at 20, *available at* http://papers.ssrn.com/sol3/papers.cfm?abstract_id=2498407: "It is often said that the EU case-law on abuse of dominance is 'form-based', with the strong suggestion that this is something undesirable. Iis far from clear what exactly is meant by the case-law being 'form-based'. If it means that the EU case-law per se prohibits the use of exclusivity rebates or other practices by dominant undertakings, it is based on a misreading of that case-law, because the case-law always provides for the possibility of objective justification".

15 For instance, it expressly covers "acts that has the object" of achieving the proscribed effects.

16 CADE has already admitted 'form-based' approaches (i.e., acknowledgement of anticompetitive nature of a practice regardless of any detailed analysis of actual or potential negative effects) to other kinds of anticompetitive practices, especially in the cases of those considered as having the *object* of limiting the competition ('by object' restrictions), such as horizontal price-fixing or minimum resale price maintenance, for example. However, such practices are outside the scope of this article.

17 *See* INTERNATIONAL COMPETITION NETWORK, *Brazil: Unilateral Conduct Working Group Questionnaire* (2006) [hereinafter ICN BRAZIL QUESTIONNAIRE], *available at* http://www.internationalcompetitionnetwork.org/uploads/questionnaires/uc%20objectives/brazil%20response.pdf. *See also* ORGANIZATION FOR ECONOMIC CO-OPERATION AND DEVELOPMENT, COMPETITION LAW AND POLICY IN BRAZIL: A PEER REVIEW (2010) [hereinafter OCDE PEER REVIEW], *available at* http://www.oecd.org/daf/competition/45154362.pdf.

(v) *Dominant Position*

Article 36 Paragraph 2 provides two basic criteria for analyzing the existence of a dominant position: structural and behavioral. The *structural* criterion establishes a rebuttable presumption based on market share threshold (20%), vesting CADE with authority to change such presumption with respect to specific sectors of the economy.[18] The *behavioral* criterion states that a dominant position may be presumed when "a company or a group of companies is able to unilaterally or coordinately change the market conditions". Neither the Brazilian Antitrust Law nor CADE's case law categorizes different levels of market power.

In practice, considering that the 20% market share thresholds for dominance presumption adopted by the Brazilian Antitrust Law is indubitably low,[19] CADE has usually proceeded with the assessment of dominance on a case-by-case basis, using a comprehensive set of criteria in such task, described below. Also in practice, CADE generally considers the 20% market share threshold as a 'soft' safe harbor–i.e., rebuttable presumption that the investigated company does not hold dominant position.[20]

---

18 Though CADE has never made use of this power.

19 According to the *ICN Report on Objectives and Dominance*, "jurisdictions which have [used market share thresholds as dominance presumptions and safe harbors] generally set their dominance presumption in the range of 33%-50% (except for Brazil which uses 20%), and their safe harbor in the range of 20% – 40% (except for Korea which uses 10%)".

20 In CADE, *Telemar Norte Leste S.A. and other v. Terra Network Brasil S/A and others (*Administrative Proceeding No. 53500.013140/2005) (April 9, 2008), involving the investigation of alleged predatory pricing (among other practices) by Telemar Internet Ltda (Oi Internet) in the market of broadband providers, CADE concluded that the company did not hold market power in view of low barriers to entry in the market and reduced market share (8 percent) of the investigated company, and decided not to proceed with the analysis of the practice, determining the dismissal of the investigation on this regard. In CADE, *DyStar Indústria e Comércio de Produtos Químicos Ltda. and other v. Bann Química Ltda.*, (Administrative Proceeding No. 08012.007189/2008-08) (October 1, 2014), regarding the investigation of alleged predatory pricing (among other practices) by DyStar Textilfarben Gmbd (DyStar) in the global market of indigo blue, CADE concluded that the company did not have dominant position on the grounds that its market share was inferior to 20%.

CADE's dominance assessment is generally intended to verify whether the company has some degree of freedom from competitive constraints or ability to act in ways that a competitively constrained company could not. Nevertheless, in some cases such analysis is not based on rigorous criteria that distinguish situations of mere *market power* (ability to price profitably above the competitive level[21]) from clear *dominance* or *substantial market power* (high degree of market power that can be maintained for a long duration[22]). For example, in *Administrative Proceeding No. 08012.000478/1998-62, Siemens Engenharia e Service Ltda. (Siemens) v. Leistung Comércio e Serviços Ltda., CADE's decision (August 31, 2010)*, regarding the investigation of alleged predatory pricing in public biddings of services of maintenance of no breaks practiced by Siemens, CADE essentially presumed Siemens' dominant position exclusively on the basis of the companies' market share (equivalent to 33.8%).[23-24]

Indeed, as the Brazilian antitrust system does not explicitly establish different sets of rules applicable only to companies clearly qualified

21 *See ICN Report on Objectives and Dominance*, *supra* note 8, at 3-4.

22 Dominance thus requires that market power be substantial and durable. *See ICN Report on Objectives and Dominance*, *supra* note 8, at 3-4.

23 After confirming the existence of dominant position based on Siemens' market share, CADE proceeded with the analysis to conclude that no violation had occurred based on the assessment of potential negative effects to competition, specially the very low barriers to entry into the market. If a more rigorous analysis of the existence of dominance was adopted, CADE might, in principle, have took into consideration the very low barriers to entry to conclude that the investigated company did not hold dominant position, promptly dismissing the case without the need to proceed with the assessment of potential anticompetitive effects.

24 Some cases involving the imposition of exclusivity arrangements by medical and dental services unions towards their associated professionals are other examples of not rigorous analysis of dominant position, usually based only on the market share criteria and irrespective of any analysis of entry barriers and other relevant aspects. For instance, in CADE, *Unimed Nordeste Goiano v. Secretariat of Economic Law*, (Administrative Proceeding No. 08012.007205/2009-35) (July 3, 2013), and CADE, *Uniodonto de Lençóis Paulista – Cooperativa Odontológica v. Sindicato Nacional das Empresas de Odontologia de Grupo – SINOG*, (Administrative Proceeding No. 08012.001503/2006-79) (December 4, 2013), *CADE's decision (December 4, 2013)*, the defendants were presumed to hold dominant positions based solely on their respective market shares of 24% and 32.32%.

as dominant[25]–as seen, Article 36 is applicable to any act capable of reaching specified effects–, in practice CADE tends to consider a rigorous differentiation between different levels of market power of little relevance for the purposes of application of the Brazilian Antitrust Law. However, in the context of unilateral conduct enforcement, it would be very useful if CADE could establish (in guidelines or even case law) more rigorous, clear-cut standards to identify a situation of genuine dominance or, at least, to create improved safe harbor (broader than the legal 20% parameter) below to which dominance would not be presumed. Such standards, together with desirable enforcement rules making clear that certain categories of unilateral conducts would only be investigated by CADE if adopted by genuine dominant firm, would serve as good 'filters' that could reduce uncertainty of the economic agents regarding compliance with unilateral conduct rules and enable CADE to focus on practices that are more capable of harming competition.[26]

In CADE's dominance review, market share and barriers to entry or expansion are commonly the two most important criteria. Market shares are used as an initial indicator or starting point for the dominance analysis (as it triggers the presumption of dominance and safe harbor). Barriers to entry, exit or expansion are also very important factors in the assessment of dominance. Entry analysis typically seeks for information on the significance of potential competitors for competition in the market concerned. CADE usually assess whether entry is theoretically possible as well as whether it will be likely, timely and sufficient to pose a credible competitive constraint to the incumbent. Market position, market behavior

---

25 As opposed to the European competition system, for example, in which the provisions of Article 102 of the Treaty on the Functioning of the European Union is only applicable to dominant firms.

26 As acknowledged by ICN, "[t]he concept of dominance or substantial market power limits the scope of application of most unilateral conduct laws. Making dominance or substantial market power a prerequisite for intervention under unilateral conduct laws serves as a filter for intervention against specific anti-competitive conduct. (...) Most jurisdictions find that a rigorous assessment of whether a firm possesses dominance/substantial market power, going well beyond market shares, is highly desirable. In jurisdictions with a more formalistic definition of dominance based on market shares, it is recommended that agencies be particularly rigorous in their analysis of the conduct at issue". *See ICN Report on Objectives and Dominance, supra* note 8, at 3-4.

of competitors and buyer power are also relevant aspects in dominance analysis, as well as presence of economies of scale and scope and network effects, access to upstream markets or essential facilities.[27]

(vi) *Anticompetitive Effects*

As described above, CADE's general framework for analysis of unilateral conducts reflects an intended 'effects-based' approach, where the assessment of specific actual or potential effects is a necessary step. However, as detailed in Section C below, a closer look at CADE's case law reveals that there is still space for development of more consistent substantive criteria to assess potential anticompetitive effects or to demonstrate actual damages to competition resulting from investigated unilateral conducts.

In relation to certain categories of practice, mainly those involving predatory pricing and refusal-to-deal concerns, CADE usually adopts a more objective, economic-articulated notion of competition harm, implementing more detailed, fact-based tests and standards to assess anticompetitive effects. To others, though, the variance in the criteria adopted to analyze negative effects to competition from one case to another shows some inconsistency in the case law, with some decisions applying a too-broad concept of "potential anticompetitive effects" that, in practice, they come close to a 'form-based' approach.[28] For instance, in *Administrative Proceeding No. 08012.009312/1998-39, CCPR – Cooperativa Central dos Produtores Rurais de Minas Gerais Ltda. (Itambé) v. Coopará – Cooperativa Reginal dos Produtores Rurais de Pará de Minas Ltda., CADE's decision (April 18, 2007),*[29] CADE expressly recognized that "the absence

[27] *See ICN Brazil Questionnaire, supra* note 17, at 6.

[28] *See* Geradin, Pereira Neto, *supra* note 11, at 42-43: "Depending on the particular case, and whether CADE puts heavy weight on the language of 'potential effects' and the 'scope of the act', the evidence (or the lack of evidence) considered sufficient to dismiss or convict a case may change dramatically. Some convictions based on lower standards of proof come close to a form-based approach, as they may simply ignore actual effects or any rigorous analysis of potential effects and impose a fine based exclusively on the scope of the conduct or its abstract potential effects. In conclusion, even though Brazilian Antitrust Law System's general approach towards vertical restraints seems in line with modern economic theory, it is necessary to develop clearer tests to evaluate actual effects and more consistent standards of proof".

[29] The *Itambé* case addressed, among other issues, an exclusive agreement for the

of factual evidence proving the occurrence of anticompetitive effects is insufficient for the dismissal of a case. (…) As explicitly stated in the last part of Article 20 [of the former Brazilian Antitrust Law], finding that the conduct actually generated anticompetitive effects is irrelevant for Brazilian Law. Therefore, even though no damage to the market was observed after 4 years [that the conduct was in place], it cannot be said that the practice did not have potential to produce such effects".[30]

In short, notwithstanding CADE's clear option for an approach necessarily based on potential or actual effects of unilateral conducts, the wide-ranging and abstract wording of the general framework, together with the lack of more precise criteria for the analysis of effects in guidelines or case law for some category of practices, have generated inconsistencies in the assessment of anticompetitive effects of unilateral conducts rules by CADE, with the inevitable consequence of uncertainty of compliance by the economic agents–which is aggravated by the lack of more rigorous standards to identify clear dominance or substantial market power, as seen above.

(vii) *Balancing Anticompetitive Effects and Justifications*

CADE generally acknowledges that unilateral conducts may generate economic benefits that are able to compensate actual or potential anticompetitive effects, such as improvement of quality of services or reduction of prices, market innovation, among others. However, to be admitted, any alleged economic justification must have an objective basis. Efficiencies that are merely speculative are normally disregarded. To be accepted, alleged efficiencies must prove not to be possible without the restrictive effect of the unilateral conduct at stake. In addition, there should be no lesser anticompetitive alternative for the advent of such efficiencies.

As to the balancing itself of negative effects and redeeming efficiencies, neither CADE's case law nor Brazilian Antitrust Law provides objective standards. CADE rarely proceeds with detailed quantitative assessment to measure net effects to competition or clearly defines objective, economic-based tests for a finding of infringement to unilateral conduct rules. In

sale of a particular brand of milk. The case was dismissed based on procedural grounds.

30 *Itambé* case, vote of CADE's Reporting Commissioner Abraham Sicsú, at 4.

several cases, CADE's decisions are based significantly on mere qualitative arguments and intuitive reasoning,[31] giving room to possible inconsistent decisions and legal uncertainty, as commented above.

(viii) *Burden of Proof and Types of Evidence Accepted*

The Brazilian Antitrust Law does not establish explicit rules regarding who bears the burden of proof regarding each element of the analysis of unilateral conducts. Like many other jurisdictions, typically CADE has the burden of proof of demonstrating the (actual or potential) anticompetitive effects, whereas the investigated companies must substantiate and, when possible, evidence the alleged justifications and defenses (mainly, efficiencies). The Brazilian Antitrust Law neither prescribes nor proscribes specific types of evidence for the analysis of unilateral conducts–along with other anticompetitive practices. CADE and the investigated company may use all kinds of evidence admitted in Brazilian law, such as quantitative and qualitative studies, expert opinions, hearings, any sort of documents, inspection on premises, etc.

(ix) *Role of Intent*

Article 36 explicitly excludes[32] subjective intent as an element required to support a finding of violation by companies.[33] Notwithstanding that, evidence of objective business rationale (or the lack of it) for the conduct may be relevant in some cases for the evaluation of the competitive effects or the presence of justification for the practice–for example, in investigations of predatory pricing or refusal-to-deal. In addition, evidence of the company's anticompetitive intent may play a role in determining the amount of fine and other sanctions to be imposed by CADE.[34]

---

31 *See* GERADIN, PEREIRA NETO, *supra* note 11, at 40.

32 According to the language of Article 36, "*regardless of the intent*, any act that has the object or otherwise is able to produce the following effects, even if such effects are not achieved, shall constitute an infringement" (emphasis added).

33 In the case of individuals, however, the imposition of fines for violation to Brazilian Antitrust Law depends on demonstration of their willful misconduct or at least negligence towards the anticompetitive practice (Article 37, II, of the Brazilian Antitrust Law).

34 Pursuant to Article 45 of the Brazilian Antitrust Law, CADE may take into consideration the "good-faith" of the investigated company in order to define the nature and amount of sanctions for the violation.

(x) *Exemptions to Specific Sectors or Entities*

The Brazilian Antitrust Law does not provide any exemption to particular sectors or entities. Quite to the contrary, Article 31 unequivocally sets forth the application of the Brazilian Antitrust Law (consequently, of the unilateral conduct rules) to state-created monopolies and state-owned companies, as well as to any individuals, companies, trade associations and any other kind of association or entity, even if temporary or with no legal personality.

(xi) *Extra-territoriality: Unilateral Conducts Carried Out Abroad*

According to Article 2 of the Brazilian Antitrust Law, the fact that the unilateral conduct was carried out abroad is not an admissible defense before CADE if the conduct has produced or is capable of producing effects in the Brazilian territory.

(xii) *Private Enforcement*

Article 47 of the Brazilian Antitrust Law expressly allows private parties to challenge unilateral conducts in courts not only to obtain reparation of the harm suffered by an anticompetitive conduct, but also to request (additionally or alternatively) a cease and desist order. There is no need for private parties to exhaust administrative remedies before initiating a court action. However, like other jurisdictions, private cases concerning unilateral conducts are extremely rare in Brazil, mainly because of difficulties in proving existence and amount of damages, availability of 'pass-on defense' and uncertainty of parameters for statute of limitation in case law.

(xiii) *Criminal Enforcement*

Unilateral conducts are not subject to criminal enforcement in Brazil. According to Law 8,137/90, as amended by the Brazilian Antitrust Law, only anticompetitive agreements may also constitute criminal offenses.

(xiv) *Possibility of Review of CADE's Decisions*

CADE's decisions are only subject to judicial review. Article 9 Paragraph 2 of the Brazilian Antitrust Law expressly voids the possibility of such review by government institutions.

Main Exclusionary Conducts

This Section addresses the current legal standards applicable to the main unilateral conducts, based on legislation, existing guidelines and case law.

(xv) *Exclusive Dealing*

Definition. Exclusive dealings refer to arrangements that require a buyer to purchase all of its requirements or a large extent thereof from one dominant seller, or a supplier to sell all of its products or services or a large extent thereof to the dominant firm.

Applicable Provisions. The practice is covered by Brazil's general unilateral conduct rules and policies. The Brazilian Antitrust Law and CADE's regulation do not establish specific rules or standards governing legal assessment of exclusive dealing arrangements. The Guidelines provides only generic, elementary orientation on the main possible anticompetitive effects associated with the practice–i.e., promoting market foreclosure as well as enabling implementation of market division (in the specific context of concerted practices among competitors).

No Formal Requirements. Considering that CADE follows an effects-based approach to exclusive dealing, the Brazilian Antitrust Law covers not only formal *de jure* but also *de facto* exclusivity. Therefore, exclusive dealing obligations do not have to be formalized (i.e., in a written agreement) to be affected by unilateral conduct rules. In the same way, the exclusivity effect may be achieved by concluding one or a number of contracts covering all or almost all of the supply or demand. In addition, the use of clauses such as English clauses[35] tends to be important in assessing exclusive dealing

[35] English clauses require the customer to report any better offer to the supplier and prohibit the customer from accepting it unless the supplier does not match it. The anticompetitive effects produced by such clauses were analyzed in *CADE, TV Globo Ltda. (Globo), União Brasileira dos Clubes de Futebol (Clube dos Treze) and others v. Chandre de Araújo Costa and others* (Administrative Proceeding No. 08012.006504/1997-11) (October 10, 2010), related to the establishment of English clauses in the agreements entered into between Clube dos Treze and Globo to the acquisition of broadcasting rights of soccer games, setting forth that whenever Clube dos Treze receives a proposal, Globo should be informed to exercise its right of first refusal within 30 days. CADE entered into a cease-and-desist commitment with the defendants, which foresees, among other measures, that the parties should refrain from establishing English clauses in their future contracts.

arrangements, as it may have effects similar to exclusivity commitments– especially when there is an obligation to reveal the identity of the competitor who makes a better offer, since this may discourage competitors to make competing offers to the dominant firm's customers.[36]

Legal Assessment. Market foreclosure is normally the main concern to CADE in assessing exclusive dealing by a dominant firm, in the way that it may impede or make more difficult for established agents to compete in the relevant market (by avoiding their access to upstream suppliers or downstream distribution channels/main costumers), and may increase barriers to entry for new competitors (by imposing them the need to enter in both downstream and upstream markets to be able to effectively compete). The fact that the non-dominant business partner requested the exclusivity arrangement does not tend to influence the legal assessment of the conduct.[37]

Foreclosure Test. CADE's assessment of market foreclosure is usually based on broad qualitative analysis of the specific circumstance of the case. Although in some cases CADE has attempted to calculate the level of market foreclosure to better assess the anticompetitive effects of certain exclusivity arrangements, its findings do not provide clear parameters to other cases. Indeed, CADE has not been capable so far of developing detailed tests and legal standards to define when the levels of market foreclosure raised by exclusive dealings should be considered harmful to competition.[38] In *Administrative Proceeding No 08012.003921/2005-10, Philip Morris Brasil S/A and Souza Cruz S/A v. CADE*, settled in *July 4, 2012*,[39] the authorities calculated the level of foreclosure for different geographic relevant markets involving the retail of cigarettes (including open spaces in different

---

36 *See* International Competition Network, *Report on Single Branding/Exclusive Dealing* (2008) [hereinafter: *ICN* Report on Exclusive Dealing], *available at* http://www.internationalcompetitionnetwork.org/uploads/library/doc355.pdf

37 *See ICN Brazil Questionnaire*, *supra* note 17, at 6.

38 *See* Geradin, Pereira Neto, *supra* note 11, at 10.

39 Souza Cruz S/A, the Brazilian Affiliate of British American Tobacco – BAT, and Philip Morris Brasil S/A, the two largest companies in the market for production and sale of tobacco in Brazil, agreed with CADE to end exclusivity arrangements with their dealers that prohibited the display of their competitors' products and in-store advertisements, putting an end to a pending antitrust investigation, which was initiated in 2005. Philip Morris and Souza Cruz agreed to pay BRL 250,000 and BRL 2.9 million, respectively.

neighborhoods, as well as airports and shopping malls). In *Administrative Proceeding No. 53500.000502/2001, Celular CRT S.A. v. Telet S.A., CADE's decision (June 4, 2008),*[40] there was also an attempt to measure the degree of market foreclosure in different municipal markets for the retail of cellular phones, but CADE expressly avoided defining a level of foreclosure below which exclusive dealing by a dominant firm would not violate the Brazilian Antitrust Law.[41]

Admissible Defenses. Dominant firms may always claim reasons and defenses, including efficiencies, intended to outweigh the possible anticompetitive effects of the conduct. CADE has expressly mentioned possible efficiencies in different cases involving exclusive dealings, such as relationship specific investments, facilitating innovation and cost reduction.[42] However, similarly to the assessment of market foreclosure, CADE usually conducts the balancing of the negative effects against the potential benefits of exclusive dealing based on qualitative arguments. More detailed quantitative analysis and definition of clear legal standards are not common.

---

40 In such case, Telet S.A claimed that Celular CRT S.A., one of the largest telecommunications operator in Brazil, aimed at foreclosing competitors by means of entering into exclusive dealings with wholesale companies in the retail of mobile phones in certain cities located in the District of Rio Grande do Sul. CADE's Tribunal decided to dismiss the case, due to the lack of evidence to confirm the potential market foreclosing arising from the wholesalers' retention.

41 The parties argued that market foreclosure below 40% would generally be acceptable, which was rejected.

42 For example, in CADE, *Companhia Vale do Rio Doce (CVRD) v. Secretariat of Economic Law (*Administrative Proceeding No. 08012.007285/1999-78) (April 28, 2004), CADE's Reporting Commissioner Thompson Almeida Andrade expressly recognized that the exclusivity clause foreseen in an investment agreement entered into by S/A Mineração Trindade (Samitri) and CVRD was justified as to protect mutual investments made by Samitri and CVRD in specific assets related to transport of iron ore. Furthermore, in CADE, *Center Norte S/A v. Condomínio Shopping D.* (Administrative Proceeding No. 08012.002841/2001-13) (January 19, 2005), Reporting Commissioner Roberto Pfeiffer acknowledged that "*exclusivity dealing is justifiable while protecting investments against undue appropriation by third parties [without proper compensation for the use]–known as the free riding effect*", at 33 (*Shopping Center Norte* case).

(xvi) *Conditional Rebates*

Definition. Conditional rebates are generally considered as discounts or rebates on units purchased of a single product, conditioned upon the level or share of purchases. The main aspect is their conditionality–they are conditional on the customers' engaging in loyal purchasing behavior. Customers are given a discount or rebate if their purchases over a defined reference period exceed a certain threshold. Discounts or rebates may be granted on all purchases (retroactive rebates) or only on those made in excess of those required to achieve the threshold (incremental rebates).

Applicable Provisions. The practice is also covered by Brazil's general unilateral conduct rules and policies, as there is no specific rules or standards governing conditional rebates in the Brazilian antitrust system.

No Formal Requirements. Similar to exclusive dealings, formal aspects of the practice will not govern legal assessment, as CADE's review is based on assessment of actual or potential effects to competition.

Legal Assessment. CADE has issued very few decisions on loyalty rebates. A detailed review of loyalty programs in Brazil was carried out by CADE in *Administrative Proceeding No. 08012.003805/2004-10, Companhia de Bebidas das Américas (AmBev) v. Primo Schincariol Indústria de Cervejas e Refrigerantes S/A., CADE's decision (July 22, 2009)*,[43] where main concerns

[43] "Tô Contigo" was a "frequent buyer" program that AmBev offers to bar and other retail outlets in the Brazilian beer market. The program offered participating outlets one point for each case of beer they buy up to certain monthly limits, exchangeable for a variety of merchandise. CADE deemed the program anticompetitive, considering that it involved non-systematic *de facto* exclusivity requirements to the outlets. According to the opinion of CADE's Reporting Commissioner Fernando Furlan in CADE, *Companhia de Bebidas das Américas – AMBEV* (Administrative Proceeding No. 08012003805/2004-10) (Oct. 9, 2009), at 68 : "As a relevant portion [almost 50%] of the [surveyed] outlets has acknowledged, the negotiation of an exclusivity arrangement (or the limitation of the possibility of purchasing competitors' beers) was considered part of the conditions for participation in the Program. Fail to comply with this requirement could lead to exclusion from the Program or the non-renewal of the contract, depending on the considered period. (...) Considering together the copy of documents obtained during the inspection [at AmBev's headquarters], field survey made by IBOPE [an independent poll institute] and the outlets' statements, the standard of proof was met so that it is possible to sustain that the Tô Contigo Program includes, even if not in a systematic way, the requirement of exclusivity of sales or at least some limitation on purchasing from third parties".

were similar to those of exclusive dealing, especially market foreclosure (*AmBev Tô Contigo* case). More recently, in 2013, Infoglobo's discount policy was subject to investigation in the *Administrative Proceeding No. 08012.003064/2005-58, Infoglobo Comunicações Ltda v. Jornal do Brasil S/A and Editora O Dia S/A, settled with CADE in August 28, 2013.*[44]

Foreclosure Test. Brazilian Antitrust Law and CADE's case law does not set forth thresholds to presume whether loyalty discount or conditional rebates are likely to foreclose competitors. In *AmBev Tô Contigo* case, CADE's review of the market foreclosure was rather superficial and relied mostly on general considerations and arguments of a typical 'form-based' approach. According to the vote of CADE's Reporting Commissioner: "Market foreclosure does not have to occur for anticompetitive effects to be ascertained; the non-linearity in the dominant firm program is sufficient".[45-46]

Price-cost Test and the Efficient-Competitor. Price-cost comparisons are one factor, among others, that CADE may use to assess whether loyalty discounts forecloses competitors by limiting their opportunities to

---

44 Infoglobo was accused of abuse of dominant position due to its discounts policy in the sales of advertisement spaces in newspapers. The company offered four types of discounts to their advertisers related to (i) the volume of advertisement spaces acquired, (ii) regularity/frequency of the acquisition of advertisement spaces; (iii) the percentage of the advertiser's budget to advertising that was allocated to Infoglobo's newspapers *(share discounts*), and (iv) the number of Infoglobo's newspapers in which the advertisement was published. The former Secretariat of Economic Law issued an opinion sustaining that the practice have the potential to lessen competition, as Infoglobo hold a dominant position in the market at stake and the discounts policy included non-linear discounts, notably the so-called share discounts. Infoglobo settled with CADE and paid a financial contribution of BRL 1,941,024.85.

45 CADE, *Companhia de Bebidas das Américas – AMBEV supra* note 43, at 84. In addition, according to the opinion, at 84: "the coverage of the program is totally determined by the defendant and its potential of expansion is significant. (...) In other words, if there was no investigation by the antitrust authorities, it would be more than lucrative to the defendant to expand such program to cover 40%, 50% or 60% of the total volume of all outlets in the national territory, instead of [confidential number]% of the national volume".

46 AmBev argued that the coverage of the program was very low, reaching only 10%-12% of outlets and around 10% of the volume of sales nationally (according to Secretariat of Economic Law legal opinion on the case, at 5, 9 and 11).

compete for sales. In *AmBev Tô Contigo* case, CADE mentioned the intent[47] to rely on the framework to review the conditional rebates stated in the *European Commission Discussion Paper* issued in 2005,[48] which proposes a standard of review aligned with a more rigorous 'effects-based' approach. However, the price-cost analysis in the case was not robust.[49] In addition, CADE considered that the discounts offered by AmBev have the ability to foreclose as-efficient competitors without conducting a proper 'equally efficient competitor' test.[50-51]

Duration and Retroactivity. In the review of foreclosure, CADE considers the time period for the offered discount as well as their scope of application. Neither Brazilian Antitrust Law nor CADE's case law provide for any guidance for assessment of the duration of conditional rebates. With respect to the scope of application, CADE considers that retroactive discounts (or backward-looking discounts) are more harmful to competition

---

47 According to the opinion of the Reporting Commissioner, at 73.

48 EUROPEAN COMMISSION. *DG Competition discussion paper on the application of Article 82 of the Treaty to exclusionary abuses,* (2005), *available at* http://ec.europa.eu/competition/antitrust/art82/discpaper2005.pdf. Such discussion paper was superseded by the following publication: EUROPEAN COMMISSION, *Guidance on the Commission's enforcement priorities in applying Article 82 of the EC Treaty to abusive exclusionary conduct by dominant undertakings* (2009), *avaliable at* http://eur-lex.europa.eu/legal-content/EN/TXT/PDF/?uri=CELEX:52009XC0224(01)&from=PT.

49 For instance, the vote mentions, at 44, that the program could be equivalent to a discount of up to 3%, but states that the equivalent value of the program "cannot be calculated" and that it is not "possible to quantify the exact dimension of such discounts", at 76.

50 The Efficient Competitor-Test aims at investigating whether the conduct is capable of excluding a competitor that is as efficient as the dominant firm. 'As efficient-competitor' is a hypothetical competitor having the same costs as the dominant firm. Therefore, foreclosure of an as-efficient competitor means that the dominant firm is pricing below its own costs.

51 According to the opinion, at 73 and 78, CADE estimated the level of discount necessary to be granted by competitors to match the savings achieved by AmBev's program, but did not review whether a competitor as efficient as AmBev would be excluded from the market if it competes with the dominant firm for the demand of the participating outlets (by analyzing at what price a competitor as efficient as the dominant firm would have to offer discounts in order to compensate the outlet for the loss of the dominant's rebate).

than non-retroactive discounts (or forward-looking discounts),[52] as the first are granted on a larger basis, encompassing all units acquired *ex-ante.*

Switching Costs. Potential losses that switching to other suppliers[53] would bring for distributors or clients engaged in conditional rebates are relevant to CADE's assessment of the anticompetitive effects of conditional rebates.[54]

Justifications and Defenses. In the review of conditional rebates, as any other anticompetitive practice, CADE considers whether the possible justifications or defenses, may outweigh its anticompetitive effects. Nonetheless, there is neither guidance nor legal standard to the review of the possible reasons and defenses in connection with the practice. In *AmBev Tô Contigo* case, the review of the efficiencies was based mostly on qualitative criteria.[55]

(xvii) *Tying and Bundling*

Definition. Tying and bundling are defined as any practice that "condition[s] the sale of a product [on] the acquisition of another or [on] contracting a service, or providing a service under the condition of using another or purchasing a product".[56]

Applicable Provisions. Conducts of this nature are also covered by Brazil's general unilateral conduct rules and policies. The Brazilian

52 Forward-looking discounts are applied to incremental units above a given threshold (incremental rebates), whereas backward-looking are applied to both units below and above the threshold.

53 Switching costs are the negative costs that a consumer incurs as a result of changing suppliers, brands or products. Although most prevalent switching costs are monetary in nature, there are also psychological, effort- and time-based switching costs.

54 In *AmBev Tô Contigo* case, the Reporting Commissioner acknowledged the relevance of the switching costs to strengthen the loyalty of distributors part of AmBev's loyalty program, once it established that the outlets would incur in the loss of certain benefits when leaving the program, such as multi-brand freezer, discounts and training (Opinion of CADE's Reporting Commissioner, at 77-78).

55 The efficiencies listed and analyzed were: (1) reduction of transaction costs, (2) protection to reputation and investments in specific assets, (3) development of economies of scale/scope, and (4) the protection of technological development in the market of origin.

56 Pursuant to Article 36, XVIII, of the Brazilian Antitrust Law.

Antitrust Law and CADE's regulation do not establish specific rules or standards governing legal assessment of tying and bundling. In this respect, the Guidelines refer only to generic, elementary orientation on the main possible anticompetitive effects associated with the practice–i.e., the leverage of market power involving different products and/or services, abusively increasing profits to the detriment of buyers, and ultimately, of the consumers, while 'blocking' the downstream segment (generally, of distribution) for actual and potential competitors (increase in barriers to entry).

Legal Assessment. In a paradigmatic precedent referring to tying, *Administrative Proceeding No. 23/1991, Xerox do Brasil S.A.(Xerox) v. Recomex Materiais e Equipamentos de Xerografia Ltda. and others, CADE's decision (March 31, 1993)*, Xerox was convicted by CADE for imposing the purchasing of Xerox's parts and supplies as a condition to provide technical assistance to its products. CADE considered that Xerox's dominant position in the rental of and in the technical assistance to its copying machines had a direct impact in the parts and supplies to relevant markets in which Xerox did not hold a dominant position. In *Administrative Proceeding No. 08012.001182/1998-3, Microsoft Informática Ltda v. Paiva Piovesan Engenharia & Informática Ltda., CADE's decision (May 19, 2004)*, CADE stated that "a tie-in sale consists on the imposition, by the seller, of a purchase of a certain product as a condition for the buyer to also acquire another good or service, and the anticompetitive effects of such practice are related to the transfer of market power from one product to another, making the abusive increase of profits and blockade in the access of the downstream segment possible in this second market (generally, the distribution) to actual and potential competitors".[57] In short, according to CADE's case law, in order for tying to be deemed anticompetitive the following requirements must be met (1) the existence of at least two different relevant markets, (2) the imposition of the purchase of a bundled product or service, (3) the presence of dominant position in at least one of the relevant markets involved, and (4) the production of actual or potential anticompetitive effects in any of the relevant markets involved.[58]

[57] Nevertheless, this specific case was dismissed on the grounds that both software programs could easily be found and purchased separately.

[58] According to the Reporting Commissioner Ricardo Ruiz's opinion in CADE, *Aceco Produtos para Escritório e Informática Ltda. v. Brazilian Federal Court of*

Different Relevant Markets and the Imposition of the Purchase of a Bundled Product. The first two requirements for anticompetitive tying involve the existence of at least two different relevant markets. There must be a different secondary market and some sort of imposition as a condition for the acquirer to access the primary product or service. In other words, if, for practical or technical characteristics of a product or a service, it is a "natural" choice for the demand to acquire the product or service as a bundle, i.e., there is no secondary relevant market, there is no anticompetitive tying.[59] In *Preliminary Inquiry No. 08012.008005/2008-19, Totvs S.A. v. Braspack, CADE's decision (March 20, 2013),*[60] CADE clarified that "[in the present case] there is no anticompetitive tying since there is no secondary market, provided that the services of customization, maintenance and updating shall be, in practice, necessarily provided for by the supplier of the ERP software".[61] On the other hand, even if there is a secondary product or service relevant market, the possibility of acquiring the secondary product or service separately also precludes the characterization of anticompetitive tying.

Dominant Position in at Least One Relevant Market. As already mentioned, anticompetitive tying requires dominant position on at least one of the relevant markets involved. Although there is no clear differentiation on the standards of dominance to be applied to tying, CADE's precedents on this kind of conduct indicate that clear dominance or high degrees of market power tend to be a requisite (as opposed to mere market share exceeding 20%)[62] in assessing the anti-competitiveness of the practice.

Increased Market Power and/or Market Foreclosure in the Bundled Relevant Market. CADE's case law does not establish a clear set of standards with respect to anticompetitive effects associated to the practice of tying

---

Auditors, (Preliminary Inquiry No. 08700.005025/2007-07) (June 23, 2010), at 12.

59 CADE, *Xerox do Brasil S.A.(Xerox) v. Recomex Materiais e Equipamentos de Xerografia Ltda. and others,*(Administrative Proceeding No. 23/1991) (March 31, 1993).

60 This case was related to the market for enterprise resource planning-ERP software and related services.

61 According to the Reporting Commissioner Alessandro Octaviani's opinion, at 12.

62 CADE, *Marimex – Despachos, Transportes e Serviços Ltda. v. Santos Brasil S.A. – Tecon and other* (Administrative Proceeding No. 08012.005967/2000-69) (February 5, 2014).

or bundling. Both the restriction of clients' choice and the potential of foreclosure are mentioned in the Guidelines and precedents.

Admissible Defenses. Accordingly to the above, possible defenses in tying cases are (1) the non-existence of separate relevant markets, (2) the lack of imposition of bundled purchase and/or availability of the secondary products and/or services separately from the primary ones, and (3) the absence of dominant position and of the potentiality of anticompetitive effects. Dominant firms may always claim reasons and defenses, including efficiencies, intended to outweigh the possible anticompetitive effects of the conduct.

(xviii) *Refusal-to-deal*

Definition. "To refuse the sale of goods or provision of services for payment terms within normal business practice and custom".[63]

Applicable Provisions. Brazil's general unilateral conduct rules and policies are applicable to refusal-to-deal. The Brazilian Antitrust Law and CADE's regulation do not establish specific rules or standards governing legal assessment of such practice. The Guidelines contain generic reference to possible anticompetitive effects associated with it–i.e., blockage to and/or increase in barriers to entry into the distribution or supply channels (including possible cost increase for rivals), as well as to the after-sales services.

Legal Assessment. The general provision regarding refusal-to-deal within normal business practices does not impose an *a priori* duty to contract in general. When addressing cases involving refusals to deal by a dominant player or even a monopolist, CADE's case law has adopted the so-called 'essential facility' doctrine as a parameter. In the case of an essential facility, CADE has required four elements to establish a refusal-to-deal claim (1) the existence of an essential input held by a monopolist, (2) economic or legal infeasibility of its duplication, (3) the refusal to grant access to the input to a competitor in the target-market, and (4) the practical ability of the monopolist providing the access to the infrastructure without

[63] According to the general definition provided in Article 36, XV, of the Brazilian Antitrust Law. For other more specific provisions regarding raw materials and inputs, as well as intellectual property, *see* Article 36, III, V, XIV and XIX, of the Brazilian Antitrust Law.

compromising the previously granted access.[64] CADE has imposed fines and duties to contract upon the holders of intellectual property[65] who have been found to violate the antitrust laws.

For instance, in *Administrative Proceeding No. 08012.000172/1998-42, Matel Tecnologia de Informatica S/A (Matec) v. Power-Tech Teleinformática Ltda., CADE's decision (March 26, 2003)*, CADE imposed fines after having found that Matec had monopoly power because it used its exclusive patents, technical data, industrial secrets, manufacturing technology, and system maintenance to leverage and expand its monopoly power into a secondary market of services.[66] This was possible precisely because some parts were

---

64 The major precedents in which CADE imposed obligations of contract based on the essential facility doctrine are: *Administrative* CADE, *TV Globo Ltda. v. TVA Sistemas de Televisão S/A (*Administrative Proceeding No. 53500.000359/1999) (June 20, 2001); CADE, *Brasil Telecom S.A. v. CADE (*Administrative Proceeding No. 08700.001291/2003-29) (Dec. 8, 2004); CADE, *Libra Terminais S/A-T-37 and others v. Secretariat of Economic Law,* (Administrative Proceeding No. 08012.007443/1999-17) (May 12, 2005); CADE, *Philips do Brasil Ltda. and other v. Gradiente Eletrônica S.A. and other (*Administrative Proceeding No. 08012.001315/2007-21) (May 13, 2009).

65 CADE, *Globosat Programadora Ltda (Globosat) and other v. Associação Neo TV* (Administrative Proceeding No.. 08012.003048/2001-31) (May 31, 2006)

66 "In addition, by holding monopoly power over parts, the Defendant leverages and enhances its power in the secondary market for services (because certain parts are available only through Matec). Two facts confirm this: (a) the near complete absence of intra-brand competition (the Defendant would be the sole exception); (b) the difference in prices charged by Power-Tech and Defendant, up to 69%, noted in the report of Secretariat of Economic Law and admitted indirectly by the Defendant (item 3.33 of the most recent brief), were attributed to the opportunistic behavior of Defendant. Price increases and exclusion from competition are indications of market power—monopolistic—of Matec. (…) Brand loyalty, even if relevant for the party that manufactures the equipment, does not appear to be fundamental, neither for those who wish to independently enter the maintenance market, and much less so for consumers, who will lose the opportunity and liberty to choose, for their account and risk, which companies they want to hire and what price they want to pay for maintenance services. Why 'tutor' consumers in order to restrict their decisions? Consumers of large central telephone networks—such as the Ericsson MD 110—are not so naïve and irrational with respect to economic matters to be incapable of differentiating the quality of after-sales services. There is no evidence that competition in the primary equipment market is sufficient to inhibit increase in prices in the secondary market. Everything indicates the

available only through Matec and Matec denied access to such inputs to its competitors in the services market. In the *Associação Neo TV* case,[67] CADE ordered Globosat to offer non-discriminatory terms for the distribution rights of Globosat channels to all cable TV operators, i.e., Globosat could no longer offer different terms to vertically related affiliates compared to terms offered to its downstream competitors.[68]

Admissible Defenses. Much like the above, possible defenses in refusal-to-deal cases are (1) the existence of alternatives sources of supply for the product or service whose essentiality is in question, (2) the economic and legal possibility of its duplication, and (3) the impossibility of the dominant player or monopolist providing the access to the infrastructure without compromising the previously granted access. Dominant firms may always claim reasons and defenses, including efficiencies, intended to outweigh the possible anticompetitive effects of the conduct.

(xix) *Predatory Pricing*

Definition. "To sell goods or [to provide] services unreasonably below the cost price".[69]

Applicable Provisions. The Guidelines provide more precise standards to the assessment of the anti-competitiveness of predatory pricing.[70] More

---

opposite, i.e., even in the case of acknowledgment of the competition amongst equipment manufacturers, it can coexist perfectly well with market power of their respective brands in the 'aftermarkets'" (Opinion of CADE's Reporting Commissioner Celso Campilongo, at 4 and 9).

67 *Id.*

68 In particular, CADE required that "[t]he OBLIGOR, from the signing of this Undertaking, [will] undertake to negotiate and engage in good faith and in accordance with transparent, objective and non-discriminatory terms and conditions in relation to the behavior practiced for the Sistema NET Brasil de Distribuição, considered as a whole, with the pay TV Operators that are not part of the Sistema NET Brasil de Distribuição potentially involved, the distribution of programming known generically in the market for pay television as 'Globosat Channels' (Sportv, Sportv 2, GNT, Multishow and Globonews. (...)", according to the settlement agreement executed with Globosat and others in May 31, 2006.

69 According to Article 36, XV, of the Brazilian Antitrust Law.

70 Not only CADE's Resolution 20, dated June 28, 1999, but also the Brazil's Secretariat for Economic Monitoring (SEAE)'s Directive 70, dated December 12, 2002, deal with predatory pricing legal assessment. Although the former was adopted under

specifically, Guidelines refer to the practice of prices below the average variable cost, seeking to eliminate competitors and then charge prices and yield profits that are closer to monopolistic levels. Furthermore, according to Guidelines, the assessment of the practice must take into consideration the actual cost and price oscillation conditions throughout the period of time investigated to exclude normal seasonal practices or other legitimate marketing strategies.

Legal Assessment. According to the methodology provided for in the Guidelines, the review of pricing strategy deemed to be predatory shall follow the steps bellow: (1) definition of relevant market and identification of market power, (2) presence of barriers to entry, (3) idle capacity or ability to increase supply to face the demand previously supplied by the excluded rivals, (4) financial capacity to endure the losses involved in the predation, (5) analysis of prices versus costs during the investigated period, and (6) evaluation of economic justification to exceptionally admit prices inferior to average total costs (e.g., abrupt contraction of the demand and/or increase in supply capacity).

Admissible Defenses. Accordingly to the above, possible defenses in predatory pricing cases are: (1) absence of market power, (2) inexistence of barriers to entry, (3) lack of idle capacity or unfeasibility of increasing supply after rivals are excluded, (4) financial restraints to endure losses involved in predation, (5) pricing justification vis-à-vis costs.

Consequences of Violation

Fines. According to Article 37 of the Brazilian Antitrust Law, CADE may impose the following fines to the companies, individuals or any other entities found to be involved in anticompetitive practices, including unlawful unilateral conducts: (1) companies: fines from 0.1% to 20% of gross revenue of the economic group to which the company belongs in the "field of business" affected by the practice, (2) officers and directors: fines ranging from 1% to 20% of the fine imposed to the company,[71] and (3) other individuals or entities: fines from BRL 50,000 to BRL 2 billion. In most of

the former Brazilian Antitrust Law, it is referred to in the CADE's case law and provides for a detailed methodology of analysis of predatory pricing.

71 Conviction of individuals for antitrust violation, however, depends on the demonstration of their malicious or at least negligent act towards the unlawful conduct.

the decisions involving unlawful unilateral conducts, CADE imposed to the company a fine close to the minimum level established by law.[72-73] In the first cases where CADE applied the thresholds of the Brazilian Antitrust Law for calculating the applicable fine to companies,[74] the fines imposed were equivalent to 0.5% and 1% of the companies' gross revenues.[75]

Other Sanctions. Article 38 of the Brazilian Antitrust Law sets forth that, regardless of any fine imposed under Article 37, CADE may also impose the following sanctions, individually or cumulatively, whenever the severity of the facts or the public interest so requires: (1) publication of a summary of the ruling in a newspaper designated for two consecutive days, (2) ineligibility for official financing or participating in public bidding processes for at least five years, (3) inclusion of the name of the company in the Brazilian Consumer Protection List, (4) recommendation that the relevant government agencies (a) grant compulsory licenses for intellectual property rights held by the offender, (b) deny the benefit of installment payments of overdue federal taxes, or order total or partial cancellation of tax incentives or public subsidies, (5) spin-off, transfer of corporate control, sale of assets, or partial discontinuance of activities of the company, (6)

---

72 Under the former Brazilian Antitrust Law, which provides for fines to companies ranging from 1% to 30% of the gross revenues of in the relevant market, the majority of fines imposed were not superior to 2% of the gross revenues.

73 The largest relative fines (in percentage of revenues) imposed by CADE for unlawful unilateral conduct occurred in the CADE, *Microsoft Informática Ltda. and TBA Informática Ltda. v. Secretariat of Economic Law*. (Administrative Proceeding No.08012.008024/1998-49) (August 25, 2014), in which the companies were fined, respectively, with 10% and 7% of their gross revenues in Brazil (*Microsoft/ TBA* case).

74 CADE shall apply the thresholds for calculating fines set forth in the Brazilian Antitrust Law in cases pending final ruling whenever such thresholds are more beneficial to the wrongdoer, even if the conduct took place totally under the period of the former Brazilian Antitrust Law. CADE, *Rodoban Segurança e Transporte de Valores Ltda. v. Embraforte Segurança e Transporte de Valores Ltda.* (Administrative Proceeding No. 08012.009757/2009-88) (February 5, 2014).

75 *See* CADE, *Uniodonto de Lençóis Paulista – Cooperativa Odontológica v. Sindicato Nacional das Empresas de Odontologia* (Administrative Proceeding No. 08012.001503/2006-79) (December 4, 2013 and CADE, *Unimed Cooperativa de Serviços de Saúde dos Vales do Taquari e Rio Pardo Ltda. v. Secretariat of Economic Law* (Administrative Proceeding No. 08012.010576/2009-02) (November 6, 2013).

prohibition of engaging in business activities for no more than five years, and (7) any other action or measure as may be required to eliminate the effects of the violation on the economy. In addition to fines, CADE usually order the wrongdoer to publish a summary of the ruling in newspaper,[76] as well as, of course, the immediate interruption of the practice (when it is still in place). It is also common that CADE order the inclusion of the name of the wrongdoer in the Brazilian Consumer Protection List.[77] The prohibition to participate in public bidding processes was imposed in the *Comepla* case.

Settlement Agreements. Article 85 of the Brazilian Antitrust Law allows CADE to enter into settlement agreements with defendants in unilateral conducts cases. The settlement agreement may be proposed at any time during the process, but the mere proposition does not stop the investigation and the defendant has only one opportunity to settle. Settlements may be reached either with an admission of guilt or without, at CADE's discretion. The agreement must contain the commitment to cease the conduct under investigation. It may provide for the payment of a financial contribution by the defendant, which must not be lower than the minimum fine fixed by the Brazilian Antitrust Law–the financial contribution is only mandatory in case of horizontal concerted practices. The agreement puts on hold the investigation while the defendant complies with the obligations. Once the commitment defined in the agreement is timely and fully met, CADE closes the investigation without any judgment on the merits.

CADE's policy is to encourage the execution of settlements to closing proceedings related to anticompetitive practices, including unilateral conducts.[78] Recent examples of settlement agreements in unilateral conduct cases are *Administrative Proceeding No. 08700.003070/2010-14, Banco do Brasil S.A. v. Federação Interestadual dos Sevidores Públicos dos Estado do*

[76] *See*, for instance, decision in the *Microsoft/TBA* case and CADE, *Comepla Indústria e Comércio and others v. Steel Placas Indústria e Comércio Ltda.*, (Administrative Proceeding No. 08012.001099/1999-71) (May 23, 2012).

[77] *See*, for example, decisions in the cases *AmBev Tô Contigo, Shopping Center Norte, Microsoft/TBA* and *Comepla*.

[78] CADE entered into more than 35 settlements agreements in 2014 (4 of them involving unilateral conduct investigation). In 2013, the agency entered into 42 settlements with several Unimed cooperatives in order to closing investigations related to exclusivity dealing in the provision of medical services.

Acre, Alagoas, Amapá and others, CADE's decision (November 9, 2011),[79] *Administrative Proceeding No. 08012.010028/2009-74, Felipe Szpigel and others v. CADE, Settled in July 30, 2014*[80] and *Administrative Proceeding No. 08012.004089/2009-01, Redecard S.A. v. Associação Brasileira de Internet, Settled in July 16, 2014.*[81]

Conclusions

Unilateral conduct rules have always been subject of considerable intellectual and practical difficulty in many jurisdictions. Despite the considerable difficulties, a consistent framework for review of such conducts is of utmost relevance. A too-broad concept of potential anticompetitive effects resulting from unilateral conducts would prevent legitimate and desirable competition. And too-high standards for demonstration (or presumption) of negative effects would deny the Brazilian Antitrust Law the achievement of its main goals, which have foundation in Brazilian Constitution.

---

79 The settlement agreement was signed in connection with the investigation of exclusive dealings in the provision of consigned credit to public bodies. Under the agreement, Banco do Brasil committed to pay almost BRL 100 million to FDD (as financial contribution as well as a fine for non-compliance with an interim order), to remove the exclusivity clause from the agreements already in force and to not foresee such provision in future contracts. Furthermore, Banco do Brasil also committed to communicate all contracts entered into with public entities within 30 days of the closing and to promote necessary changes in its operational system. In this case, CADE established a fine of BRL 10 million for the non-compliance with the terms of the agreement.

80 The case regards the investigation of the involvement of individuals in implementing and managing the AmBev loyalty program 'Tô Contigo', which offered discounts and bonus to points of sale in exchange of exclusivity or reduction in the sales of products of other competitors. AmBev, as a corporate body, was previously condemned for the institution of such program, as aforementioned. By the settlement, AmBev's executives refrain from practicing any of the conducts under investigation and to pay a financial contribution amounting to BRL 2 million to the Fund for the Defense of Diffuse Rights.

81 CADE entered into an agreement with Redecard S.A. in connection to Administrative Proceeding No. 08012.004089/2009-01 initiated to investigate alleged practices of abuse of dominant position in the nationwide market for facilitation and monitoring of commercial transactions through Internet. The settlement agreement sets forth that Redecard shall refrain from performing any conduct that might harm competition and pay fines to FDD amounting to BRL 7.45 million.

As seen, although CADE has clearly opted for an approach based on necessary assessment of potential or actual effects of unilateral conducts, the wide-ranging wording of legislation, plus the lack of rigorous standards for the review of effects in guidelines or case law, especially for the categories of practices of exclusive dealing, conditional rebates and tying/bundling, have generated inconsistencies in the application of unilateral conducts rules and uncertainty of compliance by the economic agents.

Developing a rational and operational approach to conducts by dominant firms, sound and consistent from the law and economic perspective, is a great challenge ahead.

Bibliography

Damien Geradin, Caio Mario da S. P. Neto, *For a Rigorous 'Effects-Based' Analysis of Vertical Restraints Adopted by Dominant Firms: An Analysis of the EU and Brazilian Competition Law*, June 2012, *available at* ssrn.com/abstract=2173735.

European Competition Commission, Guidance on the Commission's enforcement priorities in applying Article 82 of the EC Treaty to abusive exclusionary conduct by dominant undertakings (2009), *avaliable at* http://eur-lex.europa.eu/legal-content/EN/TXT/PDF/?uri=CELEX:52009XC0224(01)&from=PT.

International Competition Network, Brazil: Unilateral Conduct Working Group Questionnaire (2006), *available at* http://www.internationalcompetitionnetwork.org/uploads/questionnaires/uc%20objectives/brazil%20response.pdf.

_______, ICN Report on the Objectives of Unilateral Conduct Laws, Assessment of Dominance/Substantial Market Power, and State Created Monopolies (2007), *available at* http://internationalcompetitionnetwork.org/uploads/library/doc353.pdf.

_______, Unilateral Conduct Workbook Chapter 1: The Objectives and Principles of Unilateral Conduct Laws (2012), *available at* http://www.internationalcompetitionnetwork.org/uploads/library/doc827.pdf.

_______, Report on Single Branding/Exclusive Dealing (2008), *available at* http://www.internationalcompetitionnetwork.org/uploads/library/doc355.pdf.

Organization for Economic Co-Operation and Development, Competition Law and Policy in Brazil: a Peer Review (2010), *available at* http://www.oecd.org/daf/competition/45154362.pdf.

PAULO FURQUIM DE AZEVEDO, *Restrições Verticais e Defesa da Concorrência: a experiência brasileira*, Textos para Discussão da Escola de Economia de São Paulo da Fundação Getulio Vargas, July 2010, *available at* http://bibliotecadigital.fgv.br/dspace/bitstream/handle/10438/6895/TD%20264%20-%20Paulo%20Furquim%20de%20Azevedo.pdf?sequence=1&isAllowed=y.

RICHARD WHISH, *Intel v Commission: Keep Calm and Carry on!*, Journal of Economic Competition Law & Practice, Vol. 6, 2015, *available at* http://jeclap.oxfordjournals.org/content/6/1/1.full.pdf+html.

WOUTER P. J. WILS, *The judgment of the EU General Court in Intel and the so-called 'more economic approach' to abuse of dominance*, World Competition: Law and Economics Review, Vol. 37, No. 4, Sep. 2014, *available at* http://papers.ssrn.com/sol3/papers.cfm?abstract_id=2498407.

* * *

Chapter XIV

VERTICAL PRICE RESTRAINTS: RECENT DEVELOPMENTS IN BRAZILIAN ANTITRUST POLICY REGARDING RESALE PRICE MAINTENANCE (RPM) AND SUGGESTED RESALE PRICES

PRISCILA BROLIO GONÇALVES

I. Executive Summary

This paper provides a summary of the most recent trends of the Brazilian Antitrust Authority (CADE) decisions with respect to vertical price fixing and suggested retail prices. The paper begins with background information comprising legal treatment and relevant administrative precedents in CADE's history, emphasizing the decision CADE rendered in the early nineties on the Kibon precedent, concerning price caps (item 2). A comprehensive analysis of the reasons for the conviction of auto parts manufacturer SKF in 2013 follows, including comments regarding the two dissenting opinions (item 3). Next comes a brief description of commitments adopted by fiscal printer manufacturer Bematech, a case that shortly followed discussions on the SKF case (item 4). Both the SKF and Bematech cases relate to unilateral vertical price fixing – minimum RPM – established by a manufacturer as a response to distributors' claims. Item

5 is dedicated to the most recent discussion on RPM, a case involving fuel distribution, which CADE will likely decide in 2015. Conclusion and final remarks close the paper, including a table comparing Kibon and SKF, the two most emblematic cases CADE has ruled on with respect to such issues hence far, in addition to certain recommendations (item 6 and Appendix).

II. Background

Vertical price restraints, including resale price maintenance and suggested resale prices, are not a recent concern in Brazil. Since 1938, federal laws have been enacted to prevent agreements imposing resale prices, a behavior that was already regarded as prejudicial to public welfare, many years before the first Brazilian antitrust law was enacted in 1962.

From the perspective of antitrust measures, vertical price agreements and unilateral behavior with the purpose of imposing or fixing resale prices were deemed potentially harmful to consumers in Federal Laws 8,158/91, 8,884/94 and, finally, 12,529/11.

However, RPM was not considered an illegal behavior *per se* in any of these laws; quite to the contrary, all such laws determined that the potential effects of the behavior, including possible benefits and the transfer thereof to end users, in whole or in part, should be taken into account for the purpose of legal assessment.

The first precedent CADE decided on with respect to vertical price restraints involved the distribution of ice cream and its impact on retail.[1]

In 1992, two associations of bakeries and food shops filed complaints against Kibon,[2] a major ice cream manufacturer, for the use and implementation of suggested resale price schedules. Kibon was accused of imposing price caps; according to the plaintiffs, such behavior violated the retailers' constitutional right to free enterprise, and also breached the antitrust law. The Ministry of Justice decided to initiate formal proceedings and the company was notified to submit its defense.

1 CADE, *Sindicado da Indústria de Panificação e Confeitaria de São Paulo, v. Kibon.* Reporting Commissioner Leônidas Rangel Xausa (Administrative Proceeding No. 0148/1992) (Jan. 8, 1998).

2 At the time of the investigation, Kibon was part of the Philip Morris Group. Unilever purchased the company in 1997 and it has since remained as part of this group.

Kibon argued that its pricing policy was designed to prevent the abuse of monopoly power by bakeries and other retailers – many of which were able to abuse consumers due to their privileged location (for example, ice cream trucks at the beach), among other circumstances, thereby having increased the price of the ice cream – whose practice adversely affected Kibon's reputation and decreased its market share. Kibon also claimed that its suggested price caps were not able to distort price competition among retailers because the retailers did not follow the suggested prices. Still according to Kibon, the conduct increased competition among manufacturers and was designed to protect consumers from exploitation and to provide information on the price range the manufacturer deemed appropriate, thereby protecting the manufacturer's reputation in the marketplace.

CADE decided to dismiss the case by the end of the investigation, on the grounds that (i) Kibon was not in a position to exercise market power; (ii) the price schedules were not mandatory for retailers; and (iii) because prices substantially differed at the retailer's level, thus corroborating the claim that the schedules were merely a suggestion. CADE's reporting Commissioner Xausa also indicated that suggested resale price caps could benefit consumers because of their pedagogical effect. The decision was unanimous.

Since the Kibon precedent, CADE has expressly authorized some manufacturers to adopt maximum suggested retail price schedules or to print suggested price caps on products such as candy and chocolate (candy industry) and soft drinks. The implementation of resale price caps has also been deemed legal for the distribution of books. In turn, investigations concerning automotive parts and beer distribution were launched and dismissed due to the lack of evidence of either the requirement of a mandatory resale price policy or the anticompetitive effects thereof.

CADE has reviewed agreements or unilateral vertical price fixing on price floors in the cement, water filter and athletic footwear industries. Investigations were dismissed based on the lack of market power or absence of sufficient evidence on the restrictive behavior.

Minimum resale price restrictions were mentioned in the context of at least two cartel investigations, in which defendants were convicted in the administrative sphere (long steel products, in 2005, and LPG, in 2008).

In both cases, CADE considered that vertical price fixing policies had an important role in helping defendants monitor illegal horizontal agreements.

In 2013, CADE concluded a two-year trial on minimum resale prices. The defendant, auto parts manufacturer SKF,[3] was found guilty of violating the Brazilian antitrust law. The company was convicted and fined. The decision was not unanimous and CADE Commissioners have thoroughly debated the effects of the policy and the burden of proof. The majority of the commissioners decided that minimum resale price behavior should be *presumed illegal* whenever adopted in response to the distributor's initiative (rather than in view of the manufacturer's own needs).

A similar case was settled before CADE in the beginning of 2014. Printer manufacturer Bematech agreed to dismiss its minimum resale price policy after CADE commenced a formal investigation against the company and one of its top distributors.[4]

The SKF and Bematech cases have brought some new elements to the antitrust assessment of vertical price restraints in Brazil, and will be further discussed in the following items (items 3 and 4).

Finally, the most recent development in this area is less than one month old.[5] In January 2015, CADE Commissioner Oliveira Junior issued a third opinion for the conviction of oil company Shell (currently known as Raízen), after an almost ten-year long investigation. In this case, the discussion focuses on whether Shell imposed minimum resale prices to be adopted by fuel resellers. CADE has returned to the traditional debate on whether prices were suggested or mandatory (item 5) in the opinions that have been made public so far. All opinions for the conviction disagree on the definition of minimum RPM. In March 2015, Commissioner Frazão also argued for the conviction, but on the grounds that Shell would have

---

3 CADE, *PROCON-SP v. SKF and SKF do Brasil Ltda.* Relator: Cesar Costa Alves de Mattos (Administrative Proceeding No. 08012.001271/2001-44) (March 26, 2013).

4 CADE, *Bematech S.A. and Fagundez Distribuição Ltda* Reporting Commissioner Alessandro Octaviani Luis (Administrative Proceeding No. 08012.010829/2011-54) (Merger No. 08700.002692/2014-59) (May 5, 2014).

5 CADE, *Shell Brasil Ltda. and Odon de Oliveira Mendes*; Reporting Commissioner Alessandro Octaviani Luis (Administrative Proceeding No. 08012.004736/2005-42) (March 17, 2015).

"influenced uniform behavior" and not practiced RPM, due to lack of mechanisms of coercion.

III. Minimum Resale Prices or Unilaterally Adopted Margins Implemented at the Distributors' Requests: the SKF Case

The Ministry of Justice filed the antitrust investigation against auto parts manufacturer SKF upon request of a consumer protection association that received documents from an anonymous source according to which SKF had adopted a minimum mark-up policy in order to protect its distributors' profitability.

Minutes dated October 2000 and attributed to SKF indicated that the authorized distribution network had been losing profitability, due to the aggressive pricing policy of some of the authorized distributors. The cannibalization had been detected by members of the network and was reported to SKF. The minutes refer to a debate among distributors, with SKF's participation, aiming to protect the business and to establish 'fair pricing' policies, customers' satisfaction and the financial return on the investments. The first consensual measure to be adopted was the minimum mark-up on all SKF products, including bearings, retainers, greases, lubricants and such, tools in general and monitoring equipment, among others. The distribution channel would be in charge of monitoring the minimum mark-up policy.

Interestingly enough, formal proceedings were initiated against SKF, but not against the distributors, especially considering the original concern was cartel behavior within the distribution network.

After many years of stability in the field of vertical price restraints, on November 11, 2009 the SKF case caught the attention of the antitrust community when the investigative and advisory bodies of the Brazilian competition policy system suggested the dismissal of the case, submitted to CADE's review. The case divided the opinions of the CADE Commissioners; reporting Commissioner Mattos favored the dismissal of the case, based on both the absence of market power and lack of evidence of harm.

Commissioner Carvalho disagreed with Mattos and was in favor of SKF's conviction. According to Carvalho:

> *"suggested minimum price schedules, when adopted by companies with monopoly power in a market whose conditions favor collusion, may*

> *affect consumers. Even if there is price dispersion, it is "intuitive" that minimum thresholds will be used as a reference, acting, in fact, as a price floor."*

The Commissioner considered that minimum price schedules, even if solely suggestive, do have the ability to eliminate uncertainty, reason for which they facilitate collusion and generally result in price increase. According to his opinion, enforcement is not a necessary condition to define minimum resale price maintenance, since moral duress suffices to identify the practice as such.

In this specific case, Commissioner Carvalho understood that there were conditions for the exercise of coordinated market power, and also implied that the burden of proof in the absence of market power lies on the defendant.

The European concept of "restriction of competition by object"[6] is mentioned in the chapter "Guidance to the Brazilian Society" of the Commissioner's opinion:

> *"the European posture, regarding the restriction by object seems most adequate". The opinion further adds that, "when the burden of proof is shifted, defendants must tenaciously justify the existence of inter-brand competition and associated efficiencies. Such proof could be excessively difficult for CADE or society to produce, since it is a complex issue, which demands market expertise. If the company engaged in the suspected practice, it will likely have far more technical conditions to prove its point of view. The immediate effect of such guidance is to discourage RPM adventures without very consistent and convincing reasons, also discouraging frivolous statements before CADE. RPM will be accepted as legal only in exceptional cases."*

Another excerpt of Carvalho's opinion states that, "even in the presence of any justification, I believe that the burden of proof relative on the inexistence of anticompetitive risks of the said practice is on SKF".

Finally, the opinion mentions that "*the level of resale prices dispersion was not measured in this case*". Carvalho suggests that such mensuration would be unnecessary for antitrust review, since the mere possibility of price leveling would be sufficient. Such possibility, in turn, would arise

6 In European Law, the concept is limited to agreements (Article 101 of the TFEU, former Article 81 of the EC Treaty).

from the probability of exercise of coordinated market power, along with the fact that SKF was convicted for practicing cartel in France (along with competitors that also operated in the Brazilian market). According to Carvalho, by accepting fixed minimum margins, SKF assumed the risk of standardizing market prices, and not only intra-brand prices.

Commissioner Ruiz followed Carvalho's stand on the case and claimed there were strong indicia of possible exercise of market power by SKF and other manufacturers. Ruiz also highlighted that the case files indicated that the original purpose of the RPM was to avoid *"predatory competition"* between distributors, and that SKF actively cooperated in the enforcement of the price schedule.

The Commissioner discussed that, in general, RPM has the potential to reduce or eliminate intra-brand competition, and may create incentives to upstream collusion. He concluded that the alleged efficiencies SKF presented were not proved and that the existence or absence of anticompetitive intent by the defendant is irrelevant to define the conduct as illegal.

Commissioner Chinaglia in turn refuted Carvalho's and Ruiz's arguments and favored the dismissal of the charges. According to Chinaglia, the behavior would only be illegal upon the concurrent existence of three conditions: (i) market power; (ii) evidence that the behavior may limit competition; (iii) lack of efficiencies or positive effects related to the behavior. There was no evidence of market power, no structural conditions for the exercise thereof and no indication that the behavior would adversely affect competition in the SKF case.

Commissioner Furlan was in favor of the conviction on the grounds that the main purpose of SKF's RPM practice was to eliminate competition among the distributors, and that SKF's market power was proved in the case.

Commissioner Verissimo adhered to the conclusions of Commissioners Carvalho, Ruiz and Furlan. He highlighted that this was a leading case, since there were no precedents on minimum retail price fixing as a 'hardcore' violation in Brazil (the imposition of minimum resale prices is clearly considered a hardcore form of RPM since the conclusion of this investigation). He also stressed that the decision was expected to be used as reference for other cases.

Verissimo's opinion indicates that RPM (including minimum prices and minimum margins) has ambiguous economic and competitive effects. Throughout most of his opinion, Verissimo reviews laws, literature and precedents and analyzes the effects of "RPM – Minimum Prices" in the foreign and domestic laws and experience. For most jurisdictions, determining minimum prices/margins is presumably illegal. CADE's relevant precedents about the subject relate to suggested price caps, whereby such precedents are not applicable to this investigation, in his opinion.

Commissioner Verissimo determines the presumption of illegality in connection to vertical price restraints (in opposition to vertical non-price restraints – also related to distribution agreements/polices – which are considered to be less harmful). The vertical price restraints further included the difference between conducts that impose prices and those that merely suggest prices. The first category was also divided into two types: price caps and minimum prices. According to Commissioner Verissimo, the latter is of greatest concern for antitrust purposes.

Verissimo's vote expressly agrees with Carvalho's conclusions regarding the "moral duress" that even suggested retail prices schedules may have on distributors, characterizing illegal RPM.

Commissioner Carvalho's assumption, confirmed by Commissioner Verissimo, eliminates the administrative authority's burden of proving that the behavior under investigation (vertical price restraints) adversely affects competition. In such cases, CADE would only have to prove the existence of the conduct. The investigated company/individual is responsible for demonstrating that there is no market power and/or that the behavior leads to indubitable benefits that could not have been reached by any other means. A brief description of the possible defenses are as follows:

Defense No. 1: Absence of (unilateral or coordinated) Market Power. *De minimis* rule. According to Commissioner Verissimo, the proof of the absence of market power depends on the following factors, cumulatively: (i) the supplier's market share is not equal to or in excess of 20%; (ii) the distributors joint market share is not equal to or in excess of 20%; (iii) the supplier is not among the four leading market competitors, if the four leading competitors amount to 75% of the market (C4 ≥ 75%); and (iv) the distributors (considered together, as a single entity) are not among the leading market competitors in the distribution level, if the market share of the four leading competitors amounts to 75% (C4 ≥ 75% in the distribution level).

Defense No. 2. Efficiencies Defense. If the company does not fall under the *de minimis* rule, it must demonstrate the specific benefits associated to RPM to avoid conviction, and also that such benefits: (i) could not have been produced by any other means (including other types of vertical restraints); (ii) overcome the risks to competition, and (iii) benefit end users.

Defenses No. 1 and 2 are not acceptable to prevent conviction if it is proven that distributors were behind the implementation of the RPM. According to the Commissioner, this is the most "suspicious situation" of RPM. Verissimo summarizes such position as follows:

> *"If the investigated individual/entity is unable to demonstrate its classification under the de minimis rule, the presumption of unlawfulness of the behavior would only be excluded if the individual/entity demonstrated specific efficiencies related to the RPM under analysis and that such efficiencies (i) could not have been reached by other vertical restraint or by a different and less harmful mean; (ii) clearly exceed, under the market conditions of the case, the risks to competition originated by the behavior; and (iii) result in a clear benefit to consumers.*
>
> *In my opinion, CADE must not accept the aforementioned efficiencies-based defense, if it is able to prove that the distribution network is responsible for the initiative of adopting RPM. In this case, the de minimis market power defense should also not be accepted because, as has been previously mentioned, it is the most suspicious hypothesis of RPM of all, the type that receives the most severe treatment for antitrust purposes in all international jurisdictions. (...)*
>
> *In the case reviewed hereunder, the company was convicted because, once the RPM was determined: (i) SKF failed to prove that it fell under the de minimis rule, considering its market share was above 20% in some of the relevant markets; (ii) SKF was among the 4 leading competitors in the market place; (iii) the benefits SKF argued were not demonstrated; and (iv) even if the benefits had been demonstrated, there is proof that the RPM was adopted at the distributors' initiative, which in itself backs the conviction."*

Commissioner Eduardo Pontual presented a brief oral opinion, consolidating the views presented by Commissioners Carvalho, Ruiz, Furlan and Verissimo, and favored SKF's conviction, based on the illegality of the RPM practice presented on the case.

SKF was convicted by five against two opinions and the decision determined the payment of a fine of approximately BRL 2.7 million. The company filed an objection against CADE's decision before a federal court and the case is now pending judgment.

IV. Recent Developments Following the SKF Case: the Bematech Commitment

The investigation against fiscal printer manufacturer Bematech and its distributor Fagundez was filed after a retailer's complaint, accusing Bematech of illegally refusing to supply equipment justified by the retailer's failure to comply with Bematech's minimum resale price policy. The retailer informed the Ministry of Justice that the manufacturer implemented a RPM policy with punitive measures in the event of noncompliance.

The authorities filed formal proceedings against both Bematech and Fagundez. The latter was accused of requesting Bematech to refuse sales to any company that refused to comply with the pricing policy.

The case had an interesting outcome: Bematech decided to settle the case with CADE and agreed to withdraw the minimum resale price policy. Bematech agreed to exclude the references to resale prices included in its website and to refrain from imposing, suggesting or publishing resale prices for products or services, by any means. It also agreed to provide written notice to 597 retailers members of its loyalty program, "Bematech Plus" (*Bematech Mais*), indicating that it would not publish resale prices and that the retailers were free to set the business conditions with end users. The same message would be displayed in the company's website for 60 days.

Following Bematech's voluntary commitments, CADE dismissed the case against Fagundez for lack of sufficient evidence of the distributor's involvement in the illegal behavior.

V. Investigation against Shell

Filed in 2005, the investigation against Shell relates to the behavior of one employee, accused of pressuring fuel resellers (gas stations) to increase prices and encourage collusion in the downstream level.

Reporting Commissioner Octaviani ruled for Shell's conviction in mid-2014. In his opinion, Shell was guilty of minimum RPM and of trying to obtain uniform prices in the downstream market. Minimum RPM was presumed illegal and the Commissioner stated that Shell was not able to provide a reasonable reason or an efficiency defense capable of challenging it.

Although upholding the conviction, Commissioner Pontual disagreed with Commissioner Octaviani in connection to the definition of vertical price fixing. He distinguished between the attempt to influence the adoption of uniform behavior and the RPM. In the former case, the behavior resembles a cartel, lacks any efficiency and is solely aimed at raising prices to the detriment of consumers; in the latter case, a violation would only arise when the negative effects outweigh the positive since the RPM could be legitimately adopted by an upstream firm to organize its distribution chain and obtain efficiencies. The Commissioner ultimately found that it was not a RPM case, but instead an attempt by an employee of Shell to influence the adoption of a collusive behavior by gas stations.

In early 2015, Commissioners Oliveira Junior and Frazão followed Pontual's conclusion on the merits. Oliveira Junior dismissed the charge of RPM for lack of coercive tactics forcing the resellers to adhere to the prices suggested by Shell. According to the Commissioner, along with vertical relation and resale conditions set by an upstream agent, coercion is the third element that would make RPM presumably illegal. Frazão also found that Shell influenced the adoption of uniform behavior on grounds that the behavior lacked any justification other than the mere restriction to competition, and there was no indication of coercion.

VI. Final Remarks

CADE has reviewed vertical price fixing cases under the rule of reason for almost twenty years. Maximum resale price policies have been deemed legal or neutral in all cases, while minimum resale price cases have been dismissed based on the lack of evidence of behavior, absence of market power and/or lack of anticompetitive effects. Minimum resale price policies have been appointed as restrictive in cartel investigations and have played a relevant role in the administrative convictions in the long steel and LPG investigations, but never resulted in convictions themselves.

Since 2013, however, following CADE's final administrative decision in the SKF case, a new approach has prevailed for minimum resale price by which review under rule of reason has given place to a rebuttable presumption of illegal behavior.

Although the reasons that led CADE to adopt this approach in the SKF case are clear and understandable, the decision is also very controversial because it establishes presumptions that may be very difficult for the defendants to rebut. For example, under the Brazilian antitrust law, market power is presumed where individual market share is above 20%, and consequently the authorities should have the burden of proof when the defendants have a lower share or there is a claim of collective dominance (or collective exercise of market power).

Furthermore, CADE clarified that the manufacturer's imposition of minimum resale prices at the distribution chain's request is equivalent to cartel behavior and would therefore be treated as such. It is worth mentioning that SKF is currently under investigation for cartel behavior.

The tendency to treat this type of RPM strictly was confirmed in the Bematech case. The manufacturer's voluntary commitment following negotiations with CADE indicates that CADE will not tolerate minimum resale prices or mark-ups whenever requested by distributors – not even the suggestion has been admitted in this case. As such, CADE tends to change its policy regarding suggested minimum retail prices when adopted at the distributors request as well. Both Carvalho and Verissimo's opinions reveal that in the future, it is highly unlikely that CADE will be as tolerant with defenses purely based on the absence of coercive measures to enforce resale price floors.

Besides, it is clear that CADE mistrusts all tools intended to promote the policy (printed schedules, information available on websites), since they make it easier for distributors to tacitly collude.

It is very interesting that distributors were not punished in both the SKF and Bematech precedents. Distributors were not even investigated in the SKF case, despite the fact that the original complaint reported a cartel among distributors and that there seemed to be evidence of meetings for the purpose of exchanging information.

As for the Shell case, the same presumption against minimum RPM was maintained, but the majority of the opinions considered that there was not enough evidence of this type of behavior. Shell's recommended conviction is mostly based on the attempt of the company's employee to obtain a collusion in the downstream market, and is regarded as an isolated fact (pressure exercised over a filing station), instead of a business policy involving all resellers.

Finally, CADE continues to distinguish minimum from maximum resale price fixing and the approach regarding price caps does not seem to have changed.

Summary Table: Relevant Differences between KIBON and SKF	
KIBON	**SKF**
Price caps	Minimum Prices
Policy adopted by manufacturer's initiative	Policy adopted at Distributor's request
Typically unilateral behavior	Unilateral behavior with collective effects
Authorities analyzed price dispersion	Authorities did not analyze price dispersion
Clear benefits for consumers	Unclear benefits for consumers. Quite to the contrary, behavior was likely to adversely affect consumers.

General Recommendations
Minimum RPM • Use with extreme caution; • Avoid implementation at distributions' request.
Maximum RPM • Maximum RPM, at the manufacturer's initiative and associated with efficiencies or reasonable justifications, is likely to be admitted by antitrust authorities. • However, there is no safe harbor.
Suggested Retail Prices (No Coactive Measures) • Likely to be admitted in case of price caps; • For minimum prices, use rules for minimum RPM and avoid tools such as schedules and information published in websites. Any clear indication of price floors may be interpreted as coercion (moral duress).

* * *

Chapter XV

JUDICIAL REVIEW OF CADE'S DECISIONS

Pedro Paulo Salles Cristofaro

In the Brazilian legal system, the Brazilian Antitrust Authority (CADE) is in charge of the enforcement of Federal Law 12,529 (2011) (the "Antitrust Law"). CADE is the agency that has authority to investigate, prosecute, and decide on conducts that may be considered offensive to competition, as set out in Article 36 of the Antitrust Law, applying the penalties provided for in Articles 37 and 38 of said Law. CADE also has authority to approve such mergers, which, according to Article 88 of the Antitrust Law, must be submitted to review.

CADE is part of the Federal Executive Branch and reports to the Ministry of Justice. However, despite its attachment to the Executive Branch, it is legally qualified as an "*autarquia*",[1] a specific type of independent government agency, and the special legal regime established by the Antitrust Law ensures CADE a certain level of independence from

1 Under Brazilian Law, the term "*autarquia*" means the legal entity created by law to perform typical governmental activities in a decentralized way (Article 5 of the Decree Law 200/67). To a certain extent, the "*autarquias*" are equivalent to the government agencies of the U.S. system. It is important to note, however, that the translation of legal terms is always a challenge and a risk. Similar terms may have different connotations in the legal systems of each country. In this paper, certain terms were maintained in their original version in Portuguese, whereas other were used according to the approximate U.S. law terms.

the Executive Branch, which is reflected in how its representatives are chosen (CADE's Commissioners, General Superintendent and General Counsel are appointed by the President of the Republic, to act during a fixed term, through a complex mechanism that requires Senate approval of such appointments), as well as in the impossibility of review of CADE's decisions within the scope of the Executive Branch.

CADE's final decisions cannot be appealed at the administrative level and may only be challenged in court.

In the Brazilian legal system, the right to submit to the courts that are part of the Judiciary Branch any actual or threatened breach of a right is a constitutional principle that cannot even be refused by law (Brazilian Constitution of 1988 Article 5, XXXV). Acts performed by administrative authorities, such as CADE, may therefore be challenged in court.

CADE's decisions qualify as "administrative acts," which, according to the Brazilian Constitution of 1988, Article 37, shall observe, among others, the principle of legality. The principle of legality has different connotations for private law and public law. As far as private law agents are concerned, the rule is freedom of action, which can only be limited by law (Brazilian Constitution of 1988 Article 5, II). As regards public authorities, the rule is just the opposite, given that the government shall only perform acts that are either authorized or prescribed by law. Seabra Fagundes, in his classic Brazilian law textbook on the judicial review of administrative acts, states that:

> *"All government activities are limited by subordination to legal order, or, in other words, to legality. The administrative proceeding has no legal existence if it lacks a written statute, as a primary source. It is also necessary that it be conducted in accordance with the law and within the limits set forth therein. Only so will the administrative proceeding be legitimate. Any measure taken by the Government regarding a given individual circumstance, in the absence of a rule of law authorizing such measure or going beyond the scope of the permission given by the law, shall be illegal. The complete submission of the Government to the law constitutes the so-called principle of legality, universally accepted, and is a consequence of the Civil Law system and of the very nature of the administrative function. The written law, whose strongest justification is the need to exclude free will from the development of social relations, necessarily presupposes a limitation to the activities, according to its own words. Wherever there is written law, there shall be no free will. On the other hand, being the administrative function, which constitutes the purpose of the Government*

activities, essentially aimed at making the law a reality, it is not possible to understand that it could be exercised without a legal provision authorizing it, or going beyond its limits."[2]

Besides the principle of legality, the government acts are subject to the principles of impersonality, morality, publicity, and efficiency.

The principle of impersonality embodies the idea of absence of subjectivity on the part of the government. The administration must be objective, refraining from distinguishing between citizens, and not being guided by the private interests of its government agents. In J. Cretella Júnior's words:

"In the field of public law ... the prevailing rule is the idea of non-disposability, because the Government is attached to the idea of purpose. It is the principle of the non-disposability of the public interest, in which the idea of impersonality, of objectivity, is present."[3]

The principle of morality has an obvious connotation, consisting in the obligation of a moral behavior on the part of government agents; whereas the principle of publicity requires that, as a general rule, for administrative acts to be made public, the only exception being the acts to which the law assigns secrecy, in light of public interest.

Finally, the principle of efficiency, introduced in yhe Brazilian Constitution of 1988, Article 37, by Constitutional Amendment 19 (1998), requires the acts performed by the government to be capable of producing the effects that justify them. As Tercio Sampaio Ferraz Jr. explains:

"[The] principle of efficiency has the purpose of governing the administrative activity in its results and not only in its inner consistency (strict legality, morality, impersonality). In other words, it is a principle that moves outwards, rather than inwards. It is not a condition principle, but an end principle, i.e., it does not only impose limits (formal condition of authority), but also results (material condition of performance)."[4]

2 Miguel Seabra Fagundes; Gustavo Binenbojn. *O Controle dos Atos Administrativos pelo Poder Judiciário*, 115. Editora Forense, 7th ed. 2006. All quotes were translated by the author of this article.

3 José Cretella Júnior. *Comentários À Constituição de 1988*, Vol. IV, 2145. Editora Forense Universitária, 1991.

4 Tercio Sampaio Ferraz Jr. *O Poder das Agências Reguladoras à Luz do Princípio*

In view of the foregoing, and especially in what concerns their consistency with the form and the purposes prescribed by the law, the administrative acts are subject to judicial review.

The judicial review of government acts is however limited by certain restrictions deriving from the constitutional principle of separation of powers, set forth in Brazilian Constitution of 1988, Article 2, under which "*the Legislative, the Executive and the Judiciary are Branches of the Federal Union, independent and harmonious among themselves.*" Accordingly, not all aspects of the acts performed by the government are subject to judicial review.

Regarding certain acts and decisions, the Executive Branch has no freedom of choice, that is, it can only strictly apply the law, which prescribes the form and content of the administrative act. These acts are called "*atos vinculados*" (that reasonably fits the definition of "ministerial acts", as "an act that involves obedience to instructions or laws instead of discretion, judgment, or skill"[5]). On the other hand, there are certain acts, called "*atos discricionários*" ("discretionary acts") that embody decisions of a political nature that lie within the exclusive authority of the Executive Branch; it is beyond the court's authority to challenge what legal scholars refer to as the "merits" of such decisions and its authority is limited to examining their consistency with the law:

> *"Many authors summarize these aspects in the binominal opportunity and convenience. They involve interests rather than rights. The interests that are contradicted by the administrative act are not subject to the assessment of the Judiciary Branch, but only the individual rights that may have been violated by the act. The merits [of the administrative act] lie within the exclusive authority of the Executive Branch, and, should the Judiciary Branch interfere, 'it would be playing the role of the authority, thus violating the principle of separation and independence of powers.' The constituent elements [of the act] depend on political criteria and technical means peculiar to the exercise of Government authority."*[6]

da Eficiência, in Alexandre Santos de Aragão, O poder normativo das Agências Reguladoras, Editora Forense, 2nd ed., at 217.

5 Bryan A. Garner (eds.). *Black's Law Dictionary,* West Publishing Company. 7th ed. 2007.

6 Miguel Seabra Fagundes, *supra* note 2, at 181.

For example, it is the exclusive role of the President of the Republic to appoint a Minister or of the Executive Branch to decide upon the commencement of a given construction work or on the opening of a public bidding for the provision of a public service. On the other hand, only if the matter is submitted to the court in a specific process shall the court determine whether such political administrative decisions have been made by a competent authority, in the proper form, and in compliance with the law, with the Constitution, and with the legal principles applicable to the Government. The courts do not have a say on the political convenience of the choice of a Minister or on the commencement of a construction work.

The analysis of the limitations to the review of the acts performed by administrative authorities – CADE included – depends, therefore, in the first place, on assessing the legal nature of the relevant act.

I. Legal Nature of CADE's Decisions

As seen above, administrative acts are classified in two categories: "*atos vinculados*" and "*atos discricionários*."

"*Atos vinculados*" are acts that government agents may only carry out strictly in accordance with the applicable laws. The public official has no alternative as to the essence of the act performed. All its elements arise out of the law.

In Diogo de Figueiredo Moreira Neto's definition:

> *"[Ato Vinculado] is the one that the agent is competent to carry out strictly in accordance with the applicable legal requirements, expressing the intention of the government at the opportunity and for the purposes entirely foreseen in the law, without any freedom of choice to act, whether as to time or content."*[7]

As it initiates a public bidding process, for example, the government authority is required to follow certain procedures set out in the Public Procurement Law (Law 8,666 (1993)), none of which may be disregarded. Likewise, when it licenses a given enterprise, the government authority must strictly follow the law and cannot either deny a license which is in accordance with the legal requirements or grant a license that is not.

7 Diogo de Figueiredo Moreira Neto. *Curso de Direito Administrativo*, 163. Editora Forense, 16th ed., 2014.

Discretionary acts, in contrast, are acts in connection to which the government authority is granted the possibility of making choices based on *opportunity* and *convenience*. The authority has the freedom to choose among two or more alternatives when the act is to be conducted, all of which may be valid by law. It is exclusively for the authority to decide as to the convenience and opportunity to choose between one alternative or the other.

One shall once again resort to Diogo de Figueiredo Moreira Neto's lessons, for whom a discretionary act is the act in relation to which the authority:

> *"is competent to make choices, whether of opportunity or of convenience, regarding the method of implementation, the extent of its effects, its legal content, its ancillary conditions, the time of enforcement, or to whom the will of the government is addressed. There may be only one or several choices as to all these aspects under consideration, as long as [such choices are] strictly contained within the limits allowed by the law."*[8]

The textbooks on Administrative Law also refer to administrative acts provided with *technical discretion*, in which the act performed by the government is not exactly (or exclusively) based on a judgment of convenience and opportunity, but rather on technical criteria, on specific technical knowledge. Considering the issue in more depth, however, it is clear that such acts are not exactly discretionary, as the government has no freedom of choice, but is rather bound by technical criteria arising out of the application of the legal rule.

Strictly speaking, it is possible to distinguish between cases of typical and atypical technical discretion. In the first case, the public official relies on technical criteria, but still exercises a judgment of convenience and opportunity. This is what happens, for example, as pointed out by Tercio Sampaio Ferraz Jr., when technical reports recommend that a certain asset be listed as historic site, in view of its cultural value, but the authority chooses not to do so based on other reasons, of a political or economic nature, or simply for reasons of convenience and opportunity.[9] In the second case, the law resorts to concepts whose application depends on

---

8 Diogo de Figueiredo Moreira Neto, *supra 7,* note at 163.

9 Tercio Sampaio Ferraz Jr. *Discricionariedade das Decisões do CADE sobre Atos de Concentração, available at* www.terciosampaioferrazjr.com.br.

specific technical knowledge. In this case, the law enforcement agent has no leeway and must adopt the technical solution that arises from the law.

While "*atos vinculados*" (including those to be performed with "atypical technical discretion") are subject to full review by the courts, which have the authority to assess whether each of their elements complies with the legal system, discretionary acts are only partially subject to judicial review.

In what concerns the discretionary act, the courts have the role of addressing the lawful aspects of its necessary elements (the authority of the government agent who performed the act, how it was performed, the purpose for which it was intended, and its consistency with such purpose); however, the courts are not entitled to overturn the choice made by the government within the leeway provided to it by law. In this regard, it is important to note that, as highlighted by Maria Sylvia Zanella di Pietro,[10] the scope of the government's freedom of choice in the performance of the discretionary act is not limited only by the *stricto sensu* law – i.e., written statutes – but also by the law in its broader meaning, including the principles that are part of it, such as public interest, reasonableness, proportionality, etc.

Over time, there has been intense debate on the legal nature of CADE's decisions. They have an administrative character (given that CADE is an agency of the Executive Branch), as well as a "jurisdictional" nature, attributed by Article 4 of the Antitrust Law, which defines CADE as an "adjudicating entity," in the sense that it is competent to hear cases and make decisions in concrete situations as to the enforcement of the Antitrust Law in its various aspects. It is not, of course, a judicial jurisdiction (which is solely for the Judiciary Branch to exercise), but an administrative jurisdiction, which ultimately decides within the scope of the Executive Branch and whose decisions may only be challenged in court.

It is undisputed that CADE's decisions shall be based on strict compliance with the law (which describes the wrongful acts and imposes restrictions on the consummation of certain mergers), but it is also undeniable that such decisions depend on specific technical knowledge.

---

10 Maria Sylvia Zanella di Pietro. *Discricionariedade Técnica e Discricionariedade Administrativa*; *in* REDAE – Revista Eletrônica de Direito Administrativo Econômico Vol. 9, 2007, *available at* www.direitodoestado.com.

It is not possible to determine whether or not an act carried out by an economic agent is harmful to competition, or whether it qualifies as abuse of dominant position, without specific expertise regarding the behavior of the economic agents in competitive markets, the definition of the relevant market, the effects of the actions on the markets, among other aspects. It is also not possible to compare positive and negative effects of a merger without knowledge of economics.

However, such specific technical knowledge is not grounds for the government to make discretionary policy decisions, based on reasons of *convenience* and *opportunity*; rather, such specific technical knowledge makes it possible to apply to concrete cases certain undetermined legal concepts imposed by the law. In Maria Sylvia Zanella Di Pietro's words,

> *"if the undetermined concept contained in the law may be determined by the decision of the technical agency, based on scientific knowledge, one cannot refer to discretion per se, and the Judiciary Branch is entitled to review the decision of the Government."*[11]

Accordingly, other than a few exceptions expressly set out in the Antitrust Law, it is the prevailing understanding that, in the exercise of its administrative jurisdictional function, CADE carries out ministerial decision-making acts ("*atos* vinculados") or, at most, acts provided with atypical technical discretion, and thus subject to full review by the courts.

In fact, the law does not afford CADE room for choice regarding compliance with a specific procedure in order to reach a decision and regarding the necessary attention to the parties' rights in the course of the administrative proceeding. During the proceedings, CADE performs a coordinated series of administrative acts that lead to the formation of a consistent decision on the application of the Antitrust Law to a concrete case. Such administrative acts that make up the proceedings are strictly bound by specific rules and constitutional principles, such as the principle whereby parties are also entitled to the right to be heard and to the due process of law in administrative proceedings (Article 5, LV of the Brazilian Constitution). CADE's noncompliance with procedural rules causes its decisions to be null and void; consequently, all procedural acts performed by CADE are subject to judicial review.

---

[11] MARIA SYLVIA ZANELLA DI PIETRO. *Supra* note 10, at 15.

With regard to the CADE decisions concerning the economic agents' behavior, in view of the assessment of a particular case, the law does not give CADE room to decide whether an act is lawful or, on the contrary, if it constitutes anticompetitive conduct. The recognition of a cartel or the qualification of an act as abuse of dominant position is not an act of political choice for CADE. The definition of the wrong arises from the law and the application of a certain penalty is a necessary consequence of the unlawful character of the act. The decision is, therefore, also in this respect, strictly bound by law and subject to judicial review. The fact that CADE's decision depends on certain specific technical knowledge does not give room for CADE to choose between holding the party liable or finding for its innocence, but only makes it mandatory for the decision to be technically supported. The atypical technical discretion is therefore characterized, which does not take away the courts.

There is also no discretion in CADE's application of penalties. The choice of the adjudicating authority between one or another penalty does not result from reasons of convenience and opportunity, freely established by the government.

In fact, Articles 37 *et seq.* of the Antitrust Law establish a series of penalties applicable to anticompetitive conducts, as well as fines for those who fail to fulfill certain duties related to the administrative proceedings. In addition to the provisions regarding payment of fines, whose amounts must be determined in each concrete case within certain minimum and maximum limits, the Antitrust Law also lists a number of obligations to act or refrain from acting, including the conduction of "*any act or measure required to eliminate the harmful effects on competition*" (Article 38, VII of the Antitrust Law).

The determination of the applicable penalty is, however, subject to a strict principle of proportionality, which requires adherence, in the setting of the sanction, to the criteria set forth in Antitrust Law (Act. 12,529/11) Article 45, considering: "I – the seriousness of the violation; II – the offender's good faith; III – the advantage obtained or intended by the offender; IV – whether or not the violation was consummated; V – the extent of the threatened or actual injury to free competition, the national economy, consumers, or third parties; VI – the adverse economic effects on the market; VII – the offender's economic situation; and VIII – recurrence."

The fact that such concepts are undetermined and dependent, in some cases, upon specific technical knowledge, does not make the imposition of penalties a discretionary act. Consequently, the application of penalties by CADE is an "*ato vinculado*", validity of which is subject to full control by the courts.

In this respect, it is worth mentioning Tercio Sampaio Ferraz Jr.'s lesson:

> "*The lawfulness of the administrative acts – for example, in the application of penalties – includes not only the authority to perform the act and its extrinsic formalities, but also its mandatory requirements, its reasons, and its requisites by law and in fact (when binding upon the act).*"[12]

The same applies to the assessment of mergers.

In the Brazilian legal system, the rule is freedom for the economic agents. The Brazilian Constitution includes free initiative among the principles of the economic order, which are applicable to the entire legal system, and freedom to contract is one of its key elements. Certain actions defined by the Antitrust Law as mergers, provided that they meet certain objective requirements, are subject to a special condition of validity: CADE's approval. CADE's approval, in whole or in part, or rejection of an act is dictated directly by the Antitrust Law in particular and by law in general.

CADE has no choice but to approve the mergers that do not have the effects mentioned in the Antitrust Law (Law 12,529 (2011) Article 88, Paragraph 5 – elimination of competition in a substantial part of the relevant market, creation or strengthening of a dominant position or domination of a relevant market of goods or services). If the merger results in such effects, CADE must not approve it, unless the limits strictly required to achieve certain goals set out in the Antitrust Law, Article 88, Paragraph 6, are observed.

In this respect, the wording of the Antitrust Law (Law 12,529 (2011) Article 88, Paragraph 6), has made room for questions as to the nature of a CADE decision that approves a merger capable of producing the harmful effects listed in Paragraph 5. In fact, Paragraph 6 provides that, in light of certain anticompetitive effects mentioned in the Act, mergers "may be

---

12 Tercio Sampaio Ferraz Jr. *O Poder Normativo das Agências Reguladoras à Luz do Princípio da Eficiência*, 209, Editora Forense, 2006.

authorized, provided that strictly necessary limits [to achieve certain goals] are observed." Use of the term "may" could imply that CADE would be free to choose between approving or rejecting a merger falling within both Paragraphs 5-6 of Antitrust Law (Law No. 12,529 (2011) Article 88).

In our view, however, the best understanding is the one that recognizes not CADE's power, but the duty to approve mergers that fall under Paragraph 6 of Article 88 of the Antitrust Law. In a systematic interpretation of the legal system based on the economic agents' freedom to act, when the law provides that the acts capable of producing certain effects may be approved (i.e., there is no obstacle in the law to the approval), CADE has the duty to approve the merger; in other words, CADE's decision is bound by the terms of the law and it must not exercise a judgment of convenience and opportunity to approve the merger.

In this regard, Tercio Sampaio Ferraz Jr. states as follows:

> *"In cases of approval or disapproval of mergers, I understand such acts are incorrectly called technically discretionary. In fact, CADE ... makes a decision whose technical grounds do not express a judgment of convenience and opportunity, but rather an obligation to comply with certain legal dictates concerning the protection of free initiative and free competition. Its decision is therefore not a political government act, according to occasional guidelines, but an act that satisfies a State policy according to constitutional and legal guidelines.*
>
> *Accordingly, if the CADE Board acknowledges that a certain merger increases the barriers to entry, but nevertheless also recognizes that there are efficiencies that technically outweigh the damage, its approval is a ministerial, rather than a discretionary, act. The legal expression 'may authorize' ... is actually a 'power/duty,' and not a discretionary power."*[13]

The same applies to the approval of a merger subject to conditions, as allowed by Article 61 of the Antitrust Law. According to the Law, CADE shall determine the appropriate restrictions to mitigate possible adverse effects of a merger on the relevant markets affected. Paragraph 2 of Article 61 provides for a non-exhaustive list of alternatives that may be adopted. The choice among the alternatives given by the law, however, in view of each particular case, is not random and is not linked to the concepts of opportunity and convenience that define the discretionary act. The grounds

13 Tercio Sampaio Ferraz Jr. *Discricionariedade das Decisões do CADE sobre Atos de Concentração; available at* www.terciosampaioferrazjr.com.br.

for the choice are predominantly technical and are limited by the principle of reasonableness, which requires that CADE impose the least possible restrictions to mitigate the harmful effects of the merger.

As suggested by Justice Luis Roberto Barroso, of the Federal Supreme Court (STF):

> *"The principle of reasonableness is a mechanism to control legislative and administrative discretion. It allows the Judiciary Branch to overturn legislative or administrative acts when: (a) they are not suitable; (b) the measure is neither required nor necessary, and there is an alternative way to achieve the same result with a lower burden on an individual right; (c) there is no proportionality in the strict sense, that is, what is lost as a result of the measure is more relevant than what is earned.*
>
> *As a result, in the first place, there must be a rational and reasonable link between the disciplinary measure implemented and the goal to be achieved, given the factual assumption that supports the norm. In other words, there must be a logical and rational correlation between the distortion to be corrected and its remediation.*
>
> *The principle of reasonableness also requires that, among the measures used to achieve the intended goal, the one that causes the least restriction to the rights protected by the Constitution be chosen. One must ensure the presence of the binomial need/utility in the particular case, consequently preventing any excess. Finally, the measure shall be comparatively les harmful to the constitutional principles that govern the economic order than the reason for the intervention itself. In other words, the cost-benefit ratio must be positive."*[14]

As a result, the technical nature of several aspects of CADE's decisions, as well as the existence of undetermined legal concepts in the Antitrust Law, which CADE interprets in its decisions, do not provide CADE's decisions with the nature of discretionary administrative acts. CADE's decisions are, as a rule, ministerial acts ("*atos vinculados*"), which may therefore be subject to judicial review, in all their aspects.

---

14 Luís Roberto Barroso. *A Ordem Econômica Constitucional e os Limites à Atuação Estatal no Controle de Preços. in* Revista de Direito Administrativo, Vol. 226, Rio de Janeiro: Renovar, Oct./Dec. 2001, at 206.

II. Exceptions: Discretionary Acts Performed by CADE

With respect to a few acts, however, the Antitrust Law provides CADE with the power to base its decision on a judgment of convenience and opportunity:

- The execution, in the course of administrative proceedings to ascertain any anticompetitive conduct, of a "*cease-and-desist commitment in relation to the practice being investigated or its harmful effects*" (Article 85 of the Antitrust Law);
- The execution of a "leniency agreement" (Article 86 of the Antitrust Law);
- The execution of a "concentration control agreement," according to Article 125 of CADE Internal Regulations.

The object of the three abovementioned cases are agreements that may or may not be concluded by CADE. Such agreements depend on requirements defined by the law (CADE's decision is therefore bound by the existence of these requirements). However, even if such requirements are present in the particular case, CADE is not obliged to execute them. Therefore, CADE's decision to enter into a cease-and-desist commitment, a leniency agreement or a concentration control agreement is qualified as a discretionary act.

The same applies to the case of Paragraph 7 of Article 88 of the Antitrust Law. Such provision states that "within one year from the date of consummation, CADE is allowed to require the submission of mergers that do not fall within" the objective requirements set out in the Antitrust Law that make it mandatory to submit a merger in advance. It is worth mentioning that CADE does not have the power to determine the submission for approval of all acts carried out by the economic agents. It is necessary, initially, for the act to qualify as a "merger," under Article 90 of the Antitrust Law. It is also imperative that the act be potentially capable of resulting in damages to competition, otherwise there would be no justification for CADE's intervention (the submission to CADE of an act whose approval evidently could not be denied could not be requested).

However, even if the requirements that would make it possible for CADE to determine the submission for approval of the act were present in the specific case, CADE may, for reasons of convenience and opportunity, decide not to make this determination. It is therefore a discretionary act.

This does not mean that such discretionary acts cannot be challenged in court, but only that said challenge will not result in the analysis of the aspects of convenience and opportunity of CADE's act. As has been pointed out by Diogo de Figueiredo Moreira Neto, "*what is unchangeable by judicial review shall be limited solely to such largely discretionary content.*" He explains:

> "*Therefore, as an administrative act, it may always be confronted with the legal system as for all its mandatory elements, namely: the competence of those issuing it; the form which it assumes...; plus certain binding reasons..., as well as the assessment of its legality, its standards of reality and reasonableness.*"[15]

III. Limitations to the Extent of the Court Decision

As seen above, CADE decisions may be challenged in court. The Judiciary Branch is competent to examine all aspects of CADE's decisions related to legal requirements and certain aspects of the decisions that qualified as a discretionary act.

The content of the court rulings whose object are CADE decisions remains to be considered.

In view of the constitutional principle of separation of powers (Articles 2 and 60, Paragraph 4, III of the Brazilian Constitution), in the exercise of the judicial review of administrative acts, the courts are generally not authorized to take the place of the Executive Branch to render another decision that seems more correct. As stated by Diogo de Figueiredo Moreira Neto:

> "*The Judiciary Branch, under the excuse of exerting a legality control, may not replace any decision assigned by the Constitution to other Branches and independent agencies with its own decision. ... Given the unlawfulness existing in such cases, the Judiciary Branch is prohibited from replacing the defective decision with another one, whether normative or administrative, that seems better to it.*"[16]

In the exercise of the legality control of CADE's decisions, the courts are competent to overturn it in whole or in part, by assessing whether or

---

[15] Luís Roberto Barroso, *supra* note 14.

[16] Luís Roberto Barroso, *supra* note 14, at 261.

not CADE's decision is compatible with the law, in order to make it comply with the breached legal provision or to order the conduction of the act or decision by which CADE would be bound. The courts may therefore:

I. Overturn, in full, the decision rendered by CADE, either based on formal requirements or on the merits of the decision; or

II. Overturn CADE's decision in part, making it suitable to the law.

IV. Enforcing And Challenging CADE's Decisions

Under Article 93 of the Antitrust Law, decisions made by CADE's Board imposing a fine or an obligation to act or refrain from acting are extrajudicial enforcement instruments.

This means that, if CADE's decision is not complied with by the parties to the administrative proceeding at will, CADE does not need to institute a new judicial proceeding to discuss whether or not the wrongful act has taken place or the possibility to approve the merger. However, CADE does not have the coercive power to directly enforce its decisions, so that the enforcement in court is vital if the party fails to fulfill them voluntarily.[17]

According to Article 94 of the Antitrust Law, when the sole purpose of the enforcement proceedings instituted by CADE is the collection of a pecuniary fine, it will be conducted in accordance with the provisions of the Tax Collection Act (Federal Law 6,830 (1980)). The proceeding is the same adopted to tax foreclosure. As a result, if the party does not voluntarily pay the fine applied within the term established by CADE, the amount of such penalty shall be listed as overdue debt/liability ("*dívida ativa*"), which allows the institution of collection proceedings.

Once the collection proceedings are filed, the debtor is summoned to pay the debt with default interest and penalties within five days, plus the charges listed in the Certificate of Overdue Liability, or give security (Article 8 of Federal Law 6,830 (1980)). In order to ensure the enforcement

[17] The Brazilian legal system distinguishes some processes intended to declare the existence of a right ("*processos de conhecimento*"), and processes designed to enforce a right already been declared ("*processos de execução*"). As CADE's decisions are extrajudicial enforcement instruments, CADE need not to initiate a "*processo de conhecimento*" against the party, but only an enforcement proceeding ("*processo de execução*").

proceedings for the amount of the debt, the default interest and the penalties and charges listed in the Certificate of Overdue Liability, the debtor may (i) make a cash deposit; (ii) provide a bank guarantee or a guarantee insurance; (iii) offer assets for attachment, following a certain order which prioritizes the most liquid assets, such as cash and government bonds; or (iv) offer for attachment assets made available by third parties and accepted by the creditor.

When the object of the CADE decision is an obligation to act or refrain from acting, the enforcement proceedings are governed by the Brazilian Code of Civil Procedure.

In relation to the obligation to act, once the enforcement suit is filed, the party CADE finds guilty shall be summoned to perform the obligation within the term granted by the judge, if not otherwise determined in CADE's decision. If the party does not perform the obligation within the prescribed period, CADE may, in the same judicial proceedings, require the obligation to be enforced at the party's expense. In the event of an obligation to refrain from acting determined by CADE, if the party fails to comply with the decision, CADE shall request the judge to either establish a time limit for the act to be undone or to have it undone itself.

In enforcement proceedings whose object is, in addition to the collection of fines, the performance of an obligation to act or refrain from acting, the general rule is that the judge will grant specific performance or order certain measures be taken to ensure a practical outcome equivalent to the satisfaction of the decision. The conversion of the obligation to act or refrain from acting into indemnification for damages shall be without prejudice to the fines imposed and shall only be admissible if the specific performance or the achievement of the corresponding practical outcome is impossible.

When necessary for enforcement purposes, the Antitrust Law authorizes the judge to determine an intervention in the company.

The proper lawsuit to cancel the extrajudicial enforcement instrument object of the enforcement proceedings is the so-called motion to stay execution ("*Embargos à Execução*"). This motion may be based both on formal aspects of the enforcement proceedings or of the CADE administrative proceedings and on the substantive aspects of the decision rendered by CADE that could lead to the invalidity, in whole or in part, of

CADE's decision and, consequently, the invalidity, whole or in part, of the enforcement instrument.

In the case of a tax foreclosure, it is not admissible to file the motion to stay execution before securing the amount of the debt (Article 16, Paragraph 1 of the Tax Foreclosure Law). With respect to the obligation to act or refrain from acting, the motion may be filed without the offering of security (Article 736 of the Brazilian Code of Civil Procedure), but, as a rule, it does not stay the enforceability of the enforcement instrument. Under Article 739-A, Paragraph 1 of the Code of Civil Procedure, the court may, at the debtor's request, stay the proceedings when the grounds of the motion are relevant and the enforcement proceedings may clearly cause to the debtor severe damages, of difficult or uncertain remediation, and provided that the enforcement proceedings have already been guaranteed by sufficient attachment, deposit or bond. As to the guarantees necessary to stay the effects of CADE's decision, see item 6 below.

According to Article 97 of the Antitrust Law, CADE decisions must be enforced before the Federal Court of the Federal District (that is, the capital of Brazil, Brasilia) or at the court of the debtor's domicile, at CADE's discretion. The motion to stay execution must be filed with the same court.

V. Annulment Action of CADE's Decisions

The Parties to the administrative proceedings are not required to wait until CADE files the enforcement action to seek the annulment of the enforcement instrument, if it is not in accordance with the law, by means of a motion to stay execution.

The debtor may get ahead of the Agency by filing an annulment action against CADE's decision, whose purpose shall be the total or partial annulment of it. Filing of the annulment action does not depend on prior offer of security, but it will not stay the effects of CADE's decision.

Pursuant to Paragraph 4 of Article 98 of the Antitrust Law, plaintiff must produce all relevant issues in fact and in law, under penalty of estoppel (that is, loss of the right to later litigate such issues in fact and in law) in the action that seeks to annul CADE's decision. All allegations that could be raised for the pleadings to be granted are therefore deemed argued. Further, the same claims may not be submitted under different causes of action, in different lawsuits, except with regard to supervening facts.

According to recent case law of the Federal Supreme Court (Extraordinary Appeal to the Federal Supreme Court No. 627709, heard on August 2014), the rule under Article 109, Paragraph 2 of the Brazilian Constitution applies to CADE, according to which actions brought against the Agency may be filed in the Federal Court with jurisdiction over the plaintiff's domicile, over the place where the act or event which has given rise to the claim has taken place, or yet in the Federal Court for the Federal District. Such constitutional provision reads as follows:

> *"Paragraph 2 – Cases brought against the Federal Government may be filed at the judicial district where the plaintiff is domiciled, or where the act or fact giving rise to the suit occurred or where the item is located, or further, in the Federal District."*

CADE used to claim that this rule would apply only to lawsuits filed against the Federal Government, but not to actions brought against the independent government agencies (organized as "*autarquias*"), which have their own legal standing. Accordingly, being CADE an independent government agency with domicile in Brasília, in the Federal District, only the Federal Court of Brasília would be competent to prosecute lawsuits filed against it. The Agency's defense in other locations would represent a large and undue burden for the government, to the detriment of CADE's right to full hearing and of the public interest. Justice Ricardo Lewandowski, the reporting justice of the Supreme Court case, held that the jurisdiction criterion established by Article 109, Paragraph 2 shall be extended to all independent government agencies in order to facilitate access to the party that brings suit against any entities of the direct or indirect government of the Federal Government, stating as follows:

> *"[The] aforementioned rule is not designed to favor the Federal Government, but rather to benefit the other side in the lawsuit, which, if allowed to choose the venue, will more easily achieve the desired jurisdictional provision."*

VI. Stay of CADE's Decisions: Anticipatory Relief and Provisional Remedy

The mere filing of a motion to stay execution or of an annulment action against CADE's decision does not immediately stay its effects. As to the motion to stay execution, the law grants the stay of the proceedings to the secured tax foreclosure and allows for its effects be stayed pursuant to the terms of Article 16 of the Tax Foreclosure Law and Article 739-A of the Brazilian Code of Civil Procedure, as referred to in item IV above.

In annulment actions filed against CADE, it is also possible to obtain full or partial stay of CADE's decision through a motion for advanced relief ("*antecipação de tutela*"), based on Article 273 of the Brazilian Code of Civil Procedure. The first requirement of the advanced relief is the "semblance of truth of the claims." This requirement means that it is up to the court to determine the plausibility of the right claimed in view of the information provided in the record. It is not necessary to prove the alleged right, but only that it is in principle compatible with the legal system. The second requirement is the existence of damages that will be impossible or difficult to remedy. The following situations may represent damages to justify the advanced relief: (i) the enrollment of the fine as enforceable debt, which limits the ability to participate in public bids and obtain bank loans; (ii) the definitive collection of the fine; or (iii) the implementation of the effects of the obligations to act or refrain from acting determined by CADE.

The motion for advanced relief is not made in an autonomous lawsuit, and must instead be filed in the complaint or produced in the course of an annulment action of CADE's decision.

The stay of CADE's decision may also be the subject matter of a preliminary injunction ("*ação cautelar*"), an independent proceeding governed by Article 796 *et seq.* of the Brazilian Code of Civil Procedure, which may be either preparatory or incidental to the main proceedings. The preliminary injunctions aim at obtaining the necessary measures to ensure the effectiveness of the court decision.

Article 98 of the Antitrust Law states that the filing of a motion to stay execution or of any other action seeking to annul the enforcement instrument shall not stay the enforcement proceedings if guarantees are not offered in the amount of the fines imposed, in order to secure compliance with the final decision issued in the lawsuit, including in what concerns daily fines. The abovementioned provision also determines that in order to ensure performance of the obligations to act in a certain way, the judge shall establish appropriate security.

There are a number of court decisions allowing the fine to be secured not only by a deposit, but also through a bank guarantee or insurance, as expressly provided for in Article 9 of the Tax Collection Law. As for the bond related to the obligation to act or refrain from acting, it must be established by the court taking into account its general power to issue interim rulings and based on reasonable judgment.

VII. Writ of Mandamus

Under Article 5 of the Brazilian Constitution and Federal Law 12,016 (2008), "a writ of mandamus shall be granted to protect a clear and perfect right, not covered by habeas corpus or habeas data, whenever the party responsible for the illegal actions or abuse of power is a government official or a legal entity agent in the exercise of the duties of a Public Authority."

The acts carried out by CADE authorities (Board Members, Superintendent) may theoretically be the target of a writ of mandamus.

It is important to mention, however, that this measure does not allow the production of additional evidence. The writ of mandamus is only appropriate when it is possible to prove in advance the unlawful character of the decision or the abuse of power by the public authority. Save for exceptional cases, a decision on the merits rendered in a CADE proceeding cannot dispense with the examination of elements of evidence in the course of the judicial proceedings. Accordingly, the writ of mandamus is more suitable, as a rule (except in cases of flagrant illegality), when CADE's decision concerns a possible breach of procedural rules or the parties' right to full hearing in the administrative proceedings.

VIII. Appeals

The decisions rendered by Federal Judges with jurisdiction to review the lawsuits to which CADE is a party may be appealed before the Federal Regional Courts (TRF). There are five Federal Regional Courts in Brazil, each one responsible for a particular group of Brazilian states, as shown below:

TRF of the 1st Region – States of Acre, Amapá, Amazonas, Bahia, Distrito Federal, Goiás, Maranhão, Mato Grosso, Minas Gerais, Pará, Piauí, Rondônia, Roraima, and Tocantins

TRF of the 2nd Region – States of Espírito Santo and Rio de Janeiro

TRF of the 3rd Region – States of Mato Grosso do Sul and São Paulo

TRF of the 4th Region – States of Paraná, Rio Grande do Sul, and Santa Catarina

TRF of the 5th Region – States of Alagoas, Ceará, Paraíba, Pernambuco, Rio Grande do Norte and Sergipe

A large part of the case law on the application of the Antitrust Law comes from the Federal Regional Court of the 1st Region, which is competent to entertain appeals against decisions rendered by Federal Judges sitting in Brasília (Federal District). Nevertheless, especially after the Federal Supreme Court understanding regarding the possibility of filing claims against CADE in the entire national territory, one can expect an increase in the number of decisions from the Federal Regional Courts in other regions of Brazil.

In a very brief summary, two are the main appeals available against decisions rendered by first instance judges:

The first one is called "*agravo de instrumento*" (interlocutory appeal) and is filed to overturn interlocutory decisions, i.e., decisions rendered by the judge that do not terminate the proceedings (such as, for example, the decision that grants or denies interlocutory relief to stay the effectiveness of CADE's decision).

The second is called "*apelação*" (appeal) and is filed to overturn "*sentenças*" (judgments), i.e., decisions that terminate the proceeding.

In the event of breach of federal law or of dissenting opinions from other courts, the decisions rendered by the Federal Regional Courts may be subject to "*Recurso Especial*" (Special Appeal to the Superior Court of Justice), to be heard by the Superior Court of Justice (STJ) – the highest court responsible for interpreting the federal law and standardizing the case law involving federal law. In the event of violation of the Brazilian Constitution, the decisions rendered by Federal Regional Courts may be subject to "*Recurso Extraordinário*" (Extraordinary Appeal to the Federal Supreme Court), to be heard by the Federal Supreme Court, the highest court of the country, responsible for enforcing the Brazilian Constitution.

It is important to note, however, that, although the Antitrust Law is a federal law, not every claim involving its application shall give rise to a Special Appeal to the Superior Court of Justice or an Extraordinary Appeal to the Federal Supreme Court. The Superior Court of Justice and the Federal Supreme Court do not entertain appeals whose subject matter involves facts or interpretation of contracts, but only those strictly limited to matters of law. In addition, a series of conditions for their admissibility are required for the Special Appeal to the Superior Court of Justice and the Extraordinary Appeal to the Federal Supreme Court to be entertained so that they are only admissible in very limited circumstances.

Conclusion

The purpose hereof is not to exhaust all the matters related to the judicial review of CADE's decision, but only to introduce basic concepts of the Brazilian legal system.

More specifically, it is worth mentioning that although CADE has a certain level of independence, it is nevertheless an Executive Branch agency, whose decisions constitute administrative acts subject to judicial control.

Although in many cases CADE's decisions depend on specific technical knowledge, this fact does not render them discretionary acts; in other words, CADE shall strictly observe the law, and shall not make decisions based on a judgment of convenience and opportunity. CADE's decisions are subject to judicial review not only as to their formal aspects, but also as to their substantive aspects.

It is true that the courts, in order to review CADE's decisions, also needs to resort to specific technical knowledge. This, however, is not a peculiarity of the Antitrust Law. In the analysis of a number of different issues – from cases involving alleged medical malpractice to others dealing with complex power supply contracts – the judge may, and must, make use of technical knowledge, through expert reports.

This paper presents the personal views of the author on the matter. Naturally, the application of the general rules summarized above may be subject to different interpretation and shall be carefully examined in view of the particularities of each case.

BIBLIOGRAPHY:

Diogo de Figueiredo Moreira Neto. *Curso de Direito Administrativo*: Forense publishers, 16th ed. (2014).

José Cretella Júnior. *Comentários à Constituição de 1988*, Vol. IV. Forense Universitária publishers (1991).

Luís Roberto Barroso. *A Ordem Econômica Constitucional e os Limites à Atuação Estatal no Controle de Preços in Revista de Direito Administrativo*, v. 226. Rio de Janeiro: Renovar publishers (2000).

Maria Sylvia Zanella Di Pietro. *Discricionariedade Técnica e Discricionariedade Administrativa*: *in* REDAE – Revista Eletrônica de Direito Administrativo Econômico v. 9 (2007). Available at www.direitodoestado.com.

Miguel Seabra Fagundes. *O Controle dos Atos Administrativos pelo Poder Judiciário*. Updated by Gustavo Binenbojn: Forense publishers, 7th ed.

Tercio Sampaio Ferraz Jr. *Discricionariedade das Decisões do CADE sobre Atos de Concentração. Available at:* www.terciosampaioferrazjr.com.br.

______. O Poder Normativo das Agências Reguladoras à Luz do Princípio da Eficiência in *"O Poder Normativo das Agências Reguladoras"*, coord. Alexandre Santos de Aragão, 2nd ed., Editora Forense publishers (2011).

* * *

Chapter XVI

PRIVATE ANTITRUST DAMAGES

Carlos Francisco de Magalhães
Gabriel Nogueira Dias
Cristiano Rodrigo Del Debbio
Francisco Niclós Negrão

I. Introduction

From the classic judicial controversy over the validity and extension of a non-compete clause at the beginning of the twentieth century to the ground-breaking decisions on monopoly rights and market closure upheld by the Supreme Court in the 1950s, the Brazilian Judiciary Branch has always been extraordinarily active in antitrust litigation. Competition violations may take many forms and the Brazilian courts have dealt with practically every type thereof as they became progressively more complicated. Claims involving non-compete clauses and refusals to deal, exclusivity agreements, abusive conduct and predatory practices are routinely found in courts – even more so after the enactment of the Brazilian Consumer Code (Federal Law 8,078/90) and, more recently, Brazil's new Competition Law (Federal Law 12,529/11).

In more recent years, as the Brazilian Antitrust Authority (CADE) has gained visibility – and its significant investment in competition advocacy has started to mature – Brazil has also experienced a surge of class actions aimed at redressing collective damages arising out of antitrust violations to the market as a whole, most of them filed by the state and federal branches of the Prosecution Office. Although Brazil does not have the same powerful tools and incentives for collective dispute as other countries,[1] CADE has been searching for new and more effective ways to encourage victims to claim damages as a group, in order to amplify the deterrent effect of the Agency's decisions. For example, in its industrial gas cartel decision, CADE has openly encouraged associations and other injured parties to file collective claims against the defendants.[2] CADE has also decided to take a more active role in individual disputes, joining private lawsuits as *amicus curiae*, to ensure its view of the Competition Law will prevail also in the courts.

It is clear that CADE plays a prominent role in the defense of competition – so that Federal Law 12529/11 even refers to the Brazilian Antitrust Authority – CADE and the Economic Supervision Office of the Ministry of Finance (SEAE) as the sole components of the Brazilian Competition System. However, CADE's preventive and repressive functions are geared towards the protection of collective (trans-individual) rights.[3] CADE is not interested in conducts with private repercussions only – *CADE aims to protect competition, not competitors.*[4] Similarly, since

---

1 For instance, Brazil does not have a 'triple damages rule' for antitrust private litigation.

2 For example, in CADE, *Combustíveis.* Reporting Commissioner Fernando de Magalhães Furlan. (AP 08012.009888/2003-70) (Sept. 27, 2010), after rendering judgment against the companies involved in the gas cartel, CADE determined that a copy of the judgment should be delivered to several trade confederations, federations and associations for any interested parties to be notified of the possibility of filing claims for damages.

3 CADE prevents anticompetitive behavior by analyzing mergers and assessing their impact on the market. On the other hand, CADE represses anticompetitive behavior by monitoring, investigating and punishing cartels or abuse of market power.

4 CADE, *Indústria de Bebidas.* Reporting Commissioner Ruy Santacruz (PA. 08000.000146/1996-55) (Jan. 1, 2001). *See also*: CADE, *Indústria de Bebidas.* Reporting Commissioner Arthur Barrionuevo Filho (PA No. 08000.015370/97-13) (Sept. 09, 1998); CADE, *Skol de Santa Catarina.* Reporting Commissioner Marcelo Calliari (PI No. 08012.001192/98-95) (April 14, 1999); CADE, *Indústria de Bebida.* Reporting Commissioner João Bosco Leopoldino da Fonseca (AP No. 08000.000826/97-41) (Aug. 11, 1999); CADE, *Indústria de Bebidas.* Reporting Commissioner Mércio Felsky. (PA No. 0139/1993) (Oct. 1, 1999); CADE, *Cervejaria Brahma.* Reporting Commissioner Mércio Felsky (PA No. 0142/1993) (Oct. 23, 2000); CADE, *Cervejaria Skol Caracu S.A.* Reporting

the administrative activity takes into consideration the potential effects of market conduct, CADE is also not concerned with the measurement and quantification of any actual damages that may have been caused by the offender.[5] In fact, administrative sanctions have the immediate goal of punishing offenders – and that is it. Compensation for private damages for specific companies or consumers must be addressed through private actions, whether class or individual actions.

As a matter of fact, under Brazilian Law, victims are allowed to go to court even if CADE has expressly decided that no violation has occurred[6] – given that courts are not bound by CADE's judgment and therefore are free to take a different view of the matter.[7]

Article 5 (XXIV) of the Brazilian Federal Constitution establishes as a fundamental guarantee that any injury or threat to a right may be referred to the Judiciary Branch. This is the basic foundation for the prevention and redress of any and all damages under Brazilian Law. Moreover, Federal Law 10,406/2002 – the Brazilian Civil Code (CC) – sets out the right to obtain compensation for any damages suffered due

---

Commissioner Thompson Andrade (PA No. 08000.004544/97-31) (Out. 5, 2000); CADE, *Cervejaria de Brasilia S.A – CEBRASA*. Reporting Commissioner Celso Fernandes Campilongo. (AP No. 08012.009882/98-47) (Feb. 08, 2001); CADE, *Companhia de Bebida das Américas – AMBEV*. Reporting Commissioner Carlos Emmanuel Joppert Ragazzo. (PA No. 08012.004363/2000-89) (Nov. 09, 2009); CADE, *Redisbel v. AMBEV*. Reporting Commissioner Carlos Emmanuel Joppert Ragazzo.(PA No. 08012.002417/2008-45) (July 15, 2011).

5 CADE only requires a "high risk that effects will be produced, once the conduct is practiced " (CADE, *CIEFAS v. COOPANEST-BA*. Reporting Commissioner. Luiz Fernando Schuartz. (PA No. 08012.007042/2001-33). (April 26, 2006) "Antitrust Law expressly, in its art. 20, proof of exemption, that is, it is not necessary to prove the actual effects, but the potential effects" (cf. CADE, *SINDUSCON/SP v. Gerdau S.A, Siderúrgica Belgo-Mineira e Siderúrgica Barra Mansa*. Reporting Commissioner Roberto Pfeiffer. (PA No. 08012.004086/2000-21) (Nov. 7, 2005).

6 As an example, the Economic Law Office – a former part of Brazilian Competition System, now replaced by CADE – opened investigations questioning the legality of the radius clause on shopping centers, and CADE has considered such clauses illegal in certain situations. The Brazilian courts, however, have consistently upheld the validity of such same clauses.

7 Naturally, even if judges are not bound by CADE's opinion, its authority as the antitrust agency will lend considerable weight to its influence on the judicial decision.

to wrongful or unlawful behavior. This general torts rule is applicable to virtually all disputes involving competition issues. In fact, before the enactment of the Competition Law, the CC was at the heart of practically every claim involving unfair competition, abuse of economic power and contractual restrictions in general. To this day, the CC continues to regulate damages, causation and liability – and the breadth and versatility of its rules allows its enduring applicability to competition issues. In addition, Article 47 of Federal Law 12,529/11 establishes that any injured individuals may file suit to cease or to seek compensation for any violation of the economic order, on their own behalf or by means of their representatives or substitutes, regardless of any prior decision or authorization from CADE – confirming, once more, the parties' right to access the courts and to obtain civil remedies when there is an unlawful act, damage and causation. The statute of limitations on these lawsuits is of three years for injured parties in general,[8] and five years if the victim is a consumer,[9] counted from the date the damage occurred.[10]

Together with the full compensation of damages, victims are allowed to file for injunctions to prevent or stop the anticompetitive behavior. Brazilian courts, for example, may impose daily, weekly or monthly fines on the offender, in order to seek mandatory compliance therefrom. Courts structure fines according to the situation, and have broad discretion to raise their amount, if compliance is not immediate. Fines may be accompanied by any other measure required to stop the antitrust violation.[11] For example, courts have the power to suspend contractual clauses, restore unlawfully terminated agreements and impose obligations to negotiate. In extreme cases, courts may even intervene directly in the defendant's business.[12] In these situations, intervention must address the crisis in a proportional and appropriate fashion, such as appointment of a court official to supervise the defendant's activities or temporarily replace its managers. In any event, the judicial intervention must not exceed 180 days.

8 Article 206(3)(V) of the CC.

9 Article 27 of the Brazilian Consumer Protection Code (CDC).

10 Every case of damage (i.e., multiple purchases from a cartel) is counted individually.

11 Article 461 of the Brazilian Code of Civil Procedure (CPC).

12 Article 102 of Federal Law 12,529/11.

II. Jurisdiction of Brazilian Courts over Antitrust Private Damages Disputes

Under Article 88 of the CPC, Brazilian courts have jurisdiction over any dispute: a) in which the defendant, regardless of nationality, has registered office or a subsidiary in Brazil; b) in which the obligation shall be performed in Brazil; or c) that has arisen from a fact or act that took place in Brazil. The lawsuit may be filed in Brazil in the presence of any of the above conditions, regardless of the nationality of the parties.[13-14] Foreign plaintiffs, however, must post a deposit in court for the full amount of the court and attorneys' fees in order to litigate in Brazil.[15] The Brazilian Competition Law is only applicable to acts perpetrated in Brazil or that may produce effects in Brazil.[16] Therefore, competition violations perpetrated abroad by Brazilian companies that produce no effects in Brazil may still be litigated before Brazilian courts but will be governed by foreign law. Ongoing disputes abroad do not prevent the filing of the same suit in Brazil.[17] If final judgment has been rendered in a foreign court, it may be enforced in Brazil upon prior submission to the Superior Court of Justice for homologation (*exequatur*).[18]

III. Standing

The injured party or the successors thereof may file private antitrust lawsuits in Brazil. Collective lawsuits (class actions) however may only be filed by:

a) The Prosecution Office. The role of the Prosecution Office has gained visibility, as more and more class actions are filed to seek damages arising out of anticompetitive conduct. In some cases, the Prosecution

---

13 *See*, STF, *Maria José de Oliveira v. Newton João Cardoso*. Reporter Justice Sepulveda Pertence. (SEC No. 6684/EU) (Oct. 8, 2004).

14 If there is more than one defendant, as long as one is domiciled in Brazil, all the others may be jointly sued in Brazil.

15 Article 835 of the CPC. The bond must be equivalent to twenty percent of the amount in dispute (which means, as a rule, the amount requested for the award, if it is a net value).

16 Article 2 of Federal Law 12,529/11.

17 Article 90 of the CPC.

18 The Superior Court of Justice (STJ) will not analyze the merits of the foreign judgment, but determine whether it does not breach any provision of public policy or social interest.

Office has filed a lawsuit even before CADE has reached a final decision. More lawsuits are expected as prosecutors increase their cooperation with CADE.

b) The union, states, municipalities and the federal district;

c) Direct and indirect government entities and agencies; or

d) Associations existing for at least one year that include the defense of interests and rights of their members in their purpose.[19] However, the Supreme Court has decided that only members that have expressly authorized the filing of a class action will be able to enforce the relevant decision.[20] This Supreme Court precedent goes against the Superior Court of Justice precedents on the same matter and limited the scope of class actions for damages. Some precedents have recognized that in addition to the above-mentioned requirements, Courts should also evaluate if the association adequately provides representation for its members – i.e., such associations must demonstrate their ability to properly conduct the defense of the respective collective interest in Court by revealing its technical expertise and financial capability to handle the class action, among others. Finally, certain decisions require the association to show that it is comprised of at least an appropriate (minimum) number of alleged victims.

Private companies or individuals are not authorized to file class actions on behalf of the parties injured by anticompetitive behavior. Nevertheless, certain private actions based on competition issues may in fact indirectly result in some form of collective protection, such as when parties are not only seeking damages, but also filing for an injunction to immediately cease the antitrust violation (for instance, to cease misleading advertisement or any abusive or discriminating conduct).

It is important to point out that CADE usually does not intervene in private lawsuits and Courts also generally see no reason to call for CADE's intervention.[21] Also, even when called in Court as an interested third party

19 Recently established associations may file class actions, provided they prove the addressed damage has extraordinary social interest.

20 STF, *Estado do Rio Grande do Sul*. Reporter Justice Ricardo Lewandowski. (RE 573323) (Feb. 21, 2008).

21 "CADE should not intervene in lawsuits which, in fact, aim to determine the existence of damages or abuse that interfere in private contracts, lawsuits which do not aim for the correction of the market as a whole, but only damages resulting

or *amicus curiae*, CADE does not address matters which have never been or which are currently under its investigation.[22]

IV. Production of Evidence

Brazilian civil procedure does not include any phase similar to pretrial discovery: all evidence must be produced in court before the judge during the lawsuit. The CPC deems all legal means of evidence admissible, as well as those that are morally legitimate (i.e., evidence that does not unreasonably violate, for example, the intimacy or privacy of the parties). Wiretapping is generally considered illegal, whether the recording was conducted by a third party or by one of the parties to the conversation[23] – although occasionally the courts will admit the recording as evidence, if it is necessary to prove the defendant is not guilty in a criminal trial.[24]

The current CPC establishes that evidence may only be anticipated if there is a risk involved (danger in delay or *periculum in mora*) – for example, in the past, Courts have authorized an allegedly severely ill witness to be heard in connection to an investigation conducted by CADE. The recently enacted "new" Civil Procedure Code (Federal Law 13,105/2015), which will be in effect next year, will allow for a more widespread use of anticipated production of evidence, in cases in which there is no risk involved, but the evidence may help the parties reach a settlement or in cases when the production of the evidence may prevent a lawsuit altogether. This new provision may turn the anticipated production of evidence into a "Brazilian discovery phase", through which potential plaintiffs would assess the viability of their claims.

---

from the practice of conducts which might be forbidden under Law 12,529/11" TJSP, White Martins Gases Industriais Ltda. Manoel Justino Bezerra Filho. (AI 0156468-75.2012.8.26.0000) (March 19, 2013)

22 *See* CADE, SINDICAN v. ANTV. Reporting Commissioner Luiz Fernando Schuartz (PA 08012.005669/2002-31) (Dec. 20, 2007), in which CADE decided that it should not take stand on "a lawsuit with the same object as an investigation pending decision (...) lest we would see a situation of potential non-decisiveness".

23 STJ, *Arlindo Joaquim de Souza*. Reporter Justice Edson Vidigal (RT 743/208) (April 28, 1998); RF 342/307; RT 620/151; 789/293; 815/242; 828/250; JTJ 143/199; 916/221.

24 STF, *Luiz Marcos Klein*. Reporter Justice Moreira Alves. (HC No. 74.678) (Jul. 15, 1997).

There is no legal hierarchy as to the different types of evidence, so courts are free to weigh them as they see fit.[25] The burden of proof falls on the plaintiff as a general rule,[26] but litigation involving consumers may shift the burden to the defendant, if the plaintiff is deemed more vulnerable (i.e., when there is a significant asymmetry of information or economic resources between the parties). The parties must declare early on in the lawsuit the types of evidence they intend to produce or to obtain through discovery[27] – failure to comply with this rule may result in the loss of the right to produce the evidence, as judges do not usually request its production *ex officio*.[28] The most common types of evidence in Brazil, expressly regulated in the CPC, consist of: (1) the testimony of parties and witnesses; (2) documental evidence; (3) expert examination (See Section VI, infra).

A. Deposition and Testimony of Witnesses

Each party is entitled to motion for the other party to testify[29] (however, they cannot motion for their own deposition in court). The main goal of the deposition is to get the other party to confess – that is, to admit facts that are detrimental to their cause.[30] Therefore, when summoned to depose, parties cannot fail to show up in court, or refuse to answer the judge's or the other party's questions: if they do, without proper and justified cause, the judge will treat such behavior as an admission of the truth of the claims made by the other party.[31]

Parties also have the right to summon up to ten witnesses[32] – limited to three for each of the facts that the party intends to prove. Witnesses may be challenged for impediment (for example, kinship) or suspicion

---

25 Article 131 of the CPC.

26 Article 333(I) of the CPC.

27 Plaintiffs must specify the evidence they want to produce when the defendant files the claim. Defendants must specify it in their defenses.

28 Although exceptionally the judge may determine the production of evidence if deemed necessary to clarify potential doubts or if it is indispensable for the proper trial of the dispute.

29 Article 342 of the CPC.

30 Article 348 of the CPC.

31 Article 343(2) of the CPC.

32 Article 407 of the CPC.

(close friendship, or strong animosity proven through objective fact).[33] Court mediates the testimony, as parties are not allowed to ask questions directly to the witness. Witnesses are not obliged to testify on facts that may endanger them or their relatives; or on facts that they are bound to maintain confidential.[34]

(i) Documents

Parties may produce any document they possess in court. According to Brazilian law, 'document' means any material representation capable of reconstituting or preserving an image, sound, situation, idea, wish, etc. Therefore, contracts, declarations, statements, business records, photographs, digital files (e-mails) and sound recordings are considered documents. There are several rules governing the admissibility and validity of each different type of document, but, as a general rule, parties must produce the original document in court. The law establishes, however, that courts may accept copies, if properly certified by a public notary[35] or if the lawyer assumes responsibility for the accuracy of the copy.[36] If the document is not in possession of the party, courts may be asked to reclaim such documents from the opposing party or any third party.[37] In order to do so, however, the requesting party must describe the document as accurately as possible and inform the purpose of the evidence. The party must also demonstrate reasonable belief that the document exists and is in possession of the other party. As such, Brazilian law does not leave much room for 'fishing expeditions'. Refusal to surrender the document may result in the penalty of confession or the search and seizure of the document.[38] Parties are nonetheless allowed to refuse to provide documents that may subject them to the risk of a criminal action[39] – a very important limitation, especially when one is dealing with cartel cases. Any document produced in the lawsuit may be challenged for its authenticity. Documents produced

33 Article 405 of the CPC.

34 Article 406 of the CPC.

35 Article 365 of the CPC.

36 Courts may also allow regular copies, as long as the opposite party does not challenge the document.

37 Article 355 of the CPC.

38 Articles 359 and 362 of the CPC.

39 Article 363 of the CPC.

in previous lawsuits or administrative proceedings – for example, those provided to CADE or any other regulatory agency – are also admissible under Brazilian case law as 'borrowed evidence'. The same applies to documents produced in foreign legal or administrative proceedings.[40] It is noteworthy that administrative proceedings before CADE are sometimes confidential, meaning that third parties – including victims – may not have access to the evidence produced.[41] In the industrial gas cartel case, for example, part of the evidence used to convict some of the defendants is confidential and, therefore, would not be readily available to potential plaintiffs. There is no case law addressing this situation.

Courts may exceptionally admit witnesses' testimonies or the seizure of documents as a preliminary measure.[42] Witness depositions may be anticipated as long as there is a risk of the witness defaulting (for example, leaving the country) or dying.[43] Documents, on the other hand, may be obtained insofar as their content is necessary for the evaluation of a future dispute.[44]

(ii) Use of Experts

If the dispute requires the assessment of technical issues, the judge will summon an expert in the field to perform an examination, either *ex officio* or upon the parties' motion.[45] Antitrust issues usually involve the opinion of an economist or accountant, but depending on the relevant market, product or infrastructure involved in the dispute, court may summon engineers,

40 They must, however, first be duly translated into Portuguese.

41 See Opinion No. 206/2010 from Office of the General Counsel to CADE: "This Attorney believes that, as a rule, anyone may inquire or obtain copies of records of an administrative proceeding in progress with CADE, regardless of the demonstration of a private or collective interest to be defended. It is nevertheless worth mentioning that once confidentiality is granted to the files of an administrative proceeding, or to certain data, information, communication, objects or documents, it constitutes an insurmountable barrier for third parties to consult said documents or obtain copies thereof."

42 Articles 846 and 844 of the CPC.

43 Article 847. Brazilian courts have allowed some leeway, permitting the evidence to be produced early despite being outside legal cases (Appeal to the Superior Court of Justice 50492, Reporting Judge Justice Ruy Rosado).

44 Article 844 of the CPC.

45 Article 420 of the CPC.

physicians or any other expert in the related field (expert examination may involve multiple fields[46]). The court will determine the scope of the technical opinion and parties are allowed to ask questions they want the expert to address in his or her examination. In order to perform the examination, the expert may use any means available, including questioning witnesses and requesting documents held by the parties. The expert may therefore request books, records and other economic information of the parties to calculate, for example, lost profits or illegal surcharges applied to goods or services. The parties are allowed to hire their own experts to monitor and assess the work of the court expert. Though court is not obligated to follow the opinion of the expert, the examination does have exceptional weight. In addition to the court-ordered expert examination, the parties are allowed to introduce their own independent analyses, economic studies or legal opinions of jurists and authorities in order to advance their case. The courts tend to be open to these contributions, as long as they comply with due process of law – in other words, as long as they are not being used to surprise the other party or to hinder the progress of the lawsuit. CADE's decision regarding an antitrust violation will be treated as a document, as it was not produced by a court expert. Because of the authority and knowledge of the antitrust agency on the matter, however, it will have undeniable weight with the court.

V. Class Actions

According to Brazilian law, class actions may only be filed by the entities or associations determined by law and cannot be brought by a single private party or a corporation.[47]

Class actions must involve collective rights; the Brazilian system identifies three types of 'collective' rights to this end:

a) *diffuse rights*, which are considered to be indivisible, belonging to a collectivity comprised of indeterminate people (i.e., indeterminability of the subjects, there being no individuation) linked by factual circumstances;

b) that belong to a group, category or class of indeterminate, but determinable, people, linked to each other, or to the adversary party, by a standard legal relationship; and,

46 Article 431-B of the CPC.

47 With the exception of associations.

c) homogeneous individual interests or rights, are individual rights arising from a common origin,– which is usually the case with class actions aimed to redress antitrust damages.

Courts may grant provisional remedies in class actions so long as there is *prima facie* evidence on the strength of the claim and, cumulatively, there is risk of extraordinary damages resulting from procedural delay. As sound as the lawsuit may be, courts generally understand that the mere delay of the lawsuit poses no risk to claims for monetary damages. For that reason, it is very unlikely that courts will grant an injunction for a quicker payment of damages. If the class action is successful, it will benefit the whole class. A judgment against the collective plaintiff, however, will not harm the individual rights of the members of the class – who may therefore still file their own private claims against the defendant.[48] The progress of a successful class action aimed to redress antitrust injuries is divided into two phases: first, the court establishes the competition violation and the liability of the defendant, rendering a collective order;[49] next, each injured member of the class must act individually to claim its own damages.[50] However, if the individual damages effectively claims are not deemed consistent with theestimated scope and seriousness of the antitrust violation the court may assess a fine to be paid by the defendant to the Fund for the Protection of Collective Rights.[51]

VI. Calculating Damages

Victims may seek damages for all types of damages under Brazilian law, which may be either pecuniary losses (any type of pecuniary damages, including loss of profits and loss of business) or pain-and-suffering (i.e., injury to the reputation or good standing of the victim). Such damages are not to be confused with the punitive damages available in the United States, for instance, as the purpose thereof is not to penalize the offender.

The Brazilian Law does not provide a specific or mandatory form of calculating material antitrust damages. Therefore, disputes in Brazil will face the same challenges already found by other jurisdictions, mainly,

48 Article 103 (I) of the CPC.

49 Article 95 of the CPC.

50 Article 97 of the CPC.

51 Article 100 of the CDC.

the proper form of evaluating damages arising out of an anticompetitive behavior and, more specifically, by a cartel. Furthermore, it seems that a solution will indeed be assessed on a case-by-case basis, according to the elements available to the Court.

On the other hand, in order to be entitled to pain and suffering in an antitrust case, the victim must effectively prove an actual injury to reputation. There is no strong set of judicial precedents for pain-and-suffering in cases involving private antitrust litigation – although there are usually pecuniary losses involved, and with the exception of disparagement cases, the reputation or good standing of the victim is seldom tainted by a competition violation – but ordinarily the awards in such cases do not exceed five hundred times the Brazilian minimum salary.[52]

In recent years, certain class actions – especially those filed by public prosecutors – have claimed compensation for 'social' damages caused by the offender (i.e., damage to the entire market). Though such claims generally work as disguised claims for punitive damages, they have been accepted by courts in certain circumstances, mainly in cases involving labor claims or mass torts.[53] In individual actions, the award also includes the payment of attorneys' fees (to be collected by the lawyers, not the parties[54]), usually between ten percent and twenty percent of the amount under dispute. Defendants may also be subject to the payment of attorneys' fees if a private party files the class action.[55]

---

52 Approximately BRL 362,000.00.

53 The 5th Regional Federal Appellate Court upheld a judgment against companies involved in a fuel cartel for damages caused to their consumers. Court ordered the companies to cease the anticompetitive behavior and sentenced the companies to the payment of social damages of one million reais as compensation for the harm caused to society. *See* TRF5, *Liquigás, Supregasbrás, Gás Butano, Minasgás, Ultragás e Pampagás.* Fernando Quadros da Silva. (Appeal 5021730-87.2011.404.7100/RS) (June 27, 2012). *See also* STJ, *Bento Gonçalves de Transportes Ltda.* Reporting Justice Eliana Calmon. (REsp No. 1.057.274) (Dec. 1, 2009).

54 In the event that plaintiff is the losing party, plaintiff must pay attorneys' fees to the defendant.

55 *See* STJ, *Companhia Nacional de Abastecimento – CONAB.* Reporting Justice Luiz Fux. (REsp No. 200600937910) (Dec. 11, 2007).

VII. Pass-on Defenses

Brazilian Law allows defendents to argue pass-on defenses (i.e., the claim that plaintiff passed on its losses to third parties or to end consumers). The CC expressly sets out that indemnification must be measured according 'to the extent of the damage',[56] which means that it must not exceed what was effectively lost by the victim. Therefore, there is a strong body of case law stating that victims cannot claim damages for losses that have already been paid or covered by someone else (such as by an insurer or a third party), since this would not be compensation, but truly improper and unjustified enrichment. The burden of proof that the increased price was not passed on falls on the plaintiff, which in fact has better conditions to demonstrate this fact in court.

Furthermore, the Courts are paying increased attention to the victim's duty *to mitigate the damage.* It is unclear how this duty would apply in antitrust disputes. In addition, it is possible that the same defendant faces multiple lawsuits related to the same alleged cartel – for example, a lawsuit filed by a downstream buyer and a different lawsuit filed by end consumers. In this case, Courts must try to reach a coherent solution, so as to avoid *bis in idem* and ensure that each alleged victim will recover the exact extent of damages experienced.

VIII. Follow-on Litigation

Only a small fraction of Brazilian private antitrust litigation actually depends on CADE's decisions. Each dispute is litigated directly by the parties in court, even if in some disputes there is also an underlying collective issue.[57] Companies usually do not wait for CADE or even for its regulatory agencies

---

[56] Article 944.

[57] See precedents: TJRS, *Ambev.* Des. Odone Sanguiné. (Appeal n. 70018077529) (May 09, 2007); TJSP, *Cosan S.A v. Agrícola Três Meninas Ltda.* Roberto Mac Cracken (Appeal n. 990.10.279201-3) (Sept. 16, 2010); TJMG, Tarcisio Martins Costa. (Appeal n. 2.0000.00.514885-2/000) (March 02, 2005); TJMG, 11st Civil Chamber of Belo Horizonte *Vergalhões.* (Ordinary Action n. 002406984815-8) (Feb. 11, 2006); TJSP, *Sul América Cia. Nacional de Seguros.* Dyrceu Cintra. (Appeal n. 1184536-0/4) (May 30, 2008); TJSP, *Autoposto Gás Shop Ltda. v. Petrobras Distribuidora S.A.* Dyrceu Cintra. (Appeal n. 1057638-0/6) (June 28, 2006); TJRS, *Combustíveis.* Paulo Sérgio Scarparo (Appeal n. 70033651423) (Jan. 21, 2010).

to take action over matters affecting their businesses – mainly because, as previously mentioned, under Brazilian law victims are not obliged to wait for an administrative decision to seek relief in court. As a result, follow-on litigation is usually not a relevant issue for companies and entrepreneurs. As class actions for damages have caused consumers to take a more prominent role in the system,[58] however, more and more associations (and sometimes even the Prosecution Office) are turning to CADE for information and guidance regarding collective antitrust violations.

That being said, there are virtually no limitations regarding follow-on litigation in Brazilian law: CADE's decision on whether to convict or acquit a defendant does not prevent private antitrust litigation. The payment of administrative fines does not release the defendant from repairing the damages arising out of the antitrust behavior. An administrative conviction, however, may foster private antitrust ligation, since it may make it easier, faster and less costly for collective plaintiffs to demonstrate the liability of the defendant and the damages caused to the market in a civil court.[59]

58 The State Prosecution Office of São Paulo has recently filed a lawsuit against companies and individuals allegedly involved in the subway cartel claiming BRL 2.5 billion damages in compensation for pain and suffering and for the losses in contracts involving 98 trains. The State Prosecution Office of Rio Grande do Norte has also filed a lawsuit against companies that allegedly participated in a cement cartel See also the following precedents STJ, *Associação Nacional das Empresas Transportadoras de Veículos.* Reporter Justice Luiz Fux. (REsp n. 677.585/RS) (Dec. 6, 2005); STJ REsp n. 1.181.643-RS. Reporter Justice Herman Benjamin, Full Bench, (adjudged on 1 March 2011); 28 Civil Court of Belo Horizonte; *Associação de Hospitais (AHMG).* Iandara Peixoto Nogueira. Class Action (ACP 7099345-90.2009.8.13.0024) (May 19, 2009); TJRS, *Combustíveis,* Class Action (ACP 053/1.03.0002071-0) (Dec. 28, 2006); TJRS, *Combustíveis.* Class Action (ACP 027/1.05.0004158-2) (Feb. 03, 2011); TJRS, Class Action (ACP) 032/1.03.0005173-1; TJSP, *CIA de Saneamento Básico do Estado de São Paulo (SABESP)* Isador Segalla Afanasieff. Class Action (ACP 0000233-25.2011.4.03.6100) (April 4, 2011); TJRS, *Combustíveis,* Class Action (ACP 044/1.06.0002731-1) (April 11, 2007); 14 Civil Court of São Paulo, *Abbott Laboratórios do Brasil Ltda., Eli Lilly do Brasil Ltda.* Class Action (ACP 0029912-22.2001.403.6100) (Nov. 27, 2001); TRF4, Class Action (ACP) 2008.71.07.001547-0. Lenise Kleinübing Gregol (Sept. 11, 2013); TRF4, *Combustíveis,* Class Action (ACP) 2001.70.01.008206-8 (Jan. 12, 2011); TRF4, Class Action (ACP) 2002.72.07.000694-3; TRF3, *Unimed,* Class Action (ACP) 2002.61.17.000769-6 (Sept. 28, 2012); TRF4, *Anatel.* Nicolau Konkel Júnior. Class Action (ACP 2003.72.05.006266-5) (Nov. 24, 2009)..

59 Sometimes, however, according to Federal Law 12,529/11, CADE may punish

Leniency agreements or cease-and-desist agreements entered into by a defendant may involve some sort of admission regarding the antitrust behavior or the facts underlying the investigation. Should the defendant plead guilty for the purposes of such agreements, the defendant will not be allowed to discuss his or her liability in follow-on individual or collective litigation (agreements, however, are always restrictively interpreted in Brazil).[60]

IX. Privileges

Under Brazilian law, attorney–client communication is privileged.[61] This privilege covers the law firm or office, as well as to the professional tools, work product, written, electronic, telephone and telematics communications.[62] There are only two exceptions: where there is evidence indicating the authorship and material perpetration of a crime by the lawyer;[63] and when the lawyer holds an element of the *corpus delicti*[64] (Brazilian law does not differentiate between outside and in-house counsel).[65] According to the

the defendant's behavior based on its potential to cause damages to the market. In these cases, CADE does not have to show that the behavior caused actual damages. Plaintiffs on private antitrust lawsuits, however, still have the burden of proving the damages they suffered.

60 CADE has decided that "facilitating the redress of private damages resulting from anticompetitive offenses is not one of the immediate goals of the repressive action of this authority, despite being one of its likely developments" (*see* Motion No. 08700.002709/2010-44, Reporting Commissioner Olavo Chinaglia). Therefore this is usually not an issue during negotiations, as CADE could frustrate interesting and valid antitrust commitments "just because, in the remote future, it would be likely for an agent injured by the alleged offender to eventually benefit from CADE's unfavorable judgment upon seeking redress for its private damages." (Motion No. 08700.002709/2010-44, Reporting Commissioner Olavo Chinaglia). Therefore, admission of guilt generally does not involve admission of harm to specific parties.

61 Article 133 of the Brazilian Constitution.

62 Article 7 of the Federal Law 8,906/94.

63 Article 7(6) of Federal Law 8,906/94.

64 Article 243(2) of the Brazilian Code of Criminal Procedure.

65 However, in practice, in-house counsel may have documents seized (for example, during a search carried out at the company's headquarters) and the court will later select the documents that may be included in the administrative or judicial proceeding.

Brazilian Constitution, all correspondence and data communication may not be violated and therefore cannot be used for litigation purposes.[66] There is, however, no consistent body of case law defining whether this provision also encompasses e-mails or other forms of electronic communication. It is also noteworthy that several precedents have allowed the use in court of open letters and e-mails, under the principle that the Federal Constitution protects the transmission of data (the communication process) but not its content.[67]

On the other hand, the Brazilian Constitution allows wiretapping 'by court order, in the situations and in the manner provided by law for the purposes of criminal investigation or fact finding'.[68] Federal Law 9,296/96 sets forth very specific and restrictive conditions for such practice: first, the authority requesting the wiretap must demonstrate that all other means of investigation have been exhausted. Additionally, wiretapping must not exceed 30 days and the decision allowing the measure must be strongly grounded. Once the recording has been used in criminal court, parties may produce it (or the transcription thereof) as evidence in administrative proceedings or civil litigation.[69]

X. Settlement Procedures

Parties are allowed to settle disputes on disposable rights at any time. Settlements are, in fact, encouraged by Brazilian courts and may even encompass rights or obligations that are not part of the original lawsuit. A settlement in or out of court has the same weight as *res judicata*, so that, once settled, the parties may not litigate the controversy again. Under Brazilian Law, damages usually fall under the "disposable" rights category, which means parties may freely agree on and even waive their rights. Antitrust Law, however, is considered a matter of public interest. Therefore, while an agreement over damages would be enforceable, an agreement over

66 Article 5 (XII) of Federal Law 8,906/94.

67 *See* opinion in STF, *Banco do Brasil S.A*, Reporter Justice Neri da Silveira (MS 21729) (May 10, 1995); STF, *Luciano Hang Antonio Nabora Areias Bulhões*. Reporter Justice Sepulveda Pertence (RE 418416) (Dec. 19, 2006).

68 STF. *Antônio Carlos de Almeida Castro, Thiago Brugger, José Gerardo Grossi*. Reporter Justice Cezar Peluso. (Inq. 2424) (March 26, 2010).

69 STF. *Antônio Carlos de Almeida Castro, Thiago Brugger, José Gerardo Grossi*. Reporter Justice Cezar Peluso (Inq. 2424-QO-QO) (Aug. 24, 2007).

discriminatory conduct might not be, and it would also not prevent CADE from taking further action against the perpetrator.

Class actions, in comparison, allow very limited room for settlements. If the plaintiff is the Prosecution Office, Brazilian law allows the parties to enter into a Consent Decree for the purpose of ceasing the relevant behavior, often with a payment (contribution) connected thereto. The payment of a contribution in the context of a Consent Decree may prevent the application of further penalties by other authorities, as that would result in a possible *bis in idem*.

The payment of a contribution, however, irrespective of the amount, does not relieve the defendant from the obligation of redressing individual damages, as the TAC cannot set forth the individual rights of the victims.

XI. Arbitration

Under Federal Law 9,307/96 (Brazilian Arbitration Law), parties may resort to arbitration only to settle disputes on disposable property rights. Law 12,529/11 establishes that competition is a matter of public interest, narrowing the possibilities of using arbitration to deal with antitrust litigation. It is theoretically possible to refer to arbitration in Brazil to dispute the amount of damages arising out of a cartel, for example. It is very unlikely, however, for a defendant to voluntarily join an arbitration of such scope. On the other hand, agreements entered into with arbitration clauses may generate disputes involving antitrust issues – for example, contracts with exclusivity clauses. In such cases, it is possible that the arbitrators will have to face an antitrust issue as part of their brief.[70] The Brazilian Arbitration Law determines, however, that court may deem an arbitration award void if the decision conflicts with public interest provisions.[71] Moreover, the arbitration clause does not prevent the injured party from seeking an administrative decision from CADE, which will not be bound to the arbitration award, in any way. This means that CADE may decide to investigate and punish behavior or contractual clauses even if they were deemed fully lawful or enforceable by the arbitrators.

70 The Brazilian system also provides for the possibility of arbitrators suspending the procedure and remanding the decision of a matter involving inalienable rights to the Judiciary Branch (Article 25).

71 Article 32 of Federal Law 9,307/96.

XII. Indemnification and Contribution

In the event of a competition violation, Brazilian law determines that all the individuals involved in the conduct – for example, all the members of the cartel – will be jointly liable for the damages caused.[72] This means that each of the offenders may be called to answer for the full amount of damages.

However, the full implications of this rule have not been properly tested in Court yet. For example, (i) liabilities may vary when considering the different effects of the cartel over a supply chain; (ii) as mentioned, Courts have applied the duty to mitigate damages to the victim, which, again, may result in different responsibilities along the supply chain; (iii) finally, the Civil Code provides that, "if there is excessive disproportion between the agent's fault and the damage, the judge may equitably reduce the compensation to be paid to the victim". Hence, it is necessary to assess the actual behavior of each of the alleged parties. Therefore, there are many issues that can and should be further developed in future private litigation.

Furthermore, managers and sometimes employees involved in the conduct may also be liable for the damages. Brazilian law also provides for piercing of the corporate veil in the events of fraud or property commingling[73] – so that the victim, in some cases, may seek reimbursement from other companies of the same group, even if such companies were not directly involved in the violation.

XIII. Future Developments and Perspectives

The reform of the Brazilian competition system, whereby the former three administrative entities in charge of antitrust analysis and investigation – the Economic Supervision Office (SEAE), the Economic Law Office (SDE) and CADE – fused into 'SuperCADE' – has provided a significant increase in efficiency and in the rate of antitrust investigation and merger review.[74]

---

72 Article 942 of the CC.

73 Article 50 of the CC.

74 Due to the innovations of the new law, the former 182-day period to review a merger (in 2009) has been reduced to a 25-day period. Also, CADE has been able to review and decide almost twice the administrative procedures that it used to, closing many antitrust investigations. This expressive increase of quality and efficiency has rendered CADE a four-star evaluation by the Global Competition Review.

Specifically regarding antitrust investigation, CADE has announced that it will sharpen its focus,[75] and that further important investigations are on the horizon.[76]

Furthermore, Brazil is currently developing certain relevant legislation reforms aimed at improving its judicial civil procedure and consumer protection environment that will significantly affect private competition litigation.

There is the aforementioned new CPC, which is expected to reduce the cost and duration of civil lawsuits. A Legislative Senate Commission has been assigned to work on a bill for a new Consumer Protection Code. The Commission is currently studying changes in Brazilian class actions in order to encourage their further use by consumers. At the same time, several regulatory agencies are studying changes to their procedures and regulation to create more competition in regulated sectors.

In short, private antitrust litigation is entrenched in Brazilian judicial culture and will continue to flourish in the future, as companies in Brazil tend to consider the Judiciary Branch their main source of protection against unfair competitors and competition misconduct. In addition, class actions aimed at redressing collective damages caused to consumers are also expected to experience a significant boost in the near future as a result of CADE's remarkable efforts in competition advocacy.

* * *

75 CADE's Chairman, Carlos Ragazzo, stated in April 2013 that: CADE was not going "to have 200 cartel investigations anymore. The ones that we do are going to have a very high probability of conviction and they will be very, very sturdy cases." ("CADE redefining focus of cartel enforcement", MLex, October 8 2013)

76 CADE entered into 4 new leniency agreements and has currently 296 ongoing investigations (data from May 2014).

Chapter XVII

STANDARD ESSENTIAL PATENTS, FRAND COMMITMENTS AND ANTITRUST LAW FROM A BRAZILIAN PERSPECTIVE

Bruno de Luca Drago

I. Introduction

Despite the recent development of the Brazilian Antitrust System, one must still consider it a relatively premature system when compared to the US and European systems, not only in terms of its material and institutional framework, but especially in view of the limited exposure of its members and private practitioners to more complex issues involving competition law. Among such issues, it is worth mentioning those related to the new economy, including multisided markets, network externalities, technological convergence and creation of standards, which require a far more complex understanding and a more dynamic assessment. Not to mention that the commercial relationship among economic agents in the most diverse parts of the globe has been increasingly affected by technological innovation, globalization and market power.

In the context of repressive and preventive analysis involving new economy topics, it is undisputed that intellectual property rights must play a key role, to the extent in which the ultimate goal of intellectual property rights is to seek the balanced equilibrium between the level of protection required to provide incentives for investments in socially useful innovation and the guarantee of the optimum dissemination of such innovation. In order to do so, a certain level of competition exemption is allowed, so as to provide the necessary tools for recoupment of investments incurred in the innovation process. The balance lies on the correct relation between investments and their recoupment on one side, and social benefits created to end users and consumers, on the other.

In this regard, it is worth mentioning that intellectual property rights allow holders thereof to prevent their use by third parties or the distribution of any products using such rights in the market. The main principle behind such rational is to prevent free riders from benefiting from third-party investments without incurring into any costs whatsoever. Intellectual property rights thus create some level of protection against market failures Intellectual property rights often confer some level of market power over the protected technology to the holder thereof.

Notwithstanding the initial perception that the pursuit of a free competition environment and the protection of intellectual property rights may enjoy some level of antagonism, a more detailed analysis inevitably leads to the conclusion that both legal institutes seek welfare resulting from the efficient allocation of resources and from technological progress and innovation. One may further attribute a social purpose to intellectual property rights, to the extent in which they balance the exclusivity rights with the access to, and dissemination of, innovation, thus avoiding excessive protection or the undesirable prevention of access to information regarding the innovation process and interoperability. Information concerning intellectual property rights must be supplied, at a certain stage, in order to spread the innovation phenomenon. In the end, it is necessary to acknowledge that innovation is a cumulative process.

Intellectual property rights must, by no means, be understood and enforced with no further consideration to its effects on the marketplace. Once innovation is created and its rights are dully registered, giving rising to legal protection, chances are that abuses may take place, especially considering the fact that relevant tools for committing such abuses are created; as mentioned before, dominant position is usually created in such occasions. Arguably, monopolists would have the incentives to prevent their competitors from benefiting from their innovation without supporting research and development costs, in certain cases in an illegitimate fashion.

On this matter, the important role antitrust authorities play in assessing whether a conduct implemented by the holder of an intellectual property right is abusive, and may harm competition, is undisputed.

Antitrust Law shall, therefore, be invoked to correct regulatory failures or deficiencies in the industrial property system, which may impair the effective appropriation of the results of the innovation process by consumers. Although there is skepticism and diverging views regarding the correlation of an industry's concentration and resulting incentives to innovation, a rational conclusion concerning the positive interaction of the two institutes would inevitably lead to an increase in innovation whenever some level of competition is introduced or fostered.

It is noteworthy that the existence of intellectual property rights for the use of certain technology does not necessarily result in economic monopoly. It is possible, for instance, for different technologies to be used for the same purpose, thus competing with each other and enlarging the relevant market definition.

In this context, this paper intends to briefly review the legal treatment concerning abuse of market power claims involving intellectual properties rights, especially before the Brazilian Antitrust Authorities. Subsequently, the article intends to assess the issues arising from the adoption of standards on technological markets and, in particular, the issues resulting from commitments undertaken by the agents involved to allow their technology to become a standard. If such commitments are disregarded, consideration must be given to the legal tools available to the affected parties. In particular, one should look at the challenges arising out of the exercise of such tools in the Brazilian territory.

II. Industrial Property Rights and Antitrust Law in Brazil

Discussions involving industrial property rights and antitrust rules in Brazil have been limited to very few cases, which do not further develop the analysis of the particular issues faced in such circumstances. In this regard, it is worth mentioning that the new Brazilian Antitrust Law, enacted in May 2012, provides that any act intended or otherwise able to limit, restrain or in any way harm free competition or free enterprise, control a relevant market of a certain product or service, increase profits arbitrarily or abuse a dominant position, even if such effects are not achieved, will be deemed an anticompetitive practice, regardless of fault.

In addition, the Brazilian legal system has no specific statutes or guidelines to regulate the interaction between antitrust and intellectual property rights, as it is the case in other jurisdictions. Administrative penalties on companies for practicing anticompetitive activities under the Brazilian Antitrust Law may vary from 0.1% to 20% of the gross turnover of the company, group or conglomerate, in the field of business affected by the anticompetitive practice.

In turn, the Brazilian Constitution, in its Articles 5, XXIX, and 170, II, provides extensive protection to the industrial property rights. In addition, intellectual property is mainly regulated in Brazil by the Intellectual Property Law (Law 9,279, of 1996),[1] the Paris Convention and its Stockholm Revision, the several resolutions issued by the Brazilian Patent and Trademark Office (INPI) and the Central Bank of Brazil. The Intellectual Property Law consolidated the several rules governing the matter and introduced changes to the current protection of industrial property rights in Brazil. INPI is the federal agency in charge of regulating and registering patents, trademarks and industrial designs, as well as approving license agreements and any other agreements involving industrial property rights.

Furthermore, the Intellectual Property Law provides that a patent confers, to its holder, the right to prevent a third party from producing, using, offering for sale, selling or importing a product that is the object of the patent or a process or product directly obtained by a patented process,[2] without proper consent. Patent holders are also ensured the right to obtain indemnification for improper exploitation of the object of the patent.

The provision subjecting patent-holders to compulsory licensing is of special interest, which may occur in cases where the rights are exercised

---

1 The INDUSTRIAL PROPERTY LAW (Act 9.279/96) provides, in its Article 2: "*The protection of industrial property rights, considering the social interest and the technological and economic development of this country, is afforded by means of: I. the grant of invention and utility model patents; II. the grant of a registration of an industrial design; III. the grant of a registration of a trademark; IV. the repression of false geographical indication; and V. the repression of unfair competition.*"

2 A process patent right shall be deemed to have occurred when the possessor or owner does not prove, by a specific judicial ruling, that the product was obtained by a manufacturing process different than the one protected by the patent.

in an abusive manner. A non-exhaustive list of conducts that are subject to compulsory license, provided by the Intellectual Property Law, includes the non-exploitation of the object of the patent within the Brazilian territory for failure to manufacture or incomplete manufacture of the product, or also failure to make full use of the patented process, except cases where this is not economically feasible, when import shall be permitted. Also, any sale that does not satisfy the needs of the market may also be subject to compulsory licensing.[3] Finally, compulsory licenses may be granted whenever there is a situation of dependency of one patent to another, the object of the dependent patent constitutes a substantial technical progress with regard to the earlier patent and the titleholder fails to reach an agreement with the patent holder of the dependent patent on the exploitation of the former.[4] It shall be further noted that the patent holder licensed pursuant to the compulsory license provisions shall have the right to a crossed compulsory license on the dependent patent.

Pursuant to the words of Professor Denis Barbosa, what defines the patent as a type of social use of the property is the fact that it is limited by its function, thus only existing while it is socially useful.[5] The patent has, therefore, the purpose of reattributing its creator, as much as a social interest purpose aimed the technological development of the nation. In this regard, as an important tool resulting in competition restrictions, it shall inevitably be used according to its purpose; deviating from such purpose may amount to the abuse of rights, and thus to the abuse of dominance under such circumstances.

Professor Barbosa further claims that the balance between the two constitutional principles – protection of property and social interest – shall also be applied pursuant to the principle of proportionality. For instance, the

3 A license may be requested only by a person having a legitimate interest and technical and economic ability to effectively exploit the object of the patent, which shall be predominantly destined for the domestic market. It is also worth mentioning that the compulsory license shall not be granted if the patent holder justifies the non-use based on legitimate reasons, proves that serious and effective preparations for exploitation have been made, or justifies the failure to manufacture or to market on grounds of any legal obstacles.

4 A dependent patent is a patent whose exploitation necessarily depends on the use of the object of an earlier patent.

5 Denis B. Barbosa, *Uma Introdução à Propriedade Intelectual* 413 (2nd ed. 2008), *available at* http://www.denisbarbosa.addr.com/arquivos/livros/umaintro2.pdf.

use of a compulsory license shall only prevail to the exact extent required for compliance with the envisaged social interest.

Besides the legal circumstances set out in the Intellectual Property Law and which are presumed abusive, there may be several other circumstances, which are not provided in such law, but which may amount to an abusive behavior by the patent holder, aiming at excluding its rivals in downstream markets, or increasing its costs to leverage its position. For instance, an abuse of patent would include the tying of licenses, the imposition of licenses beyond the expiration of the patent, discriminatory or excessive royalties refuse to license, fixing prices of manufactured products, territorial or quantitative restrictions of patent use, among others.

The Brazilian Antitrust Authorities must review such circumstances and, in the event of abuse of monopoly power, recommend the grant of compulsory license to INPI. It is worth highlighting that the Brazilian Antitrust Authorities are not legally entitled to directly grant any compulsory license, but may only recommend it to INPI. With CADE's decision in hands, confirming the abuse committed and recommending the grant of a compulsory license, the interested party would be entitled to request the license before such authority.

In this regard, it is noteworthy that Law 12,529/11 sets forth a non-exhaustive list of infringements deemed illegal provided that they are able to produce anticompetitive effects. Specifically, the new law considers illegal the exercise or exploitation of industrial or intellectual property rights, technology or brands, in an abusive manner.

CADE's precedents have suggested that, in order for an abuse of industrial or intellectual property rights to be verified, it is necessary to prove: (i) that the ownership of the IP rights enjoys a monopoly power in the relevant market; (ii) that there are structural conditions for the abusive exercise of this power; and (iii) that there was, indeed, an abuse, with damages to competition, or that it is in fact likely, beyond any reasonable doubt.[6]

[6] CADE, *Gradiente Eletrônica S.A. and Cemaz Indústria Eletrônica da Amazônia S.A., v. Koninklijke Philips Electronics N.V. and Philips do Brasil Ltda.* Reporting Commissioner Olavo Zago Chinaglia (Preliminary Investigation No. 08012.001315/2007-21) (Aug. 11, 2009)

CADE has brief experience in investigations and decisions involving antitrust and intellectual property rights. Additionally, in some merger control cases, intellectual property rights have been the subject of discussions. In general, these were cases in which the parties acquired or shared intellectual property rights, the great majority of which were unconditionally approved by the authorities. According to the current legal framework, the Brazilian authorities may investigate and impose penalties, for instance, on any case involving misuse of patent rights, tying arrangements involving protected goods, restrictions imposed by abusive licensing agreements, refusals to deal or cartel practices involving intellectual property rights.

III. Creation of Technological Standards

When addressing the creation of technological standards, one should consider the issues under intense debate in the US and Europe, identifying the circumstances in which a conduct involving licensing of intellectual property rights, or litigation to enforce rights of standard-essential patents may amount to an abuse of a dominant position. Such debate may seem to be concentrated, and thus more intense, in these jurisdictions, in view of the fact that there is a strong dependency of external technology suppliers. Also, intellectual property rights tend to be globally negotiated from the companies' main headquarters located in these countries. Nevertheless, regional discussions also tend to take place in the context of local licensing negotiations, with local players.

The concept of a standard may be defined as "a set of technical specifications which seeks to provide a common design for a product or process."[7] In this regard, the benefits of standards are clear and straightforward, to the extent that they allow complementary or connected products from different manufactures to be used together. Such standards often increase consumer choice and convenience and reduce costs. Thus, standard settings imply a decision on the most suitable technologies to be used on a given product, for the delivery of a given service. Such technologies are inevitably protected by intellectual property rights, especially patents.

7 Damien Gerardin, *Ten Years of DG Competition Effort to Provide Guidance on the Application of Competition Rules to the Licensing of Standard-Essential Patents: Where do We Stand?* (2013), *available at* http://papers.ssrn.com/sol3/papers.cfm?abstract_id=2204359

Standards are usually created by organizations, known as standard-setting organizations (SSOs), which are comprised of members of the relevant industry. These members meet to discuss mutually acceptable technologies that may guarantee interoperability and delivery of a service or product. Their primary activities are developing, coordinating, promulgating, revising, amending, reissuing, interpreting, or otherwise producing technical standards that are intended to address the needs of some relatively wide base of affected adopters.[8] Most standards are voluntary, in the sense that they are offered for adoption without being required by law. Also, some standards become mandatory when they are adopted by regulators as legal requirements in particular domains.

There are many international standards organizations, the three largest ones being the International Organization for Standardization (ISO); the International Electro-technical Commission (IEC) and the International Telecommunication Union (ITU). They have established several thousands of standards covering almost every possible topic. Many of these are then adopted worldwide, replacing various incompatible local standards. Many have also naturally evolved from in-house designs within an industry, or by a particular country, while others have been built from scratch by groups of experts who sit in several technical committees.

In addition to said organizations there are several independent international standards organizations such as the International Engineering Task Force (IETF), the World Wide Web Consortium (W3C) and the Universal Postal Union (UPU), which develop and publish standards for a variety of international uses. Regional standard bodies also exist, such as the European Committee for Standardization (CEN), the European Committee for Electro-technical Standardization (CENELEC), the European Telecommunications Standard Institute (ETSI), and the Institute for Reference Materials and Measurements (IRMM) in Europe, among others.[9]

---

8 A technical standard is an established rule or requirement in regard to technical systems. It is usually formalized through a document that establishes uniform engineering or technical criteria, methods, processes and practices.

9 In general, each country or economy has a single recognized national standards body (NSB). A national standards body is likely the sole member from that economy in ISO; ISO currently has 161 members. National standards bodies usually do not prepare the technical content of standards, which instead is developed by national

Among the aforementioned standardization organizations, of special interest to this paper are those involved with intellectual property rights, since standards usually involve proprietary technologies, which are protected by industrial property rights-patents. As verified above, the fact that a standard usually involves several patents, downstream manufacturers are often unable to implement a standard unless a license is granted by the holders of essential patents, in which case such holders have the right to obtain compensation for the licensing agreements.

During the process of establishing a standard, SSOs must follow, if applicable, a certain intellectual property right policy, encouraging patent owners to disclose, upfront, all and any patents owned that may be indispensable for the service to be delivered. This tends to promote more efficient and accurate assessments of patents to be used and the standard to be adopted and, specifically, tends to level the playing field for negotiations of patents. It is worth mentioning that royalties are not the only issue at stake herein, but also cross-licenses and upfront fee payments.

Parallel to the disclosure of essential patents, essential patent holders (SEPs) may be also required to agree to license their patents, considered essential for the standard, on fair, reasonable and non-discriminatory terms (FRAND) to other members of the SSO. This commitment is significantly important due to the fact that after a standard is adopted, switching to alternative technologies may imply impeditive costs, increasing the bargaining power of the standard essential patent holders. This is known as the patent hold-up problem.

The Guidelines issued by the European Commission on the applicability of Article 101 to horizontal co-operation agreements determines that whenever participation in standard settings is unrestricted and the procedure for adopting the standard is transparent, standardization agreements which contain no obligation to comply with the standard and provide access to the standard on fair, reasonable and non-discriminatory terms generally will not restrict competition.[10] Thus, to ensure effective access to the standard, intellectual property right policies should require

technical societies. In Brazil, there is the Brazilian Standards Institute (ABNT).

10 European Commission, Communication, Guidelines on the applicability of Article 101 of the Treaty on the Functioning of the European Union to horizontal co-operation agreements (Text with EEA relevance) Section 280 (Jan. 11, 2011).

participants wishing to have their patents included in the standard to provide an irrevocable commitment in writing to offer to license their essential intellectual property right to all third parties on fair, reasonable and non-discriminatory terms, such commitment being made prior to the adoption of the standard. Moreover, such policies should require good faith disclosure of patents that may be essential for the implementation of the standard.

A hold-up problem may lead to situations where licensing terms are not reached between the SEP and other SSO member, and the former may even go further and file injunctions to prevent the later to use its license, which would ultimately imply in ceasing to sell final products including such standard to consumers. A controversial issue that arises in this context is whether those SEPs, which have committed to FRAND terms, should be permitted to seek injunctions against the infringing party or whether this should be considered an abuse of dominance.

IV. Relevant Case Law in the US and Europe

The first two cases discussing licensing of industrial property rights in the context of technological standards were the Rambus and Qualcomm cases,[11] which, although unable to provide further guidance on the limits between a regular exercise of industrial property rights and an abuse of such rights, have served the Commission the purpose to study the issue aiming future interpretation of the law.

In the Rambus case, for instance, the Commission claimed that the company abused its monopoly power in the market of Dynamic Random Access Memory (DRAM), by charging excessive royalties for its patents. The fact that Rambus had intentionally covered that it had patents and patent applications that were relevant to technology during the development of the JEDEC standard was not considered by the Commission as an abuse,[12] but rather the excessive royalties being charged afterwards, amounting to a patent ambush situation. In the end of 2009, the Commission entered into an *Article 9 Settlement Decision*, through which it rendered legally binding

11 European Commission, *Texas Instruments/Qualcomm, available at* http://ec.europa.eu/competition/elojade/isef/case_details.cfm?proc_code=1_39247

12 Unlike in the US, monopolization is not considered, under EU laws, as a violation of competition law.

the commitments offered by Rambus, capping the royalties it could charge for its essential patents on the JEDEC's standard for DRAM chips.

In turn, the Qualcomm case concerned six companies active in the mobile phone equipment sector (Broadcom, Texas Instrument, Panasonic, Nokia and NEC) filing complaints with the European Commission against Qualcomm's licensing terms and conditions for its essential patents in the WCDMA standard, which allegedly was not being negotiated under FRAND terms. According to Qualcomm, licensing terms were negotiated on arm's length with such large and sophisticated companies, making the case difficult for the Commission to demonstrate that there effectively was an abuse. After a long investigation, the Commission decided to close the case.

At the time, the most complex issue was how to define what a fair, reasonable and non-discriminatory term is. While the "non-discriminatory" feature may seem very straightforward, the concept of "fair and reasonable" may assume a very discretionary nature. In this regard, the Commission Guidelines on Horizontal Cooperation asserts that it is not the role of the standard-setting organization to verify whether licensing terms of participants fulfill the FRAND commitment, but rather such standard participants shall have the duty to evaluate whether the licensing terms and, in particular, the fees they charge, fulfill the FRAND commitment. As provided for in the Guidelines, the assessment on whether fees charged for access to intellectual property rights in the standard-setting context are unfair or unreasonable should be based on whether the fees bear a reasonable relationship to the economic value of the patent.[13]

The smartphone war has received more attention recently from the Commission and also from US Courts. Leading device manufacturers, such as Google, Motorola, Samsung and Nokia, have been intensely litigating in US and European courts. The patent dispute between Apple and Samsung

[13] The Guidelines provide that there are several methods available to make this assessment, such as comparing the licensing fees charged by the company for the relevant patents in a competitive environment before the industry has been locked into the standard with those charged after the industry has been locked in. Another method would be to obtain an independent expert assessment on the objective centrality and essentiality of the standard at issue of the relevant IPR portfolio, or to refer to *ex ante* disclosures of licensing terms in the context of a specific standard-setting process.

has generated several lawsuits in a variety of jurisdictions, some of which have included antitrust complaints.

It is worth mentioning that the European Commission used its decision on the merger between Google and Motorola Mobility Inc. to express its views on FRAND and the use of injunctions by SEP holders that made FRAND commitments in the context of patent litigation. The Commission has claimed that "FRAND commitments can prevent IPR holders from making the implementation of a standard difficult by refusing to license or by requesting unfair or unreasonable fees (in other words excessive fees) after the industry has been locked-in to the standard or by charging discriminatory royalty fees". It follows to say that "[a]lthough a FRAND commitment may influence a company's incentives to significantly impede effective competition, it remains true that the company would still have some ability to do so."[14] One may therefore conclude that the Commission may intervene to prevent the abuse of SEPs, specifically when companies try to breach their FRAND commitments.

But the Commission needed to bring cases represented by such conduct in order to give further guidance to the business community. Thus, in 2012, it initiated proceedings against two SEP holders active in the mobile device industry; the first one to assess whether Samsung Electronics abusively used certain of its SEPs to distort competition in European mobile device markets.[15] The Samsung SEPs in question relate to ETSI 3G UMTS standard, a key industry standard for mobile and wireless communications. Reference is made to the fact that when this standard was adopted in Europe, Samsung agreed to license the patents which it had declared essential to the standard on FRAND terms. In 2011, Samsung started to seek injunctive relief before courts in various Member States against Apple based on claimed infringements of certain of its 3G UMTS SEPs.

The Commission wanted to investigate whether SEPs were abusing their market power by seeking injunctive relief against competing mobile device manufacturers based on alleged infringements of their SEPs. The

---

14 European Commission, Press Release, Mergers: Commission approves acquisition of Motorola Mobility by Google (Feb. 13, 2012) (IP/12/129), *available at* http://europa.eu/rapid/press-release_IP-12-129_en.htm.

15 European Commission, Press Release, Antitrust: Commission opens proceedings against Samsung (Jan. 31, 2012) (IP/12/89), *available at* http://europa.eu/rapid/press-release_IP-12-89_en.htm .

understanding was that Samsung failed to comply with its commitment, made to ETSI, to license any standard essential patents relating to European mobile telephony standards.

For the sake of information, it is worth mentioning that Samsung and Apple, besides being competitors, are key commercial partners that need each other. In addition, Apple initiated the patent battle between the two companies by filing a complaint in the United States District Court for the Northern District of California in April 2011 claiming that several of Samsung's Android phones and tablets infringed Apple's intellectual property.[16] Samsung retaliated by suing Apple for breach of its SEPs in a number of jurisdictions, including some Member States.[17]

In December 2012, just before Samsung received its Statement of Objections,[18] it announced the decision to withdraw all of its requests for sales ban against Apple products on the basis of alleged violations of SEPs on a Europe-wide basis. Such fact, however, did not prevent the Commission from sending out the Statement of Objections, which mentioned that Samsung's seeking of injunctions against Apple in various Member States on the basis of its mobile phone SEPs amounted to an abuse of a dominant position prohibited by EU antitrust rules. It also pointed out that, while resorting to injunctions is a possible remedy for patent infringements, such conduct may be abusive where SEPs are concerned and the potential licensee is willing to negotiate a license on FRAND terms.

---

16 Apple, Inc. v. Samsung Elecs. Co., Ltd., N. D. Cal., 5:11-cv-01846 (April, 2011).

17 *See*, Florian Mueller, *List of 50+ Apple-Samsung lawsuits in 10 countries*, BLOG Foss Patents (April, 28, 2012 12:04 PM), *available at* http://www.fosspatents.com/2012/04/list-of-50-apple-samsung-lawsuits-in-10.html.

18 A Statement of Objections is a formal step in Commission investigations. The Commission informs the parties concerned in writing of the objections raised against them and the parties can reply in writing and request an oral hearing to present comments. The Commission takes a final decision only after the parties have exercised their rights of defense. If, after the parties have exercised their right of defense, the Commission concludes that there is sufficient evidence of an infringement, it can issue a decision prohibiting the conduct and impose a fine of up to 10% of a company's annual worldwide turnover. Press Release, European Commission Antitrust: Commission sends Statement of Objections to Samsung on potential misuse of mobile phone standard-essential patents. (Dec., 21, 2012) (IP/12-1448), *available at* http://europa.eu/rapid/press-release_IP-12-1448_en.htm.

On April 29, 2014, the European Commission disclosed the commitments made by Samsung. According to these commitments, Samsung will not seek injunctions in Europe on the basis of its SEPs for smartphones and tablets against licensees that sign up for a specified licensing framework. Under said framework, any dispute over what are fair, reasonable and non-discriminatory terms for the SEPs in question will be determined by court, or if both parties agree, by an arbitrator. The commitments therefore provide a "safe harbor" for all potential licensees of the relevant Samsung SEPs. Indeed, potential licensees that sign up to the licensing framework will be protected against SEP-based injunctions by Samsung.[19]

In the same year, 2012, the Commission initiated two formal investigations against Google's MMI.[20] The Commission wanted to further investigate whether MMI had abusively used certain of its SEPs to distort competition. According to the terms of the complaints made by Apple and Microsoft, the Commission proposed to investigate whether the seeking and enforcement of injunctions by Google's Motorola against Apple's and Microsoft's main products, such as iPhone, iPad, Windows and Xbox, on the basis of its SEPs, was indeed a failure to comply with its FRAND commitments and breach of Article 102 TFEU.[21] Both Apple and Microsoft also claimed that Motorola offered unfair licensing conditions for its standard-essential patents in violation of Article 102 TFEU.

---

19 European Commission, Press Release, Antitrust: Commission accepts legally binding commitments by Samsung Electronics on standard essential patent injunctions. (April 29, 2014) (IP/14/490), *available at*: http://europa.eu/rapid/press-release_IP-14-490_en.htm. *See also,* Memorandum from European Commission on Antitrust decisions on standard essential patents (SEPs) – Motorola Mobility and Samsung Electronics – Frequently asked questions (April 29, 2014) (MEMO/14/322), *available at* http://europa.eu/rapid/press-release_MEMO-14-322_en.htm.

20 European Commission, Press Release, Antitrust: Commission opens proceedings against Motorola (April 3, 2012) (IP/12/345), *available at* http://europa.eu/rapid/press-release_IP-12-345_en.htm.

21 Motorola has accused Microsoft of infringing five patents for the use of its Android software. For of these complaints were withdrawn and only one remained. According to ITC, this patent concerns communication among devices with wireless connection. Final decision from the ITC is pending.

In January 2013, FTC settled with Google MMI, which agreed not to use injunctions or threats of injunctions against current or future potential licensees that are willing to accept a license on FRAND terms.[22] This Order prohibited Google MMI from continuing or enforcing existing motions for injunctive relief based on FRAND commitments. In addition, they have been prohibited from bringing future claims for injunctive relief under the same circumstances. However, the Order accepts that if a potential licensee indisputably demonstrates that it is not willing to pay a reasonable fee for use of Google's SEPs, Google would be authorized to seek injunctive relief.

Thus, according to the terms of the settlement, Google is permitted to seek injunctive relief only in the following four narrowly-defined circumstances: "(1) the potential licensee is not subject to United States jurisdiction; (2) the potential licensee has stated in writing or in sworn testimony that it will not accept a license for Google's FRAND-encumbered SEPs on any terms; (3) the potential licensee refuses to enter a license agreement for Google's FRAND-encumbered SEPs on terms set for the parties by a court or through binding arbitration; or (4) the potential licensee fails to assure Google that it is willing to accept a license on FRAND terms."[23]

The European Commission has also filed formal investigations to assess whether The MathWorks Inc., a US-based software company, has distorted competition in the market for the design of commercial control systems by preventing competitors from achieving interoperability with its products.[24] The Commission investigated whether, by allegedly refusing to provide a competitor with end-user licenses and interoperability information, the company has engaged in abusive conduct. The investigation follows a complaint claiming that MathWorks had refused to provide a competitor with end-user software licenses and accompanying

---

22 Federal Trade Commission, Analysis of Proposed Consent Order to Aid Public Comment, In the Matter of Motorola Mobility LLC, and Google Inc., 6 (File No. 121-0120), *available at* http://www.ftc.gov/os/caselist/1210120/130103googlemotorolaanalysis.pdf .

23 Id.

24 MathWorks' "Simulink" and "MATLAB" software products are widely used for designing and simulating control systems. Control systems are deployed in many innovative industries such as in cruise control or anti-lock braking systems (ABS) for cars. Press Release, European Commission Antitrust: Commission opens proceedings against MathWorks. (March 1, 2012) (IP/12/208), *available at* http://europa.eu/rapid/press-release_IP-12-208_en.htm?locale=en.

interoperability information for its flagship products "Simulink" and "MATLAB", thereby preventing it from lawfully reverse-engineering in order to achieve interoperability with these two products. In September 2, 2014, the European Commission announced that it had decided to close the antitrust proceeding. The Commission provided no public details about the reasons for its decision, but it has been reported that the complainant withdrew its complain.[25]

It is also worth mentioning that Huawei Technologies Co., China's largest phone-equipment producer, filed a complaint in May 2012 regarding the SEP licensing practices of Interdigital Inc., a patent assertion entity. Huawei's complaint reportedly alleges that Interdigital has abused its dominant position by seeking an injunction in relation to the alleged SEP infringement to obtain non-FRAND licensing terms from Huawei. In March 2013, the Düsseldorf Regional Court made an Article 267 TFEU reference for a preliminary ruling from the Court of Justice in litigation between Huawei and ZTE on issues touching directly on the Commission investigations against Samsung and, arguably, Motorola.[26]

In April 25, 2014, the U.S. Court of Appeals for the Federal Circuit, in Apple Inc. and Next Software, Inc. v. Motorola, Inc., rejected a *per se* rule that injunctions are unavailable for SEPs, stating that the Supreme Court's decision in eBay "provides ample strength and flexibility for addressing the unique aspects of FRAND committed patents and industry standards in general."[27] Prior to eBay, permanent injunctive relief was virtually automatic following a District Court's finding of infringement, given the general presumption of irreparable harm. In the eBay case, a unanimous Supreme Court ruling rejected the presumption of irreparable harm and

---

[25] European Commission, Antitrust: Commission closes case against MathWorks. (AT.39840) (Sept., 2, 2014) *available at* http://ec.europa.eu/competition/antitrust/cases/dec_docs/39840/39840_1248_3.pdf.

[26] Damien Geradin, *Düsseldorf court refers five questions to the CJEU regarding standard-essential patents and Article 102 TFEU,* BLOG The Antitrust Hotch Potch (March 24, 2013 12:35 PM) Available at http://professorgeradin.blogs.com/professor_geradins_weblog/2013/03/d%C3%BCsseldorf-court-refers-five-questions-to-the-cjeu-regarding-standard-essential-patents-and-article--1.html.

[27] United States Court of Appeals, Federal Circuit, Apple Inc. and Next Software, Inc. V. Motorola, Inc. and Motorola Mobility, Inc. 71-72 (Case 2012-1548, 2012-1549) (Fed. Cir. April 25, 2014), *available at* http://www.essentialpatentblog.com/wpcontent/uploads/sites/234/2014/04/12-1548.Opinion.4-23-2014.1.pdf.

other categorical approaches in favor of a case-by-case application of "traditional equitable principles," including requiring proof of the patent holder's irreparable harm and the inadequacy of money damages.[28]

In addition to the discussions in Europe and the US, other jurisdictions have also been investigating and adopting decisions regarding the issue. In the Pacific, the Guangdong People's Court made public two decisions in April 2014, regarding a dispute between Huawei and Interdigital, affirming the lower court's FRAND royalty determination of 0.019 percent of the sales price for each Huawei product for Interdigital, Inc's 2G, 3G and 4G Chinese essential patents. The Court also held that IDC violated China's Anti-Monopoly Law (AML) by, among other things, seeking an exclusion order in the U.S. International Trade Commission (ITC) against Huawei while negotiations were still in progress regarding IDC's Chinese SEPs. China's National Development and Reform Commission (NDRC) is currently considering commitments offered by IDC in an investigation into whether IDC abused its dominant position by seeking discriminatorily high royalties on Chinese essential patents.[29]

In February 2014, the Korean Fair Trade Commission (KFTC) issued its first decision on whether seeking injunctive relief on a FRAND-encumbered SEP constitutes a violation of Korea's Fair Trade Law, concluding that, because Apple Inc. failed to engage in good faith negotiations, Samsung's injunction claims against Apple on SEPs related to 3G mobile communication technology do not constitute an abuse of dominance or unfair trade practice. KFTC also rejected Apple's contention that such conduct constitutes a refusal of access to essential facilities, concluding that FRAND-encumbered SEPs do not constitute essential facilities.[30]

The Competition Commission of India (CCI) also opened, recently, two related investigations against Ericsson, claiming that it violated its FRAND commitments by imposing discriminatory and "excessive"

---

28 Koren W. Wong-Ervin, *Standard-Essential Patents: The International Landscape*, Federal Trade Commission, Intellectual Property Committee, ABA Section of Antitrust Law, Spring 2014, *available at* http://www.ftc.gov/system/files/attachments/key-speeches-presentations/standard-essential_patents_the_intl_landscape.pdf.

29 Koren W. Wong-Ervin, *supra* note 28.

30 Koren W. Wong-Ervin, *supra* note 28.

royalty rates and using Non-Disclosure Agreements (NDAs). In its investigation order, CCI stated that "forcing" a party to execute [a] NDA" and "imposing excessive and unfair royalty rates" constitute "prima facie" abuse of dominance and violation of section 4 of the Indian Competition Act, as does "[i]mposing a jurisdiction clause debarring [licensees] from getting disputes adjudicated in the country where both parties were in business."[31-32]

Parallel to the smartphone war, one has to consider the precedents from the European [and US] Courts regarding sham litigation cases, which somewhat concerns a similar object of discussion in connection to the present one. In this regard, the *ITT Promedia case*[33] sets an extremely high bar for demonstrating sham litigation, recently confirmed by the General Court in *Protégé International.*[34] *Protégé International* was a case concerning Intellectual property litigation, and the court stated that "[a]s access to the Court is a fundamental right and a general principle ensuring the rule of law, it is only in wholly exceptional circumstances that the fact that legal proceedings are brought is capable of constituting an abuse of a dominant position". In this regard, litigation can only be abusive if each limb of the two pronged cumulative test is satisfied, the legal action must be both: (i) "manifestly unfounded", i.e., at the time the action was brought it "cannot reasonably be considered as an attempt to establish the rights of the undertaking and can therefore only serve to harass the opposite party"; and (ii) conceived in the framework of a plan whose goal is to eliminate competition.

Thus, the issue to be brought forth is whether there should be deviation from the precedents, and therefore, the tests provided by

---

31 Competition Commission of India, Micromax Informatics Ltd. v. Telefonaktiebolaget LM Ericsson 1-9 (Nov. 12, 2013) (Case 50/2013), *available at* http://cci.gov.in/May2011/OrderOfCommission/261/502013.pdf; *see also* Competition Commission of India, Intex Techn. Ltd., v. Telfonaktiebolaget LM Ericsson Paragraph 17 (Jan. 16, 2014) (Case 76/2013), *available at* http://cci.gov.in/May2011/OrderOfCommission/261/762013.pdf.

32 Koren W. Wong-Ervin, *supra* note 28.

33 European Court Reports, Alargada Court of First Instance (Fourth Chamber) (July 17, 1998) (T-111/96): ITT Promedia NY v. Comissão das Comunidades Europeias.

34 European Court Reports, Judgement of the General Court (Seventh Chamber) (Sept. 13, 2012) (T-119/09): Protégé International Ltd contra Comissão Europeia.

the Courts, in sham litigation cases, when the Commission and other authorities decide whether seeking injunction relief on SEP with FRAND commitments may be considered an abuse of dominance. The right of access to courts is a fundamental right in the European Union as much as it is in other jurisdictions, and limiting such right may pose major risks to the due process of law and fundamental guarantees of companies and individuals alike.

It seems that the Commission realized that sham litigation cases may not applicable to the situations where SEP holders seek their rights before the courts to avoid patent infringement, to the extent that they are not able to demonstrate the first requirement of the theory, since no manifestly unfounded rights are to be recognized. Therefore, it has developed a new theory, despite all the risks seen, whereby it intends to exercise certain pressure on SEP holders to license technology on FRAND commitments.

However, the effect may be quite the opposite, for technological innovative companies, which must rethink their incentives to step forward and provide FRAND commitment in the context of standard developments.

This debate clearly demonstrates the maturity of the European institution *vis-a-vis* the Brazilian legal system. Although it can be certainly noted below that cases discussing the interaction between competition and intellectual property right policies in Brazil have not reached a thorough analysis in terms of the indispensability of FRAND commitments on the context of SSOs and its resulting effects and remedies, the debate is valid to the extent that similar issues may soon cross the ocean and arrive at the tropical lands.

V. Relevant Case Law In Brazil and Available Tools

There have been attempts before the Brazilian Antitrust Authorities to recognize abuse of dominance from conducts involving intellectual property rights whose exercise allegedly restricts free competition. In most of these cases, the authorities have been unable to collect evidence to sufficiently demonstrate that there has been a competition violation beyond any reasonable doubt, ultimately deciding to shelve the cases.

In this regard, Alcoa, a major steel producer, was accused in 2006 of restricting the offer of aluminum structures for doors and windows by means of deceitful requests for registry of industrial design, patents and utility models, followed by judicial claims filed against the infringing parties.[35] In addition, Alcoa was accused of disclosing to the market intellectual property rights over aluminum structures that the company had not actually registered. The Brazilian authorities have treated the cause under the theory of sham litigation and decided, ultimately, that there was no infringement since (i) the registry of the industrial designs was submitted to the Brazilian Patent and Trademark Office (INPI), fact that suggested no opportunistic conduct in view of possible gaps in the process for the concession of intellectual property rights; and (ii) due to the fact that the disclosure to the market ultimately involved Alcoa trademarks.

Microsoft has also been under the spotlight in Brazil for alleged anticompetitive conducts. Among such investigations, in 2005 the company was accused of refusing to license its Windows 2000 operating system technology, in view of the fact that there would be no translation into Portuguese of the operating system's installation software. Visual Black 6.0 used to include a standard translation to install the software, which was excluded from the new operating system. Also, Microsoft was accused of preventing the development of software companies in the market of financial applications for Windows, since it was including the software *Money* in the Microsoft Office for Small Business package, using its dominant position to create difficulties to its competitors and preventing the development of free exploitation of industrial and intellectual technology. CADE shelved the case in 2007 based on the lack of evidence on the infringements.[36]

It is noteworthy that prior to the aforesaid investigation, Microsoft had also been accused of (i) tying the sales of its operating system with its browser and some of its applications; (ii) charging excessive prices for the update thereof; (iii) fixing its profit margin arbitrarily,; (iv) granting licenses of restrictive use, specifically with respect to the Exchange software; and (v) imposing anticompetitive clauses in the training agreements.[37] CADE also shelved this investigation in 2007 based on the lack of evidence brought forth by the Complaining parties. However, in view of similar cases and

35 CADE, *Alcoa Alumínio S.A.* Reporting Commissioner César Costa Alves de Mattos (Preliminary Investigation No. 08012.005727/2006-50) (May 13, 2010).

36 CADE, *Microsoft Informática Ltda.* Reporting Commissioner Abrabam Benzaquen Sicsú (Preliminary Investigation No. 08012.002034/2005-24) (April 11, 2007).

37 CADE, *Microsoft Informática Ltda.* Reporting Commissioner Luiz Alberto Esteves Scaloppe (Preliminary Investigation No. 08012.004570/2000-50) (Oct. 05, 2004).

convictions in other jurisdictions, CADE required its investigative agency – SDE – to further scrutinize Microsoft's conducts. Thus, SDE has filed a new investigative proceeding, which is still pending – in other words, no opinion or decision has been issued so far.[38]

Another relevant case in terms of IP-related conducts was the Monsanto case, in which the company was accused, in 1998, of conditioning the sale of transgenic soy seeds to the sale of its herbicides, as well as of preventing its competitors' access to herbicides for the seeds, in order to eliminate competition.[39] The complaining party claimed that Monsanto refused to make its genetically modified seeds available to its competitors for tests. The case was shelved based on the lack of evidence on the tying charge and based on the legitimate interest of Monsanto not to supply the seeds, in view of the fact that such seeds had not yet, at the time, been launched in the market.

The aforementioned cases may be considered the seeds of the discussions between industrial/intellectual property rights and antitrust law in Brazil, whereby the complementary nature of these two diplomas has been debated and, to a certain extent, clarified. Cases brought to the authorities involving the creation of technological standards furthered such debate, as well as the claims of refusal to deal or exploitative prices.

In terms of SSOs and technological standard creation in the country, it is important to note that the associative agreements among companies, such as the creation of patent pools, is subject to mandatory submission to the Brazilian Antitrust Authorities, which must review the competition aspects involved. In this regard, Sony, Philips, Panasonic, Hitachi, Samsung and Ciberlink filed in 2009 a Concentration Act concerning the formation of a patent pool and acquisition of interests in a future company that would globally license essential patents for the manufacturing of blue-ray products.[40] CADE approved the case unconditionally. In addition, Sony, Philips and Pioneer filed a new Concentration Act with the Brazilian

[38] CADE, *Microsoft Informática Ltda.* Reporting Commissioner Ricardo Machado Ruiz (Preliminary Investigation No. 08012.010027/2007-68) (Dec. 12, 2013).

[39] CADE, *Monsanto do Brasil Ltda.* Reporting Commissioner Luís Fernando Rigato Vasconcellos (Preliminary Investigation No. 08012.008659/1998-09) (June 05, 2007).

[40] CADE, *Sony Corporation.* Reporting Commissioner Carlos Emmanuel Joppert Ragazzo. (Merger No. 08012.008810/2009-23) (July 01, 2011).

Antitrust authorities for the purchase of One-Red LLC, a limited-liability company which would offer services for the management of certain patent-licensing software, and CADE also approved such merger.[41] Thus, the Brazilian authorities have reviewed the cases above on the context of their preventive role, scrutinizing such associative agreements to approve their effect produced in the market.

Arguably, and as has been previously mentioned, precedents concerning the licensing of intellectual property rights before the Brazilian Antitrust authorities are relatively poor, lacking a thorough assessment of the sensible issues at stake. The most recent cases were decided in 2009, concerning a complaint filed by Gradiente Eletrônica S.A. ("Gradiente") and Cemaz Indústria Eletrônica da Amazônia S.A. ("CCE") against Koninklijke Philips Eletronics, N.V. ("Philips") and Philips do Brasil Ltda. ("Philips Brasil"), as well as another complaint filed by Videolar S.A. ("Videolar") also against Philips. Both cases have been superficially dealt in view of the lack of evidence produced by the plaintiffs and the humble investigation run by the Brazilian authorities.

The first case referred to the claim that Philips was abusing its dominant position in the market of technology supply for the production of DVD players by attempting to leverage its position in the downstream market of DVD players by excluding its competitors.[42] According to the claimants, the technology for reading and reproducing DVD encompasses thirty-nine inventions, eighteen of which are protected by patents registered before INPI. The companies holding the industrial property rights were organized in two different pools – 3C and 6C pools, which, by means of royalty payments, licensed different and complementary technology. Thus, it would be necessary to license patents of both groups to be capable of, legitimately, manufacturing and marketing DVD players in the Brazilian territory.[43] Philips was part of the 3C Pool and was also in charge of

[41] CADE, *Sony Corporation.* Reporting Commissioner Olavo Zago Chinaglia. (Merger No. 08012.000734/2011-22) (June 17, 2011).

[42] CADE, *Gradiente Eletrônica S.A.* Reporting Commissioner Olavo Zago Chinaglia. (Preliminary Investigation No. 08012.001315/2007-21) (Oct. 11, 2009).

[43] Earlier in the 1990s, two high capacity optical disc drives were under development: the MultiMedia Compact Disc (MMCD), from Philips and Sony, and the Super Density Disk (SD), from Toshiba, Time-Warner, Matsushita Electric, Hitachi, Mitsubishi, Pioneer, Thomson and JVC. Foreseeing recurrence of problems that

representing the 3C Patent Pool in negotiating the licensing agreement of the technologies those companies held in Brazil.

The conducts were associated to the way in which the industrial property rights were being enforced by the respondents, which would involve: (i) threats to clients, suppliers, distributors and resellers of DVD players, of charges of undue royalties; (ii) inclusion on the patent pool of technologies which were not owned by the respondents and which were not indispensable for the manufacturing of the DVD players; (iii) charging abusive prices for the licensing of its technology, which would imply in (iv) refusal to deal on essential facility; (v) charging double royalties; and (vi) discrimination between producers of DVD players. The relevant market defined by the authorities was the market for manufacturing and sale of the hardware for reading and reproducing DVDs, on a global level.

In essence, claimants alleged that the royalties charged by the SEPs holders were abusive, which would imply a margin squeeze of the rivals' profits to the point that would prevent an effective challenge of the market power of the dominant firms. This was verifiable not only in the abusive royalties, but also in the double charging thereof, the price discrimination between different competitors, and the conducts envisaging the illegal protection of industrial property rights, which were allegedly neither essential nor followed the relevant legislation for its concession.

occurred in the 80's with VHS and Betamax VCR's, the companies decided to unify these two systems. Thus, in 1996, Panasonic, Toshiba, Mitsubishi, AOL, JVC, Hitachi, Thomson, Philips, Sony and Pioneer gathered together and formed the "DVD Consortium", aiming to develop technics for manufacturing equipment's capable of reading optical disk drives and converting their information into images accompanied by audio. Thereby, the MMCD format was abandoned by Phillips and Sony, who adopted Toshiba's format with two modifications in its technology. The first modification regarded the capacity of switching tracks, a technology developed by Philips/Sony. The second was the adoption of Philips' system EFMPlus, which presented high weather resistance despite the slightly smaller capacity in relation to the SD system. Such technology originated the DVD. In 1997, the DVD Consortium became the DVD Forum, open to all companies. There were two horizontal agreements characterizing the patent pools: the 3C Group and 6C Group, which certified and licensed different patents, essential to DVD. In 1998, the 3C Group was formed, by Philips, Sony and Pioneer, for licensing the set of patents related to their own DVD technology. In 1999, Toshiba, Panasonic, Mitsubishi, AOL, JVC and Hitachi constituted the 6C Group.

The non-bidding report SDE issued (currently CADE's General Superintendence), agency responsible for the investigation of the case at the time, concluded that there was no evidence of anticompetitive conduct, thereby suggesting the dismissal of the case. This was also the understanding of the Prosecution Office and CADE's General Attorney.

Claimants theoretically proved that the respondents had dominant position on the upstream market concerning technology for the production of DVDs, and that there were structural conditions for engaging into vertical anticompetitive conducts aimed at the leveraging of their share in the downstream market of DVD player production and sale. However, according to SDE, CADE's General Attorney and the Public Prosecutor, there were insufficient elements to conclude that the conducts under investigation had the effect of harming free competition.

In this regard, CADE's Tribunal considered that: (i) with respect to the threats, it was verified that correspondence sent by the respondents only informed that the sale of DVD players without demonstration of royalties being paid by manufacturers could imply legal action, not only against the manufacturers but also against the resellers; (ii) concerning the inclusion on the patent pool of technologies which were allegedly not owned by the respondents and which were not indispensable for the manufacturing of the DVD players, the claimants failed to identify which patents were subject to their allegations; in addition, CADE' Tribunal quoted that the DOJ had verified in more details the legality of the licensing agreements in the context of a similar investigation in the US, concluding that all the patents included in the pool were essential; also, there was a fixed and independent value of the patents negotiated that would limit the scope for antitrust intervention;[44] (iii) regarding the alleged charge of abusive prices for the licensing of its technology, which would imply in (iv) refusal to deal on essential facility, information provided in the case records was that royalties would be fixed at USD 3.50 per product sold, plus an upfront payment of ten thousand US dollars (USD 10,000.00), which was deemed insufficient information to verify whether there was any abusive pricing;[45] (v) with

44 Here, a specific reference by the Commissioner that the right to fix prices to be charged is upon industrial property holders, thus protected and in compliance with the legislation, except in essential facility cases. The Commissioner goes on to say that, in this case, there has been no refusal by the respondents.

45 CADE's precedents are in the line that excessive prices charged as the result of

respect to the allegation of double royalties charge, CADE's Commissioner argued that there were insufficient elements to conclude whether a payment was made on the origin of the supply, since claimants affirmed that royalties were charged in two moments: from suppliers of components and from the companies that assembled final products;[46] and finally (vi) concerning the claim on discrimination between producers of DVD players, since the deposit of the patents was made in certain Mercosul countries only, discriminating the players and which could affect competition of national companies *vis-a-vis* other Mercosul countries, CADE claimed this was not a competition-related issue, therefore dismissing all claims and determining the shelving of the case.

On the second case, filed by Videolar,[47] allegations were that Philips was abusing its dominant position by means of (i) eliminating competing media formats in Brazil aimed at leveraging its dominant position in the technology market; and (ii) charging abusive prices for the licensing of essential patents for digital media production.[48] The conducts were pursued in the market of manufacturing of optical media or recordable storage, specifically the CD-R and the DVD-R. The SDE investigation led to its non-binding opinion of lack of evidence against the respondent, therefore suggesting the shelving of the case, in which it was followed by CADE' General Attorney and the Public Prosecutor.

---

profits arising from legally achieved monopoly power do not characterize an antitrust violation.

46 Furthermore, CADE's Commissioner argued that even if royalties were charged twice, this would be a regular exercise of the intellectual property rights of the Respondents.

47 CADE, *Videolar S.A.* Reporting Commissioner Paulo Furquim de Azevedo. (Preliminary Investigation No. 08012.005181/2006-37) (May 22, 2009).

48 In 1979, Philips and other companies joined efforts with the research and development of a new audio media technology to be faster and with a higher storage capacity, in replacement of the magnetic technology. Thus, they established a working group comprised of technicians of several companies to establish a single technology standard, that became known as Compact Disk (CD). After the launch of the first CD, in 1982, Toshiba, Time-Warner, Matsushita Electric, Hitachi, Mitsubishi, Pioneer, Thomson and JVC formed a consortium to develop other optical medias such as CD-R and DVD-R. As a result of the consortium, a patent pool was created to develop such products and Philips became the manager of the patent pool in Brazil.

Regarding the first complaint, Videolar accused Philips of fomenting non-licensed imports of optical media of recordable storage as an exclusionary strategy of competing magnetic media, specifically VHS. The complaint focused on Philips' omission towards the non-licensed new technology. Thus, Philips' omission should be understood as an abuse of its dominant position which would tend to eliminate competing media formats in Brazil. CADE concluded that the performance and outcome of the VHS market does not relate to any conduct perpetrated by Philips, but merely results from the technological preeminence of optical medias in relation to magnetic ones, represented by better quality of reproduction, storage and durability, as a typical example of Schumpeter's creative destruction.[49] In addition, CADE also pointed out that it would be Philips prerogative to enforce its intellectual property rights. With respect to the abusive pricing allegation, claimant affirms that prices charged in Brazil were significantly higher than those charged abroad, and that it would be possible to buy CD-R and DVD-R from companies abroad with and without royalties' payment, to be delivered in Brazil. CADE's position on claims of excessive pricing was reinforced by SDE and by the Tribunal in its vote:

> *"[T]he price or its excessive increase may not be considered an illegal practice harming free competition per se; it may be considered as such only to the extent that it results from a illegal practice or is able to cause anticompetitive effects (such as elimination of competition).*
>
> *CADE's interpretation regarding the conduct under examination converges with the doctrine concerning the distinction of two different types of excessive pricing: (i) merely excessive or exploitative prices, resulting from market power. In such cases, the dominant firm charges high prices to its end consumers, with no competition; (ii) abusive prices which are exclusionary, implemented with the purpose of excluding competitors from the market (and performed by vertically integrated companies).*
>
> *In this regard, the authorities must play the role of challenging excessive prices that are exclusionary, aimed at promoting necessary working conditions for the market, correcting its possible failures, being prevented however from replacing the market mechanisms or assume the role of the private agent in the process of decision making, among which the price formation. In other words, it shall*

49 CADE, *Videolar S.A.* Reporting Commissioner Paulo Furquim de Azevedo, *supra* note 47, at 365.

occur on the competitive process, ensuring the dispute for markets to be legal, and the possible market power resulting from such dispute to be legitimate."[50]

Based on the above, CADE concluded for the lack of evidences of a strategy to exclude competitors or illicit conducts which could somehow refute the legitimacy on price increases, therefore not being characterized any infringement to competition. It was reminded that the respondent charged a fix global price for licensing its patents. Furthermore, considering the correct prices of the licensing agreements, it would be clear that claimant was actually paying less than the standard royalty fees, in view of the discounts Philips provided to reward companies performing their contractual obligations. Also, with respect to the claim that it would be possible to acquire non-licensed products abroad, it was irrelevant whether such possibility did exist, in view of the fact that all companies that sell CD-R and DVD-R products in Brazil are subject to the payment of royalties, under legal penalties for illicit practices.

Apart from the reported leading cases above, no further discussions involving the adoption of technological standards and commitments for fair, reasonable an non-discriminatory license have been carried out before CADE. In this regard, perhaps the most relevant case under scrutiny of the SBDC involving competition and IP rights, but not particularly related to standards and FRAND terms, is the case filed by the Association of Independent Auto-Parts Producers (ANFAPE) against three of the leading original equipment manufacturing (OEMs) in Brazil.[51]

In short, ANFAPE claims that OEMs abuse their market power by legally enforcing their intellectual property rights – industrial designs of external auto parts – against independent auto parts manufacturers. Such rights aim at inhibiting the production and sale of copies of protected products in the market. It is noteworthy in this regard that all judicial decisions related to the issue have confirmed OEMs' intellectual property rights, thus ordering seizure measures of the products and preventing the defendant from continuing to produce auto-parts subject to protected

50 CADE, *Videolar S.A.* Reporting Commissioner Paulo Furquim de Azevedo, *supra* note 47, at 366.

51 CADE, *ANFAPE v., Volkswagen do Brasil, Fiat Automóveis S.A, and Ford Motor Company Brasil Ltda.* Reporting Commissioner Carlos Emmanuel Joppert Ragazzo (Preliminary Investigation No. 08012.002673/2007-51) (Dec. 17, 2010).

industrial designs. SDE's non-bidding legal opinion suggested the shelving of the case, based on the arguments that the protection granted to the OEMs' industrial designs was in compliance with the Intellectual Property Law, and were validly registered. SDE also concluded, at the time, that such restriction did not foreclose the auto parts market since such companies could develop their own alternative and similar auto parts without copying the protected products. SDE recognized that the protection given by intellectual property rights is a trade-off by which society agrees to grant exclusivity to innovators, which will have, in exchange, incentives to innovate.

Notwithstanding SDE's opinion, which was ratified by the Public Prosecutors and CADE's General Attorney, CADE's Tribunal promoted the conversion of the preliminary investigation into an Administrative Proceeding in December 2010 and sent the case for further instruction and investigation by SDE – currently the General Superintendence. The Reporting Commissioner was very clear to say that (i) the IP rights grant monopoly in the aftermarket to OEM; (ii) there clearly were, lock-in effects recognized in the affected markets; (iii) competition in the primary market did not seem sufficient to ensure competition in the aftermarket; (iv) the actual exercise of market power in the aftermarket would possibly result in consumer losses; and (v) there were no plausible objective justifications of the OEMs with respect to their conducts. The case has been, since them, under further investigations conducted by SDE and, more recently, the General Superintendence.

More recently, in 2014, the General Superintendence recommended CADE's Tribunal the condemnation of Eli Lilly do Brasil Ltda. and Eli Lilly Company for Sham Litigation practice.[52] The case thus involved sham litigation in the context of IPRs. The GS's legal opinion pointed out that the company tried to maintain the exclusive sale of the Gemzar drug. According to the GS, INPI has denied the drug patent several times, and, after that, the company filed a lawsuit to obtain product exclusivity. As a result of the company's conducts, Eli Lilly obtained, between 2007 and 2008, an undue

[52] CADE, *Associação Brasileiras das Indústrias de Medicamentos Genéricos – Pró Genéricos, Defendants: Eli Lilly And Company and Eli Lilly do Brasil Ltda.* Reporting Commissioner Ana de Oliveira Frazão, pending decision.

monopoly in Brazil, which leaded to higher prices in the medicine market. The case is currently under CADE's review.[53]

Though the ANFAPE case referred to above, has not been decided, it has provided clear signs from the authorities in the sense that IP rights shall not be considered absolute and shielded from competition scrutiny. There should be instances where excessive protection may promote deadweight losses to consumers and the adequate balancing of IP protection avoiding harm to the innovation process, with the appropriation of such innovation to the benefit of consumers, shall be a task pursued by the antitrust authorities. It will be interesting to see how such balance will come up, specifically the tests to be used by the authorities and possible remedies to be implemented in this regard.

Conclusions

As may be seen based on the aforementioned cases, there has been limited exposure of the Brazilian Antitrust Authorities to cases involving IP rights protection and competition effects. A natural explanation could be the fact that Brazil enjoys a low level of innovation, therefore being very dependent on foreign technology. The context expected from such discussions, thus, would be most likely on the licensing of IP rights to local companies aiming to explore products dependent on such protected IP rights.

The references to the cases regarding the smartphone battle and other investigations involving IP rights, and more specifically, standard-essential patents, are to anticipate issues that soon tend to reach the Brazilian territory. The Brazilian Antitrust Authority and the Brazilian Courts should, therefore, be prepared for such issues to reach the nation.

It is noteworthy, as mentioned before, that most of the cases brought to the attention of the Brazilian Antitrust Authorities described above, which involve basic IP and Antitrust Law interaction issues and abusive claims of licensing, have inevitably failed to condemn the involved companies.

---

[53] On another similar case shelved by the authorities also in 2014 – CADE, *Niely do Brasil, (AI* 08012.003303/2011-18) – was being investigated by sham litigation practices. The claimants informed that they were the owners of "Gold" registration, and that they were prevented of the creation of a new product named "Novex Gold" because Niely has filed law suits claiming exclusivity over the term. GS concluded that the lawsuits filed by Niely do not constitute sham litigation practice.

However, it is worth mentioning the superficial treatment of the review not only by the authorities, but also by the claimants, which have also often failed to provide conclusive evidence on the abuses.

Notwithstanding such failures, the authorities' duties are to further investigate cases in which there is evidence of anticompetitive conduct. The asymmetry of information, usually approached by the authorities as a market failure, is particularly strong in such types of investigations involving monopolists and dominant players. Precisely for this reason, it shall be equally attacked by the authorities, which shall not be limited to evidence produced by claimants, thus requiring a more active role of the investigators.

The lack of apparatus of the Brazilian authorities up to recent days is noteworthy, however, and perhaps still its lack of experience on the investigation of such cases which, undoubtedly, demand great efforts and expertise to be implemented. With the new law, no justification for insufficient investigations is to be expected with respect to resources, although expertise may still be an obstacle.

It would be interesting, in this regard, to expect the Brazilian authorities to foster cooperation with other authorities with solid expertise in these topics, perhaps handling similar or related investigations in the country and benefitting from such cooperation. This could be the shortest way to acquire expertise on dealing with such highly complex cases in the country.

One could also argue whether the Brazilian authorities should indeed bring such cases under scrutiny or hold still for other jurisdictions to decide similar cases, following the same routes. Notwithstanding such contrary opinions, it is about time for our system to adopt a clear antitrust policy, precisely redefining and enlarging the major areas of harsh competition violation, so as to give clarity and certainty to the business community and to provide focus on the investigations to be pursued.

The Brazilian antitrust policy on cartels is very clear and has been relatively successful, although the enforcement of local conducts must be fostered and privileged by the authorities. The real value and efficiency of an antitrust authority should not be measured only by the number of leniencies and subsequent investigations opened as a result of such tools, but especially in view of the independent investigations it is able to organize and run, collecting real evidence on the violation, and assessing whether the investigated conducts may be censured with a strong level of certainty, beyond any reasonable doubt, and respecting the due process of law provided by the national legal system.

In terms of the nature of the cases submitted to the authorities' review, as has been previously mentioned, there have been few cases in which the license of essential patents for adopted standards have been discussed in the context of excessive royalty prices and refusals to deal. Such cases have been superficially approached by the authorities and do not provided secure and consistent guidance on the limits to be explored between IP rights and antitrust laws.

In this regard, the Brazilian authorities have signaled a possible shift on CADE's enforcement priorities, showing a complementary role of competition and regulatory authorities. The following aspects need to be evaluated:**(i)** abuses on the registration proceeding and **(ii)** abuses on the exercise of IP rights if contrary to economic/social interests, promoting deadweight losses to consumers.

However, such possible shift of enforcement referred to above may not be sufficient in terms of Competition policy. It is clear that standardization usually produces significant positive economic effects, driving innovation, competition and consumer benefits. More precisely, standardization promotes the development of new and improved products or markets and improved supply conditions, normally increasing competition and lowering output and sales costs, benefiting economies as a whole. Standards may also maintain and enhance quality, provide information and ensure interoperability and compatibility. In specific situations, however, it may give rise to restrictive effects on competition by potentially restricting price competition and limiting or controlling production, markets, innovation or technical development.[54]

Thus, the Brazilian authorities should be prepared for the discussions to arrive. To follow the route proposed, but expected to be abandoned, by the European Commission, which suggests that seeking injunctions before courts prevents the misappropriation of non-license IP rights shall be

54 European Commission, Communication: Guidelines on the applicability of Article 101 of the Treaty on the Functioning of the European Union to horizontal co-operation agreements Paragraph 280 (Jan. 11, 2011)

considered abusive *per se*, is a very dangerous path – especially considering that the sham litigation theory in Brazil is still being molded.

In this regard, it is noteworthy that Brazilian precedents have followed the Noerr-Pennington Doctrine, whereby the Line adopted by the authorities recognized similar conditions of the Noerr-Pennington Doctrine: "Basically an abuse of the right to petition for competition purposes would occur in case (i) of claims or petitions from which no reasonable litigator would expect, realistically, to win, and (ii) which action hides the objective to harm or, at least, interfere in its business relations with its competitors."[55]

Challenges involved in the context of the Brazilian market include discussion on how to prevent enforcement of IP rights (abuse considered) according to relevant market definitions. Also, the importance of injunctive reliefs considering high level of informal markets (piracy) and needs for technological innovation policies.

The question to be debated concerns whether limiting the possibilities of injunctions may distort the dynamics of license negotiations and, further, reduce incentives for FRAND commitments. Relevant questions also include whether concepts of FRAND are to be adopted, and what would result in the violation of a FRAND commitment by a SEP holder . Risks of false positives seem to be relatively high in new technology markets and, therefore, still constitute a major concern for the authorities.

Bibliography

Damien Gerardin. *Ten Years of DG Competition Effort To Provide Guidance On The Application of Competition Rules To The Licensing Of Standard-Essential Patents: Where do We Stand?* (2013). *Available at* http://papers.ssrn.com/sol3/papers.cfm?abstract_id=2204359

Denis B. Barbosa, *Uma Introdução à Propriedade Intelectual.* 2nd ed. (2008)

John M. Taladay; James N. Carlin Jr. Compulsory Licensing of Intellectual Property Under the Competition Laws of the United States and European Community. Geo. Mason L. Rev., vol. 11, n. 2, 2002, p. 442.

55 CADE, *SEVA Engenharia Eletrônica S.A.* Reporting Commissioner Fernando de Magalhães Furlan (Preliminary Investigation No. 08012.004484/2005-51) (Sept. 10, 2010)

KOREN W. WONG-ERVIN, *Standard-Essential Patents: The International Landscape,* Federal Trade Commission, Intellectual Property Committee, ABA Section of Antitrust Law (2014). *Available at* http://www.ftc.gov/system/files/attachments/key-speeches-presentations/standard-essential_patents_the_intl_landscape.pdf

RICHARD J. GILBERT; CARL SHAPIRO. *Unilateral refusals to license intellectual property and international competition policy.* In HOPE, Einar; MAELENG, Per (orgs.). Competition and Trade Policies – Coherence or conflict? London: Routledge, (1998).

RICHARD WHISH. *Competition Law*. 6. ed. Oxford: Oxford University Press, 2008.

* * *

Este livro foi composto na fonte Minion Pro, corpo 11,5,
diagramado pela Microart Design Editorial,
impresso em papel Offset pela Bartira Gráfica e Editora Ltda.
para a Editora Singular, em julho de 2015.